T0321916

Cambridge Tracts in Theoretical Computer Science 57

Nominal Sets

Nominal sets provide a promising new mathematical analysis of names in formal languages that is based upon symmetry. They have many applications to the syntax and semantics of programming language constructs that involve binding or localizing names. Part One provides an introduction to the basic theory of nominal sets. In Part Two, the author surveys some of the applications that have developed in programming language semantics (both operational and denotational), functional programming and logic programming.

As the first book to give a detailed account of the theory of nominal sets, it will be welcomed by researchers and graduate students in theoretical computer science.

ANDREW M. PITTS is Professor of Theoretical Computer Science at the University of Cambridge.

CAMBRIDGE TRACTS IN THEORETICAL COMPUTER SCIENCE 57

Titles in the series
A complete list of books in the series can be found at
www.cambridge.org/computerscience.
Recent titles include the following:

28. P. Padawitz *Deductive and Declarative Programming*
29. P. Gärdenfors (ed) *Belief Revision*
30. M. Anthony & N. Biggs *Computational Learning Theory*
31. T. F. Melham *Higher Order Logic and Hardware Verification*
32. R. Carpenter *The Logic of Typed Feature Structures*
33. E. G. Manes *Predicate Transformer Semantics*
34. F. Nielson & H. R. Nielson *Two-Level Functional Languages*
35. L. M. G. Feijs & H. B. M. Jonkers *Formal Specification and Design*
36. S. Mauw & G. J. Veltink (eds) *Algebraic Specification of Communication Protocols*
37. V. Stavridou *Formal Methods in Circuit Design*
38. N. Shankar *Metamathematics, Machines and Gödel's Proof*
39. J. B. Paris *The Uncertain Reasoner's Companion*
40. J. Desel & J. Esparza *Free Choice Petri Nets*
41. J.-J. Ch. Meyer & W. van der Hoek *Epistemic Logic for AI and Computer Science*
42. J. R. Hindley *Basic Simple Type Theory*
43. A. S. Troelstra & H. Schwichtenberg *Basic Proof Theory*
44. J. Barwise & J. Seligman *Information Flow*
45. A. Asperti & S. Guerrini *The Optimal Implementation of Functional Programming
     Languages*
46. R. M. Amadio & P.-L. Curien *Domains and Lambda-Calculi*
47. W.-P. de Roever & K. Engelhardt *Data Refinement*
48. H. Kleine Büning & T. Lettmann *Propositional Logic*
49. L. Novak & A. Gibbons *Hybrid Graph Theory and Network Analysis*
50. J. C. M. Baeten, T. Basten & M. A. Reniers *Process Algebra: Equational Theories
     of Communicating Processes*
51. H. Simmons *Derivation and Computation*
52. D. Sangiorgi & J. Rutten (eds) *Advanced Topics in Bisimulation and Coinduction*
53. P. Blackburn, M. de Rijke & Y. Venema *Modal Logic*
54. W.-P. de Roever et al. *Concurrency Verification*
55. Terese *Term Rewriting Systems*
56. A. Bundy et al. *Rippling: Meta-Level Guidance for Mathematical Reasoning*
57. A. M. Pitts *Nominal Sets*

Nominal Sets
Names and Symmetry in Computer Science

ANDREW M. PITTS
University of Cambridge

CAMBRIDGE
UNIVERSITY PRESS

CAMBRIDGE
UNIVERSITY PRESS

University Printing House, Cambridge CB2 8BS, United Kingdom

One Liberty Plaza, 20th Floor, New York, NY 10006, USA

477 Williamstown Road, Port Melbourne, VIC 3207, Australia

314-321, 3rd Floor, Plot 3, Splendor Forum, Jasola District Centre, New Delhi - 110025, India

79 Anson Road, #06-04/06, Singapore 079906

Cambridge University Press is part of the University of Cambridge.

It furthers the University's mission by disseminating knowledge in the pursuit of education, learning and research at the highest international levels of excellence.

www.cambridge.org
Information on this title: www.cambridge.org/9781107017788

First published 2013

A catalogue record for this publication is available from the British Library

ISBN 978-1-107-01778-8 Hardback

To Susan.
You know why.

Contents

Preface

A personal perspective

This book has its origins in my interest in semantics and logics for *locality* in programming languages. By locality, I mean the various mechanisms that exist for making local declarations, restricting a resource to a specific scope, or hiding information from the environment. Although mathematics and logic are involved in understanding these things, this is a distinctively computer science topic. I was introduced to it by Matthew Hennessy and Alley Stoughton when we all arrived at the University of Sussex in the second half of the 1980s. At the time I was interested in applying category theory and logic to computer science and they were interested in the properties of the mixture of local mutable state and higher-order functions that occurs in the ML family of languages (Milner *et al.*, 1997).

Around that time Moggi introduced the use of category-theoretic monads to structure different notions of computational effect (Moggi, 1991). That is now an important technique in denotational semantics; and thanks to the work of Wadler (1992) and others, monads are the accepted way of 'tackling the awkward squad' (Peyton Jones, 2001) of side-effects within functional programming. One of Moggi's monads models the computational effect of dynamically allocating fresh names. It is less well known than some of the other monads he uses, because it needs categories of functors and is only mentioned in (Moggi, 1989), rather than (Moggi, 1991). My Ph.D. student Ian Stark and I used this monad in a study of higher-order functions with generative names. By isolating these two features of ML in a syntactically simple language, the ν-calculus (Pitts and Stark, 1993), we illustrated how complicated the combination of these two features can be from a semantic point of view. In his thesis, Stark gives (among other things) a denotational semantics of the ν-calculus using Moggi's dynamic allocation monad on the category of pullback preserving,

Set-valued functors on the category **Inj** of injective functions between finite ordinals; see (Stark, 1994, p. 59). This functor category was well known to me
from topos theory (Johnstone, 2002), where it is called the Schanuel topos. It
is an example of an atomic topos (Barr and Diaconescu, 1980), which relates
to models of higher-order logic in a way that generalizes the relation between
complete atomic Boolean algebras and propositional logic; and it hosts the
generic model of the geometric theory of an infinite decidable object (Ščedrov,
1984).

A few years later I returned to considering the Schanuel topos with another
Ph.D. student, Jamie Gabbay, this time as a setting for initial algebra semantics for syntax modulo α-equivalence. Preferring set theory to category theory,
Gabbay pushed us towards using another known presentation of the Schanuel
topos in terms of continuous actions of the group of permutations of the set
$\mathbb{N}$ of natural numbers (topologized as a subspace of the product of countably
many copies of $\mathbb{N}$). In this form there is an obvious connection with the cumulative hierarchy of sets (with atoms) that are hereditarily finitely supported
with respect to the action of permuting atoms; this universe of sets was devised
by Fraenkel and Mostowski in the first part of the twentieth century to model
ZFA set theory without axioms of choice. Whether one emphasizes set theory
or category theory, the move from using sheaves on **Inj** to sets with a continuous action of the group G of permutations of $\mathbb{N}$ was fruitful in several ways.
For example, it certainly makes higher-order constructions in the topos easier
to describe.

However, the move from sheaves to G-sets was initially problematic in one
important respect. We were studying semantics for syntax modulo α-equi-
valence in terms of initial algebras for functors combining products and sums
(as usual for abstract syntax trees) with a functor δ for binding. This has a simple description for **Set**-valued functors on **Inj**, one which corresponds to the
shift operation used with de Bruijn style representations of syntax: the value
of δX at $n \in$ **Inj** is the value of the functor X at $n + 1$. This functor δ features
prominently in the work of Fiore *et al.* (1999), which uses presheaf categories
to model abstract syntax with variable binding and which was taking place
in parallel to our work. (An account of this, of the related semantical analysis of higher-order abstract syntax by Hofmann (1999), and of our 'nominal'
work (Gabbay and Pitts, 1999), all appeared in the same Symposium on Logic
in Computer Science.) If one uses G-sets instead of **Set**-valued functors on **Inj**,
what does δ look like? Our first answers were not very helpful. But then we
realized that the elements of δX (or $[\mathbb{A}]X$ as it is denoted in this book) can
be described as equivalence classes for a relation that captures the essence of
α-equivalence just via the permutation action, independently of the nature of

the elements of X (which may well be more complicated than just finite syntax trees). For me, this was the point at which the subject of this book took off.

Acknowledgements

My biggest debt is to the co-founder of the theory of nominal sets, Jamie Gabbay, who has done so much to develop and promote the subject. I also thank my co-authors and collaborators on this topic: James Cheney, Ranald Clouston, Maribel Fernández, Matthew Lakin, Steffen Lösch, Mark Shinwell, Ian Stark and Christian Urban. This is the first book to give an account of the theory (Part One) and applications (Part Two) of nominal sets. Original sources are cited in the text as appropriate. Some material appears here for the first time: free nominal restriction sets (Section 9.5); the use of a bi-orthogonal closed, step-indexed logical relation within nominal sets to prove correctness properties of FreshML (Section 10.11); and a construction for minimal invariant solutions of recursive domain equations for uniform directed complete posets (Section 11.4).

I am particularly pleased to be able to begin the Introduction with a quote by the late Roger Needham; he gave me, a mathematician at the time, my first job in a computer science department.

I am grateful to all those who have endured lectures on the subject matter of this book and given useful feedback, not least the members of the *FreshML* and *Computational Aspects of Nominal Sets* projects and the participants of the 2011 Midland Graduate School.

The book has been improved by comments and corrections from Johan Glimming, Steffen Lösch, Andrzej Murawski and Sam Staton. I am very grateful to the team at Cambridge University Press (David Tranah, Clare Dennison and Sarah Payne) for their support of this project and to the copy-editor, David Hemsley, for his attention to the details. The errors that remain are all my own work.

0

Introduction

This is a book about names and symmetry in the part of computer science that has to do with programming languages. Although symmetry plays an important role in many branches of mathematics and physics, its relevance to computer science may not be so clear to the reader. This introduction explains the computer science motivation for a theory of names based upon symmetry and provides a guide to what follows.

0.1 Atomic names

Names are used in many different ways in computer systems and in the formal languages used to describe and construct them. This book is exclusively concerned with what Needham calls 'pure names':

A pure name is nothing but a bit-pattern that is an identifier, and is only useful for comparing for identity with other such bit-patterns – which includes looking up in tables to find other information. The intended contrast is with names which yield information by examination of the names themselves, whether by reading the text of the name or otherwise. [...] like most good things in computer science, pure names help by putting in an extra stage of indirection; but they are not much good for anything else.

(Needham, 1989, p. 90)

We prefer to use the adjective 'atomic' rather than 'pure', because for this kind of name, internal structure is irrelevant; their only relevant attribute is their identity. Although such names may not be much good for anything other than indirection, that one thing is a hugely important and very characteristic aspect of computer science.

1

0.2 Support and freshness

The complexity of computer systems has stimulated the development of compositional methods for specifying and constructing them. If one wishes to compose a whole out of parts, then one had better have mechanisms for hiding, or at least controlling access to, the identity of the atomic names upon which each part depends. The prerequisite for devising such mechanisms and understanding their properties is a firm grasp of what it means for a piece of the system to 'depend' upon an atomic name. Although there are syntactic considerations, such as various notions of textual occurrence, this issue really concerns semantics: what does it mean for the behaviour of a software system to depend upon the identity of some atomic names?

A conventional response to this question is simply to parametrize: replace the use of structures of some kind by functions from names to structures. This book develops an alternative approach – a mathematical theory of 'name dependence' based upon the symmetries that a structure exhibits when one permutes names. The fundamental idea is to model systems involving atomic names with mathematical structures for which every permutation of names induces a transformation of the structure. In this case one says that permutations *act* upon the structure and these actions are required to satisfy some simple laws; this is the subject of Chapter 1. A finite collection of atomic names is said to *support* such a structure if any permutation that fixes each name in the collection induces a transformation that leaves the entire structure unchanged with respect to whichever notion of equality of structures is of concern. This notion of support is an old one, mathematically speaking, that we put to new use within computer science.

From this viewpoint, a structure does not depend on a particular atomic name if there is a support set for the structure that does not include that name. This may seem a rather indirect way of getting at the idea of dependence upon names, but it has advantages compared with the more common approach based upon parametrization. In particular the use of functions means that name-dependency is made explicit, whereas often one wants to leave it implicit and work instead with the complementary relation of non-dependence, or *freshness* as we will call it. Chapters 2 and 3 develop the properties of the nominal sets notions of support and freshness. Chapter 7 consider applications of these notions to a fundamental technique in programming language semantics – the use of rule-based inductive and coinductive definitions of subsets of a given set. Chapter 9 uses freshness to model language constructs for hiding the identity of a name outside a given scope.

We turn next to the topic that was the original stimulus for developing the theory of nominal sets.

0.3 Abstract syntax with binders

When defining a programming language it is customary to specify its concrete syntax using context-free grammars that generate the strings of symbols that are legal phrases in the language. Definitions of concrete syntax have to deal with many issues to do with layout, punctuation and comments that are irrelevant to the meaning of programs. If one is primarily concerned with the semantics of programming languages, then what matters is the language's abstract syntax given in terms of parse trees. The use of abstract syntax trees enables two fundamental and inter-linked tools in programming language semantics: the definition of functions on syntax by recursion over the structure of trees; and proofs of properties of syntax by induction on the structure of trees. These techniques have their origin in the classical notions of primitive recursion and induction for the natural numbers, which were extended to abstract syntax trees by Burstall (1969), Martin-Löf (1971) and others.

However, abstract syntax trees and their associated structural recursion and induction principles are in one important respect not sufficiently abstract. They do not take into account the fact that some syntax constructors involve binding atomic names to specific scopes. Various schemes have been devised for specifying binding information. One popular option is to use some form of typed λ-calculus (Church, 1940) as a meta-language and express binding forms of the object-language in terms of function abstraction at the meta-level (Pfenning and Elliott, 1988; Harper *et al.*, 1993; Miller, 2000). Some forms of binding do not fit comfortably into this approach; see the discussion in (Sewell *et al.*, 2010, section 3), which describes a flexible mechanism for incorporating binding information in grammars that is part of the Ott tool. Whatever approach is taken, such binding specifications tell us which abstract syntax trees differ only up to consistent renaming of bound names. This is the relation of α-*equivalence*, generalized from its original use in λ-calculus.

To be a 'binder' in the sense that we are using it here, a language construct should have the property that for any reasonable definition of the language's semantics, α-equivalent phrases have equal meanings. Thus in the presence of binders, many syntax-manipulating operations only respect meaning if one operates on syntax at a level of abstraction that respects α-equivalence. So it is natural to regard α-equivalence classes of parse trees, rather than the trees themselves, as the true abstract syntactical structures which are assigned a meaning in a semantics. The problem is that unlike finite syntax trees, their α-equivalence classes are in general infinite sets and so require indirect methods of construction, computation and proof.

One way round this problem is to devise a scheme for canonical representatives of α-equivalence classes; for example by using indexes instead of names in binders, following de Bruijn (1972). The well-known disadvantage of this device is that it necessitates a calculus of operations on de Bruijn indexes that does not have much to do with our intuitive view of the structure of syntax. As a result there can be a 'coding gap' between statements of results about syntax with bound names and their de Bruijn versions – and hence it is easy to get things wrong. For this reason, most work on programming language semantics that is intended for human rather than machine consumption sticks with ordinary abstract syntax trees involving explicit bound names and uses an informal approach to α-equivalence classes. Yet there is a pressing need for fully formal methods when proving properties of program semantics, caused by the desire for high assurance of correctness in situations where lives or finances are at risk, or by complexities of scale, or both.

The informal approach is usually signalled by a form of words such as 'we identify expressions up to α-equivalence'; see for example Harper (2013, section 1.2) and Remark 10.1 in this book. In this informal mode, one does not make any notational distinction between an α-equivalence class and some chosen representative of it; and if that representative is later used in some context where its particular bound names clash in some way with those in the context, then it is changed to an α-equivalent expression whose bound names are fresh. The theory of nominal sets, with its notion of freshness, is able to fully formalize these common informal practices with bound names via the notion of name abstraction, discussed next.

0.4 Name abstraction

As described above, nominal sets provide a theory of implicit dependence on names (support) and name independence (freshness) based upon the action of name permutations on structures. If one wishes to make explicit how a structure depends upon a name, the traditional approach is to abstract and form a function from names to structures. Quite what a 'function from names to structures' means depends upon the strength of the ambient logical formalism. The notion of function is not as absolute as, say, the notion of 'ordered pair'. This has a complicating effect on logical systems that combine functional representations of binders in abstract syntax with computable functions operating on those representations (Poswolsky and Schürmann, 2009; Pientka and Dunfield, 2010). The two sorts of function have to be distinguished, leading to meta-meta-distinctions that are perhaps difficult for the average user to appreciate.

Nominal sets contain a form of name abstraction that manages to avoid these problems with function abstraction. Function abstraction models α- and β-conversion (and possibly η-conversion, depending upon how extensional is the notion of function). By contrast, name-abstraction in nominal sets models α-conversion, but only the limited form of β-conversion where one substitutes a fresh name for the bound name. This is just right for representing α-equivalence classes of abstract syntax in a way that captures the informal usage mentioned above. At the same time, nominal name-abstraction has a first-order character that allows one to use formalizations of it in logical systems (Urban, 2008) and in programming languages (Shinwell, 2005b) that mix representation of syntax up to α-equivalence with computation on that syntactical data. Chapter 4 develops the properties of this kind of name abstraction. Chapter 8 uses it to represent abstract syntax modulo α-equivalence as inductive data types with associated principles of 'α-structural' recursion and induction. Chapters 10 and 12 explore the applications of name abstraction within functional programming languages and to computational aspects of logic. At the moment these applications are most accessible to the world via the Isabelle/HOL interactive theorem-proving system (Nipkow *et al.*, 2002). This is because Urban and Berghofer (2006) have implemented a 'nominal datatype' package for it based on the nominal sets notion of name abstraction. This is now part of the official Isabelle software distribution and seems to be a useful tool for formalizing proofs about operational semantics that allows users to retain familiar habits and conventions concerning bound names and their freshness; see for example Bengtson and Parrow (2009).

0.5 Orbit-finiteness

Nominal sets provide a theory for mathematical structures involving atomic names based upon the symmetries exhibited by a structure when names are permuted. Finiteness obviously plays a fundamental role in the study of data structures and algorithms on them. Taking symmetry into account allows one to extend the reach of that study to encompass structures that are infinite, but only have finitely many different forms modulo symmetry. Name-abstractions provide an extreme example; they are singletons modulo symmetry and this partly explains why it is possible to use them to develop such a well-behaved theory of representation and computation for syntax with binders. In general, the property of having only finitely many orbits for the action of name permutations seems to be a very useful relaxation of the notion of finiteness. It is studied in Chapter 5. One application of orbit-finiteness is to the denotational semantics of programs based upon the use of partial orders, where potentially infinite behaviour is modelled as a limit of finite approximations; this is explored in Chapter 11.

0.6 Alternative formulations

One approach to formalizing the notion of freshness for names is to make use of the technique of 'possible worlds' stemming from Kripke semantics for intuitionistic and modal logics (Kripke, 1965). Structures are indexed by worlds that contain (at least) the names that are known at that stage. One then has to give morphisms between structures induced by moving from one world to another, for example by adding a name not already in the current world. The mathematics of this approach is best treated as part of the category theory of *presheaves* (Borceux, 2008, vol. 3, chapter 2). Fiore *et al.* (1999) use presheaves in their algebraic treatment of abstract syntax with binders. This is closely related to the technique of using 'well-scoped' de Bruijn indexes within functional programming and interactive theorem proving based upon constructive type theory; see for example Pouillard (2012), who compares this technique with nominal ones. Techniques based upon possible worlds bring with them a certain amount of book-keeping to do with change of world, for example when a world is weakened by adding a new name. By contrast, within the theory of nominal sets dependence on names is implicit – it is a property of an object (its support), rather than extra structure that has to be explicitly specified and manipulated.

As mentioned in the Preface, nominal sets arose from presheaves, sheaves and topos theory (Johnstone, 2002). The category of nominal sets was designed to be a conveniently concrete presentation of an existing topos of sheaves, known as the *Schanuel topos*. That uses a category of worlds consisting of injective functions between finite ordinals, thought of as the number of different well-scoped indexes currently in use. The passage to nominal sets involves first replacing finite ordinals by finite subsets of some fixed, infinite collection of atomic names; and then replacing injections between finite subsets by permutations of the whole collection of names. Neither of these steps change things up to category-theoretic equivalence; but the final result, the category of nominal sets that is studied in this book, is a much simpler setting in which to carry out the constructions and calculations relevant to the topics discussed in this introduction. This is particularly noticeable when it comes to higher-order functions; exponentials of nominal sets are appreciably easier to work with than exponentials of the **Set**-valued functors that are the objects of the Schanuel topos.

Chapter 6 describes the equivalence between the Schanuel topos and nominal sets. It also discusses some other equivalent formulations, notably the concept of *named set* that arose in the work of Montanari and Pistore (2000) on automated verification for mobile processes (Milner *et al.*, 1992).

0.7 Prerequisites

A prerequisite for understanding Part One of the book, on the theory of nominal sets, is some familiarity with naive set theory and higher-order logic; see Andrews (2002), for example.

We also assume a knowledge of the basics of category theory. The first work on nominal sets (Gabbay and Pitts, 1999, 2002; Gabbay, 2000) took a set-theoretic approach. It used *FM-sets*,[1] the cumulative hierarchy of hereditarily finitely supported sets devised by Fraenkel in the 1920s and used by him and Mostowski to get independence results for Zermelo–Fraenkel set theory with atoms; see Gabbay (2011) for a discussion of these historical sources. Nominal sets are essentially the FM-sets that depend upon no particular names (that is, whose support is empty). On the other hand the universe of FM-sets can be given a category-theoretic construction; and an 'algebraic' set-theory (Joyal and Moerdijk, 1995) can be developed for it within a category of (large) nominal sets. Should one develop the theory of nominal sets using set theory or category theory; in other words, should one be 'element-oriented' or 'morphism-oriented'? Here both approaches are used, as appropriate. Nevertheless, emphasis is placed upon category-theoretic concepts, particularly the use of various universal properties that characterize constructions uniquely up to isomorphism. So familiarity with the basic concepts of category theory – category, functor, natural transformation, adjunction and equivalence – is assumed. There are many suitable introductions, some aimed specifically at computer science applications, such as those by Pierce (1991) and Crole (1993). The classic text by MacLane (1971) still holds its own; and the three volumes by Borceux (2008) are usefully comprehensive. Some familiarity is needed with

---

[1] The term 'nominal set' was first used by Pitts (2003).

the connections between category theory, typed λ-calculus and higher-order logic, as described by Lambek and Scott (1986), for example.

The distinctive feature of nominal sets is their reliance upon some simple mathematics to do with symmetric groups and their actions on sets. This is not material that is likely to be familiar to the intended reader. So the book contains a self-contained account of the small amount of this well-developed topic that is needed.

For Part Two of the book, on computer science applications of nominal sets, the reader needs to be familiar with the basic techniques of programming language semantics; see for example Winskel (1993).

0.8 Notation

Being about a new subject, the literature on nominal sets does not always agree on matters of notation. The subject-specific notations used in this book are collected in an *Index of notation*. Apart from that we use more-or-less standard notations and conventions from logic, naive set theory and category theory, some of which are listed below.

Logic We write $\varphi \wedge \psi$ for conjunction, $\varphi \vee \psi$ for disjunction, $\varphi \Rightarrow \psi$ for implication, $\varphi \Leftrightarrow \psi$ for bi-implication, and $\neg\varphi$ for negation. Quantification is written $(\mathsf{Q}\,x)\,\varphi$ with the convention that the scope of the quantifier Q extends to the right as far as possible. So, for example, $(\forall x)\,\varphi \wedge \psi$ means $(\forall x)\,(\varphi \wedge \psi)$ rather than $((\forall x)\,\varphi) \wedge \psi$.

Sets We denote by $X - Y$ the set subtraction, $\{x \in X \mid x \notin Y\}$.

Functions Function application is written without punctuation: $F\,x$ means the result of applying function F to argument x. Multiple applications associate to the left. So, for example, $G\,F\,x$ means $(G\,F)\,x$, rather than $G\,(F\,x)$. If an expression $e(x)$ denotes an element of a set Y as x ranges over the elements of a set X, then the function from X to Y that it determines will be denoted by either of the notations

$$x \in X \mapsto e(x) \in Y \quad \text{or} \quad \lambda x \in X \rightarrow e(x).$$

When the set X has some structure, we use notations for patterns; for example if $X = X_1 \times X_2$ is a cartesian product, we write $\lambda(x_1, x_2) \in X_1 \times X_2 \rightarrow e(x_1, x_2)$.

Categories If **C** is a category, its collection of objects will also be denoted **C**. If X and Y are objects of **C**, then we write $f \in \mathbf{C}(X, Y)$, or just $f : X \to Y$, to indicate that f is a morphism in **C** whose domain is X and whose codomain is Y. The identity morphism for X is written as id_X, or just id. Composition is written in application order: $g \circ f \in \mathbf{C}(X, Z)$ denotes the composition of the morphism $f \in \mathbf{C}(X, Y)$ followed by the morphism $g \in \mathbf{C}(Y, Z)$.

PART ONE

THEORY

1
Permutations

The characteristic feature of the nominal sets approach to the syntax and semantics of formal languages is the use of permutations of names. As such, it is part of an important theme in mathematics with a well-developed body of work, the study of symmetry via the theory of groups. We need only a small amount of that theory, which we review in this chapter. See Beardon (2005) for an introduction to the subject.

1.1 The category of G-sets

A *group* is a set G equipped with an element $e \in G$ (the group *unit*), a function $(g,' g') \in G \times G \mapsto g g' \in G$ (the group *multiplication* operation) and a function $g \in G \mapsto g^{-1} \in G$ (the group *inverse* operation). This structure is required to satisfy

$$(g g') g'' = g (g' g''), \qquad (1.1)$$

$$e g = g = g e, \qquad (1.2)$$

$$g^{-1} g = e = g g^{-1}, \qquad (1.3)$$

for all $g, g', g'' \in G$. Groups are the objects of a category whose morphisms are functions $\theta : G \to G'$ satisfying

$$\theta e = e, \qquad (1.4)$$

$$\theta(g g') = (\theta g)(\theta g'), \qquad (1.5)$$

$$\theta(g^{-1}) = (\theta g)^{-1}, \qquad (1.6)$$

for all $g, g' \in G$. (Since inverses are necessarily unique, property (1.6) is implied by the preceding two.) Composition and identities in the category are

13

given by the usual operations of composition and identity for functions. A *sub-group* of a group G is a subset $G' \subseteq G$ that contains e and is closed under the group multiplication and inverse operations.

Example 1.1   If A is a set, then a *permutation* of A is a bijection π from A to itself. The composition $\pi' \circ \pi$ of two functions that are permutations is another such, as is the inverse function π^{-1} of a permutation; and the identity function id on A is a permutation. Therefore, taking the group multiplication to be function composition, the permutations of A form a group, called the *symmetric group* on the set A and denoted $\mathrm{Sym}\, A$. It is a classic result of group theory (*Cayley's theorem*, a special case of the *Yoneda lemma* in category theory) that every group is isomorphic to a subgroup of a symmetric group.

An *action* of a group G on a set X is a function $G \times X \to X$ assigning to each $(g, x) \in G \times X$ an element $g \cdot x$ of X satisfying

$$g \cdot (g' \cdot x) = (g\,g') \cdot x, \tag{1.7}$$

$$e \cdot x = x, \tag{1.8}$$

for all $g, g' \in G$ and $x \in X$. This is equivalent to specifying a morphism of groups $G \to \mathrm{Sym}\, X$ (see Exercise 1.1).

Definition 1.2   If G is a group, then a *G-set* is a set X equipped with an action of G on X. We will usually refer to a G-set by naming its underlying set X, using the same notation $\_ \cdot \_$ for all group actions, whatever the set X. G-sets are the objects of a category $[G, \mathbf{Set}]$ whose morphisms from X to X' are *equivariant functions*, that is, functions $F : X \to X'$ satisfying

$$F(g \cdot x) = g \cdot (F\, x) \tag{1.9}$$

for all $g \in G$ and $x \in X$. Composition and identities in the category are the same as in the category $\mathbf{Set}$ of sets and functions.

Example 1.3   If G is any subgroup of the symmetric group $\mathrm{Sym}\, A$, we get a G-set with underlying set A by taking the G-action to be given by function application: $\pi \cdot a = \pi a$.

Example 1.4   Let Σ be a (single-sorted) algebraic signature. Thus $\Sigma = (\Sigma_n \mid n \in \mathbb{N})$ is a countably infinite family of sets. The elements of each set Σ_n are the n-ary operations of the signature. The set $\Sigma[X]$ of *algebraic terms* over Σ with variables drawn from some set X is inductively defined by the following rules:

$$\frac{x \in X}{x \in \Sigma[X]} \qquad \frac{t_1 \in \Sigma[X] \quad \cdots \quad t_n \in \Sigma[X] \quad \mathrm{op} \in \Sigma_n}{\mathrm{op}(t_1, \ldots, t_n) \in \Sigma[X]}.$$

There is an action of $\mathrm{Sym}\, X$ on $\Sigma[X]$ given by applying a permutation to variables where they occur in algebraic terms:

$$\pi \cdot x = \pi x,$$
$$\pi \cdot \mathrm{op}(t_1, \ldots, t_n) = \mathrm{op}(\pi \cdot t_1, \ldots, \pi \cdot t_n). \tag{1.10}$$

1.2 Products and coproducts

Given a group G and G-sets $X_1, \ldots, X_n$, we make the cartesian product

$$X_1 \times \cdots \times X_n \triangleq \{(x_1, \ldots, x_n) \mid x_1 \in X_1 \wedge \cdots \wedge x_n \in X_n\} \tag{1.11}$$

into a G-set by defining the group action coordinate-wise:

$$g \cdot (x_1, \ldots, x_n) \triangleq (g \cdot x_1, \ldots, g \cdot x_n). \tag{1.12}$$

In case $n = 0$, the cartesian product is just a singleton set $1 = \{()\}$ and the action is $g \cdot () = ()$. Definition (1.12) ensures that the projection functions from a product of G-sets to one of its components

$$\mathrm{proj}_i : X_1 \times \cdots \times X_n \to X_i,$$
$$\mathrm{proj}_i \triangleq \lambda(x_1, \ldots, x_n) \in X_1 \times \cdots \times X_n \to x_i \tag{1.13}$$

are all equivariant and hence give morphisms in $[G, \mathbf{Set}]$. Indeed they make $X_1 \times \cdots \times X_n$ into the categorical product of the objects X_i in $[G, \mathbf{Set}]$. For if $(F_i : X \to X_i \mid i = 1, \ldots, n)$ are some equivariant functions, then the unique function $\langle F_1, \ldots, F_n \rangle : X \to X_1 \times \cdots \times X_n$ satisfying $\mathrm{proj}_i \circ \langle F_1, \ldots, F_n \rangle = F_i$ (for $i = 1, \ldots, n$) is easily seen to be equivariant.

Example 1.5 Given any set X, the second projection function $\lambda(g, x) \in G \times X \to x$ is trivially a G-action. We call X equipped with this action the *discrete G-set* on X. If $F : X \to Y$ is an equivariant function whose domain X is a discrete G-set, then for each $x \in X$, $F x = F(g \cdot x) = g \cdot (F x)$. Thus F maps X into the subset

$$\Gamma Y \triangleq \{y \in Y \mid (\forall g \in G)\, g \cdot y = y\}. \tag{1.14}$$

(See Exercise 1.2.) The terminal object 1 is a discrete G-set and the *global sections* $1 \to X$ of any G-set X correspond to elements of ΓX. Note that ΓX may be empty even if X as a set is non-empty. For example, when $G = \mathrm{Sym}\, A$ is the symmetric group on a set A, the $\mathrm{Sym}\, A$-set A from Example 1.3 satisfies $\Gamma A = \emptyset$ so long as A has at least two elements. In this case $\mathrm{proj}_1, \mathrm{proj}_2 : A \times A \to A$ are different morphisms in $[\mathrm{Sym}\, A, \mathbf{Set}]$ that have equal compositions with every $1 \to A \times A$ (since there are no such global sections). Thus $[\mathrm{Sym}\, A, \mathbf{Set}]$

is not a well pointed category. (In general a category with a terminal object is *well pointed* if any two morphisms with equal domain and codomain are equal if their compositions with any global section are equal.)

Example 1.6   The group G is itself a G-set once we endow it with the *conjugation* action:

$$g \cdot g' \triangleq g g' g^{-1}. \tag{1.15}$$

This is not the only possible action of G on itself, unless $G = \{e\}$ is trivial; see Exercise 1.3. However it has the distinction of making the action function $F \triangleq \lambda(g, x) \in G \times X \to g \cdot x$ for any G-set X into an equivariant function $F : G \times X \to X$. For we have $F(g \cdot g', g \cdot x) = (g\, g' g^{-1}) \cdot (g \cdot x) = (g\, g' g^{-1} g) \cdot x = (g\, g') \cdot x = g \cdot F(g', x)$.

We make the disjoint union

$$X_1 + \cdots + X_n \triangleq \{(i, x) \mid i \in \{1, \ldots, n\} \land x \in X_i\} \tag{1.16}$$

into a G-set by defining the group action as follows:

$$g \cdot (i, x) \triangleq (i, g \cdot x). \tag{1.17}$$

It is easy to see that definition (1.17) inherits the required properties (1.7) and (1.8) from the actions for each X_i. It implies that the functions injecting a G-set into a disjoint union of G-sets

$$\begin{aligned} \text{inj}_i &: X_i \to X_1 + \cdots + X_n, \\ \text{inj}_i &\triangleq \lambda x \in X_i \to (i, x) \end{aligned} \tag{1.18}$$

are morphisms in $[G, \mathbf{Set}]$ and make $X_1 + \cdots + X_n$ into the coproduct of the objects X_i in $[G, \mathbf{Set}]$.

The above constructions of cartesian product and disjoint union extend from the finite to the infinite case. Thus if $(X_i \mid i \in I)$ is a family of G-sets indexed by the elements of a set I, then the cartesian product

$$\prod_{i \in I} X_i \triangleq \{(x_i \mid i \in I) \mid (\forall i \in I)\ x_i \in X_i\} \tag{1.19}$$

equipped with the G-action $g \cdot (x_i \mid i \in I) = (g \cdot x_i \mid i \in I)$ is the product of the objects X_i in $[G, \mathbf{Set}]$. Similarly, the disjoint union

$$\sum_{i \in I} X_i \triangleq \{(i, x) \mid i \in I \land x \in X_i\} \tag{1.20}$$

equipped with the G-action $g \cdot (i, x) = (i, g \cdot x)$ is their coproduct in $[G, \mathbf{Set}]$.

1.3 Natural numbers

The coproduct $\sum_{i \in I} X_i$ in the case $I = \mathbb{N} = \{0, 1, 2, \ldots\}$ and each X_i is the terminal 1, is necessarily a *natural number object* in $[G, \mathbf{Set}]$. In other words, it is a G-set N equipped with equivariant functions

$$1 \xrightarrow{\ \text{zero}\ } N \xrightarrow{\ \text{suc}\ } N \tag{1.21}$$

with the universal property that for any other such diagram in $[G, \mathbf{Set}]$

$$1 \xrightarrow{\ X_0\ } X \xrightarrow{\ F\ } X \tag{1.22}$$

there is a unique equivariant function iter $X_0\, F$ making

$$
\begin{array}{ccccc}
1 & \xrightarrow{\ \text{zero}\ } & N & \xrightarrow{\ \text{suc}\ } & N \\
\| & & \big\downarrow \text{iter} X_0\, F & & \big\downarrow \text{iter} X_0\, F \\
1 & \xrightarrow[\ X_0\ ]{} & X & \xrightarrow[\ F\ ]{} & X
\end{array}
\tag{1.23}
$$

commute.

Note that $\sum_{i \in I} X_i$ is discrete (Example 1.5) when all the X_i are discrete G-sets. In particular we can identify N with the discrete G-set on the set $\mathbb{N}$ of natural numbers equipped with the usual zero and successor functions: zero $() = 0$, suc $n = n + 1$. Given (1.22), the unique function iter $X_0\, F : \mathbb{N} \to X$ making (1.23) commute is recursively defined by

$$\text{iter}\, X_0\, F\, 0 = X_0(),$$

$$\text{iter}\, X_0\, F\, (n + 1) = F\, (\text{iter}\, X_0\, F\, n).$$

It is equivariant because $\mathbb{N}$ is discrete and X_0 and F are equivariant.

1.4 Functions

Recall that a category with finite products is cartesian closed (Borceux, 2008, vol. 1, p. 335) if every pair of objects X and Y possesses an *exponential*. This is an object Y^X equipped with a morphism app $: Y^X \times X \to Y$ satisfying the universal property that for any other morphism $F : Z \times X \to Y$, there is a unique morphism $\overline{F} : Z \to Y^X$ making the following triangle commute:

$$
\begin{array}{ccc}
Z \times X & & \\
\big\downarrow {\overline{F} \times \text{id}_X} & \searrow^{F} & \\
Y^X \times X & \xrightarrow[\ \text{app}\ ]{} & Y.
\end{array}
$$

Theorem 1.7   *For any group G, the category* $[G, \mathbf{Set}]$ *is cartesian closed.*

Proof   This theorem can be deduced from the more general fact that cate-gories of **Set**-valued functors are cartesian closed (see Johnstone, 2002, propo-sition 1.5.5, for instance); this is because each group G can be regarded as a category with a single object and whose morphisms are the group elements. However, unlike for functor categories in general, in this particular case the cartesian closed structure is almost as simple as that of the category of sets itself and is worth describing explicitly. We saw in the previous section that $[G, \mathbf{Set}]$ has finite products, inherited from **Set**. So we just have to describe exponentials.

If X and Y are G-sets for a group G, then we can make the set Y^X of functions with domain X and codomain Y into a G-set by defining the action of $g \in G$ on a function $F \in Y^X$ to be

$$g \cdot F \triangleq \lambda x \in X \to g \cdot (F(g^{-1} \cdot x)). \tag{1.24}$$

The does give a group action on functions (Exercise 1.4). Equivariant functions $F : X \to Y$ are precisely the elements of Y^X that satisfy $g \cdot F = F$ for all $g \in G$ (Exercise 1.5).

Definition (1.24) ensures that the application function

$$\begin{aligned} \mathrm{app} &: Y^X \times X \to Y, \\ \mathrm{app} &\triangleq \lambda(F, x) \in Y^X \times X \to F\,x \end{aligned} \tag{1.25}$$

is equivariant. For we have

$$\begin{aligned} &\mathrm{app}(g \cdot F, g \cdot x) \\ =\ & \{\text{definition of app}\} \\ &(g \cdot F)(g \cdot x) \\ =\ & \{\text{definition of } g \cdot F\} \\ &g \cdot (F(g^{-1} \cdot (g \cdot x))) \\ =\ & \{(1.7), (1.3) \text{ and } (1.8)\} \\ &g \cdot (F\,x) \\ =\ & \{\text{definition of app}\} \\ &g \cdot \mathrm{app}(F, x). \end{aligned}$$

The equivariance of the currying function

$$\begin{aligned} \mathrm{curry} &: Y^{Z \times X} \to (Y^X)^Z, \\ \mathrm{curry} &\triangleq \lambda F \in Y^{Z \times X}, z \in Z, x \in X \to F(z, x) \end{aligned} \tag{1.26}$$

is a similar calculation (Exercise 1.6).

It follows that app : $Y^X \times X \to Y$ gives the exponential of Y by X in $[G, \mathbf{Set}]$. For the usual properties of application and currying in **Set** imply that $\overline{F} \triangleq$

curry $F' \in (Y^X)^Z$ is the unique function satisfying app $\circ$ (curry $F' \times \mathrm{id}_X) = F'$. So we just have to see that it is equivariant and hence a morphism $Z \to Y^X$ in $[G, \mathbf{Set}]$; but this follows from the equivariance of application, of currying and of F', using Exercise 1.5. $\qquad\square$

1.5 Power sets

Let

$$\mathbb{B} \triangleq \{\text{true, false}\} \tag{1.27}$$

denote the discrete G-set (Example 1.5) on a two element set. Given any G-set X, we can use the bijection between functions $X \to \mathbb{B}$ and subsets of X to transfer the G-action on $\mathbb{B}^X$ to one on the powerset

$$\mathrm{P}X \triangleq \{S \mid S \subseteq X\}. \tag{1.28}$$

As a matter of notation, the subset of $\mathrm{P}X$ consisting of the finite subsets of X will be written

$$\mathrm{P_f}X \triangleq \{S \subseteq X \mid S \text{ is finite}\}. \tag{1.29}$$

Converting a subset $S \subseteq X$ to a corresponding function $\chi_S : X \to \mathbb{B}$

$$\chi_S\, x \triangleq \begin{cases} \text{true} & \text{if } x \in S, \\ \text{false} & \text{if } x \notin S, \end{cases} \tag{1.30}$$

and acting by $g \in G$ to get $g \cdot \chi_S$, the subset $\{x \in X \mid (g \cdot \chi_S)\,x = \text{true}\}$ gives the action of g on S. Since $\mathbb{B}$ is discrete, $(g \cdot \chi_S)\,x = g \cdot (\chi_S\,(g^{-1} \cdot x)) = \chi_S\,(g^{-1} \cdot x)$. So $(g \cdot \chi_S)\,x = \text{true}$ if and only if $g^{-1} \cdot x \in S$. Therefore

$$g \cdot S = \{x \in S \mid g^{-1} \cdot x \in S\}. \tag{1.31}$$

Note that $g^{-1} \cdot x \in S \Leftrightarrow (\exists x' \in S)\, x = g \cdot x'$ and thus

$$g \cdot S = \{g \cdot x \mid x \in S\}. \tag{1.32}$$

The associativity and unit properties of the G-action on functions transfer to give the required properties for an action on subsets: $g \cdot (g' \cdot S) = (g\, g') \cdot S$ and $e \cdot S = S$. Note also that subset inclusion is preserved by the G-action:

$$S \subseteq S' \Rightarrow g \cdot S \subseteq g \cdot S'. \tag{1.33}$$

Definition 1.8 The *equivariant subsets* of a G-set X are those $S \subseteq X$ which are closed under the G-action on X in the sense that for all $x \in X$ and $g \in G$

$$x \in S \Rightarrow g \cdot x \in S. \tag{1.34}$$

So by (1.32), $S \subseteq X$ is an equivariant subset if $g \cdot S \subseteq S$ holds for all $g \in G$. Note that in this case we have

$$S = e \cdot S = (g\,g^{-1}) \cdot S = g \cdot (g^{-1} \cdot S) \subseteq g \cdot S$$

by (1.33); and hence $g \cdot S = S$ for any $g \in G$. Thus equivariant subsets are precisely the elements of P X that are fixed by the action of any $g \in G$. Compare this with the similar characterization of equivariant functions as elements of Y^X in Exercise 1.5.

A morphism $F : Y \to X$ in a category **C** is a *monomorphism* if $F \circ F_1 = F \circ F_2$ implies $F_1 = F_2$ for any $F_1, F_2 : \cdot \to Y$. We write $F : Y \rightarrowtail X$ to indicate that F is a monomorphism. The collection of monomorphisms with codomain X is pre-ordered by the relation

$$(F_1 : Y_1 \rightarrowtail X) \le (F_2 : Y_2 \rightarrowtail X) \Leftrightarrow (\exists F : Y_1 \to Y_2)\, F_1 = F_2 \circ F. \quad (1.35)$$

A *subobject* of X is an equivalence class of monomorphisms with codomain X for the equivalence relation generated by $\le$. When the category is $[G, \mathbf{Set}]$ it is not hard to see that the subobjects of a G-set X are in bijection with the equivariant subsets of X; and under this bijection the partial order on subobjects induced by (1.35) corresponds to subset inclusion. (See Exercise 1.7.)

We saw above (Theorem 1.7) that $[G, \mathbf{Set}]$ is a cartesian closed category. It also has a subobject classifier and hence is a topos (Johnstone, 2002, example 2.1.4). This means there is an object Ω equipped with a morphism $\top : 1 \to \Omega$ so that for any monomorphism $F : Y \rightarrowtail X$ there is a unique morphism $\chi_F : X \to \Omega$ making

a pullback square in $[G, \mathbf{Set}]$. In fact $[G, \mathbf{Set}]$ is Boolean (Johnstone, 2002, p. 38), since $\Omega = 1 + 1$ is just the discrete two-element set G-set $\mathbb{B}$. For if $F : Y \rightarrowtail X$ corresponds to the equivariant subset $S \subseteq X$, then $\chi_F : X \to \Omega$ is the characteristic function (1.30), which is an equivariant function, because S is an equivariant subset.

Since $[G, \mathbf{Set}]$ is a Boolean topos, it provides a model of classical higher-order logic (Johnstone, 2002, chapter D4). Just as for the cartesian closed structure, the interpretation of higher-order logic in $[G, \mathbf{Set}]$ is the same as in **Set**.

Proposition 1.9 *Let X and Y be G-sets. The following are equivariant subsets:*

(i) *Truth* $X \subseteq X$.
(ii) *Equality* $\{(x, x') \in X \times X \mid x = x'\} \subseteq X \times X$.
(iii) *Membership* $\{(x, S) \in X \times P(X) \mid x \in S\} \subseteq X \times P(X)$.

The following are equivariant functions:

(iv) *Conjunction* $\_ \cap \_ : P(X) \times P(X) \rightarrow P(X)$.
(v) *Negation* $\neg : P(X) \rightarrow P(X)$, *where* $\neg S \triangleq \{x \in X \mid x \notin S\}$.
(vi) *Universal quantification* $\bigcap : P(P(X)) \rightarrow P(X)$, *where* $\bigcap S \triangleq \{x \in X \mid (\forall S \in S)\, x \in S\}$.
(vii) *Substitution* $f^* : P(Y) \rightarrow P(X)$, *where* $f : X \rightarrow Y$ *is an equivariant function and* $f^*S \triangleq \{x \in X \mid f(x) \in S\}$.
(viii) *Comprehension* compr $: P(X \times Y) \rightarrow P(Y)^X$, *where* compr $S \triangleq \lambda x \in X \rightarrow \{y \in Y \mid (x, y) \in S\}$.

Proof These equivariance properties follow easily from the definition of the action of G on subsets. For example,

$$x \in g \cdot (\neg S) \Leftrightarrow g^{-1} \cdot x \in \neg S \Leftrightarrow g^{-1} \cdot x \notin S \Leftrightarrow x \notin g \cdot S \Leftrightarrow x \in \neg(g \cdot S)$$

so that $g \cdot (\neg S) = \neg(g \cdot S)$. $\qquad\square$

The proposition gives a very rich collection of equivariant subsets. Consider the formulas of classical higher-order logic; they are built up from atomic formulas using equality, membership, the propositional connectives and quantification over iterated product, function and power types. If $\varphi(x_1, \ldots, x_n)$ is such a formula with free variables as indicated, and if each variable x_i is interpreted as ranging over a G-set X_i, then the Tarski interpretation of φ (with product, function and power types interpreted as cartesian products, exponentials and powersets) determines a subset of $X_1 \times \cdots \times X_n$ in the usual way. If the function and relation symbols in φ are all interpreted by equivariant functions and subsets, then Theorem 1.9 implies that the interpretation of $\varphi(x_1, \ldots, x_n)$ is an equivariant subset of $X_1 \times \cdots \times X_n$. Thus we have:

Equivariance Principle *Any function or relation that is defined from equivariant functions and relations using classical higher-order logic is itself equivariant.*

We will use this principle to avoid proving that particular constructs are equivariant on a case-by-case basis. The next section gives a first example of this. We end this section with two warnings about the Equivariance Principle.

Note 1.10   In applying the Equivariance Principle, one must take into account *all* the parameters upon which a particular construction depends. For example, regarding G as a G-set as in Example 1.6, we saw there that for any G-set X the action

$$F : G \times X \to X,$$
$$F \triangleq \lambda(g, x) \in G \times X \to g \cdot x$$

is an equivariant function. However, if we fix upon a particular $g_0 \in G$, then the function $F_0 = F(g_0, -) : X \to X$ is not in general equivariant unless G is a commutative group (or $g_0 = e$), since $g \cdot F_0 x = (g g_0) \cdot x$, whereas $F_0(g \cdot x) = (g_0 g) \cdot x$.

Note 1.11   Classical higher-order logic is sometimes formulated using the ε-operation of Hilbert, $\varepsilon x.\varphi(x)$, which satisfies $(\forall x \in X)\ \varphi(x) \Rightarrow \varphi(\varepsilon x.\varphi(x))$. Unless G is a trivial group, such an operation cannot be equivariant – see Exercise 1.8. Thus the Equivariance Principle does not apply to constructions employing this strong form of choice. Toposes of the form $[G, \mathbf{Set}]$ do satisfy a weaker, internal version of the Axiom of Choice (Johnstone, 2002, examples 4.5.2(b)). However, when we move from considering equivariance to finite support in the next chapter, even that form of choice fails; see Section 2.7.

1.6 Partial functions

Given sets X and Y, the set $X \rightharpoonup Y$ of partial functions from X to Y is the subset of $P(X \times Y)$ consisting of all subsets $F \subseteq X \times Y$ that are *single-valued*

$$(\forall x \in X)(\forall y, y' \in Y)\,(x, y) \in F \land (x, y') \in F \Rightarrow y = y'. \tag{1.36}$$

We write $F x \equiv y$ to mean that F is defined at $x \in X$ and takes value $y \in Y$. Thus

$$F x \equiv y \Leftrightarrow (x, y) \in F. \tag{1.37}$$

More generally, given partial functions $F_1 \in X_1 \rightharpoonup Y$ and $F_2 \in X_2 \rightharpoonup Y$, for all $x_1 \in X_1$ and $x_2 \in X_2$ we define

$$F_1 x_1 \equiv F_2 x_2 \Leftrightarrow (\forall y \in Y)\,(x_1, y) \in F_1 \Leftrightarrow (x_2, y) \in F_2. \tag{1.38}$$

($F x \equiv y$ is the special case of this when $F_1 = F$ and $F_2 = \mathrm{id}_Y$.) More generally still, but less formally, if e and e' are expressions denoting partially defined values we write $e \equiv e'$ to mean that e is defined if and only if e' is and in that case they are equal values. This is sometimes referred to as *Kleene equivalence*.

The *domain of definition* Dom F and the *image* Img F of a partial function $F \in X \rightharpoonup Y$ are

$$\text{Dom } F \triangleq \{x \in X \mid (\exists y \in Y)\,(x, y) \in F\}, \tag{1.39}$$

$$\text{Img } F \triangleq \{y \in Y \mid (\exists x \in X)\,(x, y) \in F\}. \tag{1.40}$$

(We reserve the notation 'dom' for the domain of a morphism in a category. Thus in the category of sets and partial functions, given $F \in X \rightharpoonup Y$ we have dom $F = X$, but Dom F may be strictly smaller than X.)

If X and Y are G-sets, then using the Equivariance Principle we have that $X \rightharpoonup Y$ is an equivariant subset of $P(X \times Y)$ and hence a G-set. As the next result shows, the G-action on partial functions agrees with the action on total functions (1.24).

Proposition 1.12 *If X and Y are G-sets and $F \in X \rightharpoonup Y$, then for all $g \in G$ and $x \in X$*

$$(g \cdot F)\,x \equiv g \cdot (F(g^{-1} \cdot x)). \tag{1.41}$$

Proof If $(g \cdot F)\,x$ is defined, say $(x, y) \in g \cdot F$, then $(g^{-1} \cdot x, g^{-1} \cdot y) = g^{-1} \cdot (x, y) \in F$; so $F(g^{-1} \cdot x)$ is defined and equal to $g^{-1} \cdot y$ and therefore $g \cdot (F(g^{-1} \cdot x)) \equiv g \cdot (g^{-1} \cdot y) = y$.

Conversely if $g \cdot (F(g^{-1} \cdot x)) \equiv y$, then the subexpression $F(g^{-1} \cdot x)$ must also be defined, that is, $(g^{-1} \cdot x, y') \in F$ for some y' with $g \cdot y' = y$. Hence $(x, y) = (g \cdot (g^{-1} \cdot x), g \cdot y') = g \cdot (g^{-1} \cdot x, y') \in g \cdot F$ and thus $(g \cdot F)\,x \equiv y$. □

The elements of Y^X are those partial functions $F \in X \rightharpoonup Y$ that are also *total relation*

$$(\forall x \in X)(\exists y \in Y)\,(x, y) \in F. \tag{1.42}$$

Thus Y^X is an equivariant subset of $P(X \times Y)$ and the proposition shows that the action of G on subsets (1.32) of products (1.12) agrees with the action on functions (1.24) when restricted to Y^X.

1.7 Quotient sets

We write $X/\!\sim$ for the set of equivalence classes $[x]_\sim \triangleq \{x' \in X \mid x \sim x'\}$ of an equivalence relation $\sim$ on a set X. Given a group G, an *equivariant equivalence relation* on a G-set X is simply an equivalence relation on the underlying set of X which is equivariant as a subset of $X \times X$ (see Definition 1.8). In this case, for each $g \in G$, the function $g \cdot \_ : X \to X$ respects the equivalence relation and hence induces a function on equivalence classes, $X/\sim \;\to\; X/\sim$, that we also write as $g \cdot \_$. Thus

$$g \cdot [x]_\sim = [g \cdot x]_\sim \qquad (1.43)$$

and we get a G-action on $X/\sim$, which we call a *quotient G-set*.

Note that by virtue of (1.43), the quotient function

$$\begin{aligned} q &: X \to X/\sim, \\ q &\triangleq \lambda x \in X \to [x]_\sim \end{aligned} \qquad (1.44)$$

is equivariant.

Any function $F : X \to Y$ that respects $\sim$,

$$x \sim x' \Rightarrow F\,x = F\,x',$$

induces a unique function $\overline{F}$ making

commute. Note that $\overline{F}$ is definable within higher-order logic from $\sim$ and F. Thus assuming $\sim$ is an equivariant equivalence relation, by the Equivariance Principle, if F is equivariant, then so is $\overline{F}$.

1.8 Finite permutations

So far in this chapter we have considered group actions for an arbitrary group G. Now we specialize to the case we need in the rest of the book, groups of finite permutations and their actions.

Definition 1.13 We will call a permutation $\pi \in \mathrm{Sym}\,A$ *finite* if $\{a \in A \mid \pi a \neq a\}$ is a finite subset of A. Note that $\mathrm{id} \in \mathrm{Sym}\,A$ is finite and that the composition and inverse of finite permutations are finite. Therefore we get a subgroup of $\mathrm{Sym}\,A$ of finite permutations, denoted $\mathrm{Perm}\,A$.

If $S \subseteq A$ is a finite subset of a set A, we will often wish to 'move' the elements of S to some other finite subset S' via a finite permutation of A that fixes elements outside $S \cup S'$. The following lemma shows we can always do this.

Lemma 1.14 (Homogeneity lemma) *For any finite subsets* $S, S' \in P_f A$ *and any bijection* $f : S \cong S'$, *there exists* $\pi \in \mathrm{Perm}\, A$ *that extends* f *to a bijection on the whole of* A *and that is the identity away from* $S \cup S'$:

$$(\forall a \in S)\, \pi a = f a \ \wedge \ (\forall a \in A - (S \cup S'))\, \pi a = a.$$

Proof Since S and S' are finite sets with the same cardinality, $|S' - S| = |S'| - |S \cap S'| = |S| - |S \cap S'| = |S - S'|$. So one can find a bijection $f' : (S' - S) \cong (S - S')$. Then the function $\pi : A \rightarrow A$, defined by

$$\pi a \triangleq \begin{cases} f a & \text{if } a \in S, \\ f' a & \text{if } a \in S' - S, \\ a & \text{if } a \in A - (S \cup S'), \end{cases}$$

is a finite permutation with the required properties. $\qquad\square$

The *transposition* (also known as *swapping*) of a pair of elements $a_1, a_2 \in A$ is the finite permutation $(a_1\ a_2) \in \mathrm{Perm}\, A$ given for all $a \in A$ by

$$(a_1\ a_2)\, a \triangleq \begin{cases} a_2 & \text{if } a = a_1, \\ a_1 & \text{if } a = a_2, \\ a & \text{otherwise.} \end{cases} \tag{1.45}$$

Note that this definition makes sense even if $a_1 = a_2$, in which case $(a_1\ a_2) = \mathrm{id}$. If $a_1 \neq a_2$, then $(a_1\ a_2)$ is a 2-cycle. In general the *n-cycle* $(a_1\ a_2\ a_3 \cdots a_n)$ is the element of $\mathrm{Perm}\, A$ that maps a_1 to a_2, a_2 to a_3, ..., a_{n-1} to a_n, and a_n to a_1, while leaving all other elements fixed; here $a_1, \ldots, a_n$ have to be n mutually distinct elements of A with $n \geq 2$.

Transpositions play a prominent role in what follows, because they generate the group $\mathrm{Perm}\, A$.

Theorem 1.15 *Every element* π *of the group* $\mathrm{Perm}\, A$ *of finite permutations on a set* A *is equal to the composition of a finite sequence of transpositions* $(a\ a')$ *with*

$$\pi a \neq a \neq a' \neq \pi a'. \tag{1.46}$$

(The sequence may be empty, in which case its composition is by definition the identity function.)

Proof We argue by induction on the size of the finite set $\{a \in A \mid \pi a \neq a\}$. In the base case when it is empty, π must be the identity function, which is the composition of the empty sequence of transpositions. For the induction step, given $\pi \in \mathrm{Perm}\, A$ with $\{a \mid \pi a \neq a\}$ non-empty, pick some a_0 in that set and consider $\pi' = \pi \circ (a_0\ \pi^{-1} a_0)$. It satisfies $\pi' a_0 = a_0$ and $(\forall a \neq a_0)\ \pi a = a \Rightarrow \pi' a = a$. Hence

$$\{a \mid \pi' a \neq a\} \subseteq \{a \mid \pi a \neq a\} - \{a_0\}. \qquad (1.47)$$

In particular $\{a \mid \pi' a \neq a\}$ is strictly smaller than $\{a \mid \pi a \neq a\}$ and so by induction hypothesis π' is a finite composition of transpositions of elements satisfying (1.46) for π' and hence also for π in view of (1.47). Hence so is π, because

$$
\begin{aligned}
&\pi \\
={}& \{\text{transpositions are idempotent!}\} \\
&\pi \circ (a_0\ \pi^{-1} a_0) \circ (a_0\ \pi^{-1} a_0) \\
={}& \{\text{definition of } \pi'\} \\
&\pi' \circ (a_0\ \pi^{-1} a_0),
\end{aligned}
$$

and this completes the induction step.   □

In view of the theorem, an action of Perm A on a set X is completely determined by the *swapping operation*

$$
\begin{aligned}
&swap : A \times A \times X \to X, \\
&swap \triangleq \lambda(a, a', x) \in A \times A \times X \to (a\ a') \cdot x.
\end{aligned}
\qquad (1.48)
$$

This is because every $\pi \in \text{Perm}\,A$ is equal to a composition of transpositions

$$\pi = (a_1\ a_1') \circ (a_2\ a_2') \circ \cdots \circ (a_n\ a_n'), \qquad (1.49)$$

and hence

$$\pi \cdot x = swap(a_1, a_1', swap(a_2, a_2', \ldots swap(a_n, a_n', x) \cdots)). \qquad (1.50)$$

The description of [Perm A, **Set**] as a category of 'sets with a name-swapping operation' is explored further in Section 6.1. Here we just note that swapping is equivariant.

Proposition 1.16   *For each* Perm A-*set* X, *the function* $swap : A \times A \times X \to X$ *defined in* (1.48) *is equivariant (regarding* A *as a* Perm A-*set as in Example 1.3).*

Proof   Note that $\pi \circ (a\ a') = (\pi a\ \pi a') \circ \pi$, for any $\pi \in \text{Perm}\,A$ and $a, a' \in A$. Therefore $\pi \cdot swap(a, a', x) = \pi \cdot ((a\ a') \cdot x) = (\pi a\ \pi a') \cdot (\pi \cdot x) = swap(\pi \cdot a, \pi \cdot a', \pi \cdot x)$.   □

1.9 Name symmetries

In the rest of this book we fix an infinite set $\mathbb{A}$ and develop some properties of Perm $\mathbb{A}$-sets that are relevant to computer science. We call the elements of $\mathbb{A}$ *atomic names*, because they are items of data whose internal structure is irrelevant; their only relevant attribute is their identity. We need $\mathbb{A}$ to be infinite, and might as well take it to be countable (see Exercise 6.2). For concreteness, we could take atomic names to be natural numbers, or bit-patterns. However, their symmetries only preserve equality and inequality, but not any other properties the concrete representation of an atomic name might have. (We will see in Section 6.2 that since we restrict attention to sets with the finite support property (Definition 2.2), the fact that we use the group of finite permutations Perm $\mathbb{A}$, rather than the group of all permutations Sym $\mathbb{A}$, is not significant.)

'Structureless' names have a rich theory with many applications, as we will see. However, it is also natural to consider structures on the set $\mathbb{A}$ that are richer than just (in)equality and to consider symmetries of that structure, that is, subgroups of Sym $\mathbb{A}$. For example, one might want a total order on names, or want to make names the vertices of a graph; in the first case one would consider order-preserving permutations[1] and in the second automorphisms of the graph. However, to get a useful theory of generalized nominal sets with versions of (at least) the notion of 'support' that we develop in the next chapter, it seems that one needs the structure on $\mathbb{A}$ and its symmetries to have homogeneity properties analogous to Lemma 1.14. For ordered names, that means $\mathbb{A}$ should be the rational numbers with the usual, dense linear order; for names with an edge relation, it means that $\mathbb{A}$ should be the random graph of Rado (1964). These are instances of *Fraïssé limits* (also known as 'universal' homogeneous structures); see Hodges (1993, section 7.1). Some of the theory of nominal sets presented in this book (particularly the material in Chapter 5) is generalized to these 'Fraïssé nominal sets' in Bojańczyk *et al.* (2011, 2012) and Bojańczyk and Place (2012), with an orientation toward automata theory; but much remains to be explored.

Exercises

1.1 If G is a group and X a G-set, show that $\lambda g \in G \to (\lambda x \in X \to g \cdot x)$ is a morphism of groups from G to the group Sym X of permutations

---

[1] For an alternative approach to ordered names that keeps within the framework of this book, see Pitts and Shinwell (2008).

of X. Show conversely that if $\theta : G \to \mathrm{Sym}\, X$ is a morphism, then $\lambda(g, x) \in G \times X \to \theta\, g\, x$ is a G-action on X.

1.2   Show that the function mapping a G-set Y to the set ΓY defined in (1.14) extends to a functor $[G, \mathbf{Set}] \to \mathbf{Set}$. Writing ΔX for the discrete G-set on a set X, show that Δ extends to a functor $\mathbf{Set} \to [G, \mathbf{Set}]$ that is left adjoint to Γ. In other words there is a bijection $[G, \mathbf{Set}](\Delta X, Y) \cong \mathbf{Set}(X, \Gamma Y)$ which is natural in X and Y.

1.3   If G is a group, show that its multiplication $(g, g') \mapsto g\, g'$ is an action of G on itself. If G' denotes the resulting G-set, show that there is no equivariant function $G \to G'$ (where G denotes the G-set from Example 1.6) unless $G = \{e\}$ is a trivial group.

1.4   Show that definition (1.24) has the properties (1.7) and (1.8) required of a group action.

1.5   Let X and Y be G-sets. Show that a function F from X to Y is equivariant (1.9) if and only if it satisfies $g \cdot F = F$ for all $g \in G$, with $g \cdot F$ as defined in (1.24).

1.6   Show that currying (1.26) is equivariant: $g \cdot \mathrm{curry}\, F' = \mathrm{curry}(g \cdot F')$.

1.7   Show that an equivariant function $F : X \to Y$ is an isomorphism in $[G, \mathbf{Set}]$ if and only if it is a bijection. Show that it is a monomorphism if and only if it is an injective function. [Hint: consider the pullback of F along itself.] Deduce that subobjects of a G-set are in bijection with equivariant subsets of X.

1.8   Let $\mathrm{P}_{\mathrm{ne}}\, X$ denote the set of non-empty subsets of a set X. Note that if X is a G-set, then the G-action (1.31) restricts to $\mathrm{P}_{\mathrm{ne}}\, X$ and makes it a G-set. Now let X be the G-set G' from Exercise 1.3 and suppose that G is non-trivial (that is, contains some element not equal to the group unit). Show that there is no equivariant function $c : \mathrm{P}_{\mathrm{ne}}\, X \to X$ satisfying $(\forall S \in \mathrm{P}_{\mathrm{ne}}\, X)\, c\, S \in S$. [Hint: consider the action of some $g \neq e$ on $c\, S$ when S is the whole of G.]

1.9   Let $\sim$, F and $\overline{F}$ be as in Section 1.7. Instead of appealing to the Equivariance Principle, show by explicit calculation that if $\sim$ and F are equivariant, then $\overline{F}$ satisfies $g \cdot (\overline{F}[x]_\sim) = \overline{F}(g \cdot [x]_\sim)$ for all $g \in G$ and $x \in X$.

1.10   (**Finite-order lemma**) Show that for each $\pi \in \mathrm{Perm}\, A$ there exists $n \in \mathbb{N}$ with $\pi^n = \mathrm{id}$. Deduce that for any $\mathrm{Perm}\, A$-set X, $\pi \in \mathrm{Perm}\, A$ and $S \in \mathrm{P}\, X$, if $S \subseteq \pi \cdot S$ or $\pi \cdot S \subseteq S$, then $\pi \cdot S = S$.

2
Support

This chapter introduces the central concept of the theory of nominal sets, the *support* of an element in a set equipped with a permutation action. From now on $\mathbb{A}$ denotes a fixed, countably infinite set whose elements $a, b, c, \ldots$ we call *atomic names*.

2.1 The category of nominal sets

Let X be a set equipped with an action of the group $\operatorname{Perm} \mathbb{A}$ of finite permutations of $\mathbb{A}$. A set of atomic names $A \subseteq \mathbb{A}$ is a *support* for an element $x \in X$ if for all $\pi \in \operatorname{Perm} \mathbb{A}$

$$((\forall a \in A)\, \pi a = a) \Rightarrow \pi \cdot x = x. \qquad (2.1)$$

The following characterization of support in terms of transpositions is helpful.

Proposition 2.1 *Suppose X is a* $\operatorname{Perm} \mathbb{A}$-*set and $x \in X$. A subset $A \subseteq \mathbb{A}$ supports x if and only if*

$$(\forall a_1, a_2 \in \mathbb{A} - A)\, (a_1\ a_2) \cdot x = x. \qquad (2.2)$$

Proof If $a_1, a_2 \in \mathbb{A} - A$, then $(a_1\ a_2)a = a$ for any $a \in A$. So if A supports x, it clearly satisfies (2.2). Conversely, suppose A satisfies (2.2) and that $\pi \in \operatorname{Perm} \mathbb{A}$ fixes each element of A. We have to show that $\pi \cdot x = x$. Recall from Theorem 1.15 that π can be written as a composition of transpositions $(a\ a')$ satisfying $\pi a \neq a \neq a' \neq \pi a'$. Since π fixes each element of A, such a transposition satisfies $a, a' \notin A$ and hence by (2.2), $(a\ a') \cdot x = x$. Therefore, letting each transposition in the sequence whose composition is π act on x in turn, we eventually conclude that $\pi \cdot x = x$, as required. □

29

Clearly each element of a Perm $\mathbb{A}$-set is supported by the whole of $\mathbb{A}$, which is an infinite set. We will be interested in elements that are *finitely supported* in the sense that there is some finite set of atomic names that is a support for the element.

Definition 2.2   A *nominal set* is a Perm $\mathbb{A}$-set all of whose elements are finitely supported. Nominal sets are the objects of a category **Nom** whose morphisms, composition and identities are as in the category of Perm $\mathbb{A}$-sets. Thus **Nom** is a full subcategory of [Perm $\mathbb{A}$, **Set**]. The dependence of **Nom** upon $\mathbb{A}$ is left implicit (see Exercise 6.2).

Proposition 2.3   *If A_1 and A_2 are finite supports for an element x of a Perm $\mathbb{A}$-set, then so is $A_1 \cap A_2$.*

Proof   By Proposition 2.1 we just have to show that if $a, a' \in \mathbb{A} - (A_1 \cap A_2)$, then $(a\ a') \cdot x = x$. The latter certainly holds if $a = a'$, so we may suppose $a \neq a'$. In that case, picking any element a'' of the infinite set $\mathbb{A} - (A_1 \cup A_2 \cup \{a, a'\})$, then

$$(a\ a') = (a\ a'') \circ (a'\ a'') \circ (a\ a''). \tag{2.3}$$

Note that either $a \notin A_1$, or $a \notin A_2$; and similarly for a'. So each of the transpositions on the right-hand side of (2.3) swaps atomic names that are either both not in the support set A_1, or both not in the support set A_2 (since a'' is definitely not in either of A_1 or A_2). So $(a\ a')$ is a composition of transpositions each of which fixes x and hence itself fixes x. $\square$

Suppose X is a nominal set and $x \in X$. Since x possesses some finite support, by the proposition

$$\mathrm{supp}_X\ x \triangleq \bigcap \{A \in P\,\mathbb{A} \mid A \text{ is a finite support for } x\} \tag{2.4}$$

is again a finite support for x and is the least one with respect to subset inclusion. We write it as $\mathrm{supp}\ x$ when X is clear from the context. Exercise 2.11 gives an equivalent formulation of $\mathrm{supp}\ x$ from Gabbay and Pitts (2002).

Example 2.4   The *nominal set of atomic names* is given by $\mathbb{A}$ regarded as a Perm $\mathbb{A}$-set as in Example 1.3. Clearly each $a \in \mathbb{A}$ is finitely supported by $\{a\}$ and this is the smallest support, so that $\mathrm{supp}\ a = \{a\}$.

Example 2.5   The *discrete nominal set* on a set X is given by the Perm $\mathbb{A}$-action of Example 1.5, for which we have $\mathrm{supp}\ x = \emptyset$ for each $x \in X$.

Example 2.6   We saw in Example 1.4 that the set $\Sigma(\mathbb{A})$ of terms over an algebraic signature Σ with variables from $\mathbb{A}$ is a Perm $\mathbb{A}$-set. It is in fact a nominal set with supp t equal to the finite set var t of variables occurring in t. This set is recursively defined by:

$$\text{var } a = \{a\},$$

$$\text{var op}(t_1, \ldots, t_n) = \text{var } t_1 \cup \cdots \cup \text{var } t_n.$$

That var t is the least support for t follows from the fact that it is a strong support in the sense of the following theorem due to Tzevelekos (2008, section 2.1.2). Property (2.5) for $A = \text{var } t$ and $x = t$ can be proved by induction on the structure of the term t.

Theorem 2.7 *We say that a set of atomic names $A \subseteq \mathbb{A}$ strongly supports an element x of a nominal set X if and only if*

$$(\forall \pi \in \text{Perm } \mathbb{A}) \, ((\forall a \in A) \, \pi \, a = a) \Leftrightarrow \pi \cdot x = x. \tag{2.5}$$

If A is a finite set of atomic names that strongly supports x, then A is the least support of x, that is, $A = \text{supp } x$.

Proof If A strongly supports x, then it certainly supports x and hence supp $x \subseteq A$. Suppose A is finite; then in particular $\mathbb{A} - A$ is non-empty and we can choose some $a' \in \mathbb{A} - A$. If $a \in A - \text{supp } x$, then $(a \, a') a = a' \neq a \in A$. So from (2.5) we conclude that $(a \, a') \cdot x \neq x$; but this contradicts the fact that $a, a' \notin \text{supp } x$. So $A - \text{supp } x$ is empty and hence $A = \text{supp } x$. □

Remark 2.8 Kurz *et al.* (2010) have given an interesting characterization of Tzevelekos' *strong nominal sets*, that is, Perm $\mathbb{A}$-sets in which every element is strongly supported by a finite set of atomic names. Let **Set**$^{P_f \mathbb{A}}$ denote the category whose objects are families of sets $(X_A \mid A \in P_f \mathbb{A})$ indexed by finite subsets of $\mathbb{A}$ and whose morphisms are $P_f \mathbb{A}$-indexed families of functions. There is a functor $U : \textbf{Nom} \rightarrow \textbf{Set}^{P_f \mathbb{A}}$ sending each $X \in \textbf{Nom}$ to $(\{x \in X \mid \text{supp } x \subseteq A\} \mid A \in P_f \mathbb{A})$. Kurz and Petrişan show not only that this functor has a left adjoint $F : \textbf{Set}^{P_f \mathbb{A}} \rightarrow \textbf{Nom}$, but also that $X \in \textbf{Nom}$ is a strong nominal set iff it is isomorphic to $F \, I$ for some $I \in \textbf{Set}^{P_f \mathbb{A}}$. See Petrişan (2011, lemma 2.4.2) for the details.

Since $\mathbb{A}$ is a Perm $\mathbb{A}$-set, so is its powerset $P \, \mathbb{A}$, as in Section 1.5. It is not hard to see that it contains elements that are not finitely supported (Exercise 2.2); but as the next result shows, we can identify exactly which subsets of $\mathbb{A}$ are finitely supported.

Proposition 2.9 *A set $A \subseteq \mathbb{A}$ of atomic names is a finitely supported element of $P \, \mathbb{A}$ if and only if either it or its complement $\mathbb{A} - A$ is finite. In the latter case one says that A is cofinite.*

Proof Note that $(a\ a') \cdot A = A$ if and only if $(a \in A \wedge a' \in A) \vee (a \notin A \wedge a' \notin A)$. So from Proposition 2.1 it follows that $A' \subseteq \mathbb{A}$ supports $A \in \mathbb{P}\,\mathbb{A}$ if and only if either $A \subseteq A'$, or $\mathbb{A} - A \subseteq A'$. Hence the result. □

Example 2.10 Each finite element of $\mathbb{P}\,\mathbb{A}$ is supported by itself and this is the least support. So we get a nominal set $P_f\,\mathbb{A}$ of finite sets A of atomic names with $\pi \cdot A = \{\pi a \mid a \in A\}$ and $\text{supp}\,A = A$. Note that A is not a strong support for A in the sense of Theorem 2.7, so long as it has at least two elements.

Proposition 2.11 *For each nominal set X the support function* $\text{supp} : X \to P_f\,\mathbb{A}$ *is equivariant:*

$$\pi \cdot (\text{supp}\,x) = \text{supp}(\pi \cdot x) \tag{2.6}$$

holds for all $\pi \in \text{Perm}\,\mathbb{A}$ and $x \in X$.

Proof In view of (2.1) and (2.4), the support function is definable within classical higher-order logic from the action function $\lambda(\pi, x) \in \text{Perm}\,\mathbb{A} \times X \to \pi \cdot x$; and we saw in Example 1.6 that the latter is equivariant. Therefore the theorem follows from the Equivariance Principle. □

We will revisit the various constructions on G-sets from Chapter 1 and see whether they preserve the property of being a nominal set. The following results about support and equivariant functions will be useful for doing this.

Lemma 2.12 *Suppose that $f : X \to Y$ is an equivariant function between* $\text{Perm}\,\mathbb{A}$-*sets.*

(i) *If A is a support for $x \in X$, then it is a support for $f\,x \in Y$. So if X and Y are nominal sets, then*

$$(\forall x \in X)\ \text{supp}_Y(f\,x) \subseteq \text{supp}_X\,x. \tag{2.7}$$

(ii) *If f is injective $((\forall x, x' \in X)\ f\,x = f\,x' \Rightarrow x = x')$, then A is a support for $x \in X$ if and only if it is a support for $f\,x \in Y$. So if Y is a nominal set, then so is X and*

$$(\forall x \in X)\ \text{supp}_X\,x = \text{supp}_Y(f\,x). \tag{2.8}$$

(iii) *If f is surjective $((\forall y \in Y)(\exists x \in X)\ f\,x = y)$ and X is a nominal set, then so is Y.*

Proof For part (i), suppose A supports $x \in X$. If $\pi \in \text{Perm}\,\mathbb{A}$ satisfies $(\forall a \in A)\ \pi a = a$, then by (2.1) $x = \pi \cdot x$ and hence $f\,x = f(\pi \cdot x) = \pi \cdot (f\,x)$ since f is equivariant. Thus A supports $f\,x$ in Y. Therefore if X and Y are nominal sets and $x \in X$, then $\text{supp}_X\,x$ supports $f\,x$ and hence contains the smallest support, $\text{supp}_Y(f\,x)$.

For part (ii), suppose f is injective and that A supports $f\,x$. So if $\pi \in \text{Perm}\,\mathbb{A}$ satisfies $(\forall a \in A)\, \pi\,a = a$, then by (2.1) $f\,x = \pi \cdot (f\,x)$ and hence $f\,x = f(\pi \cdot x)$ since f is equivariant; as it is also injective this implies $x = \pi \cdot x$. Therefore A is a support for x. So if Y is nominal, each $x \in X$ possesses a finite support, namely $\text{supp}_Y(f\,x)$; hence X is nominal. In this case $\text{supp}_Y(f\,x)$ contains the smallest support for x, $\text{supp}_X x$; and, conversely, $\text{supp}_Y(f\,x)$ is contained in $\text{supp}_X x$ by part (i).

Finally, part (iii) follows immediately from part (i), since each $y \in Y$ possesses a finite support, namely $\text{supp}_X x$, where x is some element of X such that $f\,x = y$. □

Remark 2.13 It is immediate from the definition of support that an element $x \in X$ of a nominal set X satisfies $\text{supp}\,x = \emptyset$ iff $(\forall \pi \in \text{Perm}\,\mathbb{A})\,\pi \cdot x = x$. Elements with this property are sometimes called *equivariant*. Such elements are in bijection with global sections $1 \to X$ in the category **Nom**; see Exercise 2.1.

2.2 Products and coproducts

Coproducts in **Nom** are constructed just as in [Perm $\mathbb{A}$, **Set**], by taking disjoint unions (see Section 1.2). This is because, for any set-indexed family of nominal sets $(X_i \mid i \in I)$, each element (i, x) of $\sum_{i \in I} X_i$ is supported by $\text{supp}_{X_i} x$. For if π fixes each $a \in \text{supp}_{X_i} x$, then $\pi \cdot x = x$ and hence $\pi \cdot (i, x) = (i, \pi \cdot x) = (i, x)$. Indeed, since $\text{inj}_i = \lambda x \in X_i \to (i, x)$ is an injective equivariant function from X_i to $\sum_{i \in I} X_i$, by (2.8) we have

$$\text{supp}_{\sum_{i \in I} X_i}(i, x) = \text{supp}_{X_i} x. \tag{2.9}$$

The situation for products is more complicated. Finite cartesian products of nominal sets are again nominal, but infinite products in **Nom** are not given in general by the product in [Perm $\mathbb{A}$, **Set**].

Proposition 2.14 *The product $X_1 \times \cdots \times X_n$ in [Perm $\mathbb{A}$, **Set**] of finitely many nominal sets is another such (and hence is their product in **Nom**). For each $(x_1, \ldots, x_n) \in X_1 \times \cdots \times X_n$*

$$\text{supp}_{X_1 \times \cdots \times X_n}(x_1, \ldots, x_n) = \text{supp}_{X_1} x_1 \cup \cdots \cup \text{supp}_{X_n} x_n. \tag{2.10}$$

Proof Recall from Section 1.2 that the permutation action for products is given componentwise: $\pi \cdot (x_1, \ldots, x_n) = (\pi \cdot x_1, \ldots, \pi \cdot x_n)$. So if π fixes each atomic name in $\text{supp}_{X_1} x_1 \cup \cdots \cup \text{supp}_{X_n} x_n$, then it also fixes $(x_1, \ldots, x_n)$. Therefore each $(x_1, \ldots, x_n)$ is finitely supported by $\text{supp}_{X_1} x_1 \cup \cdots \cup \text{supp}_{X_n} x_n$ and $X_1 \times \cdots \times X_n$ is a nominal set. To prove (2.10) it just remains to show that $\text{supp}_{X_1} x_1 \cup \cdots \cup \text{supp}_{X_n} x_n$ is contained in $\text{supp}(x_1, \ldots, x_n)$; but since each projection function $\text{proj}_i : X_1 \times \cdots \times X_n \to X_i$ is equivariant, by (2.7) we have $\text{supp}_{X_i} x_i = \text{supp}_{X_i}(\text{proj}_i(x_1, \ldots, x_n)) \subseteq \text{supp}(x_1, \ldots, x_n)$ for each $i \in I$. $\square$

Generalizing from finite to infinite cartesian products $\prod_{i \in I} X_i$, as in the above proof we have that an element $(x_i \mid i \in I)$ is supported by $\bigcup_{i \in I} \text{supp}_{X_i} x_i$, but that set may not be finite (Exercise 2.4). Nevertheless, the category **Nom** does have infinite products, because of the following result.

Theorem 2.15 *For each Perm $\mathbb{A}$-set X there is an equivariant function $X_{\text{fs}} \to X$ from a nominal set X_{fs} to X that is universal among all such. In other words, given any equivariant function f from a nominal set Y to X*

*there is a unique equivariant function $\overline{f}$ making the above diagram commute. (Thus **Nom** is a co-reflective subcategory of* [Perm $\mathbb{A}$, **Set**].*)*

Proof First note that if $x \in X$ is supported by $A \in P\mathbb{A}$, then for any $\pi \in$ Perm $\mathbb{A}$, $\pi \cdot x$ is supported by $\pi \cdot A$. (This is a consequence of the Equivariance Principle mentioned in Section 1.5; or one can prove it directly from the definition of support.) So

$$X_{\text{fs}} \triangleq \{x \in X \mid x \text{ is finitely supported in } X\} \tag{2.11}$$

is an equivariant subset of X and hence a Perm $\mathbb{A}$-set with permutation action inherited from X. The inclusion $X_{\text{fs}} \subseteq X$ gives an injective equivariant function and therefore X_{fs} is a nominal set by (2.8). To see that it has the required universal property it suffices to show that any $f : Y \to X$ in [Perm $\mathbb{A}$, **Set**] with $Y \in$ **Nom** maps elements of Y into the subset $X_{\text{fs}} \subseteq X$; but from part (i) of Lemma 2.12, for each $y \in Y$ we have that $\text{supp}_Y y$ is a finite support for $f y$ and hence $f y \in X_{\text{fs}}$. $\square$

Combining the description of products in [Perm $\mathbb{A}$, **Set**] from Section 1.2 with the above theorem, we get the following corollary.

Corollary 2.16 *Given a family of nominal sets X_i indexed by the elements i of some set I, their product in **Nom** is given by $(\prod_{i \in I} X_i)_{\text{fs}}$ with product projections*

$$(\textstyle\prod_{i \in I} X_i)_{\text{fs}} \subseteq \prod_{i \in I} X_i \xrightarrow{\text{proj}_i} X_i.$$

Thus infinite products in **Nom** may contain rather few elements; see Exercise 2.5.

2.3 Natural numbers

We saw in Section 1.3 that the natural numbers object in the category of G-sets is given by $\mathbb{N}$ with the discrete G-action together with the usual zero and successor functions. As we noted in Example 2.5, every discrete Perm $\mathbb{A}$-set is a nominal set. It follows that

$$1 \xrightarrow{\text{zero}} \mathbb{N} \xrightarrow{\text{suc}} \mathbb{N}$$

is also the natural numbers object in the category **Nom** of nominal sets and equivariant functions.

2.4 Functions

Recall from Section 1.4 the definition of the function G-set Y^X. When $G = \text{Perm } \mathbb{A}$, the following characterization of the support of elements of Y^X is useful.

Lemma 2.17 *Given* $X, Y \in [\text{Perm } \mathbb{A}, \textbf{Set}]$, *a set of atomic names* $A \subseteq \mathbb{A}$ *supports* $f \in Y^X$ *if and only if for all* $\pi \in \text{Perm } \mathbb{A}$

$$((\forall a \in A)\, \pi\, a = a) \Rightarrow (\forall x \in X)\, f(\pi \cdot x) = \pi \cdot (f\, x). \tag{2.12}$$

In particular, f has empty support if and only if it is an equivariant function (Definition 1.2).

Proof It follows from the definition of the action of permutations on functions (1.24) that $\pi \cdot f = f$ holds if and only if $(\forall x \in X)\, f(\pi \cdot x) = \pi \cdot (f\, x)$. □

Definition 2.18 If X and Y are nominal sets, we write $X \to_{\text{fs}} Y$ for the nominal set $(Y^X)_{\text{fs}}$ formed from Y^X as in (2.11), and call it the *nominal function set* of X and Y.

Restricting the application function app : $Y^X \times X \to Y$ to finitely supported functions, we get an equivariant function

$$
\begin{aligned}
\text{app} &: (X \to_{\text{fs}} Y) \times X \to Y, \\
\text{app} &\triangleq \lambda(f, x) \in (X \to_{\text{fs}} Y) \times X \to f\, x.
\end{aligned} \tag{2.13}
$$

Currying an equivariant function $f : Z \times X \to Y$ to get curry $f : Z \to Y^X$ as in Section 1.4, by Theorem 2.15 if Z is nominal then curry F factors through $(Y^X)_{\text{fs}} \subseteq Y^X$ to give an equivariant function

$$\text{curry } f : Z \to (X \to_{\text{fs}} Y),$$
$$\text{curry } f \triangleq \lambda z \in Z, x \in X \to f(z, x). \tag{2.14}$$

Theorem 2.19   **Nom** *is a cartesian closed category.*

Proof   We have already seen that **Nom** has finite products. Furthermore $(Y^X)_{\text{fs}}$ gives the exponential of Y by X in **Nom** for general category-theoretic reasons: **Nom** is a co-reflective full subcategory of [Perm $\mathbb{A}$, **Set**] (Theorem 2.15) and the inclusion of **Nom** into [Perm $\mathbb{A}$, **Set**] preserves finite products. Thus there are bijections of hom-sets

$$\textbf{Nom}(Z \times X, Y)$$
$= \quad \{\text{binary products in } \textbf{Nom} \text{ are as in } [\text{Perm } \mathbb{A}, \textbf{Set}]\}$
$$[\text{Perm } \mathbb{A}, \textbf{Set}](Z \times X, Y)$$
$\cong \quad \{Y^X \text{ is the exponential in } [\text{Perm } \mathbb{A}, \textbf{Set}]\}$
$$[\text{Perm } \mathbb{A}, \textbf{Set}](Z, Y^X)$$
$\cong \quad \{\text{Theorem 2.15}\}$
$$\textbf{Nom}(Z, (Y^X)_{\text{fs}})$$
$= \quad \{\text{definition of } X \to_{\text{fs}} Y\}$
$$\textbf{Nom}(Z, X \to_{\text{fs}} Y)$$

(natural in $X, Y, Z \in$ **Nom**) given by sending $F \in \textbf{Nom}(Z \times X, Y)$ to curry $F \in \textbf{Nom}(Z, X \to_{\text{fs}} Y)$. $\square$

Not every function between nominal sets is finitely supported; in other words $X \to_{\text{fs}} Y$ can be a proper subset of Y^X. Here is an example that shows this.

Example 2.20   Consider the function Perm $\mathbb{A}$-set Y^X, where X is the set $\mathbb{N}$ of natural numbers regarded as a discrete nominal set (Example 2.5) and where Y is the nominal set $P_f \mathbb{A}$ of finite sets of atomic names, as in Example 2.10. Let $f \in Y^X$ be a function that maps each natural number $n \in \mathbb{N}$ to some finite set of atomic names of cardinality n. Then there is no finite set of atomic names A that supports f in Y^X. To see this we suppose A is a finite support for f and derive a contradiction. Since each $n \in \mathbb{N}$ has empty support, A is also a support for $(f, n) \in Y^X \times X$; and then since application app $: Y^X \times X \to Y$ is equivariant, by part (i) of Lemma 2.12 we have that A is a support for $f\, n \in P_f \mathbb{A}$. We noted in Example 2.10 that the least support of a finite set of atomic names is the set itself. Therefore we have proved $(\forall n \in \mathbb{N})\, f\, n \subseteq A$. Taking n larger than the cardinality of the finite set A gives a contradiction, since by assumption on f, $f\, n$ is a set of cardinality n and so cannot be a subset of A.

Each finite permutation $\pi \in \mathrm{Perm}\,\mathbb{A}$ is in particular a function from $\mathbb{A}$ to itself. Regarding $\mathbb{A}$ as a $\mathrm{Perm}\,\mathbb{A}$-set as in Example 1.3, the $\mathrm{Perm}\,\mathbb{A}$-action on the function set $\mathbb{A}^{\mathbb{A}}$ is $\pi \cdot f = \pi \circ f \circ \pi^{-1}$. Thus $\mathrm{Perm}\,\mathbb{A}$ is an equivariant subset of $\mathbb{A}^{\mathbb{A}}$ and the $\mathrm{Perm}\,\mathbb{A}$-action it inherits from $\mathbb{A}^{\mathbb{A}}$ is the conjugation action for the group $\mathrm{Perm}\,\mathbb{A}$ (Example 1.6).

Lemma 2.21 *With the* $\mathrm{Perm}\,\mathbb{A}$-*action*

$$\pi \cdot \pi' \triangleq \pi \circ \pi' \circ \pi^{-1} \qquad (\pi, \pi' \in \mathrm{Perm}\,\mathbb{A}) \tag{2.15}$$

$\mathrm{Perm}\,\mathbb{A}$ *is a nominal set; and for all* $\pi \in \mathrm{Perm}\,\mathbb{A}$

$$\mathrm{supp}\,\pi = \{a \in \mathbb{A} \mid \pi\,a \neq a\}. \tag{2.16}$$

Proof By definition of $\mathrm{Perm}\,\mathbb{A}$, for each $\pi \in \mathrm{Perm}\,\mathbb{A}$, $A \triangleq \{a \in \mathbb{A} \mid \pi\,a \neq a\}$ is a finite set. To see that A supports π, note that if $\pi' \in \mathrm{Perm}\,\mathbb{A}$ satisfies $(\forall a \in A)\,\pi'a = a$, then $(\forall a \in \mathbb{A})\,\pi\,a = a \vee \pi'a = a$. For each $a \in \mathbb{A}$, arguing by cases according to whether or not $\pi\,a = a$ and whether or not $\pi'a = a$, in all cases one gets $\pi(\pi'a) = \pi'(\pi\,a)$; hence $\pi' \cdot \pi = \pi' \circ \pi \circ (\pi')^{-1} = \pi$.

So $\pi \in \mathrm{Perm}\,\mathbb{A}$ is supported by $\{a \in \mathbb{A} \mid \pi\,a \neq a\}$. To see that this is the least finite support $\mathrm{supp}\,\pi$, it suffices to show that $(\forall a \in \mathbb{A})\,a \notin \mathrm{supp}\,\pi \Rightarrow \pi\,a = a$. Suppose to the contrary that $a \in \mathbb{A}$ satisfies $a \notin \mathrm{supp}\,\pi$ and $\pi\,a \neq a$. Pick any a' in the infinite set $\mathbb{A} - (\mathrm{supp}\,\pi \cup \{a, \pi\,a\})$. Since $a, a' \notin \mathrm{supp}\,\pi$, by Proposition 2.1 we have $\pi = (a\,a') \cdot \pi = (a\,a') \circ \pi \circ (a\,a')$; and so $\pi\,a' = (a\,a')(\pi((a\,a')\,a')) = (a\,a')(\pi\,a) = \pi\,a$, since $\pi\,a \notin \{a, a'\}$. Therefore $a' = \pi^{-1}(\pi\,a') = \pi^{-1}(\pi\,a) = a$, contradicting the choice of a'. □

2.5 Power sets

Lemma 2.22 *If* $S \subseteq X$ *is an equivariant subset of a nominal set* X, *then restricting the* $\mathrm{Perm}\,\mathbb{A}$-*action on* X *to* S, S *is a nominal set.*

Proof By part (ii) of Lemma 2.12 applied to the inclusion $S \subseteq X$, the elements of S are finitely supported because they are so in X. □

If X is a nominal set, then we claim that its subobjects in the category **Nom** correspond to equivariant subsets of X. To see this we need to describe pullbacks in **Nom**. A *pullback* for a pair of morphisms F_1 and F_2 with common codomain in a category is a commutative square

$$
\begin{array}{ccc}
P & \xrightarrow{\ p_2\ } & X_2 \\
{\scriptstyle p_1}\downarrow & & \downarrow{\scriptstyle f_2} \\
X_1 & \xrightarrow[\ f_1\ ]{} & Y
\end{array}
$$

with the universal property that given any $g_i : Y \to X_i$ with $f_1 \circ g_1 = f_2 \circ g_2$, there is a unique morphism from Y to P making the two triangles commute:

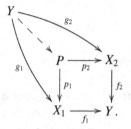

When the category is **Nom**, as for binary products, pullbacks are created by taking pullbacks of the underlying functions:

$$
\begin{aligned}
P &\triangleq \{(x_1, x_2) \in X_1 \times X_2 \mid f_1\, x_1 = f_2\, x_2\}, \\
p_i &= \lambda(x_1, x_2) \in P \to x_i .
\end{aligned}
$$

(Note that P is an equivariant subset of the product $X_1 \times X_2$ and hence by part (ii) of Lemma 2.12 is a nominal set.) By considering the pullback of a monomorphism against itself, it follows that a morphism $f : X \to Y$ in **Nom** is a monomorphism if and only if f is an injective function. Combining this observation with part (ii) of Lemma 2.12 we conclude that the subobjects of X in **Nom** are the same as its subobjects in [Perm $\mathbb{A}$, **Set**] and correspond to equivariant subsets of X.

Theorem 2.23 *The category* **Nom** *of nominal sets and equivariant functions is a Boolean topos with a natural number object.*

Proof We have already seen that **Nom** is cartesian closed and possesses a natural number object. Just as in [Perm $\mathbb{A}$, **Set**], the discrete nominal set $\mathbb{B} = \{\text{true}, \text{false}\}$ is a subobject classifier, because of the above observations about pullbacks and subobjects in **Nom**.   □

As in any topos, the exponential $X \to_{\text{fs}} \mathbb{B} = (\mathbb{B}^X)_{\text{fs}}$ of the subobject classifier by an object X gives a form of powerset object in **Nom**. The isomorphism in [Perm $\mathbb{A}$, **Set**] between $\mathbb{B}^X$ and $\mathrm{P}\,X$ (Section 1.5) restricts to an isomorphism between the finitely supported elements of $\mathbb{B}^X$ and $\mathrm{P}\,X$. However, as the next result shows, to check that $S \subseteq X$ is a finitely supported element of PX it suffices to check that containments $\pi \cdot S \subseteq S$ rather than equalities $\pi \cdot S = S$ hold for all permutations π fixing the atomic names in a support set.

Lemma 2.24 *Given* $X \in [\text{Perm}\,\mathbb{A}, \textbf{Set}]$, *a set of atomic names* $A \subseteq \mathbb{A}$ *supports* $S \in PX$ *if and only if*

$$(\forall \pi \in \text{Perm}\,\mathbb{A})((\forall a \in A)\, \pi a = a) \Rightarrow (\forall x \in S)\, \pi \cdot x \in S \,. \tag{2.17}$$

In particular, S has empty support if and only if it is an equivariant subset of X (Definition 1.8).

Proof Note that by (1.32), $(\forall x \in S)\, \pi \cdot x \in S$ is equivalent to $\pi \cdot S \subseteq S$. Note as well that any π satisfying $(\forall a \in A)\, \pi a = a$ also satisfies $(\forall a \in A)\, \pi^{-1}a = a$. So if (2.17) holds, then we have $\pi \cdot S \subseteq S$ and $\pi^{-1} \cdot S \subseteq S$ and hence $\pi \cdot S = S$. So (2.17) implies that A supports S in PX; and the converse is immediate. □

The following simple corollary of this lemma will be useful.

Proposition 2.25 *Given* $X, Y \in [\text{Perm}\,\mathbb{A}, \textbf{Set}]$, *if* $A \subseteq \mathbb{A}$ *supports both* $S \in P(X \times Y)$ *and* $x \in X$, *then it also supports* $\{y \in Y \mid (x,y) \in S\} \in PY$.

Proof Suppose $\pi \in \text{Perm}\,\mathbb{A}$ satisfies $(\forall a \in A)\, \pi a = a$. Then $\pi \cdot x = x$ and $\pi \cdot S = S$. So for all y in $\{y \in Y \mid (x,y) \in S\}$ we have $(x, \pi \cdot y) = (\pi \cdot x, \pi \cdot y) = \pi \cdot (x,y) \in \pi \cdot S = S$ and therefore $\pi \cdot y$ is also in $\{y \in Y \mid (x,y) \in S\}$. So we can apply Lemma 2.24 to deduce that A supports $\{y \in Y \mid (x,y) \in S\}$. □

Definition 2.26 If X is a nominal set, we write $P_{\text{fs}}X$ for the nominal set $(PX)_{\text{fs}}$ formed from the power $\text{Perm}\,\mathbb{A}$-set PX using (2.11). We call $P_{\text{fs}}X$ the *nominal powerset of X*.

Note that a finite subset $\{x_1, \ldots, x_n\}$ of X is supported by $\text{supp}\,x_1 \cup \cdots \cup \text{supp}\,x_n$ and hence is in $P_{\text{fs}}X$. Thus $P_f X$ is a nominal subset of $P_{\text{fs}}X$. (See Exercise 2.3.)

For any nominal set X, from parts (i)–(iii) of Proposition 1.9 we have the following equivariant and hence finitely supported subsets:

- *Truth* $X \in P_{\text{fs}}X$.
- *Equality* $\{(x, x') \in X \times X \mid x = x'\} \in P_{\text{fs}}(X \times X)$.
- *Membership* $\{(x, S) \in X \times P_{\text{fs}}X \mid x \in S\} \in P_{\text{fs}}(X \times P_{\text{fs}}X)$.

Furthermore, if $f : PX_1 \times \cdots \times PX_n \to PX$ is an equivariant function and $(S_1, \ldots, S_n) \in P_{\text{fs}}X_1 \times \cdots \times P_{\text{fs}}X_n$, then by part (i) of Lemma 2.12 and (2.10), $f(S_1, \ldots, S_n)$ is supported by the union of the supports of each S_i and hence is in $P_{\text{fs}}X$. So parts (iv)–(vii) of Proposition 1.9 give us the following equivariant functions:

- *Conjunction* $\_ \cap \_ : P_{fs} X \times P_{fs} X \rightarrow P_{fs} X$.
- *Negation* $\neg : P_{fs} X \rightarrow P_{fs} X$, where $\neg S \triangleq \{x \in X \mid x \notin S\}$.
- *Universal quantification* $\bigcap : P_{fs}(P_{fs} X) \rightarrow P_{fs} X$, where $\bigcap S \triangleq \{x \in X \mid (\forall S \in S)\, x \in S\}$.
- *Substitution* $f^* : P_{fs} Y \rightarrow P_{fs} X$, where $f : X \rightarrow Y$ is an equivariant function and $f^* S \triangleq \{x \in X \mid f\, x \in S\}$.

Finally, the analogue of part (viii) of Proposition 1.9 is the following equivariant function:

- *Comprehension* $\mathrm{compr} : P_{fs}(X \times Y) \rightarrow (X \rightarrow_{fs} P_{fs} Y)$, where $\mathrm{compr}\, S \triangleq \lambda x \in X \rightarrow \{y \in Y \mid (x, y) \in S\}$. To see that this is well defined, note that given $S \in P_{fs}(X \times Y)$ and $x \in X$, by Proposition 2.25 $\mathrm{compr}\, S\, x = \{y \in Y \mid (x, y) \in S\}$ is finitely supported by $\mathrm{supp}\, S \cup \mathrm{supp}\, x$. Hence $\mathrm{compr}\, S \in (P_{fs} Y)^X$; but since we know from Proposition 1.9 that compr is equivariant, by part (i) of Lemma 2.12 we have $\mathrm{compr}\, S \in ((P_{fs} Y)^X)_{fs} = X \rightarrow_{fs} P_{fs} Y$.

From these facts we get a version for nominal sets of the Equivariance Principle from Section 1.5:

Finite Support Principle *Any function or relation that is defined from finitely supported functions and subsets using classical higher-order logic is itself finitely supported, provided we restrict any quantification over functions or subsets to range over ones that are finitely supported.*

2.6 FM-sets

The usual *von Neumann cumulative hierarchy* of sets (Shoenfield, 1977) is the family of sets $\mathcal{V}_\alpha$ indexed by ordinal numbers α that is obtained from the empty set by iterating the powerset operation P:

$$\mathcal{V}_0 = \emptyset,$$
$$\mathcal{V}_{\alpha+1} = P\mathcal{V}_\alpha, \tag{2.18}$$
$$\mathcal{V}_\lambda = \bigcup_{\alpha < \lambda} \mathcal{V}_\alpha \quad (\lambda \text{ a limit ordinal}).$$

The *von Neumann universe* $\mathcal{V}$ is the object of the large category **Set₁** of classes and functions given by the the union of the sets $\mathcal{V}_\alpha$ as α ranges over the class of ordinals. $P\mathcal{V} = \mathcal{V}$ is the initial algebra for the functor $P : \mathbf{Set_1} \rightarrow \mathbf{Set_1}$ sending each class to the class of its sub*sets* (rather than the larger collection of all its subclasses) and sending each function to the corresponding direct image function on subsets. In other words, for any $f : P X \to X$ in $\mathbf{Set}_1$

$$\begin{array}{ccc} P \mathcal{V} & = & \mathcal{V} \\ {\scriptstyle P f} \downarrow & & \downarrow {\scriptstyle \hat{f}} \\ P X & \xrightarrow{\ f\ } & X \end{array}$$

there is a unique function $\hat{f}$ making the above diagram in $\mathbf{Set}_1$ commute, that is, satisfying $\hat{f} x = f \{ \hat{f} y \mid y \in x \}$ for all $x \in \mathcal{V}$.

Consider now what a 'nominal' version of the universe of sets should be. Every element of the universe $\mathcal{V}$ is a subset of elements of $\mathcal{V}$. We have seen that the analogue of 'subset' for nominal sets is 'finitely supported subset'; furthermore we need to consider atomic names as well as sets. Therefore we seek a universe $\mathcal{U}$ in which every element is either an atomic name, or a finitely supported subset of elements of the universe.

Definition 2.27 The cumulative hierarchy of *hereditarily finitely supported* sets is the following ordinal-indexed family of nominal sets:

$$\mathcal{U}_0 = \emptyset ,$$
$$\mathcal{U}_{\alpha+1} = \mathbb{A} + P_{\mathrm{fs}} \mathcal{U}_\alpha , \qquad\qquad (2.19)$$
$$\mathcal{U}_\lambda = \bigcup_{\alpha < \lambda} \mathcal{U}_\alpha \qquad (\lambda \text{ a limit ordinal}).$$

Thus $\mathcal{U}_0$ is the empty set, regarded as a discrete nominal set. At successor ordinals $\mathcal{U}_{\alpha+1}$ is the disjoint union $\{(0, a) \mid a \in \mathbb{A}\} \cup \{(1, S) \mid S \in P_{\mathrm{fs}} \mathcal{U}_\alpha\}$ of the nominal set of atomic names and the nominal powerset of finitely supported subsets of the nominal set $\mathcal{U}_\alpha$. At limit ordinals λ we take a union to form $\mathcal{U}_\lambda$. This gives a nominal set because the $\mathcal{U}_\alpha$ form an increasing sequence

$$\alpha \le \beta \Rightarrow \mathcal{U}_\alpha \subseteq \mathcal{U}_\beta ,$$

with the inclusions being equivariant functions. Thus the permutation actions on each $\mathcal{U}_\alpha$ extend each other as α increases and together give a permutation action on $\bigcup_{\alpha < \lambda} \mathcal{U}_\alpha$; and since each $x \in \mathcal{U}_\lambda$ is finitely supported as an element of some $\mathcal{U}_\alpha$ with $\alpha < \lambda$, it is finitely supported as an element of $\mathcal{U}_\lambda$.

Let $\mathbf{Nom}_1$ denote the large category of *nominal classes* – objects $X \in \mathbf{Set}_1$ equipped with a Perm $\mathbb{A}$-action for which all elements of X have finite support; as usual, the morphisms of $\mathbf{Nom}_1$ are the functions that are equivariant, that is, preserve the given permutation action. The functor $P_{\mathrm{fs}} : \mathbf{Nom}_1 \to \mathbf{Nom}_1$ assigns to each nominal class X the class of finitely supported subsets, with permutation action as in the previous section; the action of the functor on morphisms is given by taking images: $P_{\mathrm{fs}} f S = \{ f x \mid x \in S \}$. Combining this with the coproduct with $\mathbb{A}$, we get the functor

$$\mathbb{A} + P_{fs} \_ : \mathbf{Nom}_1 \to \mathbf{Nom}_1 \qquad (2.20)$$

sending each $X \in \mathbf{Nom}_1$ to $\mathbb{A} + P_{fs} X = \{(0,a) \mid a \in \mathbb{A}\} \cup \{(1,S) \mid S \in P_{fs} X\}$. In this context we will call the two coproduct inclusions *atm* and *set*:

$$
\begin{aligned}
atm\, a &\triangleq (0,a)\,, \\
set\, S &\triangleq (1,S)\,.
\end{aligned} \qquad (2.21)
$$

Writing $\mathcal{U} \in \mathbf{Nom}_1$ for the union of the $\mathcal{U}_\alpha$ as α ranges over the ordinals, we get $\mathbb{A} + P_{fs} \mathcal{U} = \mathcal{U}$ and this is an initial algebra for the functor (2.20). In other words, for any equivariant functions $f_0 : \mathbb{A} \to X$ and $f_1 : P_{fs} X \to X$ in $\mathbf{Nom}_1$

$$
\begin{array}{ccc}
\mathbb{A} + P_{fs}\,\mathcal{U} & = & \mathcal{U} \\
{\scriptstyle id+P_{fs}\,\hat{f}}\Big\downarrow & & \Big\downarrow{\scriptstyle \hat{f}} \\
\mathbb{A} + P_{fs}\,X & \xrightarrow[{[f_0,f_1]}]{} & X
\end{array}
$$

there is a unique $\hat{f}$ making the above diagram in $\mathbf{Nom}_1$ commute, that is, satisfying

$$
\begin{aligned}
\hat{f}(atm\, a) &= f_0\, a & (a \in \mathbb{A}), \\
\hat{f}(set\, S) &= f_1\{\hat{f}\, x \mid x \in S\} & (S \in P_{fs}\,\mathcal{U}).
\end{aligned}
$$

Definition 2.28 The *Fraenkel–Mostowski universe* $\mathcal{U}$ is the object of $\mathbf{Nom}_1$ given by the union of the increasing ordinal-indexed sequence of nominal sets $\mathcal{U}_\alpha$ from Definition 2.27. Writing $S \triangleq P_{fs}\,\mathcal{U}$, we have that $\mathcal{U} = \mathbb{A}+S$. In other words, every element of $\mathcal{U}$ is either an atom or an *FM-set*, that is, a finitely supported subset of elements of $\mathcal{U}$. The Perm $\mathbb{A}$-action on FM-sets satisfies $\pi \cdot S = \{\pi \cdot x \mid x \in S\}$; and the fact that FM-sets are finitely supported subsets means that for each $S \in S$ there is a finite set A of atomic names satisfying (2.17).

Given a nominal set $X \in \mathbf{Nom}$, we saw in the previous section that each equivariant subset S of X, equipped with the Perm $\mathbb{A}$-action obtained by restricting the given one on X, is again a nominal set (Lemma 2.22). Equivariant subsets are a special case of finitely supported subsets, namely the ones with empty support (Lemma 2.24). In general we cannot regard $S \in P_{fs} X$ as a nominal set in its own right simply because S may not be closed under the ambient permutation action; however, many of the concepts and constructs for nominal sets that we consider in the rest of this book make sense for finitely supported subsets. The Fraenkel–Mostowski universe $\mathcal{U}$ is a nominal class with a very rich collection of finitely supported subsets, the FM-sets, which is closed under the usual operations of set theory. It is possible to take an 'element-oriented' approach to the theory developed in this book and make FM-sets the primary object of study; nominal sets as we have defined them emerge as the special case of FM-sets S, where $\text{supp}\,S = \emptyset$. This was the original approach taken (Gabbay and Pitts, 2002), and this set-theoretic style (beginning with sets involving atoms that are not necessarily finitely supported) is followed in the survey by Gabbay (2011). In this book we take a 'function-oriented' approach to foundations emphasizing higher-order logic and the 'universal properties' of category theory; nominal sets come first and then FM-sets are constructed as the elements of a large nominal set S characterized by an initial algebra property. For more on the categorical algebra of set theory, see Joyal and Moerdijk (1995).

2.7 Failure of choice

Although nominal sets provide a model of classical higher-order logic, they do not model choice principles, as the following theorem shows. Indeed Fraenkel and Mostowski introduced permutations and finite supports into logic in the first place in order to construct a model of set theory with atoms not satisfying the Axiom of Choice.

Theorem 2.29 *Let* $\mathrm{P_{nefs}}\mathbb{A}$ *be the nominal set of non-empty, finitely supported subsets of* $\mathbb{A}$ *(where the* $\mathrm{Perm}\,\mathbb{A}$*-action on such subsets is as for* $\mathrm{P_{fs}}\,\mathbb{A}$*). No function* $c : \mathrm{P_{nefs}}\mathbb{A} \to \mathbb{A}$ *satisfying*

$$(\forall S \in \mathrm{P_{nefs}}\mathbb{A})\, c\,S \in S \tag{2.22}$$

can have finite support in the $\mathrm{Perm}\,\mathbb{A}$*-set* $\mathbb{A}^{\mathrm{P_{nefs}}\mathbb{A}}$.

Proof We suppose c satisfying (2.22) is supported by a finite subset $A \subseteq \mathbb{A}$ and derive a contradiction. Let S be the cofinite set $\mathbb{A} - A$. From Proposition 2.9 we have that $S \in \mathrm{P_{fs}}\,\mathbb{A}$; and, being cofinite, S is in particular non-empty. Therefore we can apply c to S to get an atomic name $a_0 \triangleq c\,S \in S = \mathbb{A} - A$. Since $A \cup \{a_0\}$ is finite and $\mathbb{A}$ is infinite, there is some $a_1 \in \mathbb{A} - (A \cup \{a_0\}) \subseteq S$. Since $a_0, a_1 \in S$, we have $(a_0\ a_1) \cdot S = S$; and since A supports C and $a_0, a_1 \notin A$, we also have $(a_0\ a_1) \cdot c = c$. So by definition of the $\mathrm{Perm}\,\mathbb{A}$-action on $(\mathrm{P_{nefs}}\mathbb{A})^{\mathbb{A}}$, $(a_0\ a_1) \cdot (c\,S) = ((a_0\ a_1) \cdot c)((a_0\ a_1) \cdot S) = c\,S$. Therefore $a_1 = (a_0\ a_1) \cdot a_0 = (a_0\ a_1) \cdot (c\,S) = c\,S = a_0$, contradicting the fact that a_1 was chosen to be distinct from a_0. $\qquad\square$

So in particular **Nom** does not model Hilbert's ε-operator mapping non-empty subsets at each type to elements of those subsets. We remarked in Note 1.11 that this is already the case for [Perm $\mathbb{A}$, **Set**] and equivariant properties. However, when we move to **Nom** and finitely supported properties, even weaker internal choice principles fail to hold. For example, the above theorem shows that **Nom** fails to satisfy the higher-order logic formula

$(\forall R \in P(X \times Y))$

$$((\forall x \in X)(\exists y \in Y)\,(x,y) \in R) \Rightarrow (\exists f \in Y^X)(\forall x \in X)\,(x, fx) \in R.$$

(To see this, interpret X as $P_{\text{nefs}}\mathbb{A}$, Y as $\mathbb{A}$ and R as $\{(S,a) \in P_{\text{nefs}}\mathbb{A} \times \mathbb{A} \mid a \in S\}$ and apply the theorem.)

Many uses of choice in computer systems for interactive theorem proving based on classical higher-order logic (such as the HOL theorem prover, Gordon and Melham, 1993) are for making definitions, where the thing defined is unique. Such restricted uses of choice are consistent with the model of higher-order logic that **Nom** provides (see Pitts, 2003, section 8).

2.8 Partial functions

If X and Y are nominal sets, we saw in Section 1.6 that the set $X \rightharpoonup Y$ of partial functions is an equivariant subset of $P(X \times Y)$. Applying $_$$_{\text{fs}}$ to it we obtain the set of finitely supported partial functions

$$X \rightharpoonup_{\text{fs}} Y \triangleq (X \rightharpoonup Y)_{\text{fs}}. \tag{2.23}$$

Thus the elements of $X \rightharpoonup_{\text{fs}} Y$ are the finitely supported subsets of $X \times Y$ that are single-valued (1.36). This gives the object of partial maps from X to Y in **Nom**; that is, there is a natural correspondence between partial maps (Johnstone, 2002, p. 100)

$$
\begin{array}{ccc}
\cdot & \longrightarrow & Y \\
\Big\downarrow & & \\
Z \times X & &
\end{array}
\tag{2.24}
$$

and morphisms $Z \to (X \rightharpoonup_{\text{fs}} Y)$. Indeed, partial maps in **Nom** correspond to *equivariant partial functions*, that is, partial functions that are equivariant as subsets. Given such an $F \in (Z \times X) \rightharpoonup Y$, the corresponding equivariant function curry $F : Z \to (X \rightharpoonup_{\text{fs}} Y)$ maps each $z \in Z$ to

$$\text{curry } F\, z = \{(x,y) \in X \times Y \mid ((z,x),y) \in F\}.$$

This is a partial function because F is one; and it is finitely supported by supp z, because of Proposition 2.25. The correspondence between F and curry F is mediated by the equivariant partial function

$$\text{app} \in (X \rightharpoonup_{\text{fs}} Y) \times X \rightharpoonup Y,$$
$$\text{app} \triangleq \{((F, x), y) \in ((X \rightharpoonup_{\text{fs}} Y) \times X) \times Y \mid (x, y) \in F\}, \tag{2.25}$$

which applies a partial function to its argument. For each F, curry F is the unique equivariant function $Z \to (X \rightharpoonup_{\text{fs}} Y)$ satisfying

$$(\forall z \in Z)(\forall x \in X)\, \text{app}(\text{curry } F\, z, x) \equiv F(z, x), \tag{2.26}$$

where $\equiv$ is Kleene equivalence – see Section 1.6. Since **Nom** is a Boolean topos (Theorem 2.23), there is a natural isomorphism between $X \rightharpoonup_{\text{fs}} Y$ and the exponential $X \to_{\text{fs}} (Y + 1)$. This is given by restricting to finitely supported elements the usual correspondence between partial functions to Y and total functions to Y augmented with an element for 'undefined', that is, to $Y + 1$.

We noted in Definition 2.26 that every finite subset of a nominal set is finitely supported. It follows that $X \rightharpoonup_{\text{fs}} Y$ contains all finite partial functions. We write the set of finite partial functions from X to Y as

$$X \rightharpoonup_{\text{f}} Y \triangleq \{f \in X \rightharpoonup Y \mid f \in P_{\text{f}}(X \times Y)\}. \tag{2.27}$$

Thus when $X, Y \in$ **Nom**, $X \rightharpoonup_{\text{f}} Y$ is a nominal set with

$$\pi \cdot f = \{(\pi \cdot x, \pi \cdot y) \mid (x, y) \in f\} \quad \text{and} \quad \text{supp } f \subseteq \bigcup_{(x,y) \in f} \text{supp } x \cup \text{supp } y,$$

for each finite partial function $f \in X \rightharpoonup Y$.

2.9 Quotient sets

In Section 1.7 we saw that if $\sim$ is an equivariant equivalence relation on a G-set, then the set $X/\sim$ of equivalence classes $[x]_\sim$ becomes a G-set once we endow it with the G-action given by (1.43). The quotient function $\lambda x \in X \to [x]_\sim$ is a surjective equivariant function $X \to X/\sim$. So if X is a nominal set, then by part (iii) of Lemma 2.12 we have that $X/\sim$ is also a nominal set. The following result provides a useful characterization of the support of an equivalence class.

Proposition 2.30 *If $\sim$ is an equivariant equivalence relation on a nominal set X and $c \in X/\sim$, then* supp $c = \bigcap\{\text{supp } x \mid x \in c\}$.

Proof By part (i) of Lemma 2.12 we have supp $[x]_\sim \subseteq$ supp x, for all $x \in X$. So supp $c \subseteq \bigcap\{\text{supp } x \mid x \in c\}$. Conversely, if $a \in \mathbb{A} -$ supp c, then choosing a representative $x \in c$ and an atomic name a' in the cofinite set $\mathbb{A} -$ supp(a, c, x), we have $(a\ a')\cdot x \in (a\ a')\cdot c = c$, since $a, a' \notin \mathrm{supp}\ c$; and since $a' \notin \mathrm{supp}\ x$, we also have $a = (a\ a')\cdot a' \notin (a\ a')\cdot \mathrm{supp}\ x = \mathrm{supp}((a\ a')\cdot x)$ by Proposition 2.11. Thus if $a \in \mathbb{A} - \mathrm{supp}\ c$, then $a \notin \bigcap\{\mathrm{supp}\ x \mid x \in c\}$. $\qquad\qquad\square$

2.10 Non-finite support

The definition of support given at the beginning of Section 2.1 makes sense whether or not support sets are finite. Restricting attention to finite ones, as we do, is a simple way of guaranteeing that a support set does not exhaust the whole countably infinite set of atomic names. We immediately exploited that fact in the proof of existence of smallest support sets (Proposition 2.3); and we will make great use of this ability to 'choose a fresh name' in the next and subsequent chapters. However, in the literature other ways have been considered for ensuring a supply of atomic names not in any given support, more subtle than just requiring the cardinality of support sets to be strictly less than the cardinality of the whole set of names.

Cheney (2006) develops a generalization of the notion of nominal set in which support sets are elements of some proper ideal of $(\mathrm{P}\,\mathbb{A}, \subseteq)$ extending the ideal $(\mathrm{P_f}\,\mathbb{A}, \subseteq)$; the extra generality is used to get completeness results for nominal logic (Pitts, 2003).

Gabbay (2007) considers supports that are infinite, but well-ordered subsets of an uncountable set of atomic names. The motivation is to get a generalization of the name-abstractions that we consider in Chapter 4 to a form of abstraction over countably infinite sequences of names. Gabbay shows how this connects with the use of an ω-indexed sequence of de Bruijn indexes when representing α-equivalence classes of syntax (de Bruijn, 1972).

Permissive-nominal sets (Dowek *et al.*, 2010), are another generalization of nominal sets that make use of non-finite supports. Gabbay (2012) uses them to get completeness results for nominal algebra (Gabbay and Mathijssen, 2009) and permissive nominal logic (Dowek and Gabbay, 2012). In the permissive-nominal theory one works with a countably infinite set of atomic names that is divided into (at least) two disjoint, infinite halves. (The division is related to the not uncommon convention of using different sorts of name for free variables and for bound variables.) Supports have to lie within 'permission sets' that, roughly speaking, contain all but finitely many names of one half and only finitely many names of the other half; see Gabbay (2012, section 2.1) for one way of making this precise. An attractive feature of the theory of permissive-nominal sets is that it yields not only clean completeness theorems for the model theory of some 'nominal' logics, but also admits constructs for abstraction over infinite lists of names, connecting with de Bruijn indexes. There is also a connection between permissive-nominal logic and the use of higher-order logic to specify languages with binders; see Dowek and Gabbay (2012).

Exercises

2.1 Show that the set $\mathbf{Nom}(1, X)$ of global sections of a nominal set X is in bijection with $\{x \in X \mid \mathrm{supp}\, x = \emptyset\}$. Give an example of a nominal set with no global section whose underlying set is non-empty. Show that **Nom** is not a well-pointed category, that is, for some $X, Y \in \mathbf{Nom}$ there exist morphisms $f, g \in \mathbf{Nom}(X, Y)$ satisfying $(\forall p \in \mathbf{Nom}(1, X))\, f \circ p = g \circ p$, but with $f \neq g$.

2.2 Give an example of an element of the power Perm $\mathbb{A}$-set $\mathrm{P}\,\mathbb{A}$ that is not finitely supported.

2.3 If X is a nominal set, for each finite subset $S \in \mathrm{P_f}\, X$, show that $\mathrm{supp}\, S = \bigcup\{\mathrm{supp}\, x \mid x \in S\}$. [Hint: consider the equivariant function $\mathrm{P_f}\, X \to \mathrm{P_f}\, \mathbb{A}$ mapping S to $\bigcup\{\mathrm{supp}\, x \mid x \in S\}$.]

2.4 Consider the product Perm $\mathbb{A}$-set $\prod_{i \in I} X_i$ for the case $I = \mathbb{N} = \{0, 1, 2, \ldots\}$ and $X_i = \mathbb{A}$ (as in Example 1.3) for each $i \in \mathbb{N}$. Let $(a_0, a_1, a_2, \ldots)$ be an element of this product that enumerates the elements of $\mathbb{A}$ in the sense that each $a \in \mathbb{A}$ is equal to a_i for some $i \in \mathbb{N}$. Show that this element is not finitely supported.

2.5 Give an example of a countably infinite family $(X_n \mid n \in \mathbb{N})$ of non-empty nominal sets whose product in the category **Nom** is empty. [Hint: for each n, consider the set of finite subsets of $\mathbb{A}$ of cardinality $n + 1$.]

2.6 Let $\mathrm{P_2}\, \mathbb{A} = \{\{a_1, a_2\} \mid a_1, a_2 \in \mathbb{A} \wedge a_1 \neq a_2\}$ be the nominal set of subsets of $\mathbb{A}$ of cardinality 2; and let $\mathbb{A}^{\#2} = \{(a_1, a_2) \mid a_1, a_2 \in \mathbb{A} \wedge a_1 \neq a_2\}$ be the nominal set of distinct ordered pairs of atomic names. Show that the surjective equivariant function

$$q : \mathbb{A}^{\#2} \to \mathrm{P_2}\, \mathbb{A}$$
$$q \triangleq \lambda(a_1, a_2) \in \mathbb{A}^{\#2} \to \{a_1, a_2\}$$

does not split, that is, there is no equivariant function $i : \mathrm{P_2}\, \mathbb{A} \to \mathbb{A}^{\#2}$ satisfying $q \circ i = \mathrm{id}$.

2.7 Regarding Perm $\mathbb{A}$ as a nominal set as in Lemma 2.21, show that it is the 'object of bijections' on $\mathbb{A}$ in the topos **Nom**. In other words it is isomorphic to the subobject of the exponential $\mathbb{A} \to_{\mathrm{fs}} \mathbb{A}$ given by the equivariant subset of functions that are both injective and surjective.

2.8   Let X be the Perm $\mathbb{A}$-set whose elements are all finite permutations of $\mathbb{A}$ and whose action is as in Exercise 1.3, that is, given by composition of permutations. Show that X is not a nominal set. [Hint: which sets of atomic names support the identity permutation with respect to this action?]

2.9   Suppose that a function $f : \mathbb{A} \to \mathbb{A}$ has the property that $S \triangleq \{a \in \mathbb{A} \mid f\,a \neq a\}$ is finite. Show that $f \in \mathbb{A} \to_{\text{fs}} \mathbb{A}$ with $\operatorname{supp} f = S \cup \{f\,a \mid a \in S\}$. Does every element of $\mathbb{A} \to_{\text{fs}} \mathbb{A}$ have this property?

2.10 Let X be a G-set for some group G. Show that for every subset $S \subseteq X$ there is a greatest equivariant subset contained in S and a least equivariant subset containing S. Is the same true for finitely supported subsets when X is a nominal set?

2.11 If X is a nominal set and $x \in X$, show that

$$\operatorname{supp} x = \{a \in \mathbb{A} \mid \{a' \in \mathbb{A} \mid (a\ a') \cdot x \neq x\} \text{ is an infinite set}\}. \qquad (2.28)$$

[Hint: see the proof of Gabbay and Pitts (2002, proposition 3.4).]

3

Freshness

In the previous chapter we explored the notion of the support of an element of a set equipped with an action of finite permutations of $\mathbb{A}$. The complementary notion of an atomic name not being in the support of an element is in many ways more important for applications of nominal sets. This is the relation of *freshness* that we explore in this chapter.

3.1 Freshness relation

Given nominal sets X and Y and elements $x \in X$ and $y \in Y$, we write $x \# y$ and say that x is *fresh for* y if the two elements have disjoint supports:

$$x \# y \Leftrightarrow \text{supp}_X \, x \cap \text{supp}_Y \, y = \emptyset. \qquad (3.1)$$

Most of the time we use the freshness relation when $X = \mathbb{A}$ and $x = a$ is an atomic name. In this case since $\text{supp} \, a = \{a\}$ (Example 2.4), $a \# y$ means that $a \notin \text{supp} \, y$, or equivalently that there is some finite support for y that does not contain a. The *finiteness* of supports compared with the *infiniteness* of $\mathbb{A}$ leads to the following simple principle that we will use very often:

Choose-a-Fresh-Name Principle *If $X_1, \ldots, X_n$ are finitely many nominal sets and if $x_1 \in X_1, \ldots, x_n \in X_n$ are elements of them, then there is an atomic name $a \in \mathbb{A}$ satisfying $a \# x_1 \wedge \cdots \wedge a \# x_n$ (indeed, there are infinitely many such names).*

Note that by Proposition 2.11 the freshness relation is equivariant:

$$x \# y \Rightarrow (\pi \cdot x) \# (\pi \cdot y). \qquad (3.2)$$

The following results restate some of the properties of supports from the previous chapter in terms of the freshness relation.

49

Proposition 3.1 *Let $x \in X$ be an element of a nominal set X. For all $a, a' \in \mathbb{A}$, if $a \mathbin{\#} x$ and $a' \mathbin{\#} x$, then $(a\, a') \cdot x = x$.*

Proof Apply Proposition 2.1.   □

Proposition 3.2 *For any atoms $a, a' \in \mathbb{A}$ and finite sets of atoms $A, A' \in P_f\, \mathbb{A}$*

$$a \mathbin{\#} a' \Leftrightarrow a \neq a',$$
$$a \mathbin{\#} A \Leftrightarrow a \notin A,$$
$$A \mathbin{\#} A' \Leftrightarrow A \cap A' = \emptyset.$$

Proof Use the facts established in Examples 2.4 and 2.10 that $\operatorname{supp} a = \{a\}$ and $\operatorname{supp} A = A$.   □

Proposition 3.3 *Let $X_1, \ldots, X_n$ be nominal sets. Then for all $x_1 \in X_1, \ldots, x_n \in X_n$, and $a \in \mathbb{A}$*

$$a \mathbin{\#} (x_1, \ldots, x_n) \in X_1 \times \cdots \times X_n \Leftrightarrow a \mathbin{\#} x_1 \wedge \cdots \wedge a \mathbin{\#} x_n$$
$$a \mathbin{\#} \operatorname{inj}_i(x_i) \in X_1 + \cdots + X_n \Leftrightarrow a \mathbin{\#} x_i.$$

Proof These follow immediately from (2.10) and (2.9).   □

Proposition 3.4 *Let X and Y be nominal sets.*

(i) *Suppose $F \in P_{fs}(X \times Y)$ is a partial function:*

$$(\forall x \in X)(\forall y, y' \in Y)\ (x, y) \in F \wedge (x, y') \in F \Rightarrow y = y'. \tag{3.3}$$

 If $(x, y) \in F$, $a \mathbin{\#} F$ and $a \mathbin{\#} x$, then $a \mathbin{\#} y$.

(ii) *Suppose $f \in X \to_{fs} Y$ and $x \in X$. If $a \mathbin{\#} f$ and $a \mathbin{\#} x$, then $a \mathbin{\#} f\, x$.*

(iii) *Suppose $f : X \to Y$ in **Nom**. For all $x \in X$, if $a \mathbin{\#} x$, then $a \mathbin{\#} f\, x$.*

Proof Part (ii) is the special case of part (i) when F is total. Part (iii) follows from part (ii), because when f is equivariant, then as noted in Lemma 2.17 $\operatorname{supp} f = \emptyset$ and hence $a \mathbin{\#} f$ always holds. So it just remains to prove part (i); and for this it suffices to show that if $(x, y) \in F$ and $A \subseteq \mathbb{A}$ supports F and x, then A supports y.

If $\pi \in \operatorname{Perm} \mathbb{A}$ satisfies $(\forall a \in \mathbb{A})\ \pi\, a = a$, then $\pi \cdot x = x$ and $\pi \cdot F = F$. Therefore $(x, \pi \cdot y) = (\pi \cdot x, \pi \cdot y) = \pi \cdot (x, y) \in \pi \cdot F = F$ and hence by (3.3), $\pi \cdot y = y$. Thus A supports y.   □

Example 3.5 Freshness is not a unary 'logical relation' for functions. Although it is the case that $a \mathbin{\#} f$ implies $(\forall x \in X)\ a \mathbin{\#} x \Rightarrow a \mathbin{\#} f\, x$, the converse is false in general. For example, given an atomic name $a \in \mathbb{A}$, consider the function $f_a : P_f \mathbb{A} \to P_f \mathbb{A}$ mapping a finite subset A to $A - \{a\}$. It is not hard to see that f_a satisfies

$$(\forall a_1, a_2 \in \mathbb{A} - \{a\}) \, (a_1 \, a_2) \cdot f_a = f_a \,,$$

and hence f_a is supported by $\{a\}$; and it also satisfies

$$(\forall a' \in \mathbb{A} - \{a\}) \, (a \, a') \cdot f_a \neq f_a \,,$$

and hence is not supported by $\emptyset$. Therefore $f_a \in P_f \mathbb{A} \to_{fs} P_f \mathbb{A}$ and $\mathrm{supp}\, f_a = \{a\}$. So it is not the case that $a \# f_a$ holds. However, f_a does satisfy

$$(\forall A \in P_f \mathbb{A}) \, a \# A \Rightarrow a \# f_a A \,,$$

since $a \notin A - \{a\} = \mathrm{supp}(A - \{a\}) = \mathrm{supp}(f_a A)$.

Note 3.6 (Proving freshness for functions and relations) Propositions 3.2 and 3.3 help one to prove instances of the freshness relation $a \# x$ in case x is a name, a tuple, or an element of a disjoint union. As Example 3.5 suggests, freshness for functions cannot in general be reduced to freshness properties for the domain and codomain of the function. So when x is a finitely supported function, or more generally a finitely supported subset of a nominal set, it can be hard to prove freshness. If we are given $a \in \mathbb{A}$ and (the description of) a finitely supported set S and wish to prove $a \# S$, one common method is as follows:

Use the Choose-a-Fresh-Name Principle to find $b \in \mathbb{A}$ satisfying $b \# S$. It suffices to use the description of S to prove $(a \, b) \cdot S = S$, since then $a = (a \, b) \cdot b \# (a \, b) \cdot S = S$ (using the equivariance property (3.2) of #).

For example, this method is used below in the proof of Proposition 4.5 and in Example 8.20.

3.2 Freshness quantifier

Here is a very common pattern when reasoning informally with fresh names. At some point in a proof one chooses *some* fresh name with certain properties; later on in the proof one may need to revise that choice to take account of extra names that have entered the current context and so one needs to know that *any* fresh name with the property would have done for the original choice. The following results show that for finitely supported properties this switch from 'some fresh' to 'any fresh' is always possible.

Lemma 3.7   *Let $S \in P_{fs} \mathbb{A}$ be a finitely supported set of atomic names, supported by $A \in P_f \mathbb{A}$ say. The following are equivalent:*

(i) $(\exists a \in \mathbb{A})\, a \notin A \wedge a \in S$.

(ii) $(\forall a' \in \mathbb{A})\, a' \notin A \Rightarrow a' \in S$.

(iii) S *is cofinite.*

Proof   If $a \in S - A$, then for any $a' \in \mathbb{A} - A$ we have $(a\ a') \cdot S = S$ since $a, a' \notin A$ and the latter supports S; so $a' = (a\ a') \cdot a \in (a\ a') \cdot S = S$. So (i) implies (ii).

We know from Proposition 2.9 that $P_{fs} \mathbb{A}$ splits up as the disjoint union of two equivariant subsets, one consisting of all the finite subsets and the other consisting of all the cofinite subsets. Condition (ii) says that S contains $\mathbb{A} - A$ and hence is not finite. Therefore (ii) implies (iii).

Finally, if S is cofinite then so is $(\mathbb{A} - A) \cap S$ and hence it is in particular non-empty. Therefore (iii) implies (i).   □

Definition 3.8   We define $\mathcal{U} \triangleq \{S \subseteq \mathbb{A} \mid \mathbb{A} - S \text{ is finite}\}$ to be the set of cofinite sets of atomic names. If φ is the description (in higher-order logic, say) of some property of atomic names a, the *freshness quantifier*

$$(\mathcal{N}a)\, \varphi \tag{3.4}$$

asserts that the set $\{a \in \mathbb{A} \mid \varphi\}$ is in $\mathcal{U}$.

Note that this is a monotone quantifier in the sense that

$$\{a \in \mathbb{A} \mid \varphi\} \subseteq \{a \in \mathbb{A} \mid \varphi'\} \Rightarrow (\mathcal{N}a)\, \varphi \Rightarrow (\mathcal{N}a)\, \varphi'. \tag{3.5}$$

By definition $(\mathcal{N}a)\, \varphi$ says that φ holds for all but finitely many atomic names; but in view of the following theorem, we can also read it as 'for some/any fresh a, φ', so long as the subset $\{a \in \mathbb{A} \mid \varphi\}$ determined by φ is finitely supported. By the Finite Support Principle stated at the end of Section 2.5, this is the case for a wide range of properties, namely those expressible in classical higher-order logic (without the axiom of choice) using finitely supported primitives.

Theorem 3.9 ('Some/any' theorem)   *Suppose that X is a nominal set and that $R \subseteq \mathbb{A} \times X$ is an equivariant subset. For each $x \in X$, the following are equivalent:*

(i) $(\exists a \in \mathbb{A})\, a \,\#\, x \wedge (a, x) \in R$.

(ii) $(\forall a \in \mathbb{A})\, a \,\#\, x \Rightarrow (a, x) \in R$.

(iii) $(\mathcal{N}a)\, (a, x) \in R$.

Proof Since R has empty support (by Lemma 2.24), it follows from Proposition 2.25 that for each $x \in X$ the subset $\{a \in \mathbb{A} \mid (a, x) \in R\}$ is supported by supp x. So we can apply Lemma 3.7 with $S = \{a \in \mathbb{A} \mid (a, x) \in R\}$ and $A = \text{supp } x$. □

The theorem expresses the freshness quantifier in terms of the freshness relation $a \# x$. The converse is also possible:

$$a \# x \Leftrightarrow (\mathsf{N}a')\, (a\, a') \cdot x = x. \tag{3.6}$$

To see this, in Theorem 3.9 take X to be $\mathbb{A} \times X$ and $R\,\{(a', (a, x)) \in \mathbb{A} \times (\mathbb{A} \times X) \mid (a\, a') \cdot x = x\}$ to deduce that $(\mathsf{N}a')\, (a\, a') \cdot x = x$ iff $(\exists a' \in \mathbb{A})\, a' \# (a, x) \land (a\, a') \cdot x = x$; but the latter is easily seen to be equivalent to $a \# x$.

As the next result shows, the freshness quantifier has very regular behaviour with respect to the Boolean operations. Exercise 3.1 explores its commutation with existential and universal quantification.

Proposition 3.10 *Suppose φ and φ' are properties of atomic names for which $\{a \in \mathbb{A} \mid \varphi\}$ and $\{a \in \mathbb{A} \mid \varphi'\}$ are finitely supported subsets of $\mathbb{A}$. Then the following properties hold:*

$$\neg(\mathsf{N}a)\, \varphi \Leftrightarrow (\mathsf{N}a)\, \neg\varphi, \tag{3.7}$$

$$((\mathsf{N}a)\, \varphi \land (\mathsf{N}a)\, \varphi') \Leftrightarrow (\mathsf{N}a)\, (\varphi \land \varphi'), \tag{3.8}$$

and hence also

$$((\mathsf{N}a)\, \varphi \lor (\mathsf{N}a)\, \varphi') \Leftrightarrow (\mathsf{N}a)\, (\varphi \lor \varphi'), \tag{3.9}$$

$$((\mathsf{N}a)\, \varphi \Rightarrow (\mathsf{N}a)\, \varphi') \Leftrightarrow (\mathsf{N}a)\, (\varphi \Rightarrow \varphi'). \tag{3.10}$$

Proof Since $S \triangleq \{a \in \mathbb{A} \mid \varphi(a)\}$ and $S' \triangleq \{a \in \mathbb{A} \mid \varphi'(a)\}$ are elements of $P_{\text{fs}}\, \mathbb{A}$, by Proposition 2.9 they are either finite or cofinite. So $S \notin \mathsf{N}$ if and only if S is finite if and only if $\mathbb{A} - S \in \mathsf{N}$; so we have (3.7). Since the union of two sets is finite if and only if they are both finite, we also have $S \cap S' \in \mathsf{N} \Leftrightarrow S \in \mathsf{N} \land S' \in \mathsf{N}$, which gives (3.8). □

3.3 Fresh names

Many constructions on syntax, especially ones involving binding operations, make use of fresh names and involve verifying that the construction is independent of which fresh name is chosen. As the following theorem shows, the notion of 'finite support' can be used to give a simple condition that guarantees this independence.

Theorem 3.11 (Freshness theorem) *Let X be a nominal set. If a finitely supported partial function $F \in \mathbb{A} \rightharpoonup_{\mathrm{fs}} X$ satisfies*

$$(\mathsf{N}a)(\exists x \in X)\, a \,\#\, x \wedge F\, a \equiv x \tag{3.11}$$

then there is a unique element $\mathrm{fresh}_X\, F \in X$ satisfying

$$(\mathsf{N}a)\, F\, a \equiv \mathrm{fresh}_X\, F. \tag{3.12}$$

Furthermore, $\mathrm{supp}(\mathrm{fresh}_X\, F) \subseteq \mathrm{supp}\, F$.

Proof   Consider the equivariant subset

$$\mathrm{fresh}_X \triangleq \{(F, x) \in (\mathbb{A} \rightharpoonup_{\mathrm{fs}} X) \times X \mid (\mathsf{N}a)\, F\, a \equiv x\}. \tag{3.13}$$

To prove the first sentence of the theorem we have to show that (3.13) is a partial function whose domain of definition contains those F satisfying (3.11); and then the second sentence follows by part (i) of Proposition 3.4. Note that

$$(F, x) \in \mathrm{fresh}_X \wedge (F, x') \in \mathrm{fresh}_X$$
$$\Rightarrow \quad \{\text{by (3.8)}\}$$
$$(\mathsf{N}a)\, (a, x) \in F \wedge (a, x') \in F$$
$$\Rightarrow \quad \{\text{since } F \text{ is single-valued}\}$$
$$x = x'.$$

So fresh_X is single-valued. If F satisfies (3.11), then by the 'some/any' theorem (Theorem 3.9) there exists $a \in \mathbb{A}$ and $x \in X$ with $a \,\#\, (F, x)$ and $(a, x) \in F$; hence $(\mathsf{N}a)\, F\, a \equiv x$ holds and therefore $F \in \mathrm{Dom}\, \mathrm{fresh}_X$.   □

Notation 3.12   If $\lambda a \in \mathbb{A} \rightarrow \varphi(a)$ is the description of some finitely supported partial function in $\mathbb{A} \rightharpoonup_{\mathrm{fs}} X$ satisfying condition (3.11) in the above theorem, then we write the element $\mathrm{fresh}_X(\lambda a \in \mathbb{A} \rightarrow \varphi(a))$ of X as

$$\mathrm{fresh}\, a \text{ in } \varphi(a). \tag{3.14}$$

Writing $a \,\#\, \varphi(a)$ for $(\exists x \in X)\, a \,\#\, x \wedge \varphi(a) \equiv x$ (in other words, the assertion that a is fresh for $\varphi(a)$ includes the assertion that $\varphi(a)$ is defined), with this notation we can summarize the freshness theorem by the formula

$$((\mathsf{N}a)\, a \,\#\, \varphi(a)) \Rightarrow (\mathsf{N}a)\, \varphi(a) \equiv (\mathrm{fresh}\, a \text{ in } \varphi(a)). \tag{3.15}$$

3.4 Separated product

Since the freshness relation (3.1) is equivariant, for any nominal sets X_1 and X_2

$$X_1 * X_2 \triangleq \{(x_1, x_2) \in X_1 \times X_2 \mid x_1 \,\#\, x_2\} \tag{3.16}$$

is again a nominal set (by Lemma 2.22). We call it the *separated product* of X_1 and X_2. It is the object part of a functor $\_ * \_ : \mathbf{Nom} \times \mathbf{Nom} \to \mathbf{Nom}$ whose effect on equivariant functions $f_1 : X_1 \to X_1'$ and $f_2 : X_2 \to X_2'$ is

$$f_1 * f_2 : X_1 * X_2 \to X_1' * X_2'$$
$$f_1 * f_2 \triangleq \lambda(x, y) \in X_1 * X_2 \to (f_1 \, x, f_2 \, y). \tag{3.17}$$

(This is well defined because by part (i) of Lemma 2.12 we have $x_1 \# x_2 \Rightarrow f_1 \, x_1 \# f_2 \, x_2$.)

Note that if X_2 is a discrete nominal set then the support of any of its elements is empty and therefore $X_1 * X_2 = X_1 \times X_2$. In particular, the terminal object 1 satisfies $X_1 * 1 = X_1 \times 1 \cong X_1$. There are also natural isomorphisms $X_1 * X_2 \cong X_2 * X_1$ and $X_1 * (X_2 * X_3) \cong (X_1 * X_2) * X_3$ inherited from those for cartesian product. Altogether $(\mathbf{Nom}, *, 1)$ is a *symmetric monoidal category* (MacLane, 1971, chapter VII) that is *affine*, in the sense that the terminal object 1 is the unit for the tensor product $*$. In fact, as the following result shows, the affine symmetric monoidal structure is *closed*.

Theorem 3.13 *For each nominal set X, the functor $\_ * X : \mathbf{Nom} \to \mathbf{Nom}$ has a right adjoint $X \rightarrowtail \_ : \mathbf{Nom} \to \mathbf{Nom}$. In other words for each $Y \in \mathbf{Nom}$ there is a nominal set $X \rightarrowtail Y$ and an equivariant function $\varepsilon : (X \rightarrowtail Y) * X \to Y$ with the universal property that given any equivariant function f as shown*

$$
\begin{array}{ccc}
Z * X & & \\
{\scriptstyle \hat{f} * \mathrm{id}_X} \downarrow & \searrow {\scriptstyle f} & \\
(X \rightarrowtail Y) * X & \xrightarrow{\quad \varepsilon \quad} & Y
\end{array}
\tag{3.18}
$$

there is a unique equivariant function $\hat{f} : Z \to (X \rightarrowtail Y)$ making the above diagram commute.

Remark 3.14 In certain cases a simple description for $X \rightarrowtail \_$ is possible, such as when $X = \mathbb{A}$; see Theorem 4.12. Schöpp (2006, section 3.3.1) gives both an abstract, category-theoretic construction for $\rightarrowtail$ (building on some previous work of Menni, 2003) and a more concrete description in terms of partial functions. The following proof, due to Clouston (2013), gives an even simpler construction for $\rightarrowtail$.

Proof of Theorem 3.13 Given nominal sets X and Y and a finitely supported partial function $F \in X \rightharpoonup_{\mathrm{fs}} Y$, note that from part (i) of Proposition 3.4 we have

$$(x, y) \in F \Rightarrow \mathrm{supp} \, y \subseteq \mathrm{supp} \, F \cup \mathrm{supp} \, x.$$

Therefore

$$\Delta_F \triangleq \bigcup \{\operatorname{supp} y - \operatorname{supp} x \mid (x, y) \in F\} \tag{3.19}$$

satisfies $\Delta_F \subseteq \operatorname{supp} F$. We single out the finitely supported partial functions F for which $\operatorname{supp} F$ is equal to Δ_F and whose domain of definition $\operatorname{Dom} F$ is equal to $\{x \in X \mid x \,\#\, F\}$:

$$X \rightarrowtail Y \triangleq \{F \in X \rightharpoonup_{\mathrm{fs}} Y \mid \operatorname{Dom} F = \{x \in X \mid x \,\#\, F\} \wedge \Delta_F = \operatorname{supp} F\}. \tag{3.20}$$

Since support and freshness are equivariant, this is an equivariant subset of $X \rightharpoonup_{\mathrm{fs}} Y$ and hence a nominal set (Lemma 2.22). Since

$$(F, x) \in (X \rightarrowtail Y) * X \Rightarrow x \in \operatorname{Dom} F,$$

the subset $\{((F, x), y) \mid (x, y) \in F\} \subseteq ((X \rightarrowtail Y) * X) \times Y$ is the graph of an equivariant function $\varepsilon : (X \rightarrowtail Y) * X \to Y$. We claim that this inherits the required universal property from the universal property of $\mathrm{app} \in (X \rightharpoonup_{\mathrm{fs}} Y) \times X \rightharpoonup Y$ described in Section 2.8.

For the existence part of the universal property, note that each $f : Z * X \to Y$ is in particular an equivariant partial function $(Z \times X) \rightharpoonup Y$ via the inclusion $Z * X \subseteq Z \times X$; so it uniquely determines an equivariant function $\operatorname{curry} f : Z \to (X \rightharpoonup_{\mathrm{fs}} Y)$ satisfying (2.26). Thus (3.19) specializes to give for each $z \in Z$

$$\Delta_{\operatorname{curry} f z} = \bigcup \{\operatorname{supp} f(z, x) - \operatorname{supp} x \mid z \,\#\, x\}. \tag{3.21}$$

We define a partial function $\hat{f} z \in X \rightharpoonup Y$ with domain of definition $\{x \in X \mid x \,\#\, \Delta_{\operatorname{curry} f z}\}$ as follows. For each $x \in X$ with $x \,\#\, \Delta_{\operatorname{curry} f z}$, let $\vec{a} = (a_1, \ldots, a_n)$ be a finite list of mutually distinct atomic names that enumerates $\operatorname{supp} z \cap \operatorname{supp} x$; pick some mutually distinct atomic names $\vec{a}' = (a_1', \ldots, a_n')$ with $\vec{a}' \,\#\, (x, z)$ and let $(\vec{a}\ \vec{a}') \in \operatorname{Perm} \mathbb{A}$ be the finite permutation that swaps a_i with a_i' for $i = 1, \ldots, n$. Note that by choice of $\vec{a}'$, we have $z \,\#\, (\vec{a}\ \vec{a}') \cdot x$ and hence also $(\vec{a}\ \vec{a}') \cdot z \,\#\, x$; so $f((\vec{a}\ \vec{a}') \cdot z, x)$ is defined and we take this to be the value of $\hat{f} z$ at x. This is independent of the choice of atomic names $\vec{a}'$ by the freshness theorem (Theorem 3.11), because

$$\vec{a}' \,\#\, f((\vec{a}\ \vec{a}') \cdot z, x). \tag{3.22}$$

To see this, note that since $x \,\#\, \Delta_{\operatorname{curry} f z}$ and $z \,\#\, (\vec{a}\ \vec{a}') \cdot x$, from (3.21) we have

$$x \,\#\, \operatorname{supp} f(z, (\vec{a}\ \vec{a}') \cdot x) - \operatorname{supp}((\vec{a}\ \vec{a}') \cdot x),$$

and hence $\{\vec{a}\} = \operatorname{supp} z \cap \operatorname{sup} z \,\#\, \operatorname{supp} f(z, (\vec{a}\ \vec{a}') \cdot x)$; applying the permutation $(\vec{a}\ \vec{a}')$ to this yields (3.22). So we get a well defined partial function $\hat{f} z \in X \rightharpoonup Y$. One can show that $\hat{f} z$ is finitely supported, indeed that

$$\operatorname{supp} \hat{f} z = \Delta_{\operatorname{curry} f z} = \Delta_{\hat{f} z}, \tag{3.23}$$

so that $\hat{f} z \in X \rightarrowtail Y$ (Exercise 3.4). Furthermore, it is not hard to see that the function $\hat{f} : Z \rightarrow (X \rightarrowtail Y)$ is equivariant. It makes (3.18) commute because when $z \mathrel{\#} x$, then in the definition of $\hat{f} z x$ we have $\vec{a} = \emptyset = \vec{a}'$ and hence $\hat{f} z x = f(z, x)$.

For the uniqueness part of the universal property, suppose $g : Z \rightarrow (X \rightarrowtail Y)$ also satisfies

$$\varepsilon \circ (g * \mathrm{id}_X) = f . \tag{3.24}$$

Then for each $z \in Z$, we claim that

$$\mathrm{supp}\, g\, z = \Delta_{\mathrm{curry}\, f\, z} . \tag{3.25}$$

For if $a \in \Delta_{\mathrm{curry}\, f\, z}$, then by (3.21) $a \in \mathrm{supp}\, f(z, x) - \mathrm{supp}\, x$ for some $x \mathrel{\#} z$; and by (3.24) this means $a \in \mathrm{supp}\, g\, z\, x - \mathrm{supp}\, x$, so that $a \in \Delta_{g\, z}$. Since $g\, z \in X \rightarrowtail Y$, $\Delta_{g\, z} = \mathrm{supp}\, g\, z$ and hence $a \in \mathrm{supp}\, g\, z$. Conversely, if $a \in \mathrm{supp}\, g\, z = \Delta_{g\, z}$, then $a \in \mathrm{supp}\, g\, z\, x - \mathrm{supp}\, x$, for some $x \in \mathrm{Dom}\, g\, z$, that is, some $x \mathrel{\#} g\, z$ (since $g\, z \in X \rightarrowtail Y$). Letting $\vec{a}$ enumerate $\mathrm{supp}\, z \cap \mathrm{supp}\, x$, we have $\vec{a} \mathrel{\#} g\, z$ and in particular $a \notin \vec{a}$; so picking $\vec{a}'$ fresh for (a, x, z), we get $a = (\vec{a}\ \vec{a}') \cdot a \in (\vec{a}\ \vec{a}') \cdot (\mathrm{supp}\, g\, z\, x - \mathrm{supp}\, x) = \mathrm{supp}\, g\, z((\vec{a}\ \vec{a}') \cdot x) - \mathrm{supp}(\vec{a}\ \vec{a}') \cdot x = \mathrm{supp}\, f(z, (\vec{a}\ \vec{a}') \cdot x) - \mathrm{supp}(\vec{a}\ \vec{a}') \cdot x$, by (3.24), since by choice of $\vec{a}'$ we have $z \mathrel{\#} (\vec{a}\ \vec{a}') \cdot x$. Thus $a \in \Delta_{\mathrm{curry}\, f\, z}$. So we do indeed have (3.25). In particular, $\mathrm{Dom}\, g\, z = \{x \in X \mid x \mathrel{\#} g\, z\} = \{x \in X \mid x \mathrel{\#} \Delta_{\mathrm{curry}\, f\, z}\} = \mathrm{Dom}\, \hat{f} z$. Furthermore, if $x \mathrel{\#} \Delta_{\mathrm{curry}\, f\, z}$, then $x \mathrel{\#} g\, z$ and so we can take $\hat{f} z x$ to be equal to $f((\vec{a}\ \vec{a}') \cdot z, x)$ with $\vec{a}, \vec{a}' \mathrel{\#} g\, z$ and hence with $(\vec{a}\ \vec{a}') \cdot (g\, z) = g\, z$. Since $(\vec{a}\ \vec{a}') \cdot z \mathrel{\#} x$, by (3.24) we have $g\, z\, x = ((\vec{a}\ \vec{a}') \cdot (g\, z))\, x = g\, ((\vec{a}\ \vec{a}') \cdot z)\, x = f((\vec{a}\ \vec{a}') \cdot z, x) = \hat{f} z x$. Thus we do indeed have $g\, z = \hat{f} z$ for all $z \in Z$. $\qquad\square$

Exercises

3.1 Show that if $X \in \mathbf{Nom}$ and $R \in \mathrm{P}_{\mathrm{fs}}\, (\mathbb{A} \times X)$, then

$$(\exists x \in X)(\mathsf{И}a)\, (a, x) \in R \Rightarrow (\mathsf{И}a)(\exists x \in X)\, (a, x) \in R , \tag{3.26}$$

$$(\mathsf{И}a)(\forall x \in X)\, (a, x) \in R \Rightarrow (\forall x \in X)(\mathsf{И}a)\, (a, x) \in R , \tag{3.27}$$

but that the reverse implications do not necessarily hold. [Hint: consider $R_1 = \{(a, a) \mid a \in \mathbb{A}\}$ and $R_2 = \{(a, a') \in \mathbb{A} \times \mathbb{A} \mid a \neq a'\}$.]

3.2 Given $X \in \mathbf{Nom}$, $A \in \mathrm{P}_f\, \mathbb{A}$ and $x \in X$ satisfying $A \mathrel{\#} x$, show that for any other finite set of atomic names $A' \in \mathrm{P}_f\, \mathbb{A}$, there exists $\pi \in \mathrm{Perm}\, \mathbb{A}$ with $(\forall a \in A)\, \pi a = a$ and $A' \mathrel{\#} \pi \cdot x$.

3.3 If $\pi, \pi' \in \mathrm{Perm}\, \mathbb{A}$, show that $\pi \mathrel{\#} \pi' \Rightarrow \pi \circ \pi' = \pi' \circ \pi$. Deduce that for any nominal set X and $\pi \in \text{Perm } \mathbb{A}$, the function $\lambda x \in X \to \pi \cdot x$ is in $X \to_{\text{fs}} X$. Can this function be equivariant even if π has non-empty support?

3.4   Complete the proof of Theorem 3.13 by proving (3.23).

4

Name abstraction

The original motivation for developing the theory of nominal sets was to extend the range of structural induction and recursion for algebraic data types to encompass quotients associated with the use of name-binding operations. Quotients of sets of algebraic terms by α-equivalence are isomorphic in **Nom** to nominal sets inductively defined using products $X \times Y$, coproducts $X + Y$ and a name abstraction construct $[\mathbb{A}]X$ for representing the domains of name-binding operations and which is the subject of this chapter.

4.1 α-Equivalence

Consider the set $\Lambda/=_\alpha$ of terms of the *untyped λ-calculus* (Barendregt, 1984), which we can take to be the quotient by α-equivalence of the set Λ of terms t given by the grammar

$$t \in \Lambda ::= a \mid \lambda a.t \mid t\, t,$$

where a ranges over $\mathbb{A}$, regarded as an infinite set of variables. The elements of Λ are sometimes called *raw terms* to distinguish them from the elements of the quotient $\Lambda/=_\alpha$.

The equivalence relation $=_\alpha$ is *α-equivalence*, which can be inductively defined by the following rules (readers unfamiliar with rule-based inductive definitions may refer to the beginning of Chapter 7 for a brief introduction):

$$\text{VAR} \frac{}{a =_\alpha a} \qquad \text{APP} \frac{t_1 =_\alpha t_2 \quad t_1' =_\alpha t_2'}{t_1\, t_1' =_\alpha t_2\, t_2'} \qquad \text{LAM} \frac{(a_1\ a) \cdot t_1 =_\alpha (a_2\ a) \cdot t_2 \quad a \notin \text{var}(a_1, t_1, a_2, t_2)}{\lambda a_1.t_1 =_\alpha \lambda a_2.t_2}. \qquad (4.1)$$

Here we are using the action of Perm $\mathbb{A}$ on terms defined as in Example 1.4;

59

and as in Example 2.6, Λ is a nominal set with supp $t = $ var t, the finite set of variables occurring in the term t:

$$\text{var } a = \{a\},$$
$$\text{var}(\lambda a.t) = \{a\} \cup \text{var } t, \qquad (4.2)$$
$$\text{var}(t\,t') = \text{var } t \cup \text{var } t'.$$

Thus the rule LAM in (4.1) can be restated neatly using the freshness quantifier (Section 3.2)

$$\frac{(\mathsf{И}a'')\,(a\,a'')\cdot t =_\alpha (a'\,a'')\cdot t'}{\lambda a.\,t =_\alpha \lambda a'.\,t'},$$

because $\{(a'', (a,t,a',t')) \mid (a\,a'')\cdot t =_\alpha (a'\,a'')\cdot t'\}$ is an equivariant subset of $\mathbb{A} \times (\mathbb{A} \times \Lambda \times \mathbb{A} \times \Lambda)$ and $a'' \# (a,t,a',t')$ holds if and only if $a'' \notin \text{var}(a\,t\,a'\,t')$.

The relation of α-equivalence is more traditionally defined to be the congruence generated by relating $\lambda a.t$ and $\lambda a'.\{a'/a\}t$ if there are no occurrences of a' in t, where $\{a'/a\}t$ is the term obtained from t by replacing all free occurrences of a with a'. The properties of this form of renaming are rather inconvenient, because the function $\lambda t \in \Lambda \to \{a'/a\}t$ does not necessarily respect α-equivalence when applied to terms that do contain occurrences of a'. This is because of the possible 'capture' of a' by binders $\lambda a'._{-}$ occurring in t. For example, if a, a_1 and a_2 are three distinct atomic names, then $\lambda a_1.a =_\alpha \lambda a_2.a$ holds, but $\{a_1/a\}(\lambda a_1.a) = \lambda a_1.a_1 \neq_\alpha \lambda a_2.a_1 = \{a_1/a\}(\lambda a_2.a)$. In the traditional development of the theory of lambda calculus (Barendregt, 1984), this inconvenient fact immediately leads to the formulation of more complicated, 'capture-avoiding' notions of renaming and substitution. However, it is possible to go in the other direction and replace $\lambda t \in \Lambda \to \{a'/a\}t$ with another, equally simple form of renaming which does respect α-equivalence, namely the action of the transposition $(a\,a')$. For if a' does not occur in t, then $\{a'/a\}t$ is α-equivalent to the term $(a\,a')\cdot t$ obtained from t by swapping all occurrences of a and a'. It is for this reason that definition (4.1) coincides with the usual definition of α-equivalence (see Gabbay and Pitts, 2002, proposition 2.2).

We noted in Example 1.6 that group action functions are equivariant; and var $: \Lambda \to \mathsf{P_f}\,\mathbb{A}$, being the support function, is equivariant by Proposition 2.11. It follows from this and the Equivariance Principle that $=_\alpha$ is equivariant:

$$t =_\alpha t' \Rightarrow \pi \cdot t =_\alpha \pi \cdot t'. \qquad (4.3)$$

It is also an equivalence relation. Proofs of the reflexivity and symmetry of $=_\alpha$ are easy, whereas the proof of its transitivity is less so; we give it in detail in Example 7.8. From Section 2.9 we have that the quotient set $\Lambda/=_\alpha$ of untyped

λ-terms is a nominal set with $\mathrm{supp}\,[t]_{=_\alpha} \subseteq \mathrm{var}\,t$. In fact the support of a λ-term is equal to the set of free variables of any representative raw term:

$$\mathrm{supp}\,[t]_{=_\alpha} = \mathrm{fv}\,t, \qquad (4.4)$$

where

$$\begin{aligned}
\mathrm{fv}\,a &= \{a\}, \\
\mathrm{fv}(\lambda a.t) &= (\mathrm{fv}\,t) - \{a\}, \qquad (4.5) \\
\mathrm{fv}(t\,t') &= \mathrm{fv}\,t \cup \mathrm{fv}\,t'.
\end{aligned}$$

This is because for all $t \in \Lambda$

$$((\forall a \in \mathrm{fv}\,t)\;\pi\,a = a) \Leftrightarrow \pi \cdot t =_\alpha t, \qquad (4.6)$$

and hence $\mathrm{fv}\,t$ strongly supports $[t]_{=_\alpha}$ in $\Lambda/{=_\alpha}$; so we can apply Theorem 2.7 to conclude that $\mathrm{supp}\,[t]_{=_\alpha}$ is equal to $\mathrm{fv}\,t$. The proof of (4.6), by induction on the size of raw terms t, is left as an exercise.

4.2 Nominal set of name abstractions

Section 4.1 gave a structurally inductive characterization of α-equivalence ($=_\alpha$) for the untyped λ-calculus that makes use of name permutations rather than more general renaming operations on λ-terms. This suggests a generalized form of α-equivalence that applies to the elements of any nominal set X and not just to nominal sets of algebraic terms. Define the binary relation $\approx_\alpha$ on $\mathbb{A} \times X$ by

$$(a_1, x_1) \approx_\alpha (a_2, x_2) \Leftrightarrow (\text{Иa})\,(a_1\;a) \cdot x_1 = (a_2\;a) \cdot x_2. \qquad (4.7)$$

Since the swapping operation is equivariant (Proposition 1.16), by Theorem 3.9 we have

$$\begin{aligned}
(a_1, x_1) \approx_\alpha (a_2, x_2) &\Leftrightarrow (\exists a \;\#\; (a_1, x_1, a_2, x_2))\,(a_1\;a) \cdot x_1 = (a_2\;a) \cdot x_2 \\
&\Leftrightarrow (\forall a \;\#\; (a_1, x_1, a_2, x_2))\,(a_1\;a) \cdot x_1 = (a_2\;a) \cdot x_2.
\end{aligned} \qquad (4.8)$$

Equivariance of swapping implies that $\approx_\alpha$ is an equivariant relation:

$$(a_1, x_1) \approx_\alpha (a_2, x_2) \Rightarrow (\pi\,a_1, \pi \cdot x_1) \approx_\alpha (\pi\,a_2, \pi \cdot x_2). \qquad (4.9)$$

Lemma 4.1 $\approx_\alpha$ *is an equivalence relation.*

Proof It is immediate from its definition that $\approx_\alpha$ is reflexive and symmetric.

Transitivity follows from the fact that the freshness quantifier commutes with conjunction:

$$(a_1, x_1) \approx_\alpha (a_2, x_2) \wedge (a_2, x_2) \approx_\alpha (a_3, x_3)$$
$\Leftrightarrow$ {by definition}
$$(\text{И}a)\,(a_1\ a) \cdot x_1 = (a_2\ a) \cdot x_2 \wedge (\text{И}a)\,(a_2\ a) \cdot x_2 = (a_3\ a) \cdot x_3$$
$\Leftrightarrow$ {by Proposition 3.10}
$$(\text{И}a)\,(a_1\ a) \cdot x_1 = (a_2\ a) \cdot x_2 \wedge (a_2\ a) \cdot x_2 = (a_3\ a) \cdot x_3$$
$\Rightarrow$
$$(\text{И}a)\,(a_1\ a) \cdot x_1 = (a_3\ a) \cdot x_3$$
$\Leftrightarrow$ {by definition}
$$(a_1, x_1) \approx_\alpha (a_3, x_3).\qquad\qquad\qquad\square$$

Lemma 4.2 *For all $a \in \mathbb{A}$ and $x_1, x_2 \in X$, $(a, x_1) \approx_\alpha (a, x_2)$ holds if and only if $x_1 = x_2$.*

Proof Immediate from the definition of $\approx_\alpha$. $\qquad\qquad\square$

Lemma 4.3 $(a_1, x_1) \approx_\alpha (a_2, x_2)$ *holds if and only if either $a_1 = a_2$ and $x_1 = x_2$, or $a_1 \mathbin{\#} (a_2, x_2)$ and $x_1 = (a_1\ a_2) \cdot x_2$.*

Proof We split the proof into two cases, according to whether or not a_1 and a_2 are equal. In case $a_1 = a_2$ we can just apply Lemma 4.2. So suppose $a_1 \neq a_2$. If $(a_1, x_1) \approx_\alpha (a_2, x_2)$, then by (4.8) $(a_1\ a) \cdot x_1 = (a_2\ a) \cdot x_2$ holds for some $a \mathbin{\#} (a_1, x_1, a_2, x_2)$. Therefore

$$a_1$$
$= \quad$ {since $a_1 \neq a_2, a$}
$$(a_2\ a) \cdot (a_1\ a) \cdot a$$
$\# \quad$ {by (3.2), since $a \mathbin{\#} x_1$}
$$(a_2\ a) \cdot (a_1\ a) \cdot x_1$$
$= \quad$ {since $(a_1\ a) \cdot x_1 = (a_2\ a) \cdot x_2$}
$$(a_2\ a) \cdot (a_2\ a) \cdot x_2$$
$= \quad$ {since $(a_2\ a) \circ (a_2\ a) = \mathrm{id}$}
$$x_2,$$

and hence also

$$(a_1\ a_2) \cdot x_2$$
$$= \quad \{\text{by Proposition 3.1, since } a_1 \# x_2 \text{ and } a \# x_2\}$$
$$(a_1\ a_2) \cdot (a_1\ a) \cdot x_2$$
$$= \quad \{\text{since } (a_1\ a_2) \circ (a_1\ a) = (a_1\ a) \circ (a_2\ a)\}$$
$$(a_1\ a) \cdot (a_2\ a) \cdot x_2$$
$$= \quad \{\text{since } (a_1\ a) \cdot x_1 = (a_2\ a) \cdot x_2\}$$
$$(a_1\ a) \cdot (a_1\ a) \cdot x_1$$
$$= \quad \{\text{since } (a_1\ a) \circ (a_1\ a) = \mathrm{id}\}$$
$$x_1\ .$$

Conversely, if $a_1 \# (a_2, x_2)$ and $x_1 = (a_1\ a_2) \cdot x_2$, then for any $a \# (a_1, x_1, a_2, x_2)$ we have

$$(a_1\ a) \cdot x_1$$
$$= \quad \{\text{since } x_1 = (a_1\ a_2) \cdot x_2\}$$
$$(a_1\ a) \cdot (a_1\ a_2) \cdot x_2$$
$$= \quad \{\text{since } (a_1\ a) \circ (a_1\ a_2) = (a_2\ a) \cdot (a_1\ a)\}$$
$$(a_2\ a) \cdot (a_1\ a) \cdot x_2$$
$$= \quad \{\text{by Proposition 3.1, since } a_1 \# x_2 \text{ and } a \# x_2\}$$
$$(a_2\ a) \cdot x_2\ .$$

Therefore $(a_1, x_1) \approx_\alpha (a_2, x_2)$, by (4.8). □

Definition 4.4 Given a nominal set X, let $\approx_\alpha$ be as in (4.7). Since $\approx_\alpha$ is an equivariant equivalence relation, from Section 2.9 we know that the quotient of $\mathbb{A} \times X$ by $\approx_\alpha$ is a nominal set. We denote this quotient by $[\mathbb{A}]X$ and call it the *nominal set of name abstractions* of elements of X. The equivalence class of $(a, x) \in \mathbb{A} \times X$ is denoted $\langle a \rangle x$ and called a *name abstraction*. Thus the Perm $\mathbb{A}$-action on $[\mathbb{A}]X$ is well defined by

$$\pi \cdot \langle a \rangle x \triangleq \langle \pi\, a \rangle (\pi \cdot x)\,. \tag{4.10}$$

We noted in Section 2.9 that an equivalence class is supported by any set of atomic names that supports a representative of the class. Therefore in $[\mathbb{A}]X$ we have $\mathrm{supp} \langle a \rangle x \subseteq \mathrm{supp}\,(a, x) = \{a\} \cup \mathrm{supp}\,x$. However, we can do better than this.

Proposition 4.5 *For any nominal set X, $a \in \mathbb{A}$ and $x \in X$, it is the case that* $\mathrm{supp} \langle a \rangle x = \mathrm{supp}\,x - \{a\}$. *Hence for all $a' \in \mathbb{A}$*

$$a' \# \langle a \rangle x \Leftrightarrow a' = a \lor a' \# x\,. \tag{4.11}$$

Proof First note that if $\pi \in \mathrm{Perm}\,\mathbb{A}$ satisfies $\pi \cdot \langle a \rangle x = \langle a \rangle x$ and $\pi\, a = a$, then by Lemma 4.2 and (4.10) it also satisfies $\pi \cdot x = x$. Therefore if $A \subseteq \mathbb{A}$ supports $\langle a \rangle x$ in $[\mathbb{A}]X$, then $A \cup \{a\}$ supports x in X. Hence $\operatorname{supp} x \subseteq \{a\} \cup \operatorname{supp} \langle a \rangle x$. Since we noted above that $\operatorname{supp}\langle a \rangle x \subseteq \{a\} \cup \operatorname{supp} x$, it just remains to show that $a \notin \operatorname{supp}\langle a \rangle x$, that is, $a \# \langle a \rangle x$. Using the Choose-a-Fresh-Name Principle to pick some $a' \# (a, x)$, from Lemma 4.3 we have $(a', (a'\ a) \cdot x) \approx_\alpha (a, x)$ and hence $(a'\ a) \cdot \langle a \rangle x = \langle a' \rangle ((a'\ a) \cdot x) = \langle a \rangle x$. Since $a' \# (a, x)$, we have $a' \# \langle a \rangle x$; so by equivariance of $\#$ we get $a = (a'\ a) \cdot a' \# (a'\ a) \cdot \langle a \rangle x = \langle a \rangle x$, as required. $\square$

Example 4.6 If X is a discrete nominal set, then $a \# x$ holds for all $a \in \mathbb{A}$ and $x \in X$. So in this case $(a_1, x_1) \approx_\alpha (a_2, x_2) \Leftrightarrow x_1 = x_2$. Thus $\langle a \rangle x \mapsto x$ is a well defined equivariant function witnessing the isomorphism

$$[\mathbb{A}]X \cong X \quad (X \text{ discrete}). \tag{4.12}$$

4.3 Concretion

In this section we compare name abstraction with the more familiar notion of function abstraction. Recall that each $\langle a \rangle x \in [\mathbb{A}]X$ is an equivalence class for the relation $\approx_\alpha$ and hence in particular is a subset of $\mathbb{A} \times X$. Lemma 4.2 implies that it is single-valued; and of course it is finitely supported. So we have an inclusion

$$[\mathbb{A}]X \subseteq (\mathbb{A} \rightarrow_{\text{fs}} X). \tag{4.13}$$

Lemma 4.7 *The domain of definition of each $F \in [\mathbb{A}]X$ regarded as a partial function from $\mathbb{A}$ to X is the cofinite set of atomic names that are fresh for it:*

$$\operatorname{Dom} F = \{a \in \mathbb{A} \mid a \# F\} = \mathbb{A} - \operatorname{supp} F.$$

Proof Suppose $F = \langle a \rangle x$. Then $\operatorname{Dom} F = \{a' \mid (\exists x')\ (a', x') \approx_\alpha (a, x)\}$. Applying Lemma 4.3, we get $\operatorname{Dom} F = \{a' \mid a' = a \lor a' \# x\}$, from which the result follows by Proposition 4.5. $\square$

Definition 4.8 Given a nominal set X, the result of applying a name abstraction $F \in [\mathbb{A}]X$, regarded as a partial function from $\mathbb{A}$ to X, to an atomic name $a \in \operatorname{Dom} F = \mathbb{A} - \operatorname{supp} F$ will be denoted $F @ a$ and called the *concretion* of F at a.

Thus from Lemma 4.3 we have for all $a, a' \in \mathbb{A}$ and $x \in X$

$$(\langle a \rangle x) @ a' \equiv \begin{cases} x & \text{if } a' = a, \\ (a\ a') \cdot x & \text{if } a' \neq a \text{ and } a' \# x, \\ \text{undefined} & \text{otherwise.} \end{cases} \tag{4.14}$$

Property (4.14) is the analogue for name abstraction/concretion of β-equivalence for function abstraction/application. The analogue of η-equivalence is given by the following result.

Proposition 4.9 *Given a nominal set X and a name abstraction $F \in [\mathbb{A}]X$, for some/any $a \# F$ it is the case that $F = \langle a \rangle (F @ a)$.*

Proof Suppose $F = \langle a' \rangle x'$. If $a \# F$ then by Proposition 4.5 either $a = a'$, or $a \# (a', x')$. In the first case $F @ a = x'$ and so $\langle a \rangle (F @ a) = \langle a' \rangle x' = F$. In the second case $F @ a = (a'\ a) \cdot x'$ and so $\langle a \rangle (F @ a) = \langle a \rangle ((a'\ a) \cdot x') = \langle a' \rangle x' = F$. $\qquad\square$

We can sum up the proposition by the formula

$$(\forall F \in [\mathbb{A}]X)(\mathsf{M}a)\ \langle a \rangle (F @ a) \equiv F,\tag{4.15}$$

which gives a form of η-equivalence for name abstractions. Just as η-equivalence for functions is connected to function extensionality, so here we have an extensionality principle for name abstractions

$$(\forall F, F' \in [\mathbb{A}]X)\ F = F' \Leftrightarrow (\mathsf{M}a)\ F @ a \equiv F' @ a.\tag{4.16}$$

For if the concretions of F and F' at $a \# (F, F')$ are equal, to $x \in X$ say, then by the proposition $F = \langle a \rangle x = F'$.

4.4 Functoriality

If $X, Y \in \mathbf{Nom}$ and $f \in X \to_{\mathrm{fs}} Y$, we can use the freshness theorem (Theorem 3.11) to get a finitely supported function

$$[\mathbb{A}]f \in [\mathbb{A}]X \to_{\mathrm{fs}} [\mathbb{A}]Y,$$
$$[\mathbb{A}]f \triangleq \lambda z \in [\mathbb{A}]X \to \mathrm{fresh}\ a\ \mathrm{in}\ \langle a \rangle (f(z @ a)),\tag{4.17}$$

satisfying

$$(\mathsf{M}a)\ [\mathbb{A}]f\,z = \langle a \rangle (f(z @ a)),\tag{4.18}$$

for all $z \in [\mathbb{A}]X$.

Lemma 4.10 $[\mathbb{A}]\mathrm{id}_X = \mathrm{id}_{[\mathbb{A}]X}$ *and* $[\mathbb{A}](f' \circ f) = ([\mathbb{A}]f') \circ ([\mathbb{A}]f)$.

Proof For each $z \in [\mathbb{A}]X$, pick some $a \# (z, f, f')$. Then by Proposition 4.9, $[\mathbb{A}]\mathrm{id}_X\,z = \langle a \rangle (\mathrm{id}_X(z @ a)) = \langle a \rangle (z @ a) = z$. Also $[\mathbb{A}]f\,z = \langle a \rangle (f(z @ a))$ and so $a \# [\mathbb{A}]f\,z$ by Proposition 4.5; therefore $[\mathbb{A}]f'([\mathbb{A}]f\,z) = \langle a \rangle (f'(([\mathbb{A}]f\,z) @ a)) = \langle a \rangle (f'(f(z @ a))) = [\mathbb{A}](f' \circ f)z$. $\qquad\square$

Note that if $f : X \to Y$ is equivariant and hence an element of $X \to_{fs} Y$ with empty support, then $[A]f$ is an equivariant function $[A]X \to [A]Y$; and in this case from (4.18) we have for all $a \in A$ and $x \in X$

$$[A]f(\langle a \rangle x) = \langle a \rangle (f\, x) \quad (f \text{ equivariant}). \tag{4.19}$$

Remark 4.11   Since **Nom** is cartesian closed, it is enriched over itself (see Johnstone, 2002, section B2.1) and in view of the lemma, the equivariant functions

$$\begin{array}{ccc} (X \to_{fs} Y) & \to & ([A]X \to_{fs} [A]Y) \\ f \in X \to_{fs} Y & \mapsto & [A]f \end{array} \quad (X, Y \in \mathbf{Nom})$$

make $[A]_-$ into a **Nom**-enriched functor. (Such functors are sometimes called *strong*.)

Theorem 4.12   *The functor* $[A]_- : \mathbf{Nom} \to \mathbf{Nom}$ *is right adjoint to the functor* $_- * A : \mathbf{Nom} \to \mathbf{Nom}$ *given by taking the separated product with* A. *Thus*

$$[A]_- \cong A \twoheadrightarrow _-,$$

where $\twoheadrightarrow$ *is as in Theorem 3.13.*

Proof   Given $X \in \mathbf{Nom}$, by Lemma 4.7 the partial operation of concretion has $([A]X) * A$ for its domain of definition and so gives an equivariant function

$$\begin{aligned} &\mathrm{conc}_X : ([A]X) * A \to X, \\ &\mathrm{conc}_x \triangleq \lambda(z, a) \in ([A]X) * A \to z \,@\, a. \end{aligned} \tag{4.20}$$

We claim this has the universal property needed for $[A]X$ to be the value of the right adjoint to $_- * A$ at X, namely that given any equivariant function f as shown:

$$\begin{array}{c} Y * A \\ {\scriptstyle \hat{f}*\mathrm{id}_A} \Big\downarrow \quad \searrow {\scriptstyle f} \\ ([A]X) * A \xrightarrow[\mathrm{conc}_X]{} X \end{array} \tag{4.21}$$

there is a unique equivariant function $\hat{f} : Y \to [A]X$ making the above diagram commute. For using the freshness theorem (Theorem 3.11) we can define

$$\hat{f} \triangleq \lambda y \in Y \to \mathrm{fresh}\, a \text{ in } \langle a \rangle (f(y, a)) \tag{4.22}$$

to get such an equivariant function. It is the unique such, since if f' is any other, then for any $y \in Y$, picking some $a \in A$ with $a \,\#\, y$, we also have $a \,\#\, f'y$

(by part (iii) of Proposition 3.4) and hence

$$
\begin{aligned}
& f' y \\
= \; & \{\text{by Proposition 4.9}\} \\
& \langle a \rangle ((f'y) \ @ \ a) \\
= \; & \{\text{since } \mathrm{conc}_X \circ (f' * \mathrm{id}_\mathbb{A}) = f\} \\
& \langle a \rangle (f(y, a)) \\
= \; & \{\text{by definition of } \hat{f}, \text{ since } a \ \# \ y\} \\
& \hat{f} y. \qquad\qquad\qquad\qquad\qquad\qquad\qquad\quad \square
\end{aligned}
$$

Theorem 4.13 *The functor* $[\mathbb{A}]_- : \mathbf{Nom} \to \mathbf{Nom}$ *has a right adjoint.*

Proof For each $X \in \mathbf{Nom}$

$$
RX \triangleq \{ f \in \mathbb{A} \to_{\mathrm{fs}} X \mid (\forall a \in \mathbb{A}) \ a \ \# \ f \ a \} \tag{4.23}
$$

is an equivariant subset of $\mathbb{A} \to_{\mathrm{fs}} X$ and hence a nominal set by Lemma 2.22. Because of the way RX is defined, we can use the partial operation of concretion from Section 4.3 and the freshness theorem (Theorem 3.11) to obtain an equivariant function

$$
\begin{aligned}
& \varepsilon_X : [\mathbb{A}](RX) \to X, \\
& \varepsilon_X \triangleq \lambda z \in [\mathbb{A}](RX) \to \text{fresh } a \text{ in } (z \ @ \ a) a.
\end{aligned} \tag{4.24}
$$

We will show that this has the universal property required to make RX the value of the right adjoint to $[\mathbb{A}]_-$ at X, namely that given any equivariant function f as shown:

$$
\begin{array}{ccc}
 & [\mathbb{A}]Y & \\
 & {\Big|} \quad \diagdown \ f & \\
[\mathbb{A}]\hat{f} \; {\Big|} & \quad\quad \diagdown & \\
 & {\Big\downarrow} \quad\quad \diagdown\!\!\!\!\searrow & \\
[\mathbb{A}](RX) & \xrightarrow[\varepsilon_X]{} & X
\end{array} \tag{4.25}
$$

there is a unique equivariant function $\hat{f} : Y \to RX$ making the above diagram commute. First note that by (4.19) and (4.24), commutation of (4.25) is equivalent to

$$
(\forall a \in \mathbb{A})(\forall y \in Y) \ \hat{f} y a = f(\langle a \rangle y). \tag{4.26}
$$

So there is at most one such $\hat{f}$. If $y \in Y$ and $a \in \mathbb{A}$, then $a \ \# \ f(\langle a \rangle y)$ (by Propositions 3.4 and 4.5) and hence $\hat{f} \triangleq \lambda y \in Y \to (\lambda a \in \mathbb{A} \to f(\langle a \rangle y))$ does indeed give an equivariant function $Y \to RX$ satisfying (4.26). $\qquad\square$

This theorem shows that $[\mathbb{A}]_-$ gives a notion of abstraction rather different from the function abstraction $\mathbb{A} \to_{\mathrm{fs}} -$, which most certainly does not have a right adjoint. To see this, note that functors with right adjoints preserve colimits. In particular, we have

$$[\mathbb{A}](X_1 + X_2) \cong ([\mathbb{A}]X_1) + ([\mathbb{A}]X_2), \tag{4.27}$$

whereas $\mathbb{A} \to_{\text{fs}} (X_1 + X_2)$ is not in general isomorphic to the disjoint union of $\mathbb{A} \to_{\text{fs}} X_1$ and $\mathbb{A} \to_{\text{fs}} X_2$. (Just consider the case $X_1 = X_2 = 1$ to see this.)

Since by Theorem 4.12 $[\mathbb{A}]_-$ has a left adjoint, it also preserves limits in **Nom**. In particular,

$$[\mathbb{A}](X_1 \times X_2) \cong ([\mathbb{A}]X_1) \times ([\mathbb{A}]X_2). \tag{4.28}$$

It is a useful exercise to construct the isomorphisms in (4.27) and (4.28) explicitly (Exercises 4.4 and 4.5).

The adjoint properties of the name abstraction functor do not explain the following somewhat surprising preservation property discovered by Gabbay (2000, corollary 9.6.9).

Proposition 4.14 *The functor* $[\mathbb{A}]_- : \mathbf{Nom} \to \mathbf{Nom}$ *preserves exponentials:*

$$[\mathbb{A}](X \to_{\text{fs}} Y) \cong [\mathbb{A}]X \to_{\text{fs}} [\mathbb{A}]Y.$$

Proof Using the partial operation of concretion and the freshness theorem (Theorem 3.11) we get equivariant functions

$$i : [\mathbb{A}](X \to_{\text{fs}} Y) \to [\mathbb{A}]X \to_{\text{fs}} [\mathbb{A}]Y, \tag{4.29}$$
$$i \triangleq \lambda u \in [\mathbb{A}](X \to_{\text{fs}} Y) \to \lambda z \in [\mathbb{A}]X \to \text{fresh } a \text{ in } \langle a \rangle((u @ a)(z @ a)),$$
$$j : ([\mathbb{A}]X \to_{\text{fs}} [\mathbb{A}]Y) \to [\mathbb{A}](X \to_{\text{fs}} Y), \tag{4.30}$$
$$j \triangleq \lambda f \in ([\mathbb{A}]X \to_{\text{fs}} [\mathbb{A}]Y) \to \text{fresh } a \text{ in } \langle a \rangle(\lambda x \in X \to f(\langle a \rangle x) @ a).$$

We will show that they are mutually inverse.

First note that for all $a \in \mathbb{A}$, $f \in X \to_{\text{fs}} Y$ and $x \in X$, the definition of @ and i give $i(\langle a \rangle f)(\langle a \rangle x) = \langle a \rangle(f x)$. Hence by definition of j we have

$$j(i(\langle a \rangle f)) = \langle a \rangle(\lambda x \in X \to (\langle a \rangle(f x)) @ a) = \langle a \rangle(\lambda x \in X \to f x) = \langle a \rangle f.$$

Thus $j \circ i = \text{id}$. Conversely, given any $f \in ([\mathbb{A}]X) \to_{\text{fs}} ([\mathbb{A}]Y)$ and $z \in [\mathbb{A}]X$, pick some $a \in \mathbb{A}$ with $a \# (f, z)$. Then by definition of j

$$(j f) @ a = \lambda x \in X \to f(\langle a \rangle x) @ a, \tag{4.31}$$

and hence

$$i(j\,f)z$$
$$= \quad \{\text{by definition of } i\}$$
$$\langle a\rangle(((j\,f) @ a)(z @ a))$$
$$= \quad \{\text{by (4.31)}\}$$
$$\langle a\rangle(f(\langle a\rangle(z @ a)) @ a))$$
$$= \quad \{\text{by Proposition 4.9}\}$$
$$\langle a\rangle((f\,z) @ a)$$
$$= \quad \{\text{by Proposition 4.9}\}$$
$$f\,z\,.$$

Thus $i \circ j = \text{id}$. $\qquad\qquad\qquad\qquad\qquad\qquad\qquad\qquad\qquad\qquad\square$

4.5 Freshness condition for binders

In this section we give analysis of what is needed to specify functions of name abstractions somewhat different from the one in Theorem 4.13. By construction, functions with domain $[\mathbb{A}]X$ correspond to functions with domain $\mathbb{A} \times X$ that respect the generalized α-equivalence relation $\approx_\alpha$. The next theorem shows that the requirement that a function respects $\approx_\alpha$ is equivalent to a simpler condition involving freshness, called the *freshness condition for binders* by Pitts (2006). At the same time the theorem embodies another common pattern when defining functions on α-equivalence classes, namely that one only specifies the function for bound names avoiding some finite set of 'bad' names. (The support of F plays this role in the theorem below.) For example, when defining capture-avoiding substitution for a λ-term $\lambda a.t$ one can just say what to do when a avoids the finite set of free variables of the term to be substituted.

Theorem 4.15 *Given $X, Y \in \textbf{Nom}$ and a finitely supported partial function $F \in (\mathbb{A} \times X) \rightarrow_{\text{fs}} Y$ satisfying*

$$(\textit{Иa})(\forall x \in X)(\exists y \in Y)\ a \mathbin{\#} y \wedge F(a, x) \equiv y \qquad\qquad (4.32)$$

there is a unique finitely supported total function $\overline{F} \in ([\mathbb{A}]X) \rightarrow_{\text{fs}} Y$ satisfying

$$(\textit{Иa})(\forall x \in X)\ F(a, x) \equiv \overline{F}(\langle a\rangle x). \qquad\qquad (4.33)$$

In this case $\text{supp}\,\overline{F} \subseteq \text{supp}\,F$.

Proof If F satisfies (4.32), then for each $z \in [\mathbb{A}]X$ we can apply the freshness theorem to the partial function $\{(a, y) \mid a \mathbin{\#} (F, z) \wedge F(a, z @ a) \equiv y\}$ to get

$$\overline{F}z \triangleq \text{fresh}\,a\ \text{in}\ F(a, z @ a). \qquad\qquad (4.34)$$

Thus for all $z \in [\mathbb{A}]X$ and $y \in Y$

$$\overline{F}z = y \Leftrightarrow (\text{И}a)(\exists x \in X)\, z = \langle a \rangle x \wedge y = F(a, x).\tag{4.35}$$

By Proposition 2.25, the right-hand side in (4.35) defines a subset of $([\mathbb{A}]X) \times Y$ that is supported by supp F; hence $\overline{F} \in ([\mathbb{A}]X) \rightarrow_{\text{fs}} Y$ and supp $\overline{F} \subseteq$ supp F. This function satisfies property (4.33), because given any $a\ \#\ (F, \overline{F})$ and $x \in X$, since $a\ \#\ (F, \langle a \rangle x)$, definition (4.34) gives us $\overline{F}(\langle a \rangle x) \equiv F(a, (\langle a \rangle x)\ @\ a) \equiv F(a, x)$; thus

$$(\forall a \in \mathbb{A})\, a\ \#\ (F, \overline{F}) \Rightarrow (\forall x \in X)\, F(a, x) \equiv \overline{F}(\langle a \rangle x)\tag{4.36}$$

and so (4.33) holds by Theorem 3.9. Finally, the uniqueness of $\overline{F}$ is immediate from property (4.33), since if F' is any other such function, then by the Choose-a-Fresh-Name Principle and Lemma 4.3 for every $z \in [\mathbb{A}]X$ we can find $a\ \#$ $(F, \overline{F}, F')$ and $x \in X$ with $z = \langle a \rangle x$ and hence with $F'z \equiv F'(\langle a \rangle x) \equiv F(a, x) \equiv \overline{F}(\langle a \rangle x) \equiv \overline{F}z$. $\qquad\qquad\square$

Notation 4.16 The theorem justifies the following use of name abstraction patterns in notation for functions with domain $[\mathbb{A}]X$. If $\lambda(a, x) \in \mathbb{A} \times X \to \varphi(a, x)$ is the description of some finitely supported partial function $F \in (\mathbb{A} \times X) \rightarrow_{\text{fs}} Y$ satisfying condition (4.32), then we write the function $\overline{F} \in ([\mathbb{A}]X) \rightarrow_{\text{fs}} Y$ from Theorem 4.15 as

$$\lambda \langle a \rangle x \in [\mathbb{A}]X \to \varphi(a, x).\tag{4.37}$$

The following corollary of the theorem gives a simple criterion for defining equivariant functions with parameters on nominal sets of name abstractions.

Corollary 4.17 *Given* $X, Y, Z \in \mathbf{Nom}$, *suppose the equivariant function* f : $X \times \mathbb{A} \times Y \to Z$ *satisfies*

$$(\forall x \in X)(\text{И}a)(\forall y \in Y)\, a\ \#\ f(x, a, y).\tag{4.38}$$

Then there is a unique equivariant function $\overline{f} : X \times [\mathbb{A}]Y \to Z$ *satisfying*

$$(\forall x \in X)(\text{И}a)(\forall y \in Y)\, \overline{f}(x, \langle a \rangle y) = f(x, a, y).\tag{4.39}$$

Proof If f satisfies (4.38), then for each $x \in X$

$$\text{curry } f\, x \in (\mathbb{A} \times Y) \rightarrow_{\text{fs}} Z,$$
$$\text{curry } f\, x = \lambda(a, y) \in \mathbb{A} \times Y \to f(x, a, y)$$

satisfies property (4.32) in Theorem 4.15. So by that theorem there is a unique

$$\overline{\text{curry } f\, x} \in ([\mathbb{A}]Y) \rightarrow_{\text{fs}} Z$$

satisfying (4.33) and with $\text{supp}(\overline{\text{curry } f\, x}) \subseteq \text{supp}(\text{curry } f\, x)$. Since curry $f\, x$

is supported by supp x (because supp $f = \emptyset$), it follows that the function $X \times [A]Y \to Z$ defined by

$$\bar{f} \triangleq \lambda(x, u) \in X \times [A]Y \to \overline{\text{curry } f \, x} \, u$$

satisfies (4.39). The uniqueness property of $\overline{\text{curry } f \, x}$ implies that

$$\pi \cdot \overline{\text{curry } f \, x} = \overline{\text{curry } f \, (\pi \cdot x)}$$

and hence that $\bar{f}$ is equivariant. It is clearly the only function satisfying (4.39), because by the Choose-a-Fresh-Name Principle and Lemma 4.3, given any $(x, u) \in X \times [A]Y$ there is some $a \in A$ with $a \, \# \, x$ and $u = \langle a \rangle y$ for some $y \in Y$. $\qquad \square$

Example 4.18 In the corollary take $X = 1 = \{()\}, Y = A, Z = A + 1 = A \cup \{()\}$ and f to be the equivariant function

$$f((), a, a') = \begin{cases} () & \text{if } a = a', \\ a' & \text{if } a \neq a'. \end{cases}$$

In this case condition (4.38) is equivalent to $(\forall a \in A)(\forall a' \in A) \, a \, \# \, f((), a, a')$, which is true. So applying the corollary we get an equivariant function $\bar{f}$: $[A]A \to A + 1$ satisfying $\bar{f}(\langle a \rangle a') = f(a, a')$ for all $a, a' \in A$. Since f is surjective, so is $\bar{f}$. It is also injective since if $\bar{f}(\langle a_1 \rangle a_1') = \bar{f}(\langle a_2 \rangle a_2')$, then $f(a_1, a_1') = f(a_2, a_2')$ and hence either $a_1 = a_1'$ and $a_2 = a_2'$, or $a_1 \neq a_1' = a_2' \neq a_2$; and hence by Lemma 4.3, $\langle a_1 \rangle a_1' = \langle a_2 \rangle a_2'$. Thus $\bar{f}$ gives an isomorphism in **Nom**:

$$[A]A \cong A + 1, \tag{4.40}$$

which using the notation as in (4.37), we can write as

$$\lambda \langle a \rangle a' \in [A]A \to \text{if } a = a' \text{ then } () \text{ else } a' \, .$$

4.6 Generalized name abstraction

Nominal sets of name abstractions can be used to model syntax involving operations that bind a single atomic name in a fixed scope; see Chapter 8. Binding operations with more complicated occurrences of both binding and bound names occur in practice; see Cheney (2005c), Pottier (2005), Sewell *et al.* (2010) and Urban and Kaliszyk (2011). In this section we consider a generalization of $[A]X$ that can model more complicated patterns of binding occurrences in operations. We replace the name a in a name abstraction $\langle a \rangle_-$ by an element x of some fixed nominal set in such a way that all the names in the support of x becoming binding occurrences in $\langle x \rangle_-$.

Given $X, Y \in \mathbf{Nom}$, $(x, y), (x', y') \in X \times Y$ and $\pi \in \mathrm{Perm}\,\mathbb{A}$, define

$$\pi : (x, y) \sim_\alpha (x', y') \tag{4.41}$$

to mean $\pi \cdot (x, y) = (x', y') \;\wedge\; \pi \,\#\, (\mathrm{supp}\,y - \mathrm{supp}\,x)$. In view of Lemma 2.21, the condition $\pi \,\#\, (\mathrm{supp}\,y - \mathrm{supp}\,x)$ is equivalent to requiring $\pi\,a = a$ for all $a \in \mathrm{supp}\,y - \mathrm{supp}\,x$. Note that if $\pi \cdot (x, y) = (x', y')$, then by Proposition 2.11

$$\mathrm{supp}\,y' - \mathrm{supp}\,x' = \mathrm{supp}(\pi \cdot y) - \mathrm{supp}(\pi \cdot x) = \pi \cdot (\mathrm{supp}\,y - \mathrm{supp}\,x).$$

So if we also have $\pi \,\#\, (\mathrm{supp}\,y - \mathrm{supp}\,x)$, then $\mathrm{supp}\,y' - \mathrm{supp}\,x'$ is equal to $\mathrm{supp}\,y - \mathrm{supp}\,x$. The following properties of $\pi : \_ \sim_\alpha \_$ follow easily from these observations.

Lemma 4.19 (i) $\mathrm{id} : (x, y) \sim_\alpha (x, y)$.
(ii) *If* $\pi : (x, y) \sim_\alpha (x', y')$, *then* $\pi^{-1} : (x', y') \sim_\alpha (x, y)$.
(iii) *If* $\pi : (x, y) \sim_\alpha (x', y')$ *and* $\pi' : (x', y') \sim_\alpha (x'', y'')$, *then* $\pi' \circ \pi : (x, y) \sim_\alpha (x'', y'')$.
(iv) *If* $\pi : (x, y) \sim_\alpha (x', y')$, *then* $\pi' \circ \pi \circ (\pi')^{-1} : (\pi' \cdot x, \pi' \cdot y) \sim_\alpha (\pi' \cdot x', \pi' \cdot y')$. $\square$

Definition 4.20 Writing $(x, y) \sim_\alpha (x', y')$ for $(\exists \pi \in \mathrm{Perm}\,\mathbb{A})\; \pi : (x, y) \sim_\alpha (x', y')$, from the lemma we have that $\sim_\alpha$ is an equivariant equivalence relation and hence that the quotient $(X \times Y)/\!\sim_\alpha$ is a nominal set. We denote this nominal set by $[X]Y$ and call it the *nominal set of X-abstractions* of elements of Y. We write the $\sim_\alpha$-equivalence class of a pair $(x, y) \in X \times Y$ as $\langle x \rangle y$.

Remark 4.21 The above notation is justified by the fact that when $X = \mathbb{A}$ the relation $\sim_\alpha \;\subseteq\; (\mathbb{A} \times Y) \times (\mathbb{A} \times Y)$ equals the relation $\approx_\alpha$ in (4.7); see Exercise 4.8. So in this case $[X]Y$ is the usual nominal set of name abstractions of elements in the nominal set Y (Definition 4.4).

Example 4.22 Taking $X = \mathrm{P}_f\,\mathbb{A}$ and $Y = \mathbb{A} \times \mathbb{A}$ in the above definition, note that for all $a, b \in \mathbb{A}$, $(a\ b) : (\{a, b\}, (a, b)) \sim_\alpha (\{a, b\}, (b, a))$. Thus $\langle \{a, b\} \rangle (a, b)$ and $\langle \{a, b\} \rangle (b, a)$ are equal elements of $[\mathrm{P}_f\,\mathbb{A}](\mathbb{A} \times \mathbb{A})$, even though $(a, b) \neq (b, a)$ (assuming a and b are distinct atomic names). So unlike the case for $[\mathbb{A}](\_)$, for which (4.13) holds, in general the elements of $[X]Y$ are not partial functions from X to Y.

The following result generalizes Proposition 4.5.

Proposition 4.23 *Given nominal sets X and Y, the support of any element $\langle x \rangle y$ of $[X]Y$ is given by:* $\mathrm{supp}\langle x \rangle y = \mathrm{supp}\,y - \mathrm{supp}\,x$.

Proof We noted above Lemma 4.19 that

$$(x, y) \sim_\alpha (x', y') \;\Rightarrow\; \mathrm{supp}\,y - \mathrm{supp}\,x = \mathrm{supp}\,y' - \mathrm{supp}\,x'.$$

So if $(x, y) \sim_\alpha (x', y')$, then $\operatorname{supp} y - \operatorname{supp} x = \operatorname{supp} y' - \operatorname{supp} x' \subseteq \operatorname{supp} x' \cup \operatorname{supp} y' = \operatorname{supp}(x', y')$. Therefore

$$\operatorname{supp} y - \operatorname{supp} x \subseteq \bigcap\{\operatorname{supp}(x', y') \mid (x, y) \sim_\alpha (x', y')\} = \operatorname{supp} \langle x \rangle y,$$

using the characterization of the support of an equivalence class given in Proposition 2.30. To prove the reverse inclusion, it suffices to show that $\operatorname{supp} y - \operatorname{supp} x$ is a support for $\langle x \rangle y$; but if $\pi \in \operatorname{Perm} \mathbb{A}$ satisfies $\pi \# (\operatorname{supp} y - \operatorname{supp} x)$, then by definition of $\sim_\alpha$ we have $\pi : (x, y) \sim_\alpha (\pi \cdot x, \pi \cdot y)$ and hence $\langle x \rangle y = \langle \pi \cdot x \rangle (\pi \cdot y) = \pi \cdot \langle x \rangle y$. $\qquad\square$

Lemma 4.24 *Given $X, Y \in \mathbf{Nom}$ and $z \in [X]Y$, for each $A \in P_f \mathbb{A}$ there exist $x \in X$ and $y \in Y$ with $A \# x$ and $z = \langle x \rangle y$.*

Proof Pick a representative (x', y') for z, so that $z = \langle x' \rangle y'$. Suppose $\operatorname{supp} x'$ consists of the distinct atomic names $a_1, \ldots, a_n$, and pick distinct atomic names $b_1, \ldots, b_n$ in the cofinite set $\mathbb{A} - (A \cup \operatorname{supp}(x', y'))$. Let $\pi = (a_1\ b_1) \circ \cdots \circ (a_n\ b_n)$, so that $A \# \pi \cdot x'$ and $\pi \# (\operatorname{supp} y' - \operatorname{supp} x')$. Hence $\pi : (x', y') \sim_\alpha (\pi \cdot x', \pi \cdot y')$, so that $z = \langle x' \rangle y' = \langle \pi \cdot x' \rangle (\pi \cdot y')$ with $A \# \pi \cdot x'$. So we can take $x = \pi \cdot x'$ and $y = \pi \cdot y'$. $\qquad\square$

The lemma says that for each abstraction in $[X]Y$ we can choose a representation $\langle x \rangle y$ with the support of the binding element x avoiding any given finite set of atomic names. Using this fact, we can make $[X]_-$ into a **Nom**-enriched functor $\mathbf{Nom} \to \mathbf{Nom}$ (cf. Section 4.4), as follows.

If $X, Y, Z \in \mathbf{Nom}$ and $f \in Y \to_{fs} Z$, there is a finitely supported function $[X]f \in [X]Y \to_{fs} [X]Z$ satisfying

$$(\forall x \in X, y \in Y)\ x \# f \Rightarrow [X]f(\langle x \rangle y) = \langle x \rangle (f\, y). \tag{4.42}$$

Indeed $[X]f \triangleq \{(\langle x \rangle y, \langle x \rangle (f\, y)) \mid x \in X \wedge x \# f \wedge y \in Y\}$ is a subset of $[X]Y \times [X]Z$ that is supported by $\operatorname{supp} f$. It is total by Lemma 4.24; and it is single-valued, because if $(x, y) \sim_\alpha (x', y')$ with $(x, x') \# f$, then by Exercise 4.8 $\pi : (x, y) \sim_\alpha (x', y')$ holds for some $\pi \in \operatorname{Perm} \mathbb{A}$ with $\operatorname{supp} \pi \subseteq \operatorname{supp}(x, x') \# f$ and hence $\pi : (x, f\, y) \sim_\alpha (x', f\, y')$.

It is not hard to see that the functions $[X]_- : (Y \to_{fs} Z) \to ([X]Y \to_{fs} [X]Z)$ are equivariant and preserve identities and composition of finitely supported functions. Generalizing Theorem 4.13, one can show that the functor $[X]_- : \mathbf{Nom} \to \mathbf{Nom}$ has a right adjoint (Exercise 4.9). However, as the following example shows, Theorem 4.12 does not hold if we replace $[\mathbb{A}]_-$ by $[X]_-$ for an arbitrary nominal set X.

Example 4.25 The functor $[P_f \mathbb{A}]_- : \mathbf{Nom} \to \mathbf{Nom}$ does not preserve products and hence cannot have a left adjoint. For if it did preserve products, then the function

$$\langle [P_f \, \mathbb{A}]\text{proj}_1, [P_f \, \mathbb{A}]\text{proj}_2 \rangle : [P_f \, \mathbb{A}](X_1 \times X_2) \to ([P_f \, \mathbb{A}]X_1) \times ([P_f \, \mathbb{A}]X_2)$$
$$\langle A \rangle (x_1, x_2) \mapsto (\langle A \rangle x_1, \langle A \rangle x_2)$$

would be an isomorphism. However, when $X_1 = X_2 = \mathbb{A}$ this function is not surjective; for example, $(\langle \emptyset \rangle a, \langle \{a\} \rangle a)$ is not in its image.

4.7 Many sorts of names

The theory of nominal sets presented so far is *single-sorted* in the sense that it is based on the actions of all (finite) permutations of a single countably infinite set $\mathbb{A}$ of atomic names. The formal languages that arise in connection with programming very often involve several different sorts of name – for example, names of identifiers, names of communication channels, names of type variables, etc. If identity is the only attribute of a particular sort of names that matters for the language's semantics, then it is appropriate to use the atomic names of the theory of nominal sets to model them. However, if the language has several different syntactic categories of name, one needs a *multi-sorted* version of nominal sets, that we sketch in this section.

Definition 4.26 A *name sorting* for the countably infinite set $\mathbb{A}$ of atomic names is given by a set *Nsort* and a function $s : \mathbb{A} \to Nsort$ with the property that for each $\mathbb{N} \in Nsort$

$$\mathbb{A}_{\mathbb{N}} \triangleq \{a \in \mathbb{A} \mid s\,a = \mathbb{N}\} \tag{4.43}$$

is countably infinite. The elements of *Nsort* are called *name-sorts* and the elements of $\mathbb{A}_{\mathbb{N}}$ are called *atomic names of sort* $\mathbb{N}$. We write

$$\text{Perm}_s \, \mathbb{A} \triangleq \{\pi \in \text{Perm} \, \mathbb{A} \mid (\forall a \in \mathbb{A}) \, s(\pi a) = s\,a\} \tag{4.44}$$

for the subgroup of finite permutations that respect the sorting.

$\text{Perm}_s \, \mathbb{A}$ contains transpositions $(a\ b)$ that are sort-respecting in the sense that $s\,a = s\,b$. These generate the group $\text{Perm}_s \, \mathbb{A}$; the proof is as for Theorem 1.15.

Definition 4.27 Given a sorting as in Definition 4.26, an *s-sorted nominal set* is a $\text{Perm}_s \, \mathbb{A}$-set X all of whose elements x are finitely supported, in the sense that there is a finite subset $A \subseteq \mathbb{A}$ satisfying $((\forall a \in A) \, \pi a = a) \Rightarrow \pi \cdot x = x$ for all $\pi \in \text{Perm}_s \, \mathbb{A}$. We write $\mathbf{Nom}_s$ for the full subcategory of $[\text{Perm}_s \, \mathbb{A}, \mathbf{Set}]$ given by such objects.

Remark 4.28   If *Nsort* only contains one name-sort, then $\text{Perm}_s \, \mathbb{A} = \text{Perm} \, \mathbb{A}$ and $\mathbf{Nom}_s = \mathbf{Nom}$.

The theory of nominal sets that we have developed so far extends smoothly to the many-sorted case. The only complication is that the *s*-sorted nominal set of atomic names $\mathbb{A}$ (Example 2.4) splits into a coproduct

$$\mathbb{A} \cong \coprod_{\mathsf{N} \in Nsort} \mathbb{A}_{\mathsf{N}}, \tag{4.45}$$

where each $\mathbb{A}_{\mathsf{N}}$ is an *s*-sorted nominal set via the $\text{Perm}_s \, \mathbb{A}$-action given by applying a permutation to an atomic name (Example 1.3). Where in the single-sorted case we used the object $\mathbb{A} \in \mathbf{Nom}$, in the many-sorted case we use $\mathbb{A}_{\mathsf{N}}$ for some $\mathsf{N} \in Nsort$. Specifically, this means working with sorted versions of the following notions:

- *Freshness quantifier* (Section 3.2): we define $\mathcal{V}_{\mathsf{N}} \triangleq \{S \subseteq \mathbb{A}_{\mathsf{N}} \mid \mathbb{A}_{\mathsf{N}} - S \text{ is finite}\}$ and write

$$(\mathcal{V}a : \mathsf{N}) \, \varphi \tag{4.46}$$

  to mean $\{a \in \mathbb{A}_{\mathsf{N}} \mid \varphi\} \in \mathcal{V}_{\mathsf{N}}$.
- *Fresh names* (Section 3.3): if $\lambda a \in \mathbb{A}_{\mathsf{N}} \to \varphi(a)$ is the description of some finitely supported partial function $f \in \mathbb{A}_{\mathsf{N}} \to_{\text{fs}} X$ satisfying $(\mathcal{V}a : \mathsf{N})(\exists x \in X) \, a \, \# \, x \wedge f \, a \equiv x$, then there is a unique element (fresh $a : \mathsf{N}$ in $\varphi(a)) \in X$ satisfying $(\mathcal{V}a : \mathsf{N}) \, f \, a \equiv (\text{fresh} \, a : \mathsf{N} \text{ in } \varphi(a))$.
- *Name abstraction* (Section 4.2): $(\mathcal{V}a : \mathsf{N}) \, (a_1 \, a) \cdot x_1 = (a_2 \, a) \cdot x_2$ gives an equivariant equivalence relation on $\mathbb{A}_{\mathsf{N}} \times X \in \mathbf{Nom}_s$ whose quotient $[\mathbb{A}_{\mathsf{N}}]X$ is the *s*-sorted nominal set of abstractions of names of sort N in elements of X.

Exercises

4.1   If $a \neq a'$ are two distinct atomic names, are $\langle a \rangle (\langle a \rangle a)$ and $\langle a \rangle (\langle a' \rangle a)$ equal elements of $[\mathbb{A}]([\mathbb{A}]\mathbb{A})$?

4.2   For each nominal set X show that there is an isomorphism making the following diagram commute:

$$\mathbb{A} * ([\mathbb{A}]X) \; \cong \; \mathbb{A} \times X.$$

$$\text{proj}_1 \searrow \qquad \swarrow \text{proj}_1$$

$$\mathbb{A}$$

4.3   Given $f : X \to Y$ in **Nom**, regarding each $z \in [\mathbb{A}]X$ as a finitely sup-
      ported partial function $\mathbb{A} \rightharpoonup_{fs} X$ as in Section 4.3, show that $[\mathbb{A}]f\,z \in [\mathbb{A}]Y$
      is equal to the composition $f \circ z = \{(a, y) \in \mathbb{A} \times Y \mid (\exists x \in X)\,(a, x) \in$
      $z \wedge f\,x = y\}$. What happens if f is finitely supported, but not equivari-
      ant? [Hint: consider the effect of $[\mathbb{A}]_{-}$ on the finitely supported function
      $1 \rightharpoonup_{fs} \mathbb{A}$ corresponding to an element $a \in \mathbb{A}$.]

4.4   Given $X_1, X_2 \in$ **Nom**, show that there is an isomorphism

$$i : ([\mathbb{A}]X_1) \times ([\mathbb{A}]X_2) \cong [\mathbb{A}](X_1 \times X_2)$$

      satisfying

$$i(\langle a_1\rangle x_1, \langle a_2\rangle x_2) = \text{fresh } a \text{ in } \langle a\rangle((a\ a_1) \cdot x_1, (a\ a_2) \cdot x_2),$$

      for all $a_1, a_2 \in \mathbb{A}$, $x_1 \in X_1$ and $x_2 \in X_2$.

4.5   Given $X_1, X_2 \in$ **Nom**, show that there is an isomorphism

$$j : ([\mathbb{A}]X_1) + ([\mathbb{A}]X_2) \cong [\mathbb{A}](X_1 + X_2)$$

      satisfying

$$j(\text{inj}_i(\langle a\rangle x_i)) = \langle a\rangle(\text{inj}_i x_i),$$

      for all $a \in \mathbb{A}$ and $x_i \in X_i$ $(i = 1, 2)$.

4.6   Given $X_1, X_2 \in$ **Nom**, show that there is an isomorphism

$$k : [\mathbb{A}](X_1 * X_2) \cong ([\mathbb{A}]X_1) * X_2 + X_1 * ([\mathbb{A}]X_2)$$

      satisfying

$$k\,\langle a\rangle(x_1, x_2) = \begin{cases} (\langle a\rangle x_1, x_2) & \text{if } a \,\#\, x_2, \\ (x_1, \langle a\rangle x_2) & \text{if } a \,\#\, x_1, \end{cases}$$

      for all $a \in \mathbb{A}$ and $(x_1, x_2) \in X_1 * X_2$.

4.7   Show that the functors $_{-} * \mathbb{A}$ and R_{-} from Theorems 4.12 and 4.13 do not
      give **Nom**-enriched adjoints for $[\mathbb{A}]_{-}$, because in general

$$(X * \mathbb{A}) \rightarrow_{fs} Y \ncong X \rightarrow_{fs} ([\mathbb{A}]Y),$$
$$([\mathbb{A}]X) \rightarrow_{fs} Y \ncong X \rightarrow_{fs} R\,Y.$$

      [Hint: consider $X = 1$ and $Y = \mathbb{B}$.]

4.8   Show that $(x, y) \sim_\alpha (x', y')$ holds iff $\pi : (x, y) \sim_\alpha (x', y')$ holds for some
      $\pi \in \text{Perm}\,\mathbb{A}$ with $\text{supp}\,\pi \subseteq \text{supp}(x, x')$. Deduce that when $a, a' \in \mathbb{A}$,
      $(a, y) \sim_\alpha (a', y')$ iff $(a, y) \approx_\alpha (a', y')$. [Hint: use the homogeneity lemma
      (Lemma 1.14).]

4.9 Generalize the proof of Theorem 4.13 to show that the functor $[X]_-$: **Nom** $\rightarrow$ **Nom** has a right adjoint R_X : **Nom** $\rightarrow$ **Nom** whose value at a nominal set Y is given by the following equivariant subset of $X \rightarrow_{\text{fs}} Y$:

$$R_X Y \triangleq \{f \in X \rightarrow_{\text{fs}} Y \mid (\forall x \in X)\; x \mathbin{\#} f\,x\}.$$

4.10 For all $X, Y, Z \in$ **Nom**, show that $[X]([Y]Z) \cong [X * Y]Z$ and $[X + Y]Z \cong ([X]Z) + ([Y]Z)$.

5
Orbit-finiteness

Taking account of symmetries to reduce the size of state spaces is an important technique in verification (see, for example, Clarke *et al.*, 2000, chapter 14). An extreme case is the reduction of infinite data structures to finite ones by quotienting by a suitable notion of symmetry. In this book we are concerned with symmetries induced by permuting the names that occur in a structure; and in this chapter we will look at the notion of 'finite modulo symmetry' within the theory of nominal sets. This aspect of nominal sets first came to the fore in the work of Montanari and Pistore (2000) on π-calculus and HD automata, albeit not using nominal sets, but rather the equivalent notion of *named sets* (Ferrari *et al.*, 2002); see Section 6.4. This has been subsumed and generalized in a program of what one might call 'orbit-finite' automata theory (Bojańczyk *et al.*, 2011; Gabbay and Ciancia, 2011; Tzevelekos, 2011; Bojańczyk and Lasota, 2012; Murawski and Tzevelekos, 2012).

These works provide a positive motivation for studying relaxations of the usual notion of finiteness in the context of nominal sets. The following theorem cuts the other way: restricting to finite nominal sets rules out any non-trivial use of name symmetry.

Theorem 5.1 *Every finite nominal set is discrete.*

Proof Recall from Example 2.5 that $X \in \mathbf{Nom}$ is said to be discrete if its permutation action is trivial, $(\forall \pi \in \operatorname{Perm} \mathbb{A}, x \in X) \, \pi \cdot x = x$; and in view of Exercise 2.1, this is equivalent to having no element with a non-empty support. So we have to show that if $X \in \mathbf{Nom}$ has a finite underlying set, then the support of each $x \in X$ is empty.

Suppose $x \in X$ and that $\operatorname{supp} x \neq \emptyset$, say $a \in \operatorname{supp} x$. For any two distinct atomic names $a' \neq a''$ satisfying $a', a'' \mathbin{\#} (a, x)$, by Proposition 2.11 we have

$$a' \in \operatorname{supp}((a \, a') \cdot x) \wedge a' \notin \operatorname{supp}((a \, a'') \cdot x),$$

so that $\text{supp}((a\,a')\cdot x) \neq \text{supp}((a\,a'')\cdot x)$ and hence $(a\,a')\cdot x \neq (a\,a'')\cdot x$.

So if $a \in \text{supp}\,x$, then the function $a' \mapsto (a\,a')\cdot x$ is an injection of the infinite set $\{a' \mid a' \,\#\, (a,x)\}$ into X. Thus if X contains an element with non-empty support, it must be infinite. □

5.1 Orbits

Let us return to the setting of Section 1.1, where we considered actions on sets of an arbitrary group G. If X is a G-set, then the *G-orbit* of an element $x \in X$ is the subset of X that can be reached from x via the action of members of the group:

$$\text{orb}\,x \triangleq \{g \cdot x \mid g \in G\}. \tag{5.1}$$

Note that G-orbits are the equivalence classes for the equivalence relation

$$x \sim_G x' \triangleq (\exists g \in G)\,g \cdot x = x'.$$

The quotient set $X/\!\sim_G$ is usually written as

$$X/G \triangleq \{\text{orb}\,x \mid x \in X\}. \tag{5.2}$$

Proposition 5.2 *Let* $\Delta : \mathbf{Set} \to [G,\mathbf{Set}]$ *be the functor sending each set to the corresponding discrete G-set (Example 1.5). For each* $X \in [G,\mathbf{Set}]$, *the set* X/G *of G-orbits is the value at* X *of a functor* $\_/G : [G,\mathbf{Set}] \to \mathbf{Set}$ *that is left adjoint to* Δ. *In other words there is an equivariant function* $\eta_X : X \to \Delta(X/G)$ *with the universal property that given any equivariant function* f *as shown:*

$$
\begin{array}{ccc}
X & \xrightarrow{\ \eta_X\ } & \Delta(X/G) \\
 & {\scriptstyle f}\searrow & \Big\downarrow{\scriptstyle \Delta\hat{f}} \\
 & & \Delta Y
\end{array}
$$

there is a unique function $\hat{f} : X/G \to Y$ *making the above diagram in* $[G,\mathbf{Set}]$ *commute.*

Proof Consider the quotient function $X \to X/G$ mapping each $x \in X$ to its G-orbit, $\text{orb}\,x$. This gives an equivariant function $\eta_X \in [G,\mathbf{Set}](X,\Delta(X/G))$, since for any $g \in G$ and $x \in X$, $\text{orb}\,(g \cdot x)$ is equal to $\text{orb}\,x$. This morphism in $[G,\mathbf{Set}]$ has the universal property needed for left adjointness: given any $Y \in \mathbf{Set}$ and

$f \in [G, \mathbf{Set}](X, \Delta Y)$ we have for all $x, x' \in X$

$$x \sim_G x'$$
$$\Rightarrow \quad \{\text{for some } g \in G\}$$
$$g \cdot x = x'$$
$$\Rightarrow \quad \{\text{since } \Delta Y \text{ is discrete and } f \text{ is equivariant}\}$$
$$f x = g \cdot (f x) = f(g \cdot x) = f x'$$
$$\Rightarrow$$
$$f x \sim_G f x'$$

so that f induces a function $\hat{f} : X/G \to Y$ satisfying $\hat{f}(\mathrm{orb}\, x) = f x$; and clearly this is the unique function $g : X/G \to Y$ satisfying $f = (\Delta g) \circ \eta_X$. □

Definition 5.3   A G-set X is *orbit-finite* if X/G is a finite set and it is *atomic* if X/G is a singleton.

Recall that subobjects of an object X in $[G, \mathbf{Set}]$ correspond to equivariant subsets of X (Definition 1.8). Note that each $O \in X/G$ is a non-empty subobject of X in $[G, \mathbf{Set}]$; and as an object $[G, \mathbf{Set}]$, O has no subobjects other than the empty set and O itself. Since X is a disjoint union of its orbits, it is isomorphic to the coproduct (Section 1.2) of the atomic G-sets $O \in X/G$:

$$X \cong \sum_{O \in X/G} O. \tag{5.3}$$

Next we recall a standard result from group theory giving a representation of each $O \in X/G$ in terms of cosets of stabilizer subgroups. If X is a G-set, then the *stabilizer* of an element $x \in X$ is

$$\mathrm{stab}\, x \triangleq \{g \in G \mid g \cdot x = x\}. \tag{5.4}$$

Note that $\mathrm{stab}\, x$ is a subgroup of G. For any subgroup $H \subseteq G$, the set of (left) *cosets*

$$\mathrm{coset}\, H \triangleq \{gH \mid g \in G\}, \tag{5.5}$$
$$gH \triangleq \{gh \mid h \in H\}$$

is the set of equivalence classes for the equivalence relation on G that relates g and g' when $g^{-1}g' \in H$. We make coset H into a G-set via left multiplication:

$$g \cdot (g'H) \triangleq (gg')H. \tag{5.6}$$

Theorem 5.4 (Orbit-stabilizer theorem)   *Let G be a group and X a G-set. For each $x \in X$ there is an isomorphism in $[G, \mathbf{Set}]$*

$$\mathrm{orb}\, x \cong \mathrm{coset}\,(\mathrm{stab}\, x).$$

Proof Note that $g \cdot x = g' \cdot x$ iff $g^{-1}g' \in \text{stab } x$ iff the cosets $g(\text{stab } x)$ and $g'(\text{stab } x)$ are equal. So there is a bijection $i : \text{orb } x \to \text{coset}(\text{stab } x)$ satisfying $i(g \cdot x) = g(\text{stab } x)$ for all $g \in \text{Perm } \mathbb{A}$. It is equivariant, because by (5.6) $g' \cdot (i(g \cdot x)) = g' \cdot (g(\text{stab } x)) = (g'g)(\text{stab } x) = i((g'g) \cdot x) = i(g' \cdot (g \cdot x))$. $\square$

5.2 Atomic nominal sets

We now specialize the material in the previous section to the case when G is $\text{Perm } \mathbb{A}$, the group of finite permutations of $\mathbb{A}$. Note that each discrete $\text{Perm } \mathbb{A}$-set is a nominal set (Example 2.5) and the orbits functor restricts to give a left adjoint to the discrete nominal set functor $\Delta : \textbf{Set} \to \textbf{Nom}$. We will write this left adjoint as

$$\Pi_0 : \textbf{Nom} \to \textbf{Set}. \tag{5.7}$$

Definition 5.5 A nominal set X is *orbit-finite* if $\Pi_0 X$ is a finite set and is *atomic* if $\Pi_0 X$ is a singleton.

Example 5.6 The nominal set $\mathbb{A}$ is atomic, since the $\text{Perm } \mathbb{A}$-orbit of any $a \in \mathbb{A}$ is the whole of $\mathbb{A}$. The product $\mathbb{A} \times \mathbb{A}$ is orbit finite since evidently there are two $\text{Perm } \mathbb{A}$-orbits, namely $\{(a, a) \mid a \in \mathbb{A}\}$ and $\{(a_1, a_2) \mid a_1 \neq a_2\}$. More generally, it is not hard to see that for each $n \in \mathbb{N}$, the set of $\text{Perm } \mathbb{A}$-orbits of the cartesian product $\mathbb{A}^n$ is in bijection with the finite set of equivalence relations on $\{0, 1, \ldots, n - 1\}$ (see Lemma 5.22). In particular, the nominal set $\mathbb{A}^{\#n}$ of pairwise distinct n-tuples of atomic names

$$\mathbb{A}^{\#n} \triangleq \{(a_1, \ldots, a_n) \in \mathbb{A}^n \mid (\forall i, j \in \{1, \ldots, n\})\ i \neq j \Rightarrow a_i \neq a_j\} \tag{5.8}$$

is atomic. In fact a nominal set is atomic iff it is a quotient of some $\mathbb{A}^{\#n}$ (Exercise 5.1). A simple example of a non-orbit-finite object of **Nom** is $\mathbb{A}^*$, the nominal set of all finite lists of atomic names is not orbit-finite, since clearly lists of different lengths belong to different $\text{Perm } \mathbb{A}$-orbits.

As in (5.3), every nominal set X is isomorphic to a coproduct $\coprod_{O \in \Pi_0 X} O$ of atomic nominal sets. Note that in view of Theorem 5.1, each atomic nominal set is either infinite, or isomorphic to the terminal object. We will give a characterization of atomic nominal sets (Theorem 5.13) based on the orbit-stabilizer Theorem 5.4.

Definition 5.7 Recall from Example 1.1 that $\text{Sym } A$ denotes the group of all permutations of a set A. Suppose $A \in P_f \mathbb{A}$ is a finite set of atomic names and that G is a subgroup of $\mathrm{Sym}\, A$. Define a subgroup $\overline{G} \subseteq \mathrm{Perm}\, \mathbb{A}$ as follows:

$$\overline{G} \triangleq \{\pi \in \mathrm{Perm}\, \mathbb{A} \mid \pi \cdot A = A \wedge (\exists g \in G)\, \pi|_A = g\}. \tag{5.9}$$

(In general, for any $A \subseteq \mathbb{A}$ we write $\pi|_A$ for the function from A to $\pi \cdot A$ given by $\lambda a \in A \to \pi a$.)

Being a subgroup of $\mathrm{Perm}\, \mathbb{A}$, $\overline{G}$ is in particular a group and so as in the previous section we get a $\mathrm{Perm}\, \mathbb{A}$-set

$$\mathrm{coset}\, \overline{G} = \{\pi\overline{G} \mid \pi \in \mathrm{Perm}\, \mathbb{A}\}, \tag{5.10}$$

$$\pi' \cdot (\pi\overline{G}) = (\pi' \circ \pi)\overline{G} \qquad\qquad (\pi', \pi \in \mathrm{Perm}\, \mathbb{A}).$$

Lemma 5.8 *Let A and G be as in the above definition. The $\mathrm{Perm}\, \mathbb{A}$-set $\mathrm{coset}\, \overline{G}$ is an atomic nominal set and for any $\pi\overline{G} \in \mathrm{coset}\, \overline{G}$, $\mathrm{supp}(\pi\overline{G}) = \pi \cdot A$.*

Proof The coset $\pi\overline{G}$ is supported by $\pi \cdot A$, because if $\pi' \in \mathrm{Perm}\, \mathbb{A}$ satisfies $(\forall a \in \pi \cdot A)\, \pi' a = a$, then $(\pi^{-1} \circ \pi' \circ \pi)|_A = \mathrm{id}|_A$; but $\mathrm{id}|_A$ is the identity element of G, so $\pi^{-1} \circ \pi' \circ \pi \in \overline{G}$ and hence $\pi\overline{G} = (\pi' \circ \pi)\overline{G} = \pi' \cdot (\pi\overline{G})$.

So $\mathrm{coset}\, \overline{G}$ is a nominal set; and it is atomic because it is equal to the orbit of $\overline{G} \in \mathrm{coset}\, \overline{G}$. So it just remains to see that $A \subseteq \mathrm{supp}\, \overline{G}$ (since then $\pi \cdot A \subseteq \pi \cdot \mathrm{supp}\, \overline{G} = \mathrm{supp}(\pi\overline{G})$, by Proposition 2.11; and we already know that $\mathrm{supp}(\pi\overline{G}) \subseteq \pi \cdot A$).

For any $a \in \mathbb{A}$, suppose $a \notin \mathrm{supp}\, \overline{G}$; we will show that $a \notin A$. Pick some $a' \,\#\, (a, A, \overline{G})$. Since $a, a' \,\#\, \overline{G}$, the action of $(a\, a')$ on elements of $\mathrm{coset}\, \overline{G}$ fixes $\overline{G}$; that is, $(a\, a')\overline{G} = \overline{G}$. Hence $(a\, a') \in \overline{G}$ and in particular $(a\, a') \cdot A = A$; so since $a' \notin A$, we cannot have $a \in A$. $\qquad\square$

Definition 5.9 For each $X \in \mathbf{Nom}$ and $x \in X$, define

$$\mathrm{stab}_f x \triangleq \{\pi \in \mathrm{Perm}\, \mathbb{A} \mid \pi \cdot x = x \wedge \mathrm{supp}\, \pi \subseteq \mathrm{supp}\, x\}. \tag{5.11}$$

Recall from Lemma 2.21 that $\mathrm{supp}\, \pi = \{a \in \mathbb{A} \mid \pi a \neq a\}$. Therefore $\mathrm{supp}\, \pi \subseteq \mathrm{supp}\, x$ holds iff π is equal to the identity on $\mathbb{A} - \mathrm{supp}\, x$. So $\{\pi \in \mathrm{Perm}\, \mathbb{A} \mid \mathrm{supp}\, \pi \subseteq \mathrm{supp}\, x\}$ is isomorphic to the finite group $\mathrm{Sym}\,(\mathrm{supp}\, x)$ and $\mathrm{stab}_f x$ is isomorphic to a subgroup of $\mathrm{Sym}\,(\mathrm{supp}\, x)$. Note that if x and x' are in the same orbit, say $x' = \pi \cdot x$, then $\mathrm{stab}_f x$ and $\mathrm{stab}_f x'$ are isomorphic groups (via conjugation with π).

Lemma 5.10 *For all $X \in \mathbf{Nom}$ and $x \in X$*

$$\mathrm{stab}\, x = \{\pi \in \mathrm{Perm}\, \mathbb{A} \mid (\exists \pi' \in \mathrm{stab}_f x)\, \pi|_{\mathrm{supp}\, x} = \pi'|_{\mathrm{supp}\, x}\}.$$

Proof First note that for all $\pi, \pi' \in \text{Perm}\,\mathbb{A}$, if $\pi|_{\text{supp}\,x} = \pi'|_{\text{supp}\,x}$, then $\pi^{-1} \circ \pi'$ fixes each $a \in \text{supp}\,x$; so $(\pi^{-1} \circ \pi') \cdot x = x$ and hence $\pi \cdot x = \pi' \cdot x$. So if $\pi|_{\text{supp}\,x} = \pi'|_{\text{supp}\,x}$ with $\pi' \in \text{stab}_f x$, it is certainly the case that $\pi \in \text{stab}\,x$. Conversely, for any $\pi \in \text{stab}\,x$ by Proposition 2.11 we have $\pi \cdot \text{supp}\,x = \text{supp}\,(\pi \cdot x) = \text{supp}\,x$. Thus π restricts to a bijection on the finite set $\text{supp}\,x$. Using the homogeneity lemma (Lemma 1.14), we can find a permutation $\pi' \in \text{Perm}\,\mathbb{A}$ that (a) agrees with π on $\text{supp}\,x$ and (b) that is the identity on $\mathbb{A} - \text{supp}\,x$. Because of (a) we have $\pi' \cdot x = \pi \cdot x = x$; and because of (b) we have $\text{supp}\,\pi' \subseteq \text{supp}\,x$. Therefore $\pi' \in \text{stab}_f x$ and $\pi|_{\text{supp}\,x} = \pi'|_{\text{supp}\,x}$. □

Proposition 5.11 *Suppose that $X \in \mathbf{Nom}$ is atomic, say $X = \text{orb}\,x$ for some $x \in X$. For each $Y \in \mathbf{Nom}$ and $y \in Y$, there is at most one equivariant function $f : X \to Y$ with $f\,x = y$; and there is one iff*

$$\text{supp}\,y \subseteq \text{supp}\,x \wedge \text{stab}_f x \subseteq \text{stab}\,y. \tag{5.12}$$

Proof Suppose $f, f' \in \mathbf{Nom}(X, Y)$ and $f\,x = y = f'x$. Then for any $x' \in X$, $x' = \pi \cdot x$ for some $\pi \in \text{Perm}\,\mathbb{A}$ and hence $f\,x' = f(\pi \cdot x) = \pi \cdot (f\,x) = \pi \cdot y = \pi \cdot (f'x) = f'(\pi \cdot x) = f'x'$. Therefore $f = f'$. Note also that $\text{supp}\,y = \text{supp}\,(f\,x) \subseteq \text{supp}\,x$ by Lemma 2.12; and for any $\pi \in \text{Perm}\,\mathbb{A}$, if $x = \pi \cdot x$, then $y = f\,x = f(\pi \cdot x) = \pi \cdot (f\,x) = \pi \cdot y$. So (5.12) is satisfied when $y = f\,x$.

Conversely, suppose x and y satisfy (5.12). If suffices to show that the equivariant subset $f \triangleq \{(\pi \cdot x, \pi \cdot y) \mid \pi \in \text{Perm}\,\mathbb{A}\} \subseteq X \times Y$ is single-valued (1.36); for then it gives a totally defined, equivariant function $X \to Y$ with $f\,x = y$. Suppose $\pi_1 \cdot x = \pi_2 \cdot x$. We wish to prove that $\pi_1 \cdot y = \pi_2 \cdot y$. Since $(\pi_2^{-1} \circ \pi_1) \in \text{stab}\,x$, by Lemma 5.10, $(\pi_2^{-1} \circ \pi_1)|_{\text{supp}\,x} = \pi'|_{\text{supp}\,x}$ for some $\pi' \in \text{stab}_f x$. By (5.12), $\pi' \cdot y = y$. Since $\text{supp}\,y \subseteq \text{supp}\,x$, π' agrees with $\pi_2^{-1} \circ \pi_1$ on $\text{supp}\,y$ and hence $y = \pi' \cdot y = (\pi_2^{-1} \circ \pi_1) \cdot y = \pi_2^{-1} \cdot (\pi_1 \cdot y)$. Therefore $\pi_2 \cdot y = \pi_1 \cdot y$, as required. □

Remark 5.12 Given $x \in X$ as in the proposition, since $\text{stab}_f x$ is a finite group, (5.12) only imposes finitely many conditions on the element $y \in Y$ for it to determine an equivariant function from X to Y. We make use of this fact in the next section (Theorem 5.16) and in Section 6.4.

Theorem 5.13 *Every atomic nominal set is isomorphic to one of the form* coset $\overline{G}$ *(Lemma 5.8) for some subgroup G of the group* Sym $\mathbb{A}$ *of permutations of some finite set of atomic names $A \in P_f\,\mathbb{A}$.*

Proof If $X \in \mathbf{Nom}$ is atomic, say $X = \text{orb}\,x$ for some $x \in X$, then we can take $A = \text{supp}\,x$ and G to consist of all permutations of $\text{supp}\,x$ that, when regarded as finite permutations of $\mathbb{A}$ by mapping each $a \in \mathbb{A} - \text{supp}\,x$ to itself, are in $\text{stab}\,x$. Clearly G is a subgroup of Sym $(\text{supp}\,x)$ and from Lemma 5.10

we have stab $x = \overline{G}$. Therefore by the orbit-stabilizer Theorem 5.4, orb $x \cong$ coset (stab x) = coset $\overline{G}$.   □

5.3 Finitely presentable objects

We review the notion of a *finitely presentable object* of a category (Gabriel and Ulmer, 1971). It gives a category-theoretic characterization of finiteness in that the finitely presentable objects in the category **Set** of sets and functions are precisely the finite sets. For the category **Nom** of nominal sets and equivariant functions we will see that 'finite' must be replaced by 'orbit finite' (Theorem 5.16).

Recall (Borceux, 2008, volume 1, definition 2.13.1) that a category **C** is said to be *filtered* if it satisfies the following three conditions (together these conditions are equivalent to requiring that there is a cocone under every finite diagram in **C**):

- There exists an object in **C**.
- If $C_1, C_2 \in \mathbf{C}$, then there exist morphisms $f_1 : C_1 \rightarrow C$ and $f_2 : C_2 \rightarrow C$ from those objects to some object $C \in \mathbf{C}$.
- If $f_1, f_2 : C_1 \rightarrow C_2$ are a parallel pair of morphisms in **C**, then there exists $f : C_2 \rightarrow C_3$ with $f \circ f_1 = f \circ f_2$.

A *filtered colimit* is the colimit of a functor whose domain is a filtered category. Filtered colimits in **Set** can be constructed as follows. Suppose $F : \mathbf{C} \rightarrow \mathbf{Set}$ is a functor with **C** small and filtered. (A category is *small* if its collections of objects and morphisms are in **Set**.) Since **C** is filtered, we get an equivalence relation $\sim$ on the disjoint union

$$\textstyle\sum_{C \in \mathbf{C}} F C = \{(C, x) \mid C \in \mathbf{C} \wedge x \in F C\} \tag{5.13}$$

by defining

$$(C_1, x_1) \sim (C_2, x_2) \triangleq (\exists C_1 \overset{f_1}{\rightarrow} C \overset{f_2}{\leftarrow} C_2) \; F f_1 \, x_1 = F f_2 \, x_2 . \tag{5.14}$$

Forming the quotient set

$$\operatorname{colim} F \triangleq (\textstyle\sum_{C \in \mathbf{C}} F C)/\!\sim , \tag{5.15}$$

and letting $[C, x]$ denote the $\sim$-equivalence class of (C, x), we get functions

$$\iota_C : F C \rightarrow \operatorname{colim} F, \tag{5.16}$$

$$\iota_C \triangleq \lambda x \in F C \rightarrow [C, x] ,$$

for each object $C \in \mathbf{C}$. These functions form a cocone under F, in the sense that for each morphism $f : C_1 \to C_2$ in $\mathbf{C}$

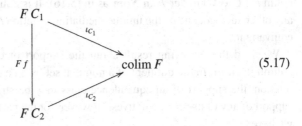

(5.17)

commutes in **Set**; for if $x_1 \in F C_1$, then

$$\iota_{C_2}(F f x_1)$$
$$= \quad \{\text{by definition of } i_{C_2}\}$$
$$[C_2, F f x_1]$$
$$= \quad \{\text{since } (C_1, x_1) \sim (C_2, F f x_1)\}$$
$$[C_1, x_1]$$
$$= \quad \{\text{by definition of } i_{C_1}\}$$
$$\iota_{C_1} x_1 .$$

Furthermore, (5.16) is a colimiting cocone: given any other cocone $(\alpha_X : F C \to X \mid C \in \mathbf{C})$ there is a unique function $\hat{\alpha} : \operatorname{colim} F \to X$ with $\hat{\alpha} \circ \iota_C = \alpha_C$ for all $C \in \mathbf{C}$:

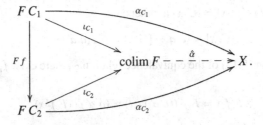

This is because any such $\hat{\alpha}$ has to satisfy

$$\hat{\alpha}\,[C, x] = \alpha_C\, c \qquad (C \in \mathbf{C}, x \in F C), \tag{5.18}$$

and this does give a well defined function on equivalence classes because if $(C_1, x_1) \sim (C_2, x_2)$, then by (5.14) and (5.17) we have $\alpha_{C_1} x_1 = \alpha_{C_2} x_2$.

This construction of filtered colimits in **Set** carries over to **Nom**. If $F : \mathbf{C} \to$ **Nom** is a small filtered diagram of nominal sets and equivariant functions, then as in Section 2.2, the disjoint union (5.13) becomes a nominal set once we endow it with the Perm $\mathbb{A}$-action $\pi \cdot (C, x) \triangleq (C, \pi \cdot x)$. The equivalence relation (5.14) is equivariant because F sends morphisms in $\mathbf{C}$ to equivariant functions;

so as in Section 2.9, the quotient $\operatorname{colim} F$ is a nominal set with permutation action satisfying $\pi \cdot [C, x] = [C, \pi \cdot x]$. Hence we get a cocone $(\iota_C : FC \to \operatorname{colim} F \mid C \in \mathbf{C})$ under F in **Nom** as in (5.16). It is colimiting because given any other such cocone α, the unique mediating function $\hat{\alpha}$ (5.18) is necessarily equivariant.

We need the following result about the support of elements of a filtered colimit in **Nom**. In the quotient of a nominal set by an equivariant equivalence relation, the support of an equivalence class may be strictly smaller than the support of any of its representatives. However, for the particular quotient (5.15) we have

$$(\forall y \in \operatorname{colim} F)(\exists C \in \mathbf{C}, x \in FC) \; y = [C, x] \wedge \operatorname{supp} y = \operatorname{supp} x. \qquad (5.19)$$

This can be proved by picking any representative (C, x) for the given equivalence class $y \in \operatorname{colim} F$ and then repeatedly applying the following lemma as many times as there are elements in $\operatorname{supp} x - \operatorname{supp} y$.

Lemma 5.14 *Suppose $F : \mathbf{C} \to \mathbf{Nom}$ is a small filtered diagram of nominal sets with colimit $(\iota_C : FC \to \operatorname{colim} F \mid C \in \mathbf{C})$, constructed as above. Then for each $a \in \mathbb{A}$, $C \in \mathbf{C}$ and $x \in FC$ we have*

$$a \mathbin{\#} \iota_C x \Rightarrow (\exists C \xrightarrow{f} C') \, a \mathbin{\#} F f x. \qquad (5.20)$$

Proof Suppose $a \mathbin{\#} \iota_C x$. Pick some $a' \mathbin{\#} (a, x)$. Then since ι_C is equivariant, by Proposition 3.4 we have $a' \mathbin{\#} \iota_C x = [C, x]$; and $a \mathbin{\#} [C, x]$ by assumption. Therefore $(a \, a') \cdot [C, x] = [C, x]$ and hence

$$[C, x] = (a \, a') \cdot [C, x] = [C, (a \, a') \cdot x].$$

So by definition (5.14) of the equivalence relation $\sim$, there exist $f, f' : C \to C'$ in $\mathbf{C}$ with

$$F f x = F f'((a \, a') \cdot x) = (a \, a') \cdot (F f' x).$$

Since $a' \mathbin{\#} x$ and $F f'$ is equivariant, we have $a' \mathbin{\#} F f' x$; and hence $a \mathbin{\#} (a \, a') \cdot (F f' x) = F f x$, as required. $\square$

Definition 5.15 Let $\mathbf{S}$ be a locally small category with small filtered colimits. (A category $\mathbf{S}$ is *locally small* if for all $X, X' \in \mathbf{S}$, the collection $\mathbf{S}(X, X')$ of all morphisms from X to X' is in **Set**.) An object $X \in \mathbf{S}$ is *finitely presentable* if the functor $\mathbf{S}(X, \_) : \mathbf{S} \to \mathbf{Set}$ preserves small filtered colimits. In other words, for each functor $F : \mathbf{C} \to \mathbf{S}$ with $\mathbf{C}$ small and filtered, the function

$$\operatorname{colim}_{C \in \mathbf{C}} \mathbf{S}(X, F C) \to \mathbf{S}(X, \operatorname{colim} F),$$

$$[C, g] \mapsto \iota_C \circ g$$

is a bijection. Splitting this requirement into injectivity and surjectivity gives
the following conditions:

$$\left(\begin{array}{ccc} X & \xrightarrow{\ g_1\ } & F C_1 \\ \forall \ \scriptstyle g_2 \downarrow & & \downarrow \scriptstyle \iota_{C_1} \\ F C_2 & \xrightarrow[\iota_{C_2}]{} & \operatorname{colim} F \end{array} \right) \left(\exists \ \begin{array}{c} C_1 \\ \scriptstyle f_1 \downarrow \\ C_2 \xrightarrow[f_2]{} C \end{array} \right) \left(\begin{array}{ccc} X & \xrightarrow{\ g_1\ } & F C_2 \\ \scriptstyle g_2 \downarrow & & \downarrow \scriptstyle F f_1 \\ F C_2 & \xrightarrow[F f_2]{} & F C, \end{array} \right) \quad (5.21)$$

$$\left(\forall \ \begin{array}{c} X \\ \ \searrow{\scriptstyle g} \\ \operatorname{colim} F \end{array} \right) \left(\exists \ g' \begin{array}{c} X \\ \downarrow \\ F C \end{array} \right) \begin{array}{c} X \\ g' \downarrow \ \searrow{\scriptstyle g} \\ F C \xrightarrow[\iota_C]{} \operatorname{colim} F . \end{array} \quad (5.22)$$

The notion of finitely presentable object is the category-theoretic generalization of the notion of a 'compact' (also known as 'isolated') element of a
lattice; and it is not hard to see that the finitely presentable objects of **Set** are
precisely the finite sets. For nominal sets we have the following result, proved
by Petrişan (2011, proposition 2.3.7) and, via the equivalent category of named
sets (Section 6.4), by Staton (2007, corollary 5.1.12).

Theorem 5.16 *A nominal set is a finitely presentable object of* **Nom** *iff it is
orbit-finite.*

Proof   We have seen that the orbits functor $\Pi_0 :$ **Nom** $\to$ **Set** has right adjoint,
namely the discrete nominal set functor $\Delta :$ **Set** $\to$ **Nom**. This functor Δ also
has a right adjoint, namely the global sections functor **Nom**$(1, \_) :$ **Nom** $\to$
Set. So Π_0 has a right adjoint that preserves filtered colimits; and from this it
follows that Π_0 maps finitely presentable objects in **Nom** to finitely presentable
objects in **Set**, that is, to finite sets. So if $X \in$ **Nom** is finitely presentable, then
it must be orbit-finite.

Conversely, to see that each orbit-finite nominal set is finitely presentable,
we first use the fact that the finitely presentable objects of a category are closed
under taking finite colimits; this follows because in **Set**, finite limits commute
with filtered colimits (MacLane, 1971, section IX.2, theorem 1). So since each
orbit-finite nominal set is a finite coproduct of atomic nominal sets, it suffices
to show that the latter are finitely presentable.

So we just need to verify that if $X \in$ **Nom** is atomic, then it satisfies conditions (5.21) and (5.22). Suppose X is equal to the Perm $\mathbb{A}$-orbit of $x \in X$. Then
for any $g, g' \in$ **Nom**(X, Y), from Proposition 5.11 we have $g = g' \Leftrightarrow g\, x = g'x$;
condition (5.21) follows from this. We can also use Proposition 5.11 to prove
condition (5.22). For suppose we have $g \in$ **Nom**$(X, \operatorname{colim} F)$. By (5.19) we can

find $C \in \mathbf{C}$ and $y \in FC$ with $g\,x = [C, y]$ and $\operatorname{supp} y = \operatorname{supp}(g\,x)$. Note that if $\pi \in \operatorname{stab}_f x$, then $[C, \pi \cdot y] = \pi \cdot (g\,x) = g(\pi \cdot x) = g\,x = [C, y]$ and hence there is some $f : C \to C'$ in $\mathbf{C}$ with $F f (\pi \cdot y) = F f y$. Since $\mathbf{C}$ is filtered and $\operatorname{stab}_f x$ is finite, we can in fact find a single $f : C \to C'$ satisfying $(\forall \pi \in \operatorname{stab}_f x)\, \pi \cdot (F f y) = F f y$. So since $\operatorname{supp}(F f y) \subseteq \operatorname{supp} y = \operatorname{supp}(g\,x) \subseteq \operatorname{supp} x$, condition (5.12) holds and by Proposition 5.11 there is an equivariant function $g' : X \to F C'$ with $g' x = F f y$. So $g\,x = [C, y] = [C', F f y] = (\iota_{C'} \circ g')\,x$ and hence $\iota_{C'} \circ g' = g$, as required for (5.22). □

Remark 5.17 **Nom** is a *locally finitely presentable* category (Borceux, 2008, volume 2, section 5.2), since it is locally small, has small colimits (in view of Sections 2.2 and 1.7) and contains a set $\{A^{\#n} \mid n \in \mathbb{N}\}$ of objects that are finitely presentable (Theorem 5.16) and that are easily seen to be conservative (Exercise 5.3). Another route to this fact is via the equivalence of **Nom** with the Schanuel topos, discussed in Section 6.3.

5.4 Orbit-finite subsets

So far we have only considered the notion of orbit-finiteness in relation to equivariant functions and relations. Now we generalize from equivariance, that is, having empty support, to finitely supported functions and relations. We have seen that any nominal set X splits into a disjoint union of equivariant subsets, its $\operatorname{Perm} \mathbb{A}$-orbits. We are interested in subsets of X that intersect only finitely many of these $\operatorname{Perm} \mathbb{A}$-orbits. Such a subset need not be finitely supported; for example $\mathbb{A}$ only has one $\operatorname{Perm} \mathbb{A}$-orbit and certainly has non-finitely supported subsets (Proposition 2.9). So we restrict attention to the following subsets.

Definition 5.18 Let X be a nominal set. A subset of X is said to be *orbit-finite* if it is finitely supported (Section 2.5) and contained in a finite union of $\operatorname{Perm} \mathbb{A}$-orbits of X. We write $P_{\text{of}} X$ for the equivariant subset of $P_{\text{fs}} X$ consisting of such subsets.

Note 5.19 Bojańczyk *et al.* (2012) use the term 'finitary' for the subsets of X that are in $P_{\text{of}} X$. I prefer to simply re-use the term 'orbit-finite' from Section 5.2. It is not hard to see that S is an orbit-finite subset of a nominal set X iff the equivariant subset $\{\pi \cdot x \mid \pi \in \operatorname{Perm} \mathbb{A} \wedge x \in X\} \subseteq X$, when regarded as a nominal set as in Lemma 2.22, is an orbit-finite nominal set in the sense of Definition 5.5. Note also that since each FM-set is a finitely supported subset of the Fraenkel–Mostowski universe $\mathcal{U}$ (Definition 2.28), it makes sense to speak of *orbit-finite FM-sets*.

Note that an orbit-finite subset may well be an infinite set. For example, $\mathbb{A}$ is an orbit-finite subset of itself. Bojańczyk *et al.* (2012) begin to investigate computation with orbit-finite data structures and algorithms (for a generalized version of nominal sets over any 'Fraïssé symmetry'). In order to compute with orbit-finite subsets one needs an effective presentation of both them and operations on them. The following notion turns out to give an alternative characterization of orbit-finite subsets that is suitable for calculation. It was introduced independently by Turner (2009, definition 3.4.3.2), by Gabbay (2009, section 3.3; 2011, definition 3.1) (see also Gabbay and Ciancia, 2011, definition 3.1) and by Bojańczyk *et al.* (2012, section 8), whose 'hull' terminology we adopt here. (See also Ciancia and Montanari, 2010, definition 6.10, whose 'closures' are hulls of the form $\text{hull}_{\text{supp}\,x-\{a\}}\{x\}$.)

Definition 5.20 For each finite set of atomic names $A \in P_f \mathbb{A}$, let

$$\text{Perm}_A\,\mathbb{A} \triangleq \{\pi \in \text{Perm}\,\mathbb{A} \mid (\forall a \in A)\,\pi\,a = a\} \qquad (5.23)$$

denote the subgroup of $\text{Perm}\,\mathbb{A}$ consisting of the finite permutations that fix each $a \in A$. For each finite subset $F \in P_f X$ of a nominal set X we define $\text{hull}_A F$ to be the union of the $\text{Perm}_A\,\mathbb{A}$-orbits of elements of F:

$$\text{hull}_A F \triangleq \{\pi \cdot x \mid \pi \in \text{Perm}_A\,\mathbb{A} \wedge x \in F\}. \qquad (5.24)$$

We call such subsets of X *orbit-finite hulls*.

Remark 5.21 Recall that for a finite permutation $\pi \in \text{Perm}\,\mathbb{A}$, $\text{supp}\,\pi = \{a \in \mathbb{A} \mid \pi\,a \neq a\}$ (Lemma 2.21). So $\text{Perm}_A\,\mathbb{A} = \{\pi \in \text{Perm}\,\mathbb{A} \mid \pi \,\#\, A\}$. If $\pi, \pi' \in \text{Perm}_A\,\mathbb{A}$, then $\pi \circ \pi' \in \text{Perm}_A\,\mathbb{A}$. Hence $\pi \,\#\, A \Rightarrow \pi \cdot \text{hull}_A F \subseteq \text{hull}_A F$ and therefore by Lemma 2.24 we have that A supports $\text{hull}_A F$ as a subset of X. Thus $\text{hull}_A F \in P_{\text{fs}} X$ and

$$\text{supp}\,(\text{hull}_A F) \subseteq A. \qquad (5.25)$$

Note that $\text{hull}_A F$ is contained in the union of the $\text{Perm}\,\mathbb{A}$-orbits of elements in F. So since F is finite, $\text{hull}_A F$ is an orbit-finite subset of X. In fact every orbit-finite subset of X is of this form (Proposition 5.25). This is a consequence of Lemma 5.24, a key technical property of orbit-finite hulls proved independently by Turner and by Bojańczyk *et al.* To prove it we make use of the following finiteness property of the cartesian product $\mathbb{A}^n$.

Lemma 5.22 *For each $n \in \mathbb{N}$ and $A \in P_f \mathbb{A}$, the nominal set $\mathbb{A}^n$ has only finitely many different $\text{Perm}_A\,\mathbb{A}$-orbits.*

Proof Identifying $n \in \mathbb{N}$ with the finite ordinal $\{0, \ldots, n-1\}$, for each partial function $f : n \rightharpoonup A$ and equivalence relation $\sim$ on $n - \mathrm{Dom}\, f$, define

$$O_{f,\sim} \triangleq \{(a_0, \ldots, a_{n-1}) \in \mathbb{A}^n \mid (\forall(i,a) \in f)\, a_i = a \,\wedge$$
$$(\forall i, j \in n - \mathrm{Dom}\, f)\, i \sim j \Leftrightarrow a_i = a_j \in \mathbb{A} - A\}.$$

Since there are only finitely many such f and $\sim$, it suffices to show that each $O_{f,\sim}$ is a $\mathrm{Perm}_A\,\mathbb{A}$-orbit and that every $\mathrm{Perm}_A\,\mathbb{A}$-orbit is of this form. This is a consequence of the following easily verified properties:

- $O_{f,\sim} \neq \emptyset$.
- $\pi \in \mathrm{Perm}_A\,\mathbb{A} \wedge \vec{a} \in O_{f,\sim} \Rightarrow \pi \cdot \vec{a} \in O_{f,\sim}$.
- $\vec{a}, \vec{b} \in O_{f,\sim} \Rightarrow (\exists \pi \in \mathrm{Perm}_A\,\mathbb{A})\, \pi \cdot \vec{a} = \vec{b}$.
- Given $(a_0, \ldots, a_{n-1}) \in \mathbb{A}^n$, then $(a_0, \ldots, a_{n-1}) \in O_{f,\sim}$, where $f \triangleq \{(i, a_i) \mid i \in n \wedge a_i \in A\}$ and $\sim \triangleq \{(i,j) \in (n - \mathrm{Dom}\, f) \times (n - \mathrm{Dom}\, f) \mid a_i = a_j\}$. $\square$

Remark 5.23 (Oligomorphic groups) A subgroup G of the group $\mathrm{Sym}\,\mathbb{A}$ of permutations of a set $\mathbb{A}$ is called *oligomorphic* if for all $n \in \mathbb{N}$, the G-set $\mathbb{A}^n$ has only finitely many orbits. A simple special case of the above lemma is the fact that $\Pi_0\,(\mathbb{A}^n)$ is in bijection with the set of equivalence relations on $\{0, \ldots, n-1\}$ and hence that $\mathrm{Perm}\,\mathbb{A}$ is oligomorphic. Then the lemma can be deduced from the following property of oligomorphic groups G (Hodges, 1993, exercise 6, p. 139): for any finite subset $A \in \mathrm{P_f}\,\mathbb{A}$, the stabilizer subgroup $G_A = \{g \in G \mid (\forall a \in A)\, g\, a = a\}$ is also oligomorphic.

The following key lemma about orbit-finite hulls was proved independently by Turner (2009, lemma 3.4.3.5) and Bojańczyk *et al.* (2012, lemma 3).

Lemma 5.24 *Suppose $A, A' \in \mathrm{P_f}\,\mathbb{A}$ are finite sets of atomic names with $A \subseteq A'$. For each $X \in \mathbf{Nom}$ and $F \in \mathrm{P_f}\, X$, there exists $F' \in \mathrm{P_f}\, X$ such that $\mathrm{hull}_A F = \mathrm{hull}_{A'} F'$.*

Proof Since $F \mapsto \mathrm{hull}_A F$ preserves unions, it suffices to show for all $A \subseteq A' \in \mathrm{P_f}\,\mathbb{A}$ and $x \in X$ that $\mathrm{hull}_A\{x\}$ is of the form $\mathrm{hull}_{A'} F'$ for some $F' \in \mathrm{P_f}\, X$.

Let $a_1, \ldots, a_n$ be the distinct elements of $\mathrm{supp}\, x$ and consider the $\mathrm{Perm}_A\,\mathbb{A}$-orbit of $(a_1, \ldots, a_n)$ in $\mathbb{A}^n$:

$$\{(\pi\, a_1, \ldots, \pi\, a_n) \mid \pi \in \mathrm{Perm}_A\,\mathbb{A}\} \subseteq \mathbb{A}^n. \tag{5.26}$$

Since $\mathrm{Perm}_{A'}\,\mathbb{A}$ is a subgroup of $\mathrm{Perm}_A\,\mathbb{A}$, (5.26) is a $\mathrm{Perm}_{A'}\,\mathbb{A}$-equivariant subset of $\mathbb{A}^n$ and so by Lemma 5.22 it has finitely many $\mathrm{Perm}_{A'}\,\mathbb{A}$-orbits. Therefore we can find $\pi_1, \ldots, \pi_m \in \mathrm{Perm}_A\,\mathbb{A}$ such that

$$(\forall \pi \in \mathrm{Perm}_A\,\mathbb{A})(\exists i \in \{1, \ldots, n\}, \pi' \in \mathrm{Perm}_{A'}\,\mathbb{A})$$
$$\pi \cdot (a_1 \ldots, a_n) = (\pi' \circ \pi_i) \cdot (a_1, \ldots, a_n). \tag{5.27}$$

We claim that $\text{hull}_A\{x\} = \text{hull}_{A'}\{\pi_1 \cdot x, \ldots, \pi_m \cdot x\}$. Since $\text{Perm}_{A'} \mathbb{A}$ is a subgroup of $\text{Perm}_A \mathbb{A}$, it is certainly the case that $\text{hull}_{A'}\{\pi_1 \cdot x, \ldots, \pi_m \cdot x\}$ is a subset of $\text{hull}_A\{x\}$. For the reverse inclusion, note that since $\text{supp}\, x = \{a_1, \ldots, a_n\}$, if $\pi \cdot (a_1 \ldots, a_n) = (\pi' \circ \pi_i) \cdot (a_1, \ldots, a_n)$, then $\pi \cdot x = \pi' \cdot (\pi_i \cdot x)$. Therefore property (5.27) implies $\text{hull}_A\{x\} \subseteq \text{hull}_{A'}\{\pi_1 \cdot x, \ldots, \pi_m \cdot x\}$. □

Proposition 5.25 *Let X be a nominal set. For each $A \in \text{P}_\text{f}\, \mathbb{A}$ and $F \in \text{P}_\text{f}\, X$, $\text{hull}_A F$ is an orbit-finite subset of X. Conversely, each orbit-finite subset $S \in \text{P}_\text{of}\, X$ is equal to $\text{hull}_{\text{supp}\, S}\, F$ for some $F \in \text{P}_\text{f}\, X$.*

Proof Each $\text{hull}_A F$ is orbit-finite since it is contained in the union of the $\text{Perm}\, \mathbb{A}$-orbits of elements in F. Conversely, suppose $S \in \text{P}_\text{of}\, X$ is contained in the union of the $\text{Perm}\, \mathbb{A}$-orbits of the elements in the finite subset $F \in \text{P}_\text{f}\, X$; in other words, $S \subseteq \text{hull}_\emptyset F$. Let $A = \text{supp}\, S$. By Lemma 5.24 there exists $F' \in \text{P}_\text{f}\, X$ with $\text{hull}_\emptyset F = \text{hull}_A F'$. We claim that $S = \text{hull}_A(F' \cap S)$.

Note that since $A = \text{supp}\, S$, we have $\pi \cdot S = S$ for any $\pi \in \text{Perm}_A \mathbb{A}$. So if $x' \in F' \cap S$, then $\pi \cdot x' \in \pi \cdot S = S$; hence $\text{hull}_A(F' \cap S) \subseteq S$. Conversely, if $x \in S$, and hence $x \in \text{hull}_A F'$, we have $x = \pi \cdot x'$ for some $\pi \in \text{Perm}_A \mathbb{A}$ and $x' \in F'$; but then $x' = \pi^{-1} \cdot x \in \pi^{-1} \cdot S = S$ and so $x \in \text{hull}_A(F' \cap S)$. □

Remark 5.26 (Name-abstractions are orbit-finite) Note that the notion of generalized name abstraction from Section 4.6 is an orbit-finite hull: given $X, Y \in \textbf{Nom}$, $x \in X$ and $y \in Y$

$$\langle x \rangle y = \text{hull}_{(\text{supp}\, y - \text{supp}\, x)}\{(x, y)\}. \tag{5.28}$$

As a special cases we have that single-name abstractions satisfy

$$\langle a \rangle x = \text{hull}_{\text{supp}\, x - \{a\}}\{(a, x)\} \quad (a \in \mathbb{A}, x \in X). \tag{5.29}$$

Thus name abstractions are 'orbit-singletons'. The same is true of elements of the free nominal restriction set $\text{Frs}\, X$ introduced in Section 9.5; see Exercise 9.4.

5.5 Uniformly supported subsets

We give an application of Proposition 5.25 that characterizes orbit-finite subsets in terms of a compactness property with respect to 'uniformly supported' directed unions. First we recall the relationship between conventional finite sets and directed unions.

Fix a set X. A set $\mathcal{S} \subseteq \text{P}\, X$ of subsets of X is *directed* if it is non-empty and for all $S_1, S_2 \in \mathcal{S}$, there is some $S \in \mathcal{S}$ with $S_1 \subseteq S$ and $S_2 \subseteq S$. Equivalently,

S is directed if the union of finitely many subsets in S is contained in some subset in S. Hence if U is a finite subset of X and S is a directed collection of subsets, then we have the following 'compactness' property:

$$U \subseteq \bigcup S \Rightarrow (\exists S \in S)\, U \subseteq S. \tag{5.30}$$

Conversely if a subset U has property (5.30) with respect to all directed sets of subsets of X, then it must be finite, since every $U \in PX$ is the union of the directed set of its finite subsets:

$$U = \bigcup \{F \mid F \in P_f X \wedge F \subseteq U\}. \tag{5.31}$$

Consider now what happens when X is a nominal set and we replace the notion of 'finite subset' by the more liberal notion of 'orbit-finite subset'. If $S \in P_{fs} X$ and $F \in P_f S$, then we have $F \subseteq \mathrm{hull}_{\mathrm{supp}\,S}\, F \subseteq S$ (since any $\pi \in \mathrm{Perm}_{\mathrm{supp}\,S}\, \mathbb{A}$ satisfies $\pi \cdot S = S$). Therefore, S can be expressed as a union of orbit-finite subsets

$$S = \bigcup \{\mathrm{hull}_{\mathrm{supp}\,S}\, F \mid F \in P_f S\} \quad (S \in P_{fs} X,\, X \in \mathbf{Nom}). \tag{5.32}$$

The set $\{\mathrm{hull}_{\mathrm{supp}\,S}\, F \mid F \in P_f S\}$ is not only directed, it also has the property that all its elements have a common support, namely $\mathrm{supp}\,S$. Following Turner and Winskel we call such subsets uniformly supported.

Definition 5.27 (Turner and Winskel, 2009, definition 1) Let X be a nominal set. A subset $S \subseteq X$ is *uniformly supported* if there exists a finite set of atomic names $A \in P_f \mathbb{A}$ that supports each $x \in S$. Note that if this is the case then for all $\pi \in \mathrm{Perm}_A \mathbb{A}$, $\pi \cdot S = \{\pi \cdot x \mid x \in S\} = S$ and hence by Lemma 2.24, S is supported by A as an element of PX. So if S is uniformly supported, it is in particular finitely supported.

Lemma 5.28 *If S is a uniformly supported subset of a nominal set, then $(\forall x \in S)\,\mathrm{supp}\,x \subseteq \mathrm{supp}\,S$.*

Proof Suppose the elements of S are all supported by $A \in P_f \mathbb{A}$. For each $x \in S$, if $a \,\#\, S$, then choosing and $a' \,\#\, (a, A)$, since $a, a' \,\#\, S$ we have $(a\ a') \cdot S = S$; so $(a\ a') \cdot x \in S$ and hence $a' \notin A \supseteq \mathrm{supp}((a\ a') \cdot x)$. Thus $a' \,\#\, (a\ a') \cdot x$ and hence $a \,\#\, x$. Therefore we have $a \,\#\, S \Rightarrow a \,\#\, x$ and hence $\mathrm{supp}\,x \subseteq \mathrm{supp}\,S$. $\square$

Remark 5.29 The uniformly supported subsets of a nominal set X are precisely the images of finitely supported functions from discrete nominal sets. For if $I \in \mathbf{Set}$ and $f \in \Delta I \to_{fs} X$, then for each $i \in I$

$$\mathrm{supp}\,(f\,i) = \mathrm{supp}\,(\mathrm{app}(f, i)) \subseteq \mathrm{supp}\,f \cup \mathrm{supp}\,i$$

(by Lemma 2.12, since application (2.13) is equivariant) and supp $i = \emptyset$ (since ΔI is discrete); so the elements of the image $\{f\, i \mid i \in I\}$ are all supported by supp f. Conversely, if $S \subseteq X$ is uniformly supported, by A say, then S is the image of the inclusion function $\Delta S \hookrightarrow X$, which is also supported by A.

Example 5.30 Clearly any finite set is uniformly supported. An example of an infinite, uniformly supported subset is $\{a\} \times \mathbb{N} \subseteq \mathbb{A} \times \mathbb{N}$ (for any $a \in \mathbb{A}$). Note that this is not an orbit-finite subset of $\mathbb{A} \times \mathbb{N}$; indeed it is the case that the only orbit-finite, uniformly supported subsets of a nominal set are the finite ones (Exercise 5.8).

Theorem 5.31 *Let X be a nominal set. Every finitely supported subset of X can be expressed as the union of a directed and uniformly supported set of orbit-finite subsets of X. Furthermore, $U \in P_{fs} X$ is orbit-finite iff it has the compactness property (5.30) with respect to all $S \subseteq P_{fs} X$ that are directed and uniformly supported.*

Proof In view of (5.32), it just remains to prove the last sentence of the theorem.

Suppose $U \in P_{fs} X$ is orbit-finite and $U \subseteq \bigcup S$ with S directed and uniformly supported. By Lemma 5.24 and Proposition 5.25, $U = \text{hull}_A F$ for some $F \in P_f X$ and some $A \in P_f \mathbb{A}$ that supports each element of S. Since F is finite, S is directed and $F \subseteq \bigcup S$, there exists $S \in S$ with $F \subseteq S$. Since A supports S, any $\pi \in \text{Perm}_A \mathbb{A}$ satisfies $\pi \cdot S = S$. So from $F \subseteq S$ we get $\text{hull}_A F \subseteq S$, that is, $U \subseteq S$.

Conversely, suppose $U \in P_{fs} X$ has the compactness property (5.30) with respect to all $S \subseteq P_{fs} X$ that are directed and uniformly supported. Then taking S as in (5.32) we have $U = \bigcup \{\text{hull}_{\text{supp}\, U} F \mid F \in P_f U\}$; it follows that $U = \text{hull}_{\text{supp}\, U} F$ for some $F \in P_f U$, so that U is orbit-finite. $\qquad \square$

This theorem provides the basis for a treatment of finiteness within the context of a nominal version of domain theory that is explored in Chapter 11.

Exercises

5.1 Show that a nominal set is atomic in the sense of Definition 5.5 iff it is isomorphic to a quotient of $\mathbb{A}^{\#n}$ for some $n \in \mathbb{N}$.

5.2 Show that orbit-finite nominal sets are closed under taking subobjects and quotients in **Nom**.

5.3 Show that $\{\mathbb{A}^{\#n} \mid n \in \mathbb{N}\}$ is a conservative set of objects in the category

Nom, in the sense that $f \in \mathbf{Nom}(X, Y)$ is an isomorphism iff for all $n \in \mathbb{N}$ the function

$$f_* : \mathbf{Nom}(\mathbb{A}^{\#n}, X) \to \mathbf{Nom}(\mathbb{A}^{\#n}, Y),$$

$$f_* \triangleq \lambda g \in \mathbf{Nom}(\mathbb{A}^{\#n}, X) \to f \circ g$$

is a bijection.

5.4 Give an example to show that $\mathrm{P_f}\,X$ need not be orbit-finite even if the nominal set X is orbit-finite.

5.5 Show that the product of two orbit-finite nominal sets is again orbit-finite. [Hint: combine Exercises 5.1 and 5.2 with Lemma 5.22.]

5.6 Show that the orbit-finite subsets of a nominal set X are closed under taking orbit-finite unions: for any orbit-finite subset $\mathcal{S} \subseteq \mathrm{P_{fs}}\,X$, if every $S \in \mathcal{S}$ is an orbit-finite subset of X, show that $\bigcup \mathcal{S} = \{x \in X \mid (\exists S \in \mathcal{S})\, x \in S\}$ is also an orbit-finite subset of X.

5.7 Show that orbit-finite subsets are closed under taking images along finitely supported functions: if $X, Y \in \mathbf{Nom}$, $f \in X \to_{\mathrm{fs}} Y$ and $S \in \mathrm{P_{of}}\,X$, show that $\{f\,x \mid x \in S\} \in \mathrm{P_{of}}\,Y$.

5.8 For any nominal set X and any uniformly supported subset $S \subseteq X$, show that S is an orbit-finite subset of X iff it is finite. [Hint: use Proposition 5.25 and Lemma 5.24.]

6

Equivalents of Nom

In this chapter we give some categories of mathematical structures considered in the literature that turn out to be equivalent to the category **Nom** of nominal sets and equivariant functions defined in Chapter 2.

6.1 Sets with name swapping

The definition of nominal sets given by Pitts (2003) emphasizes transpositions over more general permutations of atomic names. We saw in Proposition 2.1 that the support of an element of a nominal set can be defined in terms of the swapping operation

$$swap : \mathbb{A} \times \mathbb{A} \times X \to X,$$
$$swap \triangleq \lambda(a, a', x) \in \mathbb{A} \times \mathbb{A} \times X \to (a\ a') \cdot x. \tag{6.1}$$

In view of Theorem 1.15, an action of Perm $\mathbb{A}$ on a set X is completely determined by this operation; for every $\pi \in$ Perm $\mathbb{A}$ is equal to a composition of transpositions

$$\pi = (a_1\ a_1') \circ (a_2\ a_2') \circ \cdots \circ (a_n\ a_n'), \tag{6.2}$$

and hence

$$\pi \cdot x = swap(a_1, a_1', swap(a_2, a_2', \ldots swap(a_n, a_n', x) \cdots)). \tag{6.3}$$

What properties must a function $swap : \mathbb{A} \times \mathbb{A} \times X \to X$ satisfy in order for (6.3) to give a well defined Perm $\mathbb{A}$-action on X? Since the actions of a group G on a set X correspond to group homomorphisms $G \to$ Sym X (Exercise 1.1), answering this question amounts to giving a presentation of the group Perm $\mathbb{A}$ in terms of generators and relations, with the transpositions as generators.

Theorem 6.1 *For any set A, the group* Perm *A is freely generated by the transpositions (a a') (for all a, a' ∈ A) subject to the relations*

$$(a\,a) = \mathrm{id}, \tag{6.4}$$

$$(a\,a') \circ (a\,a') = \mathrm{id}, \tag{6.5}$$

$$(a\,a') \circ (b\,b') = ((a\,a') \cdot b \quad (a\,a') \cdot b') \circ (a\,a'), \tag{6.6}$$

for all a, a', b, b' ∈ A. In other words, for each group G and family $(g_{a,a'} \in G \mid a, a' \in A)$ satisfying

$$\left. \begin{array}{c} g_{a,a} = e = g_{a,a'}\, g_{a,a'}\,, \\[4pt] g_{a,a'}\, g_{b,b'} = g_{c,c'}\, g_{a,a'}\,, \\[4pt] \textit{where } c = (a\,a') \cdot b \textit{ and } c' = (a\,a') \cdot b', \end{array} \right\} \tag{6.7}$$

there is a unique homomorphism $\theta :$ Perm $A \to G$ with $\theta(a\,a') = g_{a,a'}$ for all a, a' ∈ A.

Proof   We saw in Theorem 1.15 that the group Perm A is generated by transpositions; and they certainly satisfy the identities (6.4)–(6.6). Therefore there is an epimorphism of groups to Perm A from the group freely generated by symbols $\{g_{a,a'} \mid a, a' \in A\}$) subject to the identities in (6.7). It remains to show that this epimorphism is also a monomorphism. In other words, for any word in the generators $g_{a,a'}$ whose composition of corresponding transpositions is equal to the identity permutation, we must show that the word can be proved equal to e just using the identities in (6.7). Since the word only involves finitely many generators, we can deduce this by appealing to known presentations of the finite symmetric groups. For example, if $A = \{a_0, \ldots, a_{n-1}\}$ has n elements, then Perm $A =$ Sym A is known to be freely generated by the 'adjacent' transpositions $(a_i\,a_{i+1})$ (for $i = 0, \ldots, n-2$) subject to the relations

$$(a_i\,a_{i+1})^2 = e \qquad\qquad\quad (0 \le i \le n-2),$$

$$((a_i\,a_{i+1}) \circ (a_{i+1}\,a_{i+2}))^3 = e \qquad\qquad (0 \le i \le n-3),$$

$$(a_i\,a_{i+1}) \circ (a_j\,a_{j+1}) = (a_j\,a_{j+1}) \circ (a_i\,a_{i+1}) \quad (0 \le i, j \le n-2 \wedge |i-j| > 1).$$

This can be proved by induction on $n \in \mathbb{N}$; see, for example, Johnson (1997, section 5.3). Since on the one hand each of these identities can be proved using (6.7), while on the other hand each 'non-adjacent' transposition $(a_i\,a_j)$ can be expressed as a composition of adjacent ones, the desired result follows.   □

Corollary 6.2   **Nom** *is isomorphic to the category whose objects are sets X* *equipped with a function swap* : $\mathbb{A} \times \mathbb{A} \times X \to X$ *satisfying*

$$swap(a, a, x) = x, \tag{6.8}$$

$$swap(a, a', swap(a, a', x)) = x, \tag{6.9}$$

$$swap(a, a', swap(b, b', x)) = swap((a\,a')\,b, (a\,a')\,b', swap(a, a', x)), \tag{6.10}$$

and such that for all $x \in X$ *there exists* $A \in P_f\,\mathbb{A}$ *with*

$$(\forall a, a' \in \mathbb{A} - A)\ swap(a, a', x) = x. \tag{6.11}$$

The morphisms of the category are functions $F : X \to Y$ *satisfying*

$$F(swap(a, a', x)) = swap(a, a', F\,x). \tag{6.12}$$

Composition and identities are given by the usual composition and identities for functions.

Proof If $X \in \mathbf{Nom}$, then (6.1) gives a function satisfying (6.8)–(6.10), because transpositions satisfy (6.4)–(6.6), and satisfying (6.11) by Proposition 2.1. Conversely, if X is a set equipped with a function $swap : \mathbb{A} \times \mathbb{A} \times X \to X$ satisfying (6.8)–(6.10), then for each $a, a' \in \mathbb{A}$, we get $g_{a,a'} \triangleq swap(a, a', \_) \in$ Sym X. These permutations satisfy (6.7). So by Theorem 6.1 we get a group homomorphism Perm $\mathbb{A} \to$ Sym X and hence a Perm $\mathbb{A}$-action on X satisfying $(a\,a') \cdot x = g_{a,a'}\,x = swap(a, a', x)$, for all $a, a' \in \mathbb{A}$ and $x \in X$. If $swap$ also satisfies (6.11), then by Proposition 2.1 every element of X has a finite support with respect to this action. So X is a nominal set.

These mappings between nominal sets and 'sets with swapping' are mutually inverse. Furthermore, under this bijection the property of being an equivariant function corresponds to property (6.12), since by Theorem 1.15, a function preserving the action of transpositions is equivalent to it preserving the action of arbitrary finite permutations. □

6.2 Continuous G-sets

Instead of restricting attention to special kinds of finite permutation (the transpositions), one can relax the condition of finiteness and consider the symmetric group Sym $\mathbb{A}$ of *all* permutations of the countably infinite set $\mathbb{A}$ (Example 1.1). If a set X possesses an Sym $\mathbb{A}$-action, the notion of 'support' from Section 2.1 makes sense for its elements. So we can consider the full subcategory $\mathbf{C}$ of [Sym $\mathbb{A}$, **Set**] whose objects are Sym $\mathbb{A}$-sets whose elements have finite support. Every such Sym $\mathbb{A}$-set gives a nominal set when we restrict the action to finite permutations. Conversely, given a nominal set X it is not hard to see that because of the finite support property, the action $\text{Perm}\,\mathbb{A} \times X \to X$ extends uniquely to an action $\text{Sym}\,\mathbb{A} \times X \to X$ and that $X \in \mathbf{C}$ (see Gadducci *et al.*, 2006, proposition 13, for the details). Hence $\mathbf{C}$ is isomorphic to **Nom**.

There is an alternative, topological characterization of the finite support property. We make $\text{Sym}\,\mathbb{A}$ into a topological space as a subspace of *Baire space* $\mathbb{N}^{\mathbb{N}}$, the topological product of countably many copies of the discrete topological space of natural numbers; this has basic open sets of the form $\{f \in \mathbb{N}^{\mathbb{N}} \mid (\forall i \in \{1, \ldots, k\})\ f\,m_i = n_i\}$ for some $k \in \mathbb{N}$ and $(m_1, \ldots, m_k), (n_1, \ldots, n_k) \in \mathbb{N}^k$. Fixing an enumeration $\mathbb{A} \cong \mathbb{N}$ of the atomic names, we get $\text{Sym}\,\mathbb{A} \subseteq \mathbb{A}^{\mathbb{A}} \cong \mathbb{N}^{\mathbb{N}}$ and take the subspace topology on $\text{Sym}\,\mathbb{A}$. This makes $\text{Sym}\,\mathbb{A}$ into a topological group – the operations of composition and taking inverses are continuous.

If G is a topological group, a G-set X is *continuous* if, regarding X as a discrete topological space, the action function $G \times X \to X$ is continuous. Write $\mathbf{B}(G)$ for the category of continuous G-sets and equivariant functions. It is a standard result of topological group theory that a G-set is continuous iff for each $x \in X$, the *stabilizer subgroup*

$$\text{stab}\,x \triangleq \{g \in G \mid g \cdot x = x\}$$

is an open set. In case $G = \text{Sym}\,\mathbb{A}$, this is equivalent to asking that each $\{\pi \in \text{Sym}\,\mathbb{A} \mid \pi \cdot x = x\}$ contain a basic open neighbourhood of the identity permutation; in other words there should be $a_1, \ldots, a_k \in \mathbb{A}$ such that $(\forall i \in \{1, \ldots, k\})\ \pi\,a_i = a_i \Rightarrow \pi \cdot x = x$. This is precisely the requirement that each $x \in X$ be finitely supported. Thus $\mathbf{B}(\text{Sym}\,\mathbb{A})$ is isomorphic to the full subcategory $\mathbf{C} \hookrightarrow [\text{Sym}\,\mathbb{A}, \mathbf{Set}]$ of finitely supported $\text{Sym}\,\mathbb{A}$-sets, and hence is isomorphic to **Nom**.

6.3 The Schanuel topos

Nominal sets provide a mathematical theory for objects that 'depend' upon names, via the notion of support studied in Chapter 2. The support of an element of a nominal set is defined in terms of the given action of name permutations; so name-dependency is an implicit property, rather than being given explicitly as extra structure. An alternative approach is to make name-dependency explicitly part of the structure and give, for each finite set of atomic names $A \in P_f\,\mathbb{A}$, a set $F\,A$ of elements 'in world A'. One then has to specify the relation between $F\,A$ and $F\,B$ for different worlds A and B. Such considerations have led to the use of categories of presheaves, that is functor categories valued in the category of sets, for modelling abstract syntax involving binders (Fiore *et al.*, 1999; Hofmann, 1999). It has been known since the beginning of work on nominal techniques (Gabbay and Pitts, 1999, section 6) that nominal sets are equivalent to special kinds of presheaf satisfying a sheaf condition equivalent to pullback preservation. The category of such sheaves is known as the Schanuel topos, because Schanuel first investigated its properties (unpublished). Although the Schanuel topos has the same category-theoretic properties as **Nom**, the emphasis that the latter puts on permutations of names has proved very fruitful.

We give the equivalence between **Nom** and the Schanuel topos. For background on categories of presheaves and sheaves see MacLane and Moerdijk (1992), or volume three of the encyclopaedic work of Borceux (2008).

Definition 6.3 Let C be a small category. A (covariant) *presheaf* on C is a functor $F : C \to \mathbf{Set}$. Such an F acts on the objects A and morphisms $f : A \to B$ of C to produce sets $F A$ and functions $F f : F A \to F B$, preserving identities ($F \, \mathrm{id}_A = \mathrm{id}_{FA}$) and compositions ($F(g \circ f) = F g \circ F f$). Presheaves are the objects of a category $[C, \mathbf{Set}]$ whose morphisms $\alpha : F \to F'$ are natural transformations, that is, families of functions ($\alpha_A : F A \to F'A \mid A \in C$) such that for each morphism $f : A \to B$ in C the following square of functions commutes:

$$
\begin{array}{ccc}
F A & \xrightarrow{\;\alpha_A\;} & F'A \\
{\scriptstyle F f}\big\downarrow & & \big\downarrow{\scriptstyle F'f} \\
F B & \xrightarrow[\;\alpha_B\;]{} & F'B \, .
\end{array}
\tag{6.13}
$$

Remark 6.4 In Chapter 1 we used the notation $[G, \mathbf{Set}]$ for the category of G-sets and equivariant functions associated with a group G. As the notation suggests, this is a special case of a presheaf category, once we regard G as the morphisms of a category with a single object.

Definition 6.5 Let I be the category whose objects are finite subsets of the fixed set $\mathbb{A}$ of atomic names and whose morphisms are injective functions. Identities and composition are as in **Set**.

For each nominal set $X \in \mathbf{Nom}$ and finite set of atomic names $A \in I$, let $I_*X A$ denote the subset of X consisting of elements supported by A:

$$
I_*X A \triangleq \{x \in X \mid \mathrm{supp}\, x \subseteq A\} .
\tag{6.14}
$$

We make this into the object part of a presheaf $I_*X \in [I, \mathbf{Set}]$ as follows. Given $i : A \to B$ in I and $x \in I_*X A$ define

$$
I_*X \, i \, x \triangleq \pi \cdot x \quad \text{where } \pi \in \mathrm{Perm}\, \mathbb{A} \text{ satisfies } \pi|_A = i.
\tag{6.15}
$$

This is well defined, because first there is some $\pi \in \text{Perm}\,\mathbb{A}$ that agrees with i (by the homogeneity lemma (Lemma 1.14); and secondly if π and π' are two such permutations, then $\pi^{-1} \circ \pi'$ fixes each element of A, which supports x, so that $(\pi^{-1} \circ \pi') \cdot x = x$ and hence $\pi' \cdot x = \pi \cdot x$. Furthermore

$$\text{supp}(I_*X\,i\,x) = \text{supp}(\pi \cdot x) = \pi \cdot \text{supp}\,x \subseteq \pi \cdot A \subseteq B.$$

So each $i : A \to B$ in **I** yields a function $I_*X\,i : I_*X\,A \to I_*X\,B$. Since we just saw that we are free to choose π in (6.15) to be any permutation agreeing with i, it is clear that $I_*X\,\text{id}_A = \text{id}_{I_*X\,A}$ and that $(I_*X\,j) \circ (I_*X\,i) = I_*X\,(j \circ i)$. Therefore I_*X is indeed a presheaf.

Given $f : X \to Y$ in **Nom**, we define a natural transformation $I_*f : I_*X \to I_*Y$. Its component at any $A \in \mathbf{I}$ is the function $(I_*f)_A : I_*X\,A \to I_*Y\,A$ mapping each $x \in I_*X\,A$ to

$$(I_*f)_A\,x \triangleq f\,x, \tag{6.16}$$

which is an element of $I_*Y\,A$, because $\text{supp}(f\,x) \subseteq \text{supp}\,x \subseteq A$ (using part (i) of Lemma 2.12). The naturality condition (6.13) holds because for any $i : A \to B$ in **I**

$$\begin{aligned}
&(I_*f)_B(I_*X\,i\,x)\\
=\ &\{\text{by (6.15), where } \pi|_A = i\}\\
&(I_*f)_B(\pi \cdot x)\\
=\ &\{\text{by (6.16)}\}\\
&f(\pi \cdot x)\\
=\ &\{\text{since } f \text{ is equivariant}\}\\
&\pi \cdot (f\,x)\\
=\ &\{\text{by (6.15)}\}\\
&I_*Y\,i\,(f\,x)\\
=\ &\{\text{by (6.16)}\}\\
&I_*Y\,i\,((I_*f)_A\,x)\,.
\end{aligned}$$

It is immediate from (6.16) that $I_*\text{id}_X = \text{id}_{I_*X}$ and $I_*(g \circ f) = (I_*g) \circ (I_*f)$. So we get a functor $I_* : \mathbf{Nom} \to [\mathbf{I}, \mathbf{Set}]$.

Lemma 6.6 *The functor* $I_* : \mathbf{Nom} \to [\mathbf{I}, \mathbf{Set}]$ *is:*

- faithful: *if* $f, f' : X \to Y$ *in* **Nom** *and* $I_*f = I_*f'$, *then* $f = f'$;
- full: *if* $\alpha : I_*X \to I_*Y$ *in* $[\mathbf{I}, \mathbf{Set}]$, *then* $\alpha = I_*f$ *for some* $f : X \to Y$ *in* **Nom**.

Proof Given $f, f' : X \to Y$ in **Nom** with $I_*f = I_*f'$, then for each $x \in X$, by (6.16) we have

$$f\,x = (I_*f)_{\text{supp}\,x}\,x = (I_*f')_{\text{supp}\,x}\,x = f'x\,.$$

So U is faithful.

Given $\alpha : I_* X \to I_* Y$ in $[\mathbf{I}, \mathbf{Set}]$, define a function $f : X \to Y$ by mapping each $x \in X$ to $\alpha_{\mathrm{supp}\,x}\, x$. For each $\pi \in \mathrm{Perm}\,\mathbb{A}$ and $x \in \mathbb{A}$, recalling that $\pi \cdot (supp\,x) = \mathrm{supp}(\pi \cdot x)$ (Proposition 2.11), we get a morphism $i : \mathrm{supp}\,x \to \mathrm{supp}(\pi \cdot x)$ in $\mathbf{I}$ given by $\lambda(a \in \mathrm{supp}\,x) \to \pi\,a$. Then the naturality property (6.13) of α gives $\alpha_{\mathrm{supp}(\pi \cdot x)}(I_* X\, i\, x) = I_* Y\, i\,(\alpha_{\mathrm{supp}\,x}\, x)$; so $f(\pi \cdot x) = \alpha_{\mathrm{supp}(\pi \cdot x)}(\pi \cdot x) = \alpha_{\mathrm{supp}(\pi \cdot x)}(I_* X\, i\, x) = I_* Y\, i\,(\alpha_{\mathrm{supp}\,x}\, x) = \pi \cdot (\alpha_{\mathrm{supp}\,x}\, x) = \pi \cdot (f\, x)$. Therefore f is an equivariant function. We claim that this $f : X \to Y$ in $\mathbf{Nom}$ satisfies $\alpha = I_* f$. For if $A \in \mathbf{I}$ and $x \in I_* X A$, letting $i : \mathrm{supp}\,x \to A$ be the morphism of $\mathbf{I}$ given by the inclusion $\mathrm{supp}\,x \subseteq A$, by naturality of α we have $\alpha_A(I_* X\, i\, x) = I_* Y\, i\,(\alpha_{\mathrm{supp}\,x}\, x)$; so $\alpha_A\, x = \alpha_A(\mathrm{id} \cdot x) = \alpha_A(I_* X\, i\, x) = I_* Y\, i\,(\alpha_{\mathrm{supp}\,x}\, x) = \mathrm{id} \cdot (\alpha_{\mathrm{supp}\,x}\, x) = \alpha_{\mathrm{supp}\,x}\, x = f\, x = (I_* f)_A\, x$. $\square$

Lemma 6.7 *The functor $I_* : \mathbf{Nom} \to [\mathbf{I}, \mathbf{Set}]$ has a left adjoint, which we denote by $I^* : [\mathbf{I}, \mathbf{Set}] \to \mathbf{Nom}$.*

Proof Given $F \in [\mathbf{I}, \mathbf{Set}]$, restricting F to inclusion functions $A \hookrightarrow B$ (where $A, B \in \mathbf{I}$ and $A \subseteq B$) we get a directed family of sets and functions; let $I^* F$ be its colimit. Thus $I^* F$ is the quotient

$$I^* F \triangleq \{(A, x) \mid A \in \mathbf{I} \wedge x \in F A\}/\sim , \tag{6.17}$$

where $\sim$ is the equivalence relation that relates (A, x) and (A', x') if for some $B \supseteq A \cup A'$ it is the case that $F(A \hookrightarrow B)x = F(A' \hookrightarrow B)x'$. We will write $[A, x]$ for the equivalence class of (A, x).

Given $\pi \in \mathrm{Perm}\,\mathbb{A}$ and $A \in \mathbf{I}$, we write $\pi|_A : A \to \pi \cdot A$ for the morphism of $\mathbf{I}$ given by restricting π to A. If $F(A \hookrightarrow B)x = F(A' \hookrightarrow B)x'$, then by (6.15) and functoriality of F we have $F(\pi \cdot A \hookrightarrow \pi \cdot B)(F\, \pi|_A\, x) = F(\pi|_B)(F(A \hookrightarrow B)x) = F(\pi|_B)(F(A' \hookrightarrow B)x') = F(\pi \cdot A' \hookrightarrow \pi \cdot B)(F\, \pi|_{A'}\, x')$. Therefore $(A, x) \sim (A', x') \Rightarrow (\pi \cdot A, F\, \pi|_A\, x) \sim (\pi \cdot A', F\, \pi|_{A'}\, x')$. So we get a well defined action of $\mathrm{Perm}\,\mathbb{A}$ on $I^* F$ by defining

$$\pi \cdot [A, x] \triangleq [\pi \cdot A, F\, \pi|_A\, x]. \tag{6.18}$$

Furthermore, if $(\forall a \in A)\, \pi\, a = a$, then $\pi \cdot A = A$ and $\pi|_A = \mathrm{id}_A$; so $\pi \cdot [A, x] = [\pi \cdot A, F\, \pi|_A\, x] = [A, F\, \mathrm{id}_A\, x] = [A, x]$. Hence A supports $[A, x]$ with respect to this action. Therefore $I^* F$ is a nominal set.

Since $\mathrm{supp}\,[A, x] \subseteq A$, we have that $[A, x] \in I_*(I^* F) A$. So we get a function $(\eta_F)_A : F A \to I_*(I^* F) A$ mapping each $x \in F A$ to

$$(\eta_F)_A\, x \triangleq [A, x]. \tag{6.19}$$

It is not hard to see that these functions are natural in A and thus for each $F \in [\mathbf{I}, \mathbf{Set}]$ we get a natural transformation $\eta_F : F \to I_*(I^* F)$. We claim that this has the universal property needed for I^*F to be the value of the left adjoint to I_* at F, namely that given any nominal set X and natural transformation α as shown:

$$
\begin{array}{c}
F \xrightarrow{\;\eta_F\;} I_*(I^*F) \\[2pt]
\quad\searrow_{\alpha} \quad\;\; \Big| I_*\hat{\alpha} \\[2pt]
\qquad\qquad I_*X
\end{array}
\tag{6.20}
$$

there is a unique equivariant function $\hat{\alpha} : I^*F \to X$ making the above diagram commute. Indeed there can only be one such $\hat{\alpha}$, since if (6.20) does commute, then for any $[A, x] \in I^*F$

$$
\begin{aligned}
&\hat{\alpha}\,[A, x] \\
=\ & \{\text{by (6.16), since } [A, x] \in I_*(I^*F)\,A\,\} \\
&(I_*\hat{\alpha})_A[A, x] \\
=\ & \{\text{by (6.19)}\} \\
&(I_*\hat{\alpha})_A((\eta_F)_A\, x) \\
=\ & \{\text{since } \alpha_A = (I_*\hat{\alpha})_A \circ (\eta_F)_A\} \\
&\alpha_A\, x\,.
\end{aligned}
$$

So one just has to check that the mapping $(A, x) \mapsto \alpha_A\, x$ induces a well defined equivariant function $I^*F \to X$. But if $(A, x) \sim (A', x')$ is witnessed by $F(A \hookrightarrow B)x = F(A' \hookrightarrow B)x'$, then

$$
\begin{aligned}
&\alpha_A\, x \\
=\ & \\
&\text{id} \cdot (\alpha_A\, x) \\
=\ & \{\text{by (6.15)}\} \\
&I_*X(A \hookrightarrow B)(\alpha_A\, x) \\
=\ & \{\text{by naturality of } \alpha\} \\
&\alpha_B(F(A \hookrightarrow B)\, x) \\
=\ & \{\text{since } F(A \hookrightarrow B)x = F(A' \hookrightarrow B)x'\} \\
&\alpha_B(F(A' \hookrightarrow B)\, x') \\
=\ & \ \cdots \\
&\alpha_{A'}\, x'
\end{aligned}
$$

and for any $\pi \in \text{Perm}\,A$

$$\pi \cdot (\hat{\alpha}[A, x])$$
$$=$$
$$\pi \cdot (\alpha_A\, x)$$
$$= \quad \{\text{by (6.15)}\}$$
$$I_* X\, \pi|_A\, (\alpha_A\, x)$$
$$= \quad \{\text{by naturality of } \alpha\}$$
$$\alpha_{\pi \cdot A}(F\, \pi|_A\, x)$$
$$=$$
$$\hat{\alpha}[\pi \cdot A, F\, \pi|_A\, x]$$
$$= \quad \{\text{by (6.18)}\}$$
$$\hat{\alpha}(\pi \cdot [A, x]). \qquad \qquad \square$$

Theorem 6.8 **Nom** *is equivalent to the full subcategory* **Sch** *of* [**I**, **Set**] *whose objects are the functors* **I** → **Set** *that preserve pullbacks.*

Proof In view of Lemma 6.6, it suffices to show that **Sch** is the essential image of $I_* : \mathbf{Nom} \to [\mathbf{I}, \mathbf{Set}]$. Pullbacks in **I** are created by the inclusion of **I** into **Set**. Given such a pullback

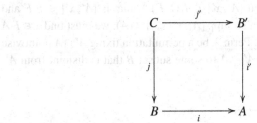

it factors as follows:

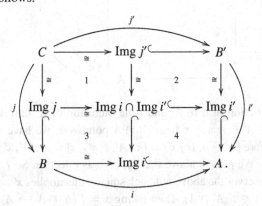

The pullback squares 1, 2 and 3 are automatically preserved by any functor, because of the presence of isomorphisms ($\cong$). Thus a functor $\mathbf{I} \to \mathbf{Set}$ preserves pullbacks iff it preserves pullback of the special form 4, given by intersection of subsets:

$$
\begin{array}{ccc}
B \cap B' & \hookrightarrow & B' \\
\big\uparrow & & \big\uparrow \\
B & \hookrightarrow & A\,.
\end{array}
\qquad (6.21)
$$

Given $X \in \mathbf{Nom}$, definition (6.15) together with the fact that supports are closed under intersection (Proposition 2.3) imply that $I_*X \in [\mathbf{I}, \mathbf{Set}]$ preserves such pullbacks. Conversely, if $F \in [\mathbf{I}, \mathbf{Set}]$ preserves pullbacks, we will show that the unit $\eta_F : F \to I_*(I^*F)$ of the adjunction in Lemma 6.7 is an isomorphism, that is, for each $A \in \mathbf{I}$ the function $(\eta_F)_A : FA \to I_*(I^*F)A$ is a bijection.

First note that since F preserves pullbacks, it also preserves monomorphisms. Thus each $F(A \hookrightarrow B) : FA \to FB$ is injective and hence by definition of $\sim$, $(A, x) \sim (A, x')$ implies $x = x'$. Therefore if $(\eta_F)_A\, x = (\eta_F)_A\, x'$, that is $[A, x] = [A, x']$, then $x = x'$. So each $(\eta_F)_A$ is injective. To see that it is also surjective, suppose given $[A', x'] \in I_*(I^*F)A$, that is $[A', x'] \in I^*F$ and $\operatorname{supp} [A', x'] \subseteq A$ (and hence also $\operatorname{supp}[A', x'] \subseteq A' \cap A$); we must find $x \in FA$ with $[A, x] = [A', x']$. Let $\pi \in \operatorname{Perm} \mathbb{A}$ be a permutation fixing $A' \cap A$ pointwise and moving the elements of $A' - A$ to some subset B that is disjoint from A'. So we get a pullback

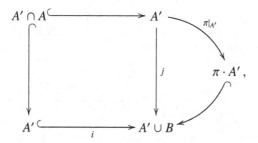

with j the restriction of π to A' and i the inclusion of A' into $A' \cup B$. Since $\operatorname{supp}[A', x'] \subseteq A' \cap A$ and π fixes $A' \cap A$ pointwise, we have $\pi \cdot [A', x'] = [A', x']$. Therefore $[A' \cup B, F\, j\, x'] = [\pi \cdot A', F\, \pi|_{A'}\, x] = \pi \cdot [A', x'] = [A', x'] = [A' \cup B, F\, i\, x']$. We proved above that $(\eta_F)_{A' \cup B}$ is injective. So $F\, j\, x' = F\, i\, x'$; and since F preserves the above pullback square, this implies $x' = F(A' \cap A \hookrightarrow A')y$ for some $y \in F(A' \cap A)$. Then taking $x = F(A' \cap A \hookrightarrow A)y \in FA$, we have $F(A \hookrightarrow A' \cup A)x = F(A \hookrightarrow A' \cup A)(F(A' \cap A \hookrightarrow A)y) = F(A' \hookrightarrow$

$A' \cup A)(F(A' \cap A \hookrightarrow A')y) = F(A' \hookrightarrow A' \cup A)x'$, so that $(A, x) \sim (A', x')$. Thus $x \in F A$ is mapped to $[A', x']$ by $(\eta_F)_A$, as required. □

Remark 6.9 Note that $\mathbf{I}$ is equivalent to the category **Inj** whose objects are finite ordinals $n = \{0, \ldots, n-1\}$ ($n \in \mathbb{N}$) and whose morphisms are all injective functions. Therefore, **Sch** is equivalent to the full subcategory of $[\mathbf{Inj}, \mathbf{Set}]$ given by pullback preserving functors. This is known as the *Schanuel topos*. It is a (Grothendieck) topos because the condition that $F \in [\mathbf{Inj}, \mathbf{Set}]$ preserve pullbacks can be shown to be equivalent to satisfying the sheaf condition for the coverage on **Inj** given by singleton families; see Johnstone (2002, examples 2.1.11(h)).

Remark 6.10 For an alternative proof of Theorem 6.8 making use of a notion of support for objects of the Schanuel topos, see Gadducci *et al.* (2006, section 3).

6.4 Named sets

The notion of 'named set' was introduced by Montanari and Pistore (2000) in their work on the π-calculus and HD automata. A category of named sets was subsequently shown to be equivalent to **Nom** independently by Gadducci *et al.* (2006) and Staton (2007). From the perspective of this equivalence, named sets provide a way of presenting the orbit-finite nominal sets from Chapter 5 in terms of completely finite data structures. We describe this equivalence of categories using the definition of named sets and their morphisms from Gadducci *et al.* (2006, section 4).

Definition 6.11 A *named set* (Q, A, G) is specified by the following data:

- A set Q.
- A Q-indexed family $A = (A_q \mid q \in Q)$ of finite subsets of $\mathbb{A}$.
- A Q-indexed family $G = (G_q \mid q \in Q)$ of groups G_q of permutations of A_q (in other words each G_q is a subgroup of $\mathrm{Sym}\, A_q$).

A morphism of named sets $(f, I) : (Q, A, G) \to (R, B, H)$ is specified by the following data:

- A function $f : Q \to R$.
- A Q-indexed family $I = (I_q \subseteq \mathbf{I}(B_{fq}, A_q) \mid q \in Q)$ of sets of injective

functions satisfying the following conditions for each $q \in Q$:

$$I_q \neq \emptyset, \tag{6.22}$$

$$(\forall g \in G_q, i \in I_q, h \in H_{fq})\, g \circ i \circ h \in I_q, \tag{6.23}$$

$$(\forall i, i' \in I_q)(\exists h \in H_{fq})\, i' = i \circ h. \tag{6.24}$$

The composition of morphisms

$$(Q, A, G) \xrightarrow{(f, I)} (R, B, H) \xrightarrow{(f', I')} (S, C, K)$$

is well defined by

$$(f', I') \circ (f, I) \triangleq (f' \circ f, (\{i \circ i' \mid i \in I_q \wedge i' \in I'_{f_q}\} \mid q \in Q)), \tag{6.25}$$

which is associative and has identities given by

$$\mathrm{id}_{(I, A, G)} \triangleq (\mathrm{id}_Q, (G_q \mid q \in Q)) \tag{6.26}$$

(noting that $G_q \subseteq \mathbf{I}(A_q, A_q)$ satisfies (6.22)–(6.24), because it is a subgroup of Sym A_q). So we get a category of named sets and their morphisms, denoted by **Nset**.

Intuitively, a named set consists of some states $q \in Q$ that each involve finitely many names A_q in their make up, in a way that is captured by a group G_q of symmetries of those names. The definition of a morphism between named sets is less intuitive, but becomes clearer in light of the following characterization (Lemma 6.12) of equivariant functions between atomic nominal sets.

Recall from Theorem 5.13 that up to isomorphism each atomic nominal set (Definition 5.5) is of the form coset $\overline{G}$ for some subgroup G of Sym A with $A \in P_f\, \mathbb{A}$. Given another such, say coset $\overline{H}$, where H is a subgroup of Sym B and $B \in P_f\, \mathbb{A}$, define a binary relation on the set $\mathbf{I}(B, A)$ of injective functions from B to A as follows:

$$\sim_{G,H}\, \subseteq \mathbf{I}(B, A) \times \mathbf{I}(B, A),$$
$$i \sim_{G,H} i' \triangleq (\forall g \in G)(\exists h \in H)\, g \circ i' = i \circ h. \tag{6.27}$$

It is not hard to see that $\sim_{G,H}$ is a partial equivalence relation on $\mathbf{I}(B, A)$; in other words it is a symmetric and transitive relation. So $\sim_{G,H}$ restricts to an equivalence relation on $\{i \in \mathbf{I}(B, A) \mid i \sim_{G,H} i\}$. We will write the corresponding quotient set as

$$\mathbf{I}(B, A)/\sim_{G,H}. \tag{6.28}$$

It is straightforward to see that the elements of this quotient set are the subsets

$I \subseteq \mathbf{I}(B, A)$ satisfying the three properties used in (6.22)–(6.24):

$$I \neq \emptyset, \tag{6.29}$$

$$(\forall g \in G, i \in I, h \in H)\ g \circ i \circ h \in I, \tag{6.30}$$

$$(\forall i, i' \in I)(\exists h \in H)\ i' = i \circ h. \tag{6.31}$$

Lemma 6.12 *There is a bijection*

$$\mathbf{Nom}(\mathrm{coset}\,\overline{G}, \mathrm{coset}\,\overline{H}) \cong \mathbf{I}(B, A)/{\sim}_{G,H}. \tag{6.32}$$

Under this bijection the identity on $\mathrm{coset}\,\overline{G}$ *corresponds to* $\overline{G} \in \mathbf{I}(A, A)/{\sim}_{G,G}$; *and if* $f \in \mathbf{Nom}(\mathrm{coset}\,\overline{G}, \mathrm{coset}\,\overline{H})$ *and* $f' \in \mathbf{Nom}(\mathrm{coset}\,\overline{H}, \mathrm{coset}\,\overline{K})$ *correspond to* $I \in \mathbf{I}(B, A)/{\sim}_{G,H}$ *and* $I' \in \mathbf{I}(C, B)/{\sim}_{H,K}$ *respectively, then* $f' \circ f$ *corresponds to* $I \circ I' \triangleq \{i \circ i' \mid i \in I \wedge i' \in I'\}$.

Proof Given $f \in \mathbf{Nom}(\mathrm{coset}\,\overline{G}, \mathrm{coset}\,\overline{H})$ and $\pi \in \mathrm{Perm}\,\mathbb{A}$, if $f\overline{G} = \pi\overline{H}$, then

$$\pi \cdot B$$
$$= \quad \{\text{by Lemma 5.8}\}$$
$$\mathrm{supp}\,\pi\overline{H}$$
$$=$$
$$\mathrm{supp}\,(f\overline{G})$$
$$\subseteq \quad \{\text{by Lemma 2.12}\}$$
$$\mathrm{supp}\,\overline{G}$$
$$= \quad \{\text{by Lemma 5.8}\}$$
$$A$$

and hence $\pi|_B \in \mathbf{I}(B, A)$. So for each $f \in \mathbf{Nom}(\mathrm{coset}\,\overline{G}, \mathrm{coset}\,\overline{H})$

$$\theta f \triangleq \{\pi|_B \mid f\overline{G} = \pi\overline{H}\}$$

is a subset of $\mathbf{I}(B, A)$; and it is not hard to see that it has properties (6.29)–(6.31). Therefore we get a function

$$\theta : \mathbf{Nom}(\mathrm{coset}\,\overline{G}, \mathrm{coset}\,\overline{H}) \to \mathbf{I}(B, A)/{\sim}_{G,H}.$$

The function θ is injective, because if $\theta f_1 = \theta f_2$, then choosing $\pi_1, \pi_2 \in \mathrm{Perm}\,\mathbb{A}$ such that $f_i\overline{G} = \pi_i\overline{H}$ for $i = 1, 2$, we have $\pi_1|_B \sim_{G,H} \pi_2|_B$. Therefore $\pi_2|_B = \pi_1|_B \circ h$ for some $h \in H$; hence $\pi_2^{-1} \circ \pi_1 \in \overline{H}$ and $f_1\overline{G} = \pi_1\overline{H} = \pi_2\overline{H} = f_2\overline{G}$. So $f_1 = f_2$ by Proposition 5.11.

The function θ is also surjective. To see this, suppose that $i \in \mathbf{I}(B, A)$ satisfies $i \sim_{G,H} i$, that is

$$(\forall g \in G)(\exists h \in H)\ g \circ i = i \circ h. \tag{6.33}$$

By the homogeneity lemma (Lemma 1.14), we can find $\pi \in \mathrm{Perm}\,\mathbb{A}$ with

$\pi|_B = i$ and $\operatorname{supp} \pi \subseteq B \cup A$. Then we can apply Proposition 5.11 with $X = \operatorname{coset} \overline{G}$, $Y = \operatorname{coset} \overline{H}$, $x = \overline{G}$ and $y = \pi \overline{H}$; for $\operatorname{supp} y = \pi \cdot B = iB \subseteq A$ and $\operatorname{stab}_f x \subseteq \operatorname{stab} y$ holds because of (6.33). So by the proposition there is $f \in$ **Nom**$(\operatorname{coset} \overline{G}, \operatorname{coset} \overline{H})$ with $f\overline{G} = \pi \overline{H}$; in particular θf is the $\sim_{G,H}$-equivalence class of $\pi|_B = i$.

Finally, the facts that $\theta \operatorname{id}_{\operatorname{coset} \overline{G}} = \overline{G}$ and that $\theta(f' \circ f) = (\theta f) \circ (\theta f')$ follow easily from the definition of θ. □

As noted by Staton (2007, section 5.1.1), the step from Lemma 6.12 to the equivalence of **Nom** with **Nset** is provided by the construction of the free co-product completion of a (small) category.

Definition 6.13 Given a small category **C**, the category Fam **C** has:

- objects that are set-indexed families $(C_q \mid q \in Q)$ of objects of **C** (thus $Q \in$ **Set** and $C_q \in$ **C** for each $q \in Q$);
- morphisms $(C_q \mid q \in Q) \to (D_r \mid r \in R)$ are pairs $(f, (i_q \mid q \in Q))$ where $f \in$ **Set**(Q, R) and $i_q \in$ **C**(C_q, D_{fq}) for each $q \in Q$.

The composition of morphisms

$$(C_q \mid q \in Q) \xrightarrow{(f,(i_q \mid q \in Q))} (D_r \mid r \in R) \xrightarrow{(f',(i'_r \mid r \in R))} (E_s \mid s \in S)$$

is $(f' \circ f, (i'_{fq} \circ i_q \mid q \in Q))$; and the identity morphism for $(C_q \mid q \in Q)$ is $(\operatorname{id}_Q, (\operatorname{id}_{C_q} \mid q \in Q))$.

It is not hard to see that Fam **C** has small coproducts (given by disjoint union of families) and that there is a functor from **C** to Fam **C** (sending each object of **C** to a one-element family). Indeed Fam **C** is universal with these two proper-ties (in an up-to-equivalence sense appropriate to bicategories). However, for our purposes we need the following categorical characterization of categories of the form Fam **C**.

Lemma 6.14 *Suppose* **S** *is a locally small category with small coproducts. Suppose that* **C** *is a set of objects of* **S** *satisfying:*

(i) *For each* $C \in$ **C**, *the functor* **S**$(C, \_) :$ **S** $\to$ **Set** *preserves small coproducts.*

(ii) *Every object of* **S** *is isomorphic to the coproduct of a set of objects in* **C**.

Then regarding **C** *as a full subcategory of* **S**, *Fam* **C** *and* **S** *are equivalent cat-egories.*

Proof Taking coproducts in **S** gives a functor $\coprod$: Fam **C** → **S**, which is essentially surjective by property (ii) and is full and faithful because

$$\mathbf{S}(\coprod(C_q \mid q \in Q), \coprod(D_r \mid r \in R))$$
$$\cong \{\text{universal property of coproducts}\}$$
$$\textstyle\prod_{q \in Q} \mathbf{S}(C_q, \coprod(D_r \mid r \in R))$$
$$\cong \{\text{by property (i)}\}$$
$$\textstyle\prod_{q \in Q} \coprod_{r \in R} \mathbf{S}(C_q, D_r)$$
$$\cong \{\text{dependently typed choice, applied in Set}\}$$
$$\textstyle\coprod_{f \in R^Q} \prod_{q \in Q} \mathbf{S}(C_q, D_{fq})$$
$$\cong \{\text{definition of Fam } \mathbf{C}\}$$
$$\text{Fam } \mathbf{C}((C_q \mid q \in Q), (D_r \mid r \in R)).$$

□

Theorem 6.15 **Nom** *and* **Nset** *are equivalent categories.*

Proof Combining the definition of **Nset** (Definition 6.11) with Lemma 6.12, we have that it is equivalent to Fam **G**, where **G** is the small full subcategory of **Nom** given by objects of the form coset $\overline{G}$ where G is a subgroup of Sym A for some $A \in P_f \mathbb{A}$. So it just remains to see that Fam **G** is equivalent to **Nom**.

We noted in Section 5.2 that every nominal set X is isomorphic to a small coproduct of atomic nominal sets, namely the disjoint union $\sum_{O \in \Pi_0 X} O$. Note that for any atomic nominal set O, **Nom**$(O, \_)$: **Nom** → **Set** preserves coproducts, because the latter are given by disjoint union (Section 2.2) and any orbit in a disjoint union $\sum_{i \in I} X_i$ must be contained in a single summand X_i. So in view of Theorem 5.13, Lemma 6.14 implies that **Nom** is indeed equivalent to Fam **G**. □

Exercises

6.1 Show that under the equivalence of **Nom** with the Schanuel topos (Remark 6.9):

(a) the nominal set $\mathbb{A}^{\#n}$ (5.8) corresponds to the representable functor **Inj**$(n, \_) \in [\mathbf{Inj}, \mathbf{Set}]$;

(b) the name abstraction functor $[\mathbb{A}](\_)$: **Nom** → **Nom** from Chapter 4 corresponds with the 'shift functor' δ, which is given on objects by $\delta F n = F(n+1)$.

6.2 The category **Nom** is defined relative to some fixed infinite set $\mathbb{A}$. At the beginning of Chapter 2 we took this to be a countably infinite set, but countability does not affect the category-theoretic properties of nominal sets. To see this, writing **Nom**(A) to indicate the dependence upon the particular set A, show that **Nom**(A) and **Nom**(A′) are equivalent categories for any two infinite sets A and A′. [Hint: combine Remark 6.9 with the fact that the proof of Theorem 6.8 does not depend upon the cardinality of A.]

PART TWO

APPLICATIONS

7

Inductive and coinductive definitions

In this chapter we consider the implications of the theory of nominal sets for a fundamental technique in programming language semantics – the use of inductive and coinductive definitions of subsets of a given set. Such definitions are often specified via a set of rules. Taking into account equivariance and, more generally, finite support properties of the rules can be very useful when reasoning about the properties of such rule-based definitions.

7.1 Inductively defined subsets

A *rule* over a set X is a pair (H, c), where $H \subseteq X$ is the rule's *hypotheses* and $c \in X$ is its *conclusion*. Given a set of rules $R \subseteq PX \times X$, we say that a subset $S \subseteq X$ is *closed* under the rules in R if

$$H \subseteq S \Rightarrow c \in S \tag{7.1}$$

holds for all $(H, c) \in R$. Note that the intersection of a collection of such subsets is another such. Therefore

$$\bigcap \{S \in PX \mid S \text{ is closed under the rules in } R\} \tag{7.2}$$

is the smallest (with respect to inclusion) subset of X that is closed under the rules in R. We call it the *inductively defined subset* of X specified by the set of rules R.

A rule (H, c) over a set X is *finitary* if its set of hypotheses H is finite. When a subset S is inductively defined by a set R of finitary rules, it is conventional to display an individual rule $(H, c) \in R$ in the form

$$\text{LABEL} \; \frac{h_1 \in S \; \cdots \; h_n \in S}{c \in S},$$

113

where $h_1, \ldots, h_n$ are the distinct elements of H. Most of the inductively defined subsets we use in this book are specified by sets of finitary rules. However, it is rarely the case that the set R is itself finite. So we usually describe infinite sets of finitary rules 'schematically' using a finite set of *scheme* of the following form:

$$\text{LABEL} \, \frac{h_1(\vec{x}) \in S \quad \cdots \quad h_n(\vec{x}) \in S \qquad side\_condition(\vec{x})}{c(\vec{x}) \in S}. \qquad (7.3)$$

Here the $h_i(\vec{x})$ and $c(\vec{x})$ are expressions in some metalanguage that denote elements of X when the meta-variables $\vec{x} = x_1, \ldots, x_n$ are suitably instantiated; and $side\_condition(\vec{x})$ is an expression in the metalanguage that denotes a boolean when the $\vec{x}$ are instantiated. Then the scheme denotes the set of rules that we can get by instantiating the meta-variables in such a way that $side\_condition(\vec{x})$ becomes true.

Example 7.1   We gave an inductive definition of the relation of α-equivalence $=_\alpha \, \subseteq \Lambda \times \Lambda$ in Section 4.1 that used the above notational conventions for schematic rules:

$$\text{VAR} \, \frac{}{a =_\alpha a} \qquad \text{APP} \, \frac{t_1 =_\alpha t_2 \quad t_1' =_\alpha t_2'}{t_1 \, t_1' =_\alpha t_2 \, t_2'} \qquad \text{LAM} \, \frac{(a_1 \, a) \cdot t_1 =_\alpha (a_2 \, a) \cdot t_2 \qquad a \notin var(a_1, t_1, a_2, t_2)}{\lambda a_1.t_1 =_\alpha \lambda a_2.t_2}. \qquad (7.4)$$

For example, the rule scheme LAM stands for the infinite collection of rules of the form

$$(\{((a_1 \, a) \cdot t_1, (a_2 \, a) \cdot t_2)\}, (\lambda a_1.t_1, \lambda a_2.t_2))$$

as t_1, t_2 range over raw λ-terms, a, a_1, a_2 over atomic names, and a does not occur in (a_1, t_1, a_2, t_2).

7.2 Rule induction

The construction in (7.2) of the subset inductively defined by a set of rules leads immediately to the following proof principle:

Rule Induction Principle   *If S is the subset of X inductively defined by a set of rules R, then given $P \in \mathrm{P}X$, to prove $S \subseteq P$ it suffices to prove that P is closed under each of the rules in R.*

When R is specified by a set of rule schemes (7.3) and P is specified by some property φ of elements of X, the Rule Induction Principle says that $(\forall x \in S)$ $\varphi(x)$ holds if for each rule scheme in the inductive definition one can prove

$$(\forall \vec{x})\ side\_condition(\vec{x}) \wedge \varphi(h_1(\vec{x})) \wedge \cdots \wedge \varphi(h_n(\vec{x})) \Rightarrow \varphi(c(\vec{x})).$$

As a corollary of Rule Induction we have the following inversion principle:

Rule Inversion Principle *If S is the subset of X inductively defined by a set of rules R, then for every element $x \in S$, there is a rule $(H, c) \in R$ with $H \subseteq S$ and $c = x$.*

Proof We use the Rule Induction Principle to show that

$$P \triangleq \{c \in X \mid (\exists H)\ (H, c) \in R \wedge H \subseteq S\}$$

contains S. Note that since S is closed under the rules in R, by definition of P we have $c \in P \Rightarrow c \in S$. So if $(H, c) \in R$ satisfies $H \subseteq P$, then $H \subseteq S$ and hence by definition of P, $c \in P$. Therefore P is indeed closed under each rule in R and so contains S. $\qquad\qquad\square$

Rule-based inductive definitions of subsets abound in the *structural* approach to operational semantics of programming languages (Plotkin, 1981). In that setting, the elements of the set X usually have some structure related to the programming language in question and which is reflected in the collection of rules. Then when applying the above Rule Inversion Principle, precisely which rules (H, c) have their conclusion equal to any given $x \in S$ is determined by the structure of x. In this case one speaks of *syntax-directed* rules.

Example 7.2 The relation of α-equivalence between raw λ-terms is inductively defined in Example 7.1 by rule schemes that are syntax-directed, because for each syntactic form of raw λ-term (variables, applications and λ-abstractions) there is exactly one rule scheme whose conclusion mentions that form. So, for example, if $\lambda a_1.t_1 =_\alpha t$ holds, when we apply the Rule Inversion Principle we can conclude that $t = \lambda a_2.t_2$, for some a_2, t_2 and some $a \notin var(a_1, t_1, a_2, t_2)$ with $(a_1\ a) \cdot t_1 =_\alpha (a_2\ a) \cdot t_2$.

7.3 Equivariant rules

Suppose we have a set R of rules on a set X equipped with a G-action, for some group G. Using the definitions from Chapter 1, the group action on X extends to one on rules and on sets of rules:

$$g \cdot (H, c) = (g \cdot H, g \cdot c) = (\{g \cdot h \mid h \in H\}, g \cdot c)$$
$$g \cdot R = \{(g \cdot H, g \cdot c) \mid (H, c) \in R\}.$$

We say that R is an *equivariant set of rules* if it is an equivariant subset of the G-set $P X \times X$; in other words, for all $g \in G$, if $(H, c) \in R$, then $(g \cdot H, g \cdot c) \in R$.

When G is the group Perm $\mathbb{A}$ of finite permutations of atomic names, we can generalize from equivariant rule sets to ones that possess a support in the sense of Chapter 2. In view of Lemma 2.24, a set $A \subseteq \mathbb{A}$ of atomic names supports a rule set R if for all $\pi \in$ Perm $\mathbb{A}$

$$((\forall a \in A) \, \pi \, a = a) \Rightarrow (\forall (H, c) \in R) \, (\pi \cdot H, \pi \cdot c) \in R. \qquad (7.5)$$

The following theorem implies that if a set of rules is finitely supported, then so is the associated inductively defined subset of X.

Theorem 7.3 *Suppose X is a Perm $\mathbb{A}$-set, $R \subseteq P X \times X$ is a set of rules and $S \subseteq X$ is the subset inductively defined by R. If R is supported by $A \subseteq \mathbb{A}$, then so is S. In particular, if R is an equivariant subset, then so is S.*

Proof Suppose R is supported by $A \subseteq \mathbb{A}$. To see that A also supports S, we apply Lemma 2.24. So suppose $\pi \in$ Perm $\mathbb{A}$ satisfies $(\forall a \in A) \, \pi \, a = a$. We have to show that $\pi \cdot S \subseteq S$, or equivalently, that $S \subseteq \pi^{-1} \cdot S$. To see this it suffices to check that $\pi^{-1} \cdot S$ is closed under the rules in R and hence contains the smallest such subset, S. But if $(H, c) \in R$, then since A supports R, by Lemma 2.24 we have $(\pi \cdot H, \pi \cdot c) \in R$. So if $H \subseteq \pi^{-1} \cdot S$, then $\pi \cdot H \subseteq S$ and since S is closed under the rule $(\pi \cdot H, \pi \cdot c) \in R$, we get $\pi \cdot c \in S$ and hence $c \in \pi^{-1} \cdot S$. So $\pi^{-1} \cdot S$ is indeed closed under the rules in R, as required. The last part of the theorem follows from the first, since as noted in Lemma 2.24, being an equivariant subset is the same as having empty support. □

Remark 7.4 This result also can be proved as a corollary of a more general result for monotone functions on complete lattices; see Section 7.5.

Example 7.5 (CCS) The process calculus CCS (Milner, 1989) provides an example of the above theorem in action: if a set of CCS process definitions is finitely supported, then so is the associated labelled transition system. We use the finitary version of CCS from section 4.2 of Sangiorgi (2011). The set of *processes* is given by the grammar

$$P \in Pr ::= P \mid P \mid P + P \mid \mu.P \mid va \, P \mid 0 \mid K,$$

where $a \in \mathbb{A}$, μ ranges over the set of *actions* given by the grammar

$$\mu \in Act ::= a \mid \bar{a} \mid \tau,$$

and K ranges over a set *Cons* of (recursively defined) *process constants*. Given a relation $D \subseteq Cons \times Act \times Pr$ specifying the behaviour of each process constant, the associated *labelled transition relation* $\mathcal{T}(D) \subseteq Pr \times Act \times Pr$ is inductively defined by the rules schemes shown below, where we write $P \xrightarrow{\mu} P'$ to mean $(P, \mu, P') \in \mathcal{T}(D)$, leaving D implicit, and where in the rule scheme COM, the action $\bar{\mu}$ is defined by

$$\bar{\mu} \triangleq \begin{cases} \bar{a} & \text{if } \mu = a, \\ a & \text{if } \mu = \bar{a}, \\ \tau & \text{if } \mu = \tau. \end{cases}$$

$$\text{PARL} \ \frac{P_1 \xrightarrow{\mu} P_1'}{P_1 \mid P_2 \xrightarrow{\mu} P_1' \mid P_2} \qquad\qquad \text{PARR} \ \frac{P_2 \xrightarrow{\mu} P_2'}{P_1 \mid P_2 \xrightarrow{\mu} P_1 \mid P_2'}$$

$$\text{COM} \ \frac{P_1 \xrightarrow{\mu} P_1' \quad P_2 \xrightarrow{\bar{\mu}} P_2'}{P_1 \mid P_2 \xrightarrow{\tau} P_1' \mid P_2'} \qquad \text{SUML} \ \frac{P_1 \xrightarrow{\mu} P_1'}{P_1 + P_2 \xrightarrow{\mu} P_1'} \qquad \text{SUMR} \ \frac{P_2 \xrightarrow{\mu} P_2'}{P_1 + P_2 \xrightarrow{\mu} P_2'}$$

$$\text{PRE} \ \frac{}{\mu.P \xrightarrow{\mu} P} \qquad \text{RES} \ \frac{P \xrightarrow{\mu} P' \quad \mu \notin \{a, \bar{a}\}}{va\,P \xrightarrow{\mu} va\,P'} \qquad \text{DEF} \ \frac{(K, \mu, P) \in D}{K \xrightarrow{\mu} P} \ .$$

For example, if D contains $(K_1, a_1, a.K_1)$ and $(K_2, a_2, \bar{a}.K_2)$, then $\mathcal{T}(D)$ contains the following labelled transitions:

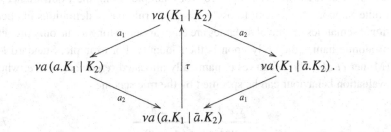

Permutations of $\mathbb{A}$ act on processes and actions as in Example 1.4 and in this way Pr and Act become nominal sets, with $\operatorname{supp} P$ and $\operatorname{supp} \mu$ equal to the set of atomic names occurring in the process $P \in Pr$ and action $\mu \in Act$ (see Example 2.6). Note that the Perm $\mathbb{A}$-action on Pr restricts to a trivial action on process constants; in other words, for all $K \in Cons$, $\pi \cdot K = K$. (This follows from the $n = 0$ case of (1.10), constants being regarded as 0-ary operations.)

Taking X to be the nominal set $Pr \times Act \times Pr$, it is not hard to see that if A supports $D \subseteq Cons \times Act \times Pr$, then the set of rules on X specified by the above rule schemes for CCS is supported by $A \subseteq \mathbb{A}$; and hence by Theorem 7.3, the labelled transition relation $\mathcal{T}(D) \subseteq Pr \times Act \times Pr$ is also supported by A. Therefore if D is finitely supported, then so is $\mathcal{T}(D)$. In particular, if $Cons = \{K_1, \ldots, K_m\}$ is finite and for each $K_i \in Cons$

$$\{(\mu, P) \mid (K_i, \mu, P) \in D\} = \{(\mu_{i,1}, P_{i,1}), \ldots, (\mu_{i,n_i}, P_{i,n_i})\}$$

is finite, so that D amounts to the recursive definition

$$K_1 \;=\; \mu_{1,1}.P_{1,1} + \cdots + \mu_{1,n_1}.P_{1,n_1},$$
$$\vdots$$
$$K_m \;=\; \mu_{m,1}.P_{m,1} + \cdots + \mu_{m,n_m}.P_{m,n_m},$$

then D is finitely supported by $\bigcup_{i=1,\ldots,m, j=1,\ldots,n_i} \mathrm{supp}(\mu_{i,j}.P_{i,j})$.

Remark 7.6 Although we do not do so here, it is semantically natural to consider the name restriction operation $va\,(\_)$ on CCS processes to be a binder and to quotient Pr by the corresponding notion of α-equivalence. Just as for λ-terms, the quotient is again a nominal set, with the least support of an α-equivalence class of processes being the finite set of free names of any of its representatives (see Section 4.1). Alpha-equivalence classes of raw λ-terms and of CCS processes are instances of a general notion of 'nominal algebraic data type' that we develop in Chapter 8.

Example 7.7 (Dynamic allocation) In practice it is usually easy to see from their schematic form whether the rules of an inductive definition are equivariant, or at least finitely supported (for example, using the Equivariance, or Finite Support Principles). Loosely speaking, rule-based definitions in operational semantics that involve names are equivariant so long as the only property of atomic names they rely upon is their identity. For example, Standard ML (Milner *et al.*, 1997) features dynamically allocated *references*, $\mathtt{ref}\,e$, whose evaluation behaviour can be specified by the rule scheme

$$\frac{s, e \Downarrow s', v \qquad a \,\#\, s'}{s, \mathtt{ref}\,e \Downarrow s'(a \mapsto v), a}, \tag{7.6}$$

where s and s' (states) are finite partial functions from names of locations a to values v, and where $s'(a \mapsto v)$ is the state mapping a to v and otherwise acting like s'. The instances of the above scheme form an equivariant subset (with respect to permuting location names), as do the other rule schemes in the definition of Standard ML, and therefore the inductively defined evaluation relation $\Downarrow$ is equivariant.

One says that the location name a in the above scheme is *dynamically allocated*; and all the above rule says about a is that it should be fresh for the current state s' (that is, not in the domain of definition of s' and not free in any of the values in the range of s'). As a result, evaluation is only deterministic up to permuting dynamically allocated location names. One can make evaluation truly deterministic by replacing the above rule scheme with

$$\frac{s, e \Downarrow s', v \qquad a = next(\text{supp } s')}{s, \text{ref } e \Downarrow s'(a \mapsto v), a},$$ (7.7)

where $next : \mathrm{P_f}\, \mathbb{A} \to \mathbb{A}$ is some function mapping each finite set of names A to a name with the property $next\, A \notin A$. (For example, fix a linear order of the set of names and take $next\, A$ to be the first name with respect to the order that is not in A.) However, no such function can be equivariant (see Section 2.7) and as a result the evaluation relation inductively defined using this rule would not be equivariant. Another example of non-equivariant operational semantics occurs in languages with 'pointer arithmetic'. The names of storage locations are taken to be integers upon which arithmetic operations can be carried out; so the meaning of expressions certainly is not invariant under permuting pointer names.

For equivariant sets of rules, Theorem 7.3 gives extra information about the inductively defined subset S that can be exploited in Rule Induction arguments in the following way. The 'induction hypothesis' is some subset $P \subseteq X$ that we wish to show contains the inductively defined one. Usually P is constructed from S using higher-order logic and so the Equivariance Principle tells us that P is equivariant, because S is. This invariance of P under the action of name permutations may be useful for showing that P is closed under the rules. We give a couple of examples to illustrate this technique. Further examples occur in Chapter 8.

Example 7.8 (Transitivity of α-equivalence) The set of rules in Example 7.1 inductively defining the relation of α-equivalence between raw λ-terms is equivariant. For if we apply a permutation to rules derived from the first two schemes in (7.4), clearly another such results; and the same is true for rules derived from the third scheme, because the swapping function is equivariant by Proposition 1.16 and the function var : $\Lambda \to \mathrm{P_f}\, \mathbb{A}$ is equivariant by Proposition 2.11, since var t is the support of a raw λ-term. So by Theorem 7.3, the binary relation $=_\alpha$ inductively defined by (7.4) is equivariant. We will use this fact to give a proof by Rule Induction that $=_\alpha$ is transitive.

Proof Consider $P \triangleq \{(t_1, t_2) \in \Lambda \times \Lambda \mid (\forall t \in \Lambda)\, t_2 =_\alpha t \Rightarrow t_1 =_\alpha t\}$. Note that P is an equivariant subset of $\Lambda \times \Lambda$, because $=_\alpha$ is equivariant. Transitivity of

$=_\alpha$ amounts to showing that P contains $=_\alpha$ and by Rule Induction it suffices to show that P is closed under the rules in (7.4).

Closure under the first rule scheme is trivial, since clearly P is reflexive.

For closure under the second rule scheme, suppose $(t_1, t_2), (t_1', t_2') \in P$. We have to show $(t_1\, t_1', t_2\, t_2') \in P$. So suppose $t_2\, t_2' =_\alpha t$. Then by the Rule Inversion Principle it must be the case that $t = t_3\, t_3'$ for some $t_3, t_3' \in \Lambda$ with $t_2 =_\alpha t_3$ and $t_2' =_\alpha t_3'$. By definition of P, this implies $t_1 =_\alpha t_3$ and $t_1' =_\alpha t_3'$ and hence applying the appropriate rule defining $=_\alpha$, that $t_1\, t_1' =_\alpha t_3\, t_3' = t$. Thus we do indeed have $(t_1\, t_1', t_2\, t_2') \in P$, as required.

For closure under the third rule scheme, suppose

$$((a_1\ a) \cdot t_1, (a_2\ a) \cdot t_2) \in P, \tag{7.8}$$

with $a \notin \mathrm{var}(a_1, t_1, a_2, t_2)$. We have to show that $(\lambda a_1.t_1, \lambda a_2.t_2) \in P$. So suppose $\lambda a_2.t_2 =_\alpha t$. Then by the Rule Inversion Principle it must be the case that $t = \lambda a_3.t_3$ for some a_3 and t_3 for which there exists $a' \notin \mathrm{var}(a_2\, t_2\, a_3\, t_3)$ with

$$(a_2\ a') \cdot t_2 =_\alpha (a_3\ a') \cdot t_3. \tag{7.9}$$

To proceed we really need $a' \notin \mathrm{var}(a_1, t_1)$ as well; and since this may not be the case, we use a permutation to move a' to a fresher name. So pick some $a'' \notin \mathrm{var}(a_1, t_1, a_2, t_2, a_3, t_3, a, a')$. Since $=_\alpha$ is equivariant, applying $(a'\ a'') \cdot {}_-$ to both sides of (7.9), we get

$$(a_2\ a'') \cdot t_2 =_\alpha (a_3\ a'') \cdot t_3. \tag{7.10}$$

Since P is equivariant, applying $(a\ a'') \cdot {}_-$ to (7.8), we get

$$((a_1\ a'') \cdot t_1, (a_2\ a'') \cdot t_2) \in P. \tag{7.11}$$

From (7.10) and (7.11) we get $(a_1\ a'') \cdot t_1 =_\alpha (a_3\ a'') \cdot t_3$; and since $a'' \notin \mathrm{var}(a_1, t_1, a_3, t_3)$ we can apply the third rule scheme defining $=_\alpha$ to deduce that $\lambda a_1.t_1 =_\alpha \lambda a_3.t_3 = t$. Thus we do indeed have $(\lambda a_1.t_1, \lambda a_2.t_2) \in P$, as required. $\qquad\square$

Example 7.9 (Weakening property of type assignment) McKinna and Pollack (1999) note that the use of named bound variables interferes with a simple use of Rule Induction for proving weakening properties of type systems. Taking account of equivariance circumvents the problem. For example, consider the relation

$$\Gamma \vdash e : T \tag{7.12}$$

for assigning simple types T over some collection of ground types G

$$Type \triangleq \{T ::= G \mid T \to T\}$$

to λ-terms

$$e \in \Lambda/=_\alpha = \{[t]_{=_\alpha} \mid t ::= a \mid \lambda a.t \mid t\,t\}$$

where in (7.12), Γ ranges over $\mathbb{A} \rightharpoonup_f Type$, the set of typing environments given by finite partial functions from atomic names to types. When writing elements of $\Lambda/=_\alpha$ we will make use of a common notational convention that blurs the distinction between a raw λ-term t and the α-equivalence class $[t]_{=_\alpha}$ that it determines. So we write:

- a for $[a]_{=_\alpha}$ (where $a \in \mathbb{A}$);
- $e\,e'$ for $[t\,t']_{=_\alpha}$ if $e = [t]_{=_\alpha}$ and $e' = [t']_{=_\alpha}$;
- $\lambda a.e$ for $[\lambda a.t]_{=_\alpha}$ if $e = [t]_{=_\alpha}$.

The type assignment relation (7.12) is inductively defined by the following rule schemes, where in the third scheme, $\Gamma(a : T_1)$ denotes the typing environment that maps a to T_1 and otherwise acts like Γ:

$$\text{VarTy}\ \frac{(a, T) \in \Gamma}{\Gamma \vdash a : T} \qquad \text{AppTy}\ \frac{\Gamma \vdash e : T_1 \to T_2 \quad \Gamma \vdash e' : T_1}{\Gamma \vdash e\,e' : T_2} \qquad \text{LamTy}\ \frac{\Gamma(a : T_1) \vdash e : T_2 \quad a \notin \text{Dom}\,\Gamma}{\Gamma \vdash \lambda a.e : T_1 \to T_2}.$$

It is clear from the form of these schemes that they define an equivariant set of rules. (The action of permutations on λ-terms is as in Section 4.1; the action on simple types is trivial; and the action on typing environments is as in Section 2.8.) So by Theorem 7.3, the type assignment relation is equivariant:

$$\Gamma \vdash e : T \Rightarrow \pi \cdot \Gamma \vdash \pi \cdot e : T. \tag{7.13}$$

We wish to prove the following weakening property by Rule Induction:

$$\Gamma \vdash e : T \wedge a' \notin \text{Dom}\,\Gamma \Rightarrow \Gamma(a' : T') \vdash e : T \tag{7.14}$$

and to do so we must show that

$$P \triangleq \{(\Gamma, e, T) \mid (\forall a', T')\, a' \notin \text{Dom}\,\Gamma \Rightarrow \Gamma(a' : T') \vdash e : T\}$$

is closed under the above rule schemes.

Proof The only difficult case is for the rule scheme LamTy and here we can use the fact that P is an equivariant subset, because of the Equivariance Principle and (7.13). Suppose that

$$(\Gamma(a : T_1), e, T_2) \in P \tag{7.15}$$

with $a \notin \text{Dom}\,\Gamma$. We have to show that $(\Gamma, \lambda a.e, T_1 \to T_2) \in P$, that is, $\Gamma(a' : T') \vdash \lambda a.e : T_1 \to T_2$ holds for any $a' \notin \text{Dom}\,\Gamma$ and any T'. Given any

$a' \notin \mathrm{Dom}\,\Gamma$ it may be that $a' = a$, in which case $a' \in \mathrm{Dom}\,\Gamma(a : T')$ and we cannot apply the defining property of P to (7.15). To avoid this clash we use a permutation to move a 'out of the way'. Picking any $a''\ \#\ (\mathrm{Dom}\,\Gamma, a, a', e)$, since P is equivariant when we apply $(a\ a'') \cdot {}_-$ to (7.15) we get

$$(\Gamma(a'' : T_1), (a\ a'') \cdot e, T_2) \in P \qquad (7.16)$$

(using the fact that $(a\ a'') \cdot \Gamma = \Gamma$, since $a, a''\ \#\ \mathrm{Dom}\,\Gamma = \mathrm{supp}\,\Gamma$). Since $a' \notin \mathrm{Dom}\,\Gamma(a'' : T')$, we can use the definition of P to deduce from (7.16) that $\Gamma(a'' : T_1)(a' : T') \vdash (a\ a'') \cdot e : T_2$. Since $a'' \notin \mathrm{Dom}\,\Gamma(a' : T')$, we can apply the rule scheme LᴀᴍTʏ to this to deduce that $\Gamma(a' : T') \vdash \lambda a''.(a\ a'') \cdot e : T_1 \to T_2$. Note that since $a''\ \#\ (a, e)$, from the definition of $=_\alpha$ we have $\lambda a''.(a\ a'') \cdot e = \lambda a.e$ and hence we do indeed have $\Gamma(a' : T') \vdash \lambda a.e : T_1 \to T_2$, as required. □

Remark 7.10 ('Strong' induction principles)   A pattern emerges from Examples 7.8 and 7.9. Rules that introduce a bound name in their conclusion usually have side-conditions in their hypotheses requiring the name to be sufficiently fresh. In the two examples the schemes Lᴀᴍ and LᴀᴍTʏ give rise to such rules. When reasoning 'bottom up' about a property of inductively defined subsets using the Rule Inversion Principle, we can conclude that some bound name exists satisfying the freshness side-conditions; later, when putting facts together 'top down' using the rules, we may need to know that the property holds not just for *some* bound name, but in fact for *any* name satisfying the freshness side-condition. This 'some/any' feature of reasoning about inductive definitions involving bound names was noted by McKinna and Pollack (1999) and independently by the author and Gabbay (Gabbay, 2000; Gabbay and Pitts, 2002) when they introduced the freshness quantifier $(\mathsf{N}a)\,\varphi$ discussed in Section 3.2.

In the two examples we used Theorem 7.3 to 'freshen up' bound names on the fly using permutations. However, this pattern of reasoning is sufficiently common to justify formalizing it in some way. One such way is to develop a formal language for inductive definitions involving the freshness quantifier; this has led to work on nominal logic programming – see Section 12.3. Instead of using non-standard logical forms, one can stick with ordinary higher-order logic and prove (using the techniques described in this book) a 'strong' induction principle involving universal rather than existential name-quantification in rule hypotheses. This is the approach taken by Urban *et al.* (2007) and implemented in the Nominal package for the Isabelle/HOL interactive theorem prover (Urban, 2008).

7.4 Tarski's fixed-point theorem

A subset inductively defined by a set of rules (Section 7.1) is an instance of the notion of the 'least fixed-point of a monotone function on a complete lattice'. The advantage of this more abstract view of inductive definitions is that it smoothly dualizes to give a notion of coinductively defined subset. In this section we recall briefly the basic notions associated with fixed points of monotone functions; see chapter 3 of Sangiorgi (2011) for a more leisurely introduction. Then we will examine how these concepts interact with the theory of nominal sets.

Definition 7.11   Recall that a *partially ordered set* (*poset*) is a set D equipped with a *partial order*, a binary relation $\sqsubseteq$ on D that is:

- *reflexive*: $(\forall d \in D)\, d \sqsubseteq d$;
- *transitive*: $(\forall d, d', d'' \in D)\, d \sqsubseteq d' \wedge d' \sqsubseteq d'' \Rightarrow d \sqsubseteq d''$;
- *anti-symmetric*: $(\forall d, d' \in D)\, d \sqsubseteq d' \wedge d' \sqsubseteq d \Rightarrow d = d'$.

The poset is a *complete lattice* if every subset $S \in \mathrm{P}D$ possesses a *join* (*least upper bound*), that is, an element $\bigsqcup S$ of D satisfying

$$(\forall d \in D)\, ((\forall d' \in S)\, d' \sqsubseteq d) \Leftrightarrow \bigsqcup S \sqsubseteq d. \tag{7.17}$$

Note that this property determines $\bigsqcup S$ uniquely, because of the anti-symmetric property of $\sqsubseteq$. Furthermore, the existence of all joins of subsets S implies the existence of a *meet* (*greatest lower bound*) $\bigsqcap S$ for each subset $S \in \mathrm{P}D$, satisfying the dual property

$$(\forall d \in D)\, ((\forall d' \in S)\, d \sqsubseteq d') \Leftrightarrow d \sqsubseteq \bigsqcap S. \tag{7.18}$$

(See Exercise 7.1.) If $(D, \sqsubseteq)$ is a poset, we say that a function $F : D \to D$ is *monotone* if it preserves the partial order

$$(\forall d, d' \in D)\, d \sqsubseteq d' \Rightarrow F\,d \sqsubseteq F\,d'. \tag{7.19}$$

An element $d \in D$ is a *pre-fixed-point* of F if it satisfies $F\,d \sqsubseteq d$, a *post-fixed-point* if $d \sqsubseteq F\,d$, and a *fixed-point* if $F\,d = d$.

The following is a very standard result; for a proof, see for example Winskel (1993, section 5.5).

Theorem 7.12 (Tarski's fixed-point theorem)   *For any monotone function $F : D \to D$ on a complete lattice there is an element* $\mathrm{lfp}\,F \in D$ *which is a least pre-fixed-point for F:*

$$\begin{aligned} F(\mathrm{lfp}\,F) \sqsubseteq \mathrm{lfp}\,F\,, \\ (\forall d \in D)\, F\,d \sqsubseteq d \Rightarrow \mathrm{lfp}\,F \sqsubseteq d\,. \end{aligned} \tag{7.20}$$

lfp F *is given by the meet of all pre-fixed-points*

$$\text{lfp } F = \sqcap \{d \in D \mid F\, d \sqsubseteq d\}. \tag{7.21}$$

Furthermore, lfp F *is actually a fixed-point for f and hence it is the* least *fixed-point of F.*   □

For any set X, the binary relation $\subseteq$ of subset inclusion is of course a partial order on the powerset $P\,X$ that makes the latter into a complete lattice, with joins and meets given by union and intersection respectively. Given a set of rules $R \subseteq P\,X \times X$, consider the function

$$\begin{aligned}
&\Phi_R : P\,X \to P\,X, \\
&\Phi_R\, S \triangleq \{x \in X \mid (\exists (H, c) \in R)\ H \subseteq S \wedge c = x\}.
\end{aligned} \tag{7.22}$$

It is easy to see that Φ_R is monotone for $\subseteq$. In fact any monotone function $F : P\,X \to P\,X$ is of the form Φ_R for some set of rules; see Exercise 7.2. Note also that $S \in P\,X$ is closed under the rules in R if and only if S is a pre-fixed-point of Φ_R. So comparing (7.2) with (7.21) we have the following corollary of Theorem 7.12.

Corollary 7.13 *The subset of a set X inductively defined by a set of rules $R \subseteq P\,X \times X$ is equal to the least fixed-point* lfp Φ_R *of the monotone function $\Phi_R : P\,X \to P\,X$ associated with R as in (7.22).*   □

7.5 Equivariant fixed-points

Now we investigate how permutation actions and the notion of support interact with fixed-points of monotone functions. Suppose a poset D is equipped with a G-action for some group G. We call D an *equivariant poset* if $\sqsubseteq$ is an equivariant subset of $D \times D$:

$$(\forall g \in G)(\forall d, d' \in D)\ d \sqsubseteq d' \Rightarrow g \cdot d \sqsubseteq g \cdot d'. \tag{7.23}$$

Note that in this case, since $g \cdot \_ : D \to D$ is a monotone bijection with monotone inverse $g^{-1} \cdot \_ : D \to D$, the action of $g \in G$ preserves any joins or meets that happen to exist in D:

$$g \cdot (\bigsqcup S) = \bigsqcup\{g \cdot d \mid d \in S\} \qquad g \cdot (\bigsqcap S) = \bigsqcap\{g \cdot d \mid d \in S\}. \tag{7.24}$$

When they do all exist, we call D an *equivariant complete lattice*. We are mainly interested in this notion when G is the group Perm $\mathbb{A}$ of finite permutations of the set $\mathbb{A}$ of atomic names.

Proposition 7.14 *Suppose D is a* Perm $\mathbb{A}$-*set that is an equivariant complete lattice and that $F : D \to D$ is a monotone function. If F is supported by $A \subseteq \mathbb{A}$ as an element of the function* Perm $\mathbb{A}$-*set D^D, then its least fixed-point* lfp $F \in D$ *is also supported by A.*

Proof Let $[D, D] \subseteq D^D$ denote the subset of monotone functions. It is an equivariant subset, since $d \sqsubseteq d'$ implies $(\pi \cdot F)\, d = \pi \cdot (F(\pi^{-1} \cdot d)) \sqsubseteq \pi \cdot (F(\pi^{-1} \cdot d')) = (\pi \cdot F)\, d'$, using monotonicity of $\pi \cdot (\_)$, F and $\pi^{-1} \cdot (\_)$. Hence $[D, D]$ is a Perm $\mathbb{A}$-set. Furthermore, the function assigning least fixed-points, lfp $: [D, D] \to D$ (whose existence is given by Theorem 7.12) is equivariant: one can deduce this from the formula (7.21) defining lfp F in terms of F, either by applying the Equivariance Principle, or more concretely, by a simple calculation:

$$
\begin{aligned}
&\pi \cdot (\text{lfp}\, F) \\
=\ & \{(7.21) \text{ and } (7.24)\} \\
&\textstyle\bigsqcap\{\pi \cdot d \mid F\, d \sqsubseteq d\} \\
=\ & \{\pi \cdot (\_) \text{ and } \pi^{-1} \cdot (\_) \text{ are mutually inverse}\} \\
&\textstyle\bigsqcap\{d' \mid F(\pi^{-1} \cdot d') \sqsubseteq \pi^{-1} \cdot d'\} \\
=\ & \{\text{definition of } \pi \cdot F \text{ and monotonicity of } \pi^{-1} \cdot (\_)\} \\
&\textstyle\bigsqcap\{d' \mid (\pi \cdot F)\, d' \sqsubseteq d'\} \\
=\ & \{(7.21)\} \\
&\text{lfp}(\pi \cdot F).
\end{aligned}
$$

Since lfp $: [D, D] \to D$ is equivariant, we can apply Lemma 2.12(i) to deduce that A supports lfp F if it supports F. □

Lemma 7.15 *Suppose X is a* Perm $\mathbb{A}$-*set and that R is a set of rules on X. If $A \subseteq \mathbb{A}$ supports R as an element of the* Perm $\mathbb{A}$-*set* $P\,X \times X$, *then the monotone function $\Phi_R : P\,X \to P\,X$ associated with R as in (7.22) is also supported by A in the function* Perm $\mathbb{A}$-*set* $(P\,X)^{P\,X}$.

Proof Given its definition (7.22), the fact that the function $R \mapsto \Phi_R$ is equivariant follows from the Equivariance Principle. So we can apply Lemma 2.12(i) to deduce the result. □

Combining Corollary 7.13 with Proposition 7.14 and Lemma 7.15, we get an alternative proof of Theorem 7.3. The advantage of the more abstract approach via complete lattices is that it is self-dual and so immediately gives a similar result for coinductively defined subsets, as we explain in the next section.

Remark 7.16 (Internalizing Tarski's fixed-point theorem) Since **Nom** is a boolean topos (Theorem 2.23), the proof of Theorem 7.12 can be carried out within its internal higher-order logic. To apply this internal version of the fixed point theorem to inductively defined subsets, one can restrict attention to finitely supported sets of rules R on a nominal set X, each of whose hypotheses are finitely supported sets (for example, because the rule is finitary); in other words R is an element of the nominal set $P_{fs} (P_{fs} X \times X)$. As discussed above, finitely supported sets of finitary rules occur very commonly in the operational semantics of languages involving names. If $R \in P_{fs} (P_{fs} X \times X)$, the Finite Support principle implies first that (7.22) gives a monotone and finitely supported function $\Phi_R \in P_{fs} X \to_{fs} P_{fs} X$; and secondly that the proof of Tarski's theorem gives the existence of least and greatest fixed-points for Φ_R in $P_{fs} X$. (Note that although $P_{fs} X$, being the power object of X in the topos **Nom**, is a complete lattice in the internal higher-order logic of the topos, it is not necessarily complete in the usual, external sense; see Exercise 7.4.)

Theorem 7.3 is more general than this 'internal' instance of Tarski's theorem in two ways. First, it applies whether or not the rules have finitely supported hypothesis sets. Secondly, even if $R \in P_{fs} (P_{fs} X \times X)$, the theorems tell us that the usual inductively defined subset, constructed by intersecting all pre-fixed subsets, coincides with the internal one constructed from finitely supported pre-fixed subsets.

7.6 Coinductively defined subsets

If $(D, \sqsubseteq)$ is a poset, then the *opposite* poset $(D, \sqsubseteq^{op})$ has the same underlying set of elements, partially ordered by: $d \sqsubseteq^{op} d' \Leftrightarrow d' \sqsubseteq d$. When the partial order is understood from the context, it is usual to write D^{op} for $(D, \sqsubseteq^{op})$.

Since a poset has joins of all subsets if and only if it has meets of all subsets (cf. Exercise 7.4), D is a complete lattice if and only if D^{op} is one. Furthermore, $F : D \to D$ is monotone if and only if it is monotone as a function from D^{op} to D^{op}. Therefore, given a monotone function $F : D \to D$ on a complete lattice, Theorem 7.12 dualizes: there is a greatest post-fixed-point

$$\begin{aligned} &\text{gfp}\, F \sqsubseteq F(\text{gfp}\, F), \\ &(\forall d \in D)\, d \sqsubseteq F\, d \Rightarrow d \sqsubseteq \text{gfp}\, F, \end{aligned} \qquad (7.25)$$

given by

$$\text{gfp}\, F = \bigsqcup \{ d \in D \mid d \sqsubseteq F\, d \}, \qquad (7.26)$$

and it is in fact the greatest fixed-point of F. When $D = PX$ is the complete lattice of subsets of a set X, one says that $\text{gfp}\, F = \bigcup \{ S \in PX \mid S \subseteq FS \}$ is the *coinductively defined subset* of X determined by the monotone function

$F : PX \to PX$. Applying Proposition 7.14 when $D = (PX)^{\mathrm{op}}$ we get the following support property for coinductively defined subsets.

Corollary 7.17 *Suppose X is a Perm $\mathbb{A}$-set and that $S \subseteq X$ is the subset coinductively defined by a monotone function $F : PX \to PX$. If F is supported by $A \subseteq \mathbb{A}$ (as an element of the function Perm $\mathbb{A}$-set $(PX)^{PX}$), then S is also supported by A. In particular if F is an equivariant function then S is an equivariant subset of X.* □

We noted above that every monotone $F : PX \to PX$ is the function Φ_R associated with some set of rules $R \subseteq PX \times X$ as in (7.22); indeed, we can take R to consist of all the rules (H, c), where $H \subseteq X$ and $c \in FH$ (Exercise 7.2). In this case we know from Lemma 7.15 that A supports F if it supports R. Phrasing the support property (7.5) directly in terms of F, we have that a monotone function $F : PX \to PX$ is supported by $A \subseteq \mathbb{A}$ iff

$$(\forall \pi \in \mathrm{Perm}\,\mathbb{A}) \, ((\forall a \in A)\, \pi a = a) \Rightarrow$$
$$(\forall H \in PX, c \in X)\, c \in FH \Rightarrow \pi \cdot c \in F(\pi \cdot H). \quad (7.27)$$

In particular, F is equivariant iff it satisfies

$$(\forall \pi \in \mathrm{Perm}\,\mathbb{A}, H \in PX, c \in X)\, c \in FH \Rightarrow \pi \cdot c \in F(\pi \cdot H). \quad (7.28)$$

If, as is usually the case, F can be defined as

$$\lambda H \in PX \to \{c \in X \mid \varphi(c, H)\},$$

where $\varphi(c, H)$ is a formula of higher-order logic, then equivariance of F follows from the Equivariance Principle, whether or not it is monotone. More well known is the fact that such an F is indeed monotone provided the free occurrences of H in $\varphi(c, H)$ are all positive, that is, to the left of an even number of nested implications.

Remark 7.18 Coinductively defined subsets that occur in programming language semantics are sometimes specified by a rule-based definition (that is, as gfp Φ_R for a suitable set of rules R), but this is less common than for inductively defined sets, where rule-based definitions prevail. Quite often a coinductive definition is more easily phrased in terms of a monotone operation rather than a set of rules. This seems especially to be the case for various notions of bisimulation (Sangiorgi, 2011), of which the following is an example.

Example 7.19 (Bisimilarity) Let X be the nominal set $Pr \times Pr$, where Pr is the nominal set of CCS processes from Example 7.5. In that example we saw that a finitely supported definition $D \subseteq Cons \times Act \times Pr$ of the process constants gives rise to a finitely supported labelled transition system $\mathcal{T}(D) \subseteq$ $Pr \times Act \times Pr$. As for any labelled transition system, we can use $\mathcal{T}(D)$ to define an equivalence relation of *bisimilarity* between CCS processes, $\sim \subseteq Pr \times Pr$; see section 3.10 of (Sangiorgi, 2011), for example. Thus $\sim = \text{gfp}\, F$, where $F : \mathrm{P}(Pr \times Pr) \to \mathrm{P}(Pr \times Pr)$ is the monotone function given by

$$FR \triangleq \{(P, Q) \in Pr \times Pr \mid (\forall \mu)$$
$$(\forall P')\, P \xrightarrow{\mu} P' \Rightarrow (\exists Q')\, Q \xrightarrow{\mu} Q' \wedge (P', Q') \in R \tag{7.29}$$
$$\wedge (\forall Q')\, Q \xrightarrow{\mu} Q' \Rightarrow (\exists P')\, P \xrightarrow{\mu} P' \wedge (P', Q') \in R\}.$$

Using (7.27), it is not hard to see that if $A \subseteq \mathbb{A}$ supports $\mathcal{T}(D)$, then it also supports this F. So by Corollary 7.17, when a CCS process definition D is supported by A, the associated relation of bisimilarity is also supported by A; that is, if $\pi \in \text{Perm}\, \mathbb{A}$ fixes each $a \in A$, then $P \sim Q \Rightarrow \pi \cdot P \sim \pi \cdot Q$.

Exercises

7.1   Show that if a poset $(D, \sqsubseteq)$ has joins for all subsets, then $\bigsqcup\{d \in D \mid (\forall d' \in S)\, d \sqsubseteq d'\}$ is a meet for $S \in \mathrm{P}\, D$.

7.2   If $F : \mathrm{P}X \to \mathrm{P}X$ is monotone for subset inclusion, show that $F = \Phi_R$ where Φ_R is defined as in (7.22) from the set of rules $R \triangleq \{(H, c) \in \mathrm{P}X \times X \mid c \in F H\}$.

7.3   Show that a monotone function $F : \mathrm{P}X \to \mathrm{P}X$ is equal to Φ_R with R a finitary set of rules (Section 7.1) if and only if it preserves joins of directed sets. In general, we say that a subset S of a complete lattice D is *directed* if every finite subset of S possesses an upper bound in S; and $F : D \to D$ is said to *preserve joins of directed sets* if for every directed subset S, $F(\bigsqcup S) = \bigsqcup\{F d \mid d \in S\}$. [Hint: every element $S \in \mathrm{P}\, X$ is the join of the directed set consisting of all the finite subsets of S.]

7.4   Show that $\mathrm{P}_{\mathrm{fs}}\, \mathbb{A}$ is not a complete lattice with respect to subset inclusion. [Hint: consider the union of $\emptyset \subseteq \{a_0\} \subseteq \{a_0, a_2\} \subseteq \{a_0, a_2, a_4\} \subseteq \cdots$ where $a_0, a_1, a_2, \ldots$ is some enumeration of $\mathbb{A}$.]

8

Nominal algebraic data types

In this chapter we consider initial algebras for functorial constructions on nominal sets that combine products and coproducts with the name-abstraction construction from Chapter 4. Such initial algebras give a semantics for languages involving names and name-binding operations where term equality is α-equivalence. This generalizes the classic initial algebra semantics of algebraic data types (Goguen *et al.*, 1977) and associated principles of structural recursion and induction.

8.1 Signatures

In the literature of programming language theory, the syntax of a language is usually specified by an *algebraic signature*. This gives a number of sorts, or 'syntactic categories', into which the terms of the language are divided, together with a number of operations for constructing terms of the various sorts. As well as giving the sorts and the operations, the signature specifies the type of each operation, namely how many arguments each operation takes, what the sorts of those arguments are, and what sort of term the operation constructs. We will use the notation

$$\text{op} : S_1 , \ldots , S_n \to S \tag{8.1}$$

to indicate that an operation op constructs a term $\text{op}(t_1 , \ldots , t_n)$ of sort S from terms $t_1, \ldots, t_n$ of sorts $S_1, \ldots, S_n$. (When $n = 0$ such an operation amounts to a *constant* of sort S.)

The following two related features of languages that occur in practice are not covered by this notion of algebraic signature, but are so common that it is worth enhancing the notion to formalize them:

- *Some syntactic categories are 'sorts of name'.* Language terms of such a sort form an infinite collection of elements whose only attribute, from the point of view of the semantics of the language, is their identity. For example, there might be sorts of 'identifier' and 'type variable' whose terms are represented concretely by strings of alphanumeric characters formed according to specific grammatical rules; but such concrete details are usually irrelevant to the semantics of the language, so we abstract away from such details and just assume there are disjoint infinite sets of atomic names of sort 'identifier' and 'type variable'.

- *Some operations are binders.* That is, the sorts of one or more of their arguments are sorts of name in the above sense; and when the operation is applied to form a term, such an argument ('binding name') is linked, in some way that has to be specified for the binding operation, to occurrences of the same name ('bound names') elsewhere in the term. The concrete detail of which particular name is used for a binding-bound linkage is usually irrelevant to the semantics of the language. In other words, whatever the meaning of a term, it should be invariant under 'α-converting' such a linkage to use another, so far unused name.

To take account of these two features, following (Urban *et al.*, 2004) we will use sorts that are built up from name-sorts N and data-sorts D according to the following grammar:

$$S ::= N \mid D \mid 1 \mid N . S \mid S , S. \tag{8.2}$$

The compound sort $N . S$ classifies terms that bind a name of sort N in a scope given by a term of sort S. The compound sort S_1 , S_2 classifies terms that are pairs of terms of the indicated sorts. Iterating, we get sorts of the form $S_1 , \ldots , S_n$ classifying tuples, with the $n = 0$ case given by the unit sort 1.

Notation 8.1 To reduce parentheses in sort expressions, we take $\_ . \_$ to bind more tightly than $\_ , \_$ and make the latter associate to the left. Thus, for example, $S_1 , N . S_2 , S_3$ stands for $(S_1 , (N . S_2)) , S_3$.

Definition 8.2 A *nominal algebraic signature* is specified by a set *Nsort* of *name-sorts*, a set *Dsort* of *data-sorts* and a set *Oper* of operations, together with typing information for each op $\in$ *Oper* of the form op : $S \rightarrow D$, where $D \in$ *Dsort* and S is a compound sort given by the grammar in (8.2). Given such a signature Σ, fixing a countably infinite set $\mathbb{A}$ of atomic names and a sorting $s : \mathbb{A} \rightarrow$ *Nsort* (Section 4.7), the sets $\Sigma(S)$ of *raw terms* of sort S are inductively defined by the following rules:

$$\frac{a \in \mathbb{A}_N}{a \in \Sigma(N)} \qquad \frac{t \in \Sigma(S) \qquad op : S \to D}{op\, t \in \Sigma(D)} \qquad \frac{}{() \in \Sigma(1)}$$

$$\frac{t_1 \in \Sigma(S_1) \qquad t_2 \in \Sigma(S_2)}{t_1 , t_2 \in \Sigma(S_1 , S_2)} \qquad \frac{a \in \mathbb{A}_N \qquad t \in \Sigma(S)}{a . t \in \Sigma(N . S)}.$$

Note that operations of a nominal algebraic signature construct terms of data-sort, but not of name-sort; this is because we wish each name-sort to classify terms that are atomic names without any compound structure. Note also that the usual notion of (many-sorted) algebraic signature can be regarded as the special case of Definition 8.2 in which the set of name-sorts is empty.

Remark 8.3 We call the elements generated by the above rules *raw* terms to distinguish them from the objects of primary interest, nominal algebraic terms, which are quotients of raw terms by the relation of α-equivalence to be introduced in the next section. Pitts (2006) uses the phrase 'term' for what we call a raw term and 'α-term' for its α-equivalence class.

Example 8.4 Here is a nominal algebraic signature for the untyped λ-calculus (Barendregt, 1984). It has a name-sort Var for variables, a data-sort Term for terms, and operations

$$V : Var \to Term,$$
$$L : Var . Term \to Term,$$
$$A : Term , Term \to Term.$$

For example, if x and y are atomic names of sort Var, then the raw term L(x . A(V x , V y)) represents the λ-term $\lambda x.x\,y$.

Example 8.5 Here is a nominal algebraic signature for the π-calculus (Sangiorgi and Walker, 2001, definition 1.1.1). It has a name-sort Chan for channel names, data-sorts Proc, Sum and Pre for processes, summations and prefixed processes, and operations

$$S : \mathtt{Sum} \to \mathtt{Proc},$$
$$\mathtt{Comp} : \mathtt{Proc}, \mathtt{Proc} \to \mathtt{Proc},$$
$$\mathtt{Nu} : \mathtt{Chan} . \mathtt{Proc} \to \mathtt{Proc},$$
$$! : \mathtt{Proc} \to \mathtt{Proc},$$
$$P : \mathtt{Pre} \to \mathtt{Sum},$$
$$\mathtt{O} : 1 \to \mathtt{Sum},$$
$$\mathtt{Plus} : \mathtt{Sum}, \mathtt{Sum} \to \mathtt{Sum},$$
$$\mathtt{Out} : \mathtt{Chan}, \mathtt{Chan}, \mathtt{Proc} \to \mathtt{Pre},$$
$$\mathtt{In} : \mathtt{Chan}, \mathtt{Chan} . \mathtt{Proc} \to \mathtt{Pre},$$
$$\mathtt{Tau} : \mathtt{Proc} \to \mathtt{Pre},$$
$$\mathtt{Match} : \mathtt{Chan}, \mathtt{Chan}, \mathtt{Pre} \to \mathtt{Pre}.$$

Thus there are two operations involving binding, $\mathtt{Nu}$ and $\mathtt{In}$. Assuming x and z are atomic names of sort $\mathtt{Chan}$ and that P is a raw term of sort $\mathtt{Proc}$, then the raw terms $\mathtt{Nu}(x . P)$ and $\mathtt{In}(x , (z . P))$ of sort $\mathtt{Proc}$ represent restricted and input-prefixed processes that are written in the π-calculus as $vx\,P$ and $x(z).P$, respectively.

Both the above examples are signatures with a single name-sort. Chapter 10 gives an example of a signature with several name-sorts (see Figure 10.3).

8.2 α-Equivalence

In a nominal algebraic signature, sorts of the form $\mathtt{N} . S$ are used in the type of an operation to indicate where it binds names. From this typing information one can generate a version of α-equivalence that identifies raw terms up to renaming such bound names. We use the theory of nominal sets to define this equivalence relation and develop its properties. In general this requires the 'many-sorted' extension of the theory of nominal sets discussed in Section 4.7, to cope with the fact that a nominal algebraic signature may have many name-sorts. For simplicity's sake, in the rest of this chapter we restrict attention to signatures with at most one name-sort; the general case is treated by Pitts (2006). We will also only consider nominal algebraic signatures that are *finite*, in the sense of having only finitely many data-sorts and operations.

Let Σ be such a finite nominal algebraic signature with a single name-sort $\mathtt{N}$. We use elements of the fixed set $\mathbb{A}$ as the atomic names of sort $\mathtt{N}$. For each sort S, the set $\Sigma(S)$ of raw terms of sort S possesses a Perm $\mathbb{A}$-action, extending the definition of the Perm $\mathbb{A}$-action for ordinary algebraic terms given in Example 1.4. It is defined for all sorts simultaneously as follows:

$$\pi \cdot a = \pi a,$$
$$\pi \cdot \mathsf{op}\, t = \mathsf{op}(\pi \cdot t),$$
$$\pi \cdot () = (), \tag{8.3}$$
$$\pi \cdot (t_1, t_2) = \pi \cdot t_1, \pi \cdot t_2,$$
$$\pi \cdot (a \cdot t) = (\pi a) \cdot (\pi \cdot t).$$

One can prove by induction on the structure of t that:

- $t \in \Sigma(S)$ implies $\pi \cdot t \in \Sigma(S)$;
- $(\pi, t) \mapsto \pi \cdot t$ has the properties (1.7) and (1.8) required of an action;
- with respect to this action, each $t \in \Sigma(S)$ is strongly supported (*cf.* Theorem 2.7) by the finite set of atomic names occurring in any position in t.

Thus each $\Sigma(S)$ is a nominal set with:

$$\mathsf{supp}\, a = \{a\},$$
$$\mathsf{supp}(\mathsf{op}\, t) = \mathsf{supp}\, t,$$
$$\mathsf{supp}() = \emptyset, \tag{8.4}$$
$$\mathsf{supp}(t_1, t_2) = \mathsf{supp}\, t_1 \cup \mathsf{supp}\, t_2,$$
$$\mathsf{supp}(a \cdot t) = \{a\} \cup \mathsf{supp}\, t.$$

The way we defined α-equivalence for untyped λ-terms in Section 4.1 extends in a straightforward way from the signature in Example 8.4 to arbitrary nominal algebraic signatures.

Definition 8.6 Given a nominal algebraic signature Σ (with single name sort), the binary relations of α-*equivalence* $=_\alpha \subseteq \Sigma(S) \times \Sigma(S)$ for each sort S, are simultaneously inductively defined by the following rules:

$$\frac{a \in \mathbb{A}}{a =_\alpha a} \qquad \frac{t =_\alpha t'}{\mathsf{op}\, t =_\alpha \mathsf{op}\, t'} \qquad \frac{}{() =_\alpha ()}$$

$$\frac{t_1 =_\alpha t_1' \qquad t_2 =_\alpha t_2'}{t_1, t_2 =_\alpha t_1', t_2'} \qquad \frac{(a_1\ a) \cdot t_1 =_\alpha (a_2\ a) \cdot t_2 \qquad a \mathrel{\#} (a_1, t_1, a_2, t_2)}{a_1 \cdot t_1 =_\alpha a_2 \cdot t_2}.$$

The first four of these rules express congruence properties of $=_\alpha$, while the fifth one combines a congruence property

$$t_1 =_\alpha t_2 \Rightarrow a \cdot t_1 =_\alpha a \cdot t_2, \tag{8.5}$$

with a renaming property (*cf.* Lemma 4.3)

$$a \# (a_1, t_1) \Rightarrow a_1 \cdot t_1 =_\alpha a \cdot (a_1 \, a) \cdot t_1 . \tag{8.6}$$

Both (8.5) and (8.6) are simple consequences of the definition of $=_\alpha$ and the fact that it is equivariant. This and the property of being an equivalence relation can be proved using Theorem 7.3, generalizing the proof in Example 7.8.

Lemma 8.7 *The relations $=_\alpha$ are equivariant equivalence relations.* □

Remark 8.8 Note that $=_\alpha$ is a decidable relation (given a suitable Gödel numbering of raw terms). A decision procedure is implicit in the inductive definition, because of the syntax-directed nature of the rules in Definition 8.6 and the fact that the size (number of symbols) of raw terms goes down reading the rules for compound terms bottom-up. (Note that the size function is equivariant: the size of $\pi \cdot t$ is equal to the size of t for any $\pi \in \text{Perm}\,A$.)

Definition 8.9 For each sort S of a nominal algebraic signature Σ, the elements of the quotient nominal set

$$\Sigma_\alpha(S) \triangleq \Sigma(S)/=_\alpha \tag{8.7}$$

are called *nominal algebraic terms* of sort S. We call nominal sets of the form $\Sigma_\alpha(S)$ *nominal algebraic data types*.

Proposition 8.10 *For each sort S of a nominal algebraic signature Σ, the least support* supp e *of a nominal algebraic term $e \in \Sigma_\alpha(S)$ is equal to the finite set* fn t *of free names of any representative raw term t:*

$$e = [t]_{=_\alpha} \Rightarrow \text{supp}\, e = \text{fn}\, t, \tag{8.8}$$

where

$$\text{fn}\, a = \{a\},$$
$$\text{fn}(\text{op}\, t) = \text{fn}\, t,$$
$$\text{fn}() = \emptyset, \tag{8.9}$$
$$\text{fn}(t_1 \, , \, t_2) = \text{fn}\, t_1 \cup \text{fn}\, t_2,$$
$$\text{fn}(a \cdot t) = (\text{fn}\, t) - \{a\}.$$

Proof One can prove that fn t strongly supports $[t]_{=_\alpha}$ in exactly the same way as for the special case of λ-terms in Section 4.1. Hence by Theorem 2.7, $\text{supp}([t]_{=_\alpha}) = \text{fn}\, t$. □

When working with languages involving binders, it is common to use notation that blurs the distinction between a raw term t and the α-equivalence class

$[t]_{=_\alpha}$ it determines. Accordingly, we use the following notation for nominal algebraic terms.

Definition 8.11

$$\text{op } e \triangleq [\text{op } t]_{=_\alpha}, \qquad \text{where } e = [t]_{=_\alpha}, \tag{8.10}$$

$$e_1 , e_2 \triangleq [t_1 , t_2]_{=_\alpha}, \qquad \text{where } e_1 = [t_1]_{=_\alpha} \text{ and } e_2 = [t_2]_{=_\alpha}, \tag{8.11}$$

$$a . e \triangleq [a . t]_{=_\alpha}, \qquad \text{where } e = [t]_{=_\alpha}. \tag{8.12}$$

We will also abbreviate $[a]_{=_\alpha}$ to a and $[()]_{=_\alpha}$ to $()$ when it is clear from the context that we are referring to nominal algebraic terms.

These notational conventions are justified by the following properties of $=_\alpha$, which are simple consequences of its definition and of Lemma 8.7:

- For each operation op : S → D there is a function $\Sigma_\alpha(S) \to \Sigma_\alpha(D)$, well defined by $[t]_{=_\alpha} \mapsto [\text{op } t]_{=_\alpha}$.
- Given sorts S_1 and S_2, there is a function $\Sigma_\alpha(S_1) \times \Sigma_\alpha(S_2) \to \Sigma_\alpha(S_1 , S_2)$, well defined by $([t_1]_{=_\alpha}, [t_2]_{=_\alpha}) \mapsto [t_1 , t_2]_{=_\alpha}$.
- For each sort S there is a function $\mathbb{A} \times \Sigma_\alpha(S) \to \Sigma_\alpha(N . S)$, well defined by $(a, [t]_{=_\alpha}) \mapsto [a . t]_{=_\alpha}$.
- For each $a \in \mathbb{A}$, the equivalence class $[a]_{=_\alpha}$ is the singleton $\{a\}$.
- The equivalence class $[()]_{=_\alpha}$ is the singleton $\{()\}$.

8.3 Algebraic functors

To each finite nominal algebraic signature Σ, with a single name-sort N and n data-sorts $D_1, \ldots, D_n$, we associate a functor T : **Nom**^{n} → **Nom**^{n}. To do so we first re-organize the typing information for a signature's operations so as to present, for each data-sort, the different ways of constructing terms of that sort. Thus

$$D_1 = \text{op}_{1,1}(S_{1,1}) \mid \cdots \mid \text{op}_{1,m_1}(S_{1,m_1})$$

$$\vdots \tag{8.13}$$

$$D_n = \text{op}_{n,1}(S_{n,1}) \mid \cdots \mid \text{op}_{n,m_n}(S_{n,m_n})$$

is the signature with operations $\text{op}_{i,j} : S_{i,j} \to D_i$ $(i = 1, \ldots, n, \ j = 1, \ldots, m_i)$. For example, the signature in Example 8.5 written in this way looks like this:

```
Proc =  S(Sum) | Comp(Proc , Proc) | Nu(Chan . Proc) | !(Proc)
Sum  =  P(Pre) | O(1) | Plus(Sum , Sum)
Pre  =  Out(Chan , Chan , Proc) | In(Chan , Chan . Proc)
     |  Tau(Proc) | Match(Chan , Chan , Pre).
```

The sorts $S_{i,j}$ in (8.13) are built up from $D_1, \ldots, D_n$ and the name-sort N as in (8.2). Given an n-tuple of nominal sets $X = (X_1, \ldots, X_n) \in \mathbf{Nom}^n$, each such sort S gives rise to a nominal set $[\![S]\!]X$, defined by recursion on the structure of S as follows:

$$[\![N]\!]X = \mathbb{A},$$
$$[\![D_i]\!]X = X_i,$$
$$[\![1]\!]X = 1, \tag{8.14}$$
$$[\![S_1, S_2]\!]X = [\![S_1]\!]X \times [\![S_2]\!]X,$$
$$[\![N . S]\!]X = [\mathbb{A}]([\![S]\!]X).$$

The mapping $X \mapsto [\![S]\!]X$ extends to a functor $[\![S]\!] : \mathbf{Nom}^n \to \mathbf{Nom}$ using the functoriality of products and of name abstraction (Section 4.4).

Definition 8.12 If Σ is the signature given by (8.13), then the associated functor $T : \mathbf{Nom}^n \to \mathbf{Nom}^n$ has components $T_i : \mathbf{Nom}^n \to \mathbf{Nom}$ (for $i = 1, \ldots, n$) given by mapping each $X = (X_1, \ldots, X_n) \in \mathbf{Nom}^n$ to

$$T_i X \triangleq [\![S_{i,1}]\!]X + \cdots + [\![S_{i,m_i}]\!]X, \tag{8.15}$$

and similarly for n-tuples of equivariant functions. We call functors that arise in this way *nominal algebraic functors*.

Example 8.13 If Σ is the signature from Example 8.4, then the associated functor $\mathbf{Nom} \to \mathbf{Nom}$ maps a nominal set X to $\mathbb{A} + ([\mathbb{A}]X) + (X \times X)$. Whereas for the signature in Example 8.5, the associated functor $\mathbf{Nom}^3 \to \mathbf{Nom}^3$ maps a triple of nominal sets (X_1, X_2, X_3) to the triple whose components are

$$X_2 + (X_1 \times X_1) + [\mathbb{A}]X_1 + X_1,$$
$$X_3 + 1 + (X_2 \times X_2),$$
$$(\mathbb{A} \times \mathbb{A} \times X_1) + (\mathbb{A} \times [\mathbb{A}]X_1) + X_1 + (\mathbb{A} \times \mathbb{A} \times X_3).$$

In the next section we will need to use the fact that the action of nominal algebraic functors on equivariant functions extends to one on all finitely supported functions. Given $X = (X_1 \ldots, X_n)$ and $Y = (Y_1 \ldots, Y_n)$ in $\mathbf{Nom}^n$, define

$$X \to_{\mathrm{fs}}^n Y \triangleq (X_1 \to_{\mathrm{fs}} Y_1) \times \cdots \times (X_n \to_{\mathrm{fs}} Y_n). \tag{8.16}$$

This is the hom-object in $\mathbf{Nom}$ for the $\mathbf{Nom}$-enriched category $\mathbf{Nom}^n$. We noted in Remark 4.11 that the functor $[\mathbb{A}]\_ : \mathbf{Nom} \to \mathbf{Nom}$ is $\mathbf{Nom}$-enriched; and the same is true for the product and coproduct functors for more standard reasons. Using these we get a $\mathbf{Nom}$-enrichment for each T. Concretely this means that there are equivariant functions

$$(X \to_{\mathrm{fs}}^n Y) \to (TX \to_{\mathrm{fs}}^n TY) \quad (X, Y \in \mathbf{Nom}^n) \tag{8.17}$$

that preserve identity and composition and agree with the application of T to equivariant functions (recalling that these are the elements of $X \rightarrow^n_{fs} Y$ with empty support). Following (8.15), the functions in (8.17) are defined using coproduct (disjoint union) from **Nom**-enrichments

$$(X \rightarrow^n_{fs} Y) \rightarrow ([\![S]\!]X \rightarrow_{fs} [\![S]\!]Y) \quad (X, Y \in \mathbf{Nom}^n) \tag{8.18}$$

for the functors $[\![S]\!] : \mathbf{Nom}^n \rightarrow \mathbf{Nom}$; and following (8.14), these are defined by recursion on the structure of the sort S using the enrichments for product and name abstraction. Thus given $F \in X \rightarrow^n_{fs} Y$, the function $[\![S]\!] F \in [\![S]\!]X \rightarrow_{fs} [\![S]\!]Y$ has the following properties according to the structure of S:

$$[\![N]\!] F a = a,$$
$$[\![S_i]\!] F d = F_i d,$$
$$[\![1]\!] F () = (), \tag{8.19}$$
$$[\![S_1, S_2]\!] F (d_1, d_2) = ([\![S_1]\!] F d_1, [\![S_2]\!] F d_2),$$
$$a \mathrel{\#} F \Rightarrow [\![N . S]\!] F (\langle a \rangle d) = \langle a \rangle ([\![S]\!] F d),$$

where the last, conditional equation uses the functorial action of $[\mathbb{A}]\_$ on finitely supported functions (4.18).

8.4 Initial algebra semantics

Let Σ be the signature given by (8.13) and define $D \in \mathbf{Nom}^n$ to be

$$D \triangleq (\Sigma_\alpha(D_1), \dots, \Sigma_\alpha(D_n)). \tag{8.20}$$

We can define equivariant functions $I_S : [\![S]\!]D \rightarrow \Sigma_\alpha(S)$ by recursion on the structure of sorts S as follows (using the notational conventions of Definition 8.11 and, in the last clause, the definition (4.19) of the action of $[\mathbb{A}]\_$ on equivariant functions):

$$I_N a = a,$$
$$I_{D_i} e = e,$$
$$I_1 () = (), \tag{8.21}$$
$$I_{S_1, S_2}(d_1, d_2) = I_{S_1} d_1, I_{S_2} d_2,$$
$$I_{N.S}(\langle a \rangle d) = a . I_S d.$$

If $T : \mathbf{Nom}^n \rightarrow \mathbf{Nom}^n$ is the functor associated with Σ as in Definition 8.12, then using these functions for each $i = 1, \dots, n$ we get an equivariant function

$I_i : T_i D = [\![S_{i,1}]\!]D + \cdots + [\![S_{i,m_i}]\!]D \to \Sigma_\alpha(D_i)$, given by

$$I_i(\mathrm{inj}_j \, d) = \mathrm{op}_{i,j}(I_{S_{i,j}} \, d) \quad (j = 1, \ldots, m_i, \, d \in [\![S_{i,j}]\!]D). \tag{8.22}$$

So altogether we get a morphism in **Nom**^{n}:

$$I \triangleq (I_1, \ldots, I_n) : T D \to D. \tag{8.23}$$

We will show that this gives an *initial* T-*algebra* for the functor $T : \mathbf{Nom}^n \to \mathbf{Nom}^n$. Thus given any T-algebra, that is, any morphism $F : T X \to X$, there is a unique morphism $\hat{F} : D \to X$ making the following diagram commute:

$$
\begin{array}{ccc}
T D & \overset{T\hat{F}}{\dashrightarrow} & T X \\
{\scriptstyle I} \downarrow & & \downarrow {\scriptstyle F} \\
D & \underset{\hat{F}}{\dashrightarrow} & X.
\end{array}
\tag{8.24}
$$

In particular, I is an isomorphism, by a well-known lemma of Lambek (1968).

In general, the initial T-algebra property is of interest because it gives rise to recursion principles for the initial algebra. In this particular case, in order to capture some common informal uses of recursion in the presence of α-equivalence, we need to establish a stronger version of (8.24), one in which equivariant functions are generalized to finitely supported functions. The following familiar example illustrates the need for this.

Example 8.14   Let Σ be the signature for untyped λ-calculus from Example 8.4. In this case $D = \Sigma_\alpha(\mathtt{Term})$ is the nominal set of λ-terms modulo α-equivalence from Section 4.1; the functor $T : \mathbf{Nom} \to \mathbf{Nom}$ is $\mathbb{A} + ([\mathbb{A}]\_) + (\_ \times \_)$; and the morphism $I : \mathbb{A} + [\mathbb{A}]D + D \times D \to D$ satisfies

$$
\begin{aligned}
I(\mathrm{inj}_1 \, a) &= \mathsf{V} \, a, \\
I(\mathrm{inj}_2(\langle a \rangle e)) &= \mathsf{L} \, a \, . \, e, \\
I(\mathrm{inj}_3(e_1, e_2)) &= \mathsf{A}(e_1, e_2).
\end{aligned}
\tag{8.25}
$$

A T-algebra is given by equivariant functions $F_1 : \mathbb{A} \to X$, $F_2 : [\mathbb{A}]X \to X$ and $F_3 : X \times X \to X$. The unique $\hat{F} : D \to X$ making (8.24) commute satisfies the following recursion equations:

$$
\begin{aligned}
\hat{F}(\mathsf{V} \, a_1) &= F_1 \, a_1, \\
\hat{F}(\mathsf{L} \, a_1 \, . \, e_1) &= F_2(\langle a_1 \rangle(\hat{F} \, e_1)), \\
\hat{F}(\mathsf{A}(e_1, e_2)) &= F_3(\hat{F} \, e_1, \hat{F} \, e_2).
\end{aligned}
\tag{8.26}
$$

Contrast this with the operation $[a := e] : D \to D$ of *capture-avoiding substitution* of a λ-term e for all free occurrences of a variable $\mathsf{V} \, a$ in a λ-term. Being finitely supported by $\{a\} \cup \mathrm{fv}\, e$, this operation cannot be an instance of the above initial T-algebra property (with $X = \Sigma_\alpha(\mathrm{Term})$), since that produces an emptily supported function $\hat{F}$ from emptily supported functions (F_1, F_2, F_3). Nevertheless, it has a recursive specification that is quite similar to (8.26):

$$[a := e](\mathsf{V}\, a_1) = F_1\, a_1\,,$$

$$a_1 \notin \{a\} \cup \mathrm{fv}\, e \Rightarrow [a := e](\mathsf{L}\, a_1 \,.\, e_1) = F_2(\langle a_1\rangle([a := e]e_1))\,, \qquad (8.27)$$

$$[a := e](\mathsf{A}(e_1\, ,\, e_2)) = F_3([a := e]e_1, [a := e]e_2)\,,$$

where $F_1 \in \mathbb{A} \to_{\mathrm{fs}} D$ is $\lambda a_1 \in \mathbb{A} \to$ if $a_1 = a$ then e else $\mathsf{V}\, a_1$ (which has support $\{a\} \cup \mathrm{fv}\, e$), and where F_2 and F_3 are the equivariant functions $I \circ \mathrm{inj}_2$ and $I \circ \mathrm{inj}_3$ from (8.25).

The middle clause in (8.27) is the essence of the capture-avoiding aspect of this form of substitution: it is only necessary to say how to unwind the recursive definition for sufficiently fresh bound variables a_1. Since $[a := e]$ is uniquely determined by (F_1, F_2, F_3) and the latter has support $\{a\} \cup \mathrm{fv}\, e$, this middle clause can be rephrased using a freshness quantifier

$$(\mathsf{N}a_1)\, [a := e](\mathsf{L}\, a_1 \,.\, e_1) = F_2(\langle a_1\rangle([a := e]e_1))\,.$$

It turns out that this use of the freshness quantifier corresponds exactly to the way it occurs in the definition of the action of the functor $[\mathbb{A}]_-$ on finitely supported functions, as in (4.18). Thus the recursive definition of $[a := e]$ is an instance of the following initial algebra property of nominal data types.

Theorem 8.15 (Initial algebra theorem for nominal algebraic data types)
Let Σ be a nominal algebraic signature with a single name-sort N, with n data-sorts $\mathsf{D}_1, \ldots, \mathsf{D}_n$, and with operations as shown in (8.13). The n-tuple of nominal algebraic data types

$$D = (\Sigma_\alpha(\mathsf{D}_1), \ldots, \Sigma_\alpha(\mathsf{D}_n))$$

*equipped with the morphism (8.23) is an initial algebra for the **Nom**-enriched functor* $\mathrm{T} : \mathbf{Nom}^n \to \mathbf{Nom}^n$ *associated with Σ as in Section 8.3. In other words, for each $X \in \mathbf{Nom}^n$ and $F \in \mathrm{T}X \to_{\mathrm{fs}}^n X$ there is a unique $\hat{F} \in D \to_{\mathrm{fs}}^n X$ satisfying*

$$F \circ (\mathrm{T}\hat{F}) = \hat{F} \circ I\,. \qquad (8.28)$$

Moreover, $\mathrm{supp}\, \hat{F} \subseteq \mathrm{supp}\, F$.

Remark 8.16 The fact that any nominal algebraic functor T has a **Nom**-enriched initial algebra follows from general, category-theoretic considerations. It can be constructed by taking the colimit of the countable chain

$$\emptyset \to \mathrm{T}\emptyset \to \mathrm{T}(\mathrm{T}\emptyset) \to \cdots$$

and using the fact that the **Nom**-enriched functor T preserves such colimits. So the force of the theorem is that this initial algebra can be presented in terms of the sets of nominal algebraic terms associated with the signature.

Proof of existence of $\hat{F}$ Define relations $\overline{F}_S \subseteq \Sigma(S) \times [\![S]\!]X$, as S ranges over sorts, inductively by the following rules:

$$
\frac{a \in \mathbb{A}}{(a, a) \in \overline{F}_N}
\qquad
\frac{(t, d) \in \overline{F}_{S_{i,j}} \qquad i \in \{1, \ldots, n\} \quad j \in \{1, \ldots, m_i\}}{(\mathrm{op}_{i,j}\, t, F_i(\mathrm{inj}_j\, d)) \in \overline{F}_{D_i}}
$$

$$
\frac{}{((), ()) \in \overline{F}_1}
\qquad
\frac{(t_1, d_1) \in \overline{F}_{S_1} \qquad (t_2, d_2) \in \overline{F}_{S_2}}{(t_1 , t_2, (d_1, d_2)) \in \overline{F}_{S_1, S_2}}
\tag{8.29}
$$

$$
\frac{((a_1\, a) \cdot t, (a_2\, a) \cdot d) \in \overline{F}_S \qquad a \mathbin{\#} (a_1, t, a_2, d, F)}{(a_1\, .\, t, \langle a_2 \rangle d) \in \overline{F}_{N.S}}\, .
$$

These relations have the following properties:

(i) Each $\overline{F}_S$ is supported by supp F as a subset of the nominal set $\Sigma(S) \times [\![S]\!]X$; this follows by Theorem 7.3, because the set of rules in (8.29) is supported by this finite set.

(ii) The relations respect α-equivalence in their first components and they are single-valued:

$$
(t, d) \in \overline{F}_S \wedge t =_\alpha t' \Rightarrow (t', d) \in \overline{F}_S ,
\tag{8.30}
$$

$$
(t, d) \in \overline{F}_S \wedge (t, d') \in \overline{F}_S \Rightarrow d = d' .
\tag{8.31}
$$

These properties can be proved, simultaneously for all sorts S, by Rule Induction for the rules in (8.29). The only interesting induction step is for name abstractions, which uses a typical 'some/any' argument (like those in Examples 7.8 and 7.9) to replace the atomic name a in the hypothesis of the last rule in (8.30) by one that is also fresh for some $a'\, .\, t'$ (for the first property), or for some $\langle a' \rangle d'$ (for the second property).

(iii) The relations are total:

$$
(\forall t \in \Sigma(S))(\exists d \in [\![S]\!]X)\, (t, d) \in \overline{F}_S .
\tag{8.32}
$$

For this we prove a slightly stronger property, namely that the sort-indexed family of subsets

$$
H_S \triangleq \{t \in \Sigma(S) \mid (\forall \pi \in \mathrm{Perm}\,\mathbb{A})(\exists d \in [\![S]\!]X)\, (\pi \cdot t, d) \in \overline{F}_S\}
$$

is closed under the rules in Definition 8.2 inductively defining the sets $\Sigma(S)$ of raw terms of each sort, and hence that $H_S = \Sigma(S)$. (The quantification over all finite permutations $\pi \in \mathrm{Perm}\,\mathbb{A}$ in the definition of H_S is there to ensure that these subsets are equivariant, despite the fact that $\overline{F}_S$ may have non-empty support; indeed, it is easy to see from the definition that we have $t \in H_S \Rightarrow \pi \cdot t \in H_S$.) The only non-trivial induction step is for closure of the subsets under formation of raw terms of the form $a \cdot t$, which is proved as follows.

Suppose $t \in H_S$ and $a \in \mathbb{A}$; we prove that $a \cdot t \in H_{\mathbb{N}.S}$. Given any $\pi \in \text{Perm } \mathbb{A}$ we can use the Choose-a-Fresh-Name Principle to pick some $a' \# (a, \pi, t, F)$. Since $t \in H_S$, there exists $d \in [\![S]\!]X$ with

$$((\pi a \, a') \cdot \pi \cdot t, d) \in \overline{F}_S. \tag{8.33}$$

Now pick some $a'' \# (a, \pi, t, F, a', d)$; applying $(a' \, a'')$ to (8.33) and using the fact that $a', a'' \notin \text{supp } F \supseteq \sup \overline{F}_S$, we get $((\pi a \, a'') \cdot \pi \cdot t, (a' \, a'') \cdot d) \in \overline{F}_S$. Hence by definition of $\overline{F}$, $((\pi a) \cdot (\pi \cdot t), \langle a' \rangle d) \in \overline{F}_{\mathbb{N}.S}$. Therefore $a \cdot t \in H_{\mathbb{N}.S}$, as required.

In view of properties (i)–(iii), for each sort S the relation $\overline{F}_S$ induces a function from $\Sigma_\alpha(S)$ to $[\![S]\!]X$ that is supported by $\text{supp } F$. Taking S to be D_i this gives us a function $\hat{F}_i \in \Sigma_\alpha(D_i) \to_{\text{fs}} X_i$ satisfying

$$(\forall t \in \Sigma(D_i)) \, (t, \hat{F}_i[t]_{=_\alpha}) \in \overline{F}_{D_i}. \tag{8.34}$$

So we have constructed $\hat{F} = (\hat{F}_1, \ldots, \hat{F}_n) \in D \to_{\text{fs}}^n X$ supported by $\text{supp } F$ and it remains to prove that it satisfies (8.28), that is, $F_i \circ (T_i \hat{F}) = \hat{F}_i \circ I_i$ holds for $i = 1, \ldots, n$. From the definitions of T_i and I_i, this amounts to proving that for all $j = 1, \ldots, m_i$ and all $d \in [\![S_{i,j}]\!]D$

$$F_i(\text{inj}_j([\![S_{i,j}]\!] \, \hat{F} \, d)) = \hat{F}_i(\text{op}_{i,j}(I_{S_{i,j}} \, d)). \tag{8.35}$$

One can see this by proving for all sorts S, all $d \in [\![S]\!]D$ and all $t \in \Sigma(S)$ that

$$I_S \, d = [t]_{=_\alpha} \Rightarrow (t, [\![S]\!] \, \hat{F} \, d) \in \overline{F}_S. \tag{8.36}$$

For then if $I_{S_{i,j}} \, d = [t]_{=_\alpha}$, we have $(t, [\![S_{i,j}]\!] \, \hat{F} \, d) \in \overline{F}_{S_{i,j}}$ and therefore by definition of $\overline{F}$, also $(\text{op}_{i,j} \, t, F_i(\text{inj}_j([\![S_{i,j}]\!] \, \hat{F} \, d))) \in \overline{F}_{D_i}$; but then (8.34) and (8.31) together imply (8.35).

That leaves the proof of property (8.36). This can be done by induction on the structure of the sort S. The induction step when $S = D_i$ uses (8.34); and the induction step for name abstraction sorts uses the fact that every $d \in [\![\mathbb{N}.S]\!]D = [\mathbb{A}]([\![S]\!]D)$ is of the form $\langle a \rangle d'$ for some $a \# F$, together with the fact that

$$a \# F \wedge (t, d) \in \overline{F}_S \Rightarrow (a \cdot t, \langle a \rangle d) \in \overline{F}_{\mathbb{N}.S}, \tag{8.37}$$

which is a consequence of the definition of $\overline{F}$ and the fact that it is supported by $\text{supp } F$. $\qquad\square$

Proof of uniqueness of $\hat{F}$ Suppose $F' \in D \rightarrow^n_{\mathrm{fs}} X$ also satisfies $F \circ (TF') = F' \circ I$ and hence for all $i = 1, \ldots, n$, all $j = 1, \ldots, m_i$ and all $d \in [\![S_{i,j}]\!]D$

$$F_i(\mathrm{inj}_j([\![S_{i,j}]\!] F' d)) = F'_i(\mathrm{op}_{i,j}(I_{S_{i,j}} d)). \tag{8.38}$$

From this it follows by induction on the structure of sorts S that for all $d \in [\![S]\!]D$ and all $t \in \Sigma(S)$

$$I_S d = [t]_{=_\alpha} \Rightarrow (t, [\![S]\!] F' d) \in \overline{F}_S. \tag{8.39}$$

Taking $S = D_i$, this gives $(t, F'_i[t]_{=_\alpha}) \in \overline{F}_{D_i}$ for each $t \in \Sigma(D_i)$. Combining this with (8.34) and (8.31), we get $F'_i[t]_{=_\alpha} = \hat{F}_i[t]_{=_\alpha}$ for all $t \in \Sigma(D_i)$ and all $i = 1, \ldots, n$. Therefore $F' = \hat{F}$.   □

8.5 Primitive recursion

The initial algebra property of ordinary algebraic data types is equivalent to a familiar and widely used principle of structural recursion for such data. When we add names and name abstraction to get nominal algebraic data types, it turns out that the initial algebra property (Theorem 8.15) gives rise to a principle of structural recursion 'modulo α-equivalence'. This justifies many common informal uses of structural recursion in the presence of binding operations, where one identifies α-equivalence classes with representative raw terms, dynamically freshening bound names as necessary. Pitts (2006) investigates this 'α-structural' recursion in some generality. Together with the associated induction principle (Section 8.6), it forms the basis for the Nominal package for the Isabelle/HOL interactive theorem prover (Urban, 2008). Here we will just treat one simple example of α-structural recursion, for untyped λ-terms.

Let Σ be the signature from Example 8.4. The associated nominal algebraic functor **Nom** $\rightarrow$ **Nom** is $T = \mathbb{A} + [\mathbb{A}]_- + (_- \times _-)$. Thus to give a T-algebra $F \in TX \rightarrow_{\mathrm{fs}} X$ is equivalent to giving a nominal set X equipped with three finitely supported functions, $F_1 \in \mathbb{A} \rightarrow_{\mathrm{fs}} X$, $F_2 \in ([\mathbb{A}]X) \rightarrow_{\mathrm{fs}} X$ and $F_3 \in X \times X \rightarrow_{\mathrm{fs}} X$. By Theorem 4.15, F_2 is induced by a finitely supported partial function $(\mathbb{A} \times X) \rightarrow_{\mathrm{fs}} X$ satisfying (4.32). It seems that the added generality of using a *partial* function in this case is not needed in practice; so we will use a total function $F'_2 \in (\mathbb{A} \times X) \rightarrow_{\mathrm{fs}} X$, for which condition (4.32) becomes $(\mathsf{N}a)(\forall x \in X)\, a\, \#\, F'_2(a, x)$. In particular, the initial T-algebra $\Sigma_\alpha(\mathrm{Term})$ is the nominal set of λ-terms modulo α-equivalence equipped with the equivariant functions

$$I_1 : \mathbb{A} \to \Sigma_\alpha(\text{Term}),$$

$$I_1 \triangleq \lambda a \in \mathbb{A} \to V\, a,$$

$$I_2' : \mathbb{A} \times \Sigma_\alpha(\text{Term}) \to \Sigma_\alpha(\text{Term}),$$

$$I_2' \triangleq \lambda(a, e) \in \mathbb{A} \times \Sigma_\alpha(\text{Term}) \to L\, a\, .\, e,$$

$$I_3 : \Sigma_\alpha(\text{Term}) \times \Sigma_\alpha(\text{Term}) \to \Sigma_\alpha(\text{Term}),$$

$$I_3 \triangleq \lambda(e_1, e_2) \in \Sigma_\alpha(\text{Term}) \times \Sigma_\alpha(\text{Term}) \to A(e_1\, ,\, e_2).$$

The initial algebra theorem for nominal algebraic data types in this case gives the following recursion principle for λ-terms.

Theorem 8.17 (α-**Structural primitive recursion for** λ-**terms**) *Let Σ be the signature from Example 8.4. Given a nominal set X and finitely supported functions*

$$F_1 \in \mathbb{A} \to_{\text{fs}} X,$$

$$F_2 \in \mathbb{A} \times \Sigma_\alpha(\text{Term}) \times X \to_{\text{fs}} X,$$

$$F_3 \in \Sigma_\alpha(\text{Term}) \times \Sigma_\alpha(\text{Term}) \times X \times X \to_{\text{fs}} X,$$

with F_2 satisfying the following 'freshness condition for binders':

$$(\text{И}a)(\forall e \in \Sigma_\alpha(\text{Term}))(\forall x \in X)\, a \,\#\, F_2(a, e, x), \tag{8.40}$$

there is a unique finitely supported function $\hat{F} \in \Sigma_\alpha(\text{Term}) \to_{\text{fs}} X$ satisfying

$$(\forall a \in \mathbb{A})\, \hat{F}(V\, a) = F_1\, a,$$

$$\wedge\ (\text{И}a)(\forall e \in \Sigma_\alpha(\text{Term}))\, \hat{F}(L\, a\, .\, e) = F_2(a, e, \hat{F}\, e), \tag{8.41}$$

$$\wedge\ (\forall e_1, e_2 \in \Sigma_\alpha(\text{Term}))\, \hat{F}(A(e_1\, ,\, e_2)) = F_3(e_1, e_2, \hat{F}\, e_1, \hat{F}\, e_2).$$

Proof Let $D = \Sigma_\alpha(\text{Term})$. Define $G_1 \in \mathbb{A} \to_{\text{fs}} (X \times D)$, $G_2 \in [\mathbb{A}](X \times D) \to_{\text{fs}} (X \times D)$ and $G_3 \in (X \times D) \times (X \times D) \to_{\text{fs}} (X \times D)$ as follows:

$$G_1 \triangleq \lambda a \in \mathbb{A} \to (F_1\, a, V\, a),$$

$$G_2 \triangleq \lambda\langle a\rangle(x, e) \in [\mathbb{A}](X \times D) \to (F_2(a, e, x), L\, a\, .\, e),$$

$$G_3 \triangleq \lambda((x_1, e_1), (x_2, e_2)) \in (X \times D) \times (X \times D) \to (F_3(e_1, e_2, x_1, x_2), A(e_1\, ,\, e_2)).$$

The definition of G_2 uses the name abstraction pattern notation introduced after Theorem 4.15. Thus G_2 is the unique function corresponding as in that theorem to $(a, (x, e)) \mapsto (F_2(a, e, x), L\, a\, .\, e)$; it is well defined, because $(\text{И}a)(\forall(x, e) \in X \times D)\, a \,\#\, (F_2(a, e, x), L\, a\, .\, e)$ holds by (8.40) and Proposition 8.10.

From (G_1, G_2, G_3) we get a T-algebra $G \in \text{T}(X \times D) \to_{\text{fs}} (X \times D)$ for the functor $T = \mathbb{A} + [\mathbb{A}]_- + (\_ \times \_)$. Applying Theorem 8.15, there is a unique $\hat{G} \in D \to_{fs} (X \times D)$ satisfying $G \circ (T\hat{G}) = \hat{G} \circ I$. Define

$$F \triangleq \text{proj}_1 \circ \hat{G} \in D \to_{fs} X$$
$$J \triangleq \text{proj}_2 \circ \hat{G} \in D \to_{fs} D.$$

Then $G \circ (T\hat{G}) = \hat{G} \circ I$ gives

$$(\forall a \in \mathbb{A}) \, (F(\text{V}\,a), J(\text{V}\,a)) = (F_1\,a, \text{V}\,a)$$
$$\wedge \; (\mathsf{N}a)(\forall e \in D) \, (F(\text{L}\,a \,.\, e), J(\text{L}\,a \,.\, e)) = (F_2(a, J\,e, F\,e), \text{L}\,a \,.\, (J\,e))$$
$$\wedge \; (\forall e_1, e_2 \in D) \, (F(\text{A}(e_1 \,,\, e_2)), J(\text{A}(e_1 \,,\, e_2)))$$
$$= (F_3(J\,e_1, J\,e_2, F\,e_1, F\,e_2), \text{A}((J\,e_1) \,,\, (J\,e_2))). \tag{8.42}$$

The second components of the equalities in (8.42) give

$$(\forall a \in \mathbb{A}) \, J(\text{V}\,a) = \text{V}\,a$$
$$\wedge \; (\mathsf{N}a)(\forall e \in D) \, J(\text{L}\,a \,.\, e) = \text{L}\,a \,.\, (J\,e)$$
$$\wedge \; (\forall e_1, e_2 \in D) \, J(\text{A}(e_1 \,,\, e_2)) = \text{A}((J\,e_1) \,,\, (J\,e_2)).$$

So J satisfies $I \circ (T\,J) = J \circ I$; but so does id_D and by Theorem 8.15 there is only one such function corresponding to the T-algebra $I : T\,D \to D$. Therefore $J = \text{id}_D$ and hence the first components of the equalities in (8.42) imply that we can take $\hat{F} = F$ to satisfy (8.41).

For the uniqueness of $\hat{F}$, note that if F' is any other such function, then $G' \triangleq \langle F', \text{id}_D \rangle \in D \to_{fs} (X \times D)$ satisfies $G \circ (T\,G') = G' \circ I$. So by the uniqueness part of Theorem 8.15, $G' = \hat{G}$ and hence $F' = \text{proj}_1 \circ G' = \text{proj}_1 \circ \hat{G} = F = \hat{F}$. □

Note The proof of the theorem uses a standard technique for deriving primitive recursion from the more simple, 'iterative' form of recursion inherent in the existence part of the initial algebra property, using the uniqueness part of initiality. The 'freshness condition on binders' (8.40) ensures that the functions F_1, F_2 and F_3 induce a T-algebra structure on X. Similar conditions can be given for any nominal algebraic signature: see Pitts (2006, theorem 5.1).

Example 8.18 (Counting λ-abstractions) Here is a simple example to illustrate the use of Theorem 8.17. Taking X to be the discrete nominal set of natural numbers $\mathbb{N}$ (Section 2.3), consider the functions F_1, F_2, F_3 given by

$$F_1\,a \triangleq 0,$$
$$F_2(a, e, x) \triangleq x + 1, \tag{8.43}$$
$$F_3(e_1, e_2, x_1, x_2) \triangleq x_1 + x_2.$$

Note that these functions have empty support; and since every element of $\mathbb{N}$ has empty support, the freshness condition for binders (8.40) is trivially satisfied. So the theorem gives us a function $|\_| \triangleq \hat{F} : \Sigma_\alpha(\text{Term}) \to \mathbb{N}$ satisfying

$$|V\,a| = 0,$$
$$|L\,a\,.\,e| = |e| + 1, \qquad\qquad (8.44)$$
$$|A(e_1\,,\,e_2)| = |e_1| + |e_2|.$$

Note also that the theorem tells us that $|\_|$ is supported by $\text{supp}(F_1, F_2, F_3) = \emptyset$ and hence is equivariant.

For example $|L\,a\,.\,V\,a| = |V\,a| + 1 = 0 + 1 = 1$ and in general $|e|$ is the number of occurrences of λ-abstractions in the λ-term e. Although the fact that such a function is well defined is a simple application of the theorem, it is interesting to note that previous formal recursion schemes for α-equivalence classes of raw λ-terms find it troublesome: see Gordon and Melham (1996, section 3.3) and Norrish (2004, section 3). It is also interesting to compare the ease with which $|\_|$ can be defined compared with schemes for primitive recursion based on using higher-order abstract syntax: see Schürmann *et al.* (2001, example 4.4).

Example 8.19 (Capture-avoiding substitution) Suppose $a \in \mathbb{A}$ and that $e \in \Sigma_\alpha(\text{Term})$. If in Theorem 8.17 we take $X = \Sigma_\alpha(\text{Term})$ and

$$F_1\,a_1 \triangleq \text{if } a_1 = a \text{ then } e \text{ else } V\,a_1\,,$$
$$F_2(a_1, e_1, x_1) \triangleq L\,a_1\,.\,x_1\,,$$
$$F_3(e_1, e_2, x_1, x_2) \triangleq A(x_1\,,\,x_2)\,,$$

then F_2 clearly satisfies the freshness condition for binders (8.40) and the function $\hat{F}$ given by the theorem is the operation $[a := e] \in \Sigma_\alpha(\text{Term}) \to_{\text{fs}} \Sigma_\alpha(\text{Term})$ of capture-avoiding substitution from Example 8.14.

In the previous two examples it was easy to verify that the freshness condition for binders (8.40) held. The following example illustrates that this is not always the case.

Example 8.20 (Counting bound variable occurrences) We wish to define a function $cbv : \Sigma_\alpha(\text{Term}) \to \mathbb{N}$ that counts the number of occurrences of bound variables in a λ-term. For example, assuming a and b are distinct, the λ-term $(\lambda a.\lambda b.a)\,b$ contains a single bound variable occurrence (named a in the raw term we have used to represent the λ-term) and correspondingly we want the value of cbv at $A(L\,a\,.\,L\,b\,.\,V\,a\,,\,V\,b) \in \Sigma_\alpha(\text{Term})$ to be 1.

We define cbv using the approach of Schürmann *et al.* (2001, example 4.3).

We first define an auxiliary function *cbvs* satisfying

$$cbvs(V\,a)\rho = \rho\,a,$$
$$cbvs(L\,a\,.\,e)\rho = (cbvs\,e)(\rho[a \mapsto 1]),$$
$$cbvs(A(e_1\,,\,e_2)) = (cbvs\,e_1\,\rho) + (cbvs\,e_2\,\rho), \qquad (8.45)$$

where ρ ranges over environments mapping atomic names to numbers; in the second clause above, $\rho[a \mapsto 1]$ indicates the updated environment mapping a to 1 and otherwise acting like ρ. Then we define $cbv\,e \triangleq cbvs\,e\,\rho_0$ where ρ_0 is the environment mapping all atomic names to 0.

For environments we do not use arbitrary functions from names to numbers, but rather finitely supported ones. Then as a first attempt to use α-structural primitive recursion to prove the existence of a function *cbvs* satisfying (8.45), in Theorem 8.17 one could try taking X to be $(A \to_{fs} N) \to_{fs} N$ and using the functions F_1, F_2, F_3 given by

$$F_1\,a \triangleq \lambda\rho \in (A \to_{fs} N) \to \rho\,a,$$
$$F_2(a, e, x) \triangleq \lambda\rho \in (A \to_{fs} N) \to x(\rho[a \mapsto 1]), \qquad (8.46)$$
$$F_3(e_1, e_2, x_1, x_2) \triangleq \lambda\rho \in (A \to_{fs} N) \to x_1\,\rho + x_2\,\rho.$$

The problem is that F_2 does not satisfy the freshness condition for binders; in other words there is an $a \in A$ and $x \in (A \to_{fs} N) \to_{fs} N$ for which $a \,\#\, \lambda\rho \in (A \to_{fs} N) \to x(\rho[a \mapsto 1])$ does not hold (see Exercise 8.3(b)).

To solve this problem we identify a property of environment functionals that is preserved by the operations needed in (8.45). (This is analogous to 'strengthening the induction hypothesis' in a proof by induction, given the close relationship that exists between recursion and induction.) Specifically, we cut down to those $x \in (A \to_{fs} N) \to_{fs} N$ whose value at an environment ρ only depends on the values of ρ at names in the support of x. More precisely, consider the nominal subset of $(A \to_{fs} N) \to_{fs} N$ given by

$$X \triangleq \{x \in (A \to_{fs} N) \to_{fs} N \mid (\text{Ⅶ}a)(\forall\rho \in A \to_{fs} N)(\forall n \in N)\ x(\rho[a \mapsto n]) = x\rho\}.$$

It is not hard to see that the functions F_1, F_2, F_3 defined in (8.46) are equivariant and satisfy

$$F_1\,a \in X,$$
$$x \in X \Rightarrow F_2(a, e, x) \in X,$$
$$x_1, x_2 \in X \Rightarrow F_3(e_1, e_2, x_1, x_2) \in X.$$

So they give morphisms in **Nom**:

$$F_1 : \mathbb{A} \to X,$$
$$F_2 : \mathbb{A} \times \Sigma_\alpha(\text{Term}) \times X \to X,$$
$$F_3 : \Sigma_\alpha(\text{Term}) \times \Sigma_\alpha(\text{Term}) \times X \times X \to X.$$

Furthermore, F_2 satisfies the freshness condition for binders (8.40), because for any $a \in \mathbb{A}$ and $x \in X$, using the Choose-a-Fresh-Name Principle to pick $a_1 \mathbin{\#} (a, x, \lambda\rho \to x(\rho[a \mapsto 1]))$, we have

$$a$$
$$=$$
$$(a\ a_1) \cdot a_1$$
$$\#\quad \{\text{since } a_1 \mathbin{\#} \lambda\rho \to x(\rho[a \mapsto 1])\}$$
$$(a\ a_1) \cdot (\lambda\rho \to x(\rho[a \mapsto 1]))$$
$$=\quad \{\text{by definition of the action of permutations on functions}\}$$
$$\lambda\rho \to (a\ a_1) \cdot (x(((a\ a_1) \cdot \rho)[a \mapsto 1]))$$
$$=\quad \{\text{by Exercise 8.3(a) and since } a_1 \neq a\}$$
$$\lambda\rho \to (a\ a_1) \cdot (x(\rho[a \mapsto 1][a_1 \mapsto \rho\,a]))$$
$$=\quad \{\text{since } x \in X \text{ and } a_1 \mathbin{\#} x\}$$
$$\lambda\rho \to (a\ a_1) \cdot (x(\rho[a \mapsto 1]))$$
$$=\quad \{\text{since } x(\rho[a \mapsto 1]) \in \mathbb{N} \text{ and hence has empty support}\}$$
$$\lambda\rho \to x(\rho[a \mapsto 1]).$$

Therefore we can apply Theorem 8.17 to get $\hat{F} \in \Sigma_\alpha(\text{Term}) \to_{\text{fs}} X$ satisfying (8.41); and since $\text{supp}(F_1, F_2, F_3) = \emptyset$, this implies that we do have the required recursion properties (8.45) once we take $cbvs = \hat{F}$.

8.6 Induction

Initial algebras $I : TD \to D$ for functors $T : \mathbf{C} \to \mathbf{C}$ automatically satisfy a category-theoretic induction principle: if a subobject of D, given by a monomorphism $M : P \rightarrowtail D$ say, is such that $I \circ TM$ factors through M:

$$\begin{array}{ccc}
TP & \xrightarrow{\ TM\ } & TD \\
\big\downarrow & & \big\downarrow{\scriptstyle I} \\
P & \xrightarrow[\ M\ ]{} & D,
\end{array}$$

(8.47)

then the subobject is necessarily the whole of D, that is, M is an isomorphism. We leave the proof of this as an exercise (Exercise 8.4).

When C is **Nom**, we know from Section 2.5 that subobjects correspond to equivariant subsets. Just as for recursion, in order to capture some common informal uses of induction in the presence of α-equivalence, we need to establish a stronger version of this induction principle, one that applies to finitely supported subsets rather than just equivariant ones. To do so we exploit the fact that not only do nominal algebraic functors preserve monomorphisms and hence act on subobjects, but also this action internalizes to **Nom**'s power objects, the nominal sets of finitely supported subsets. (See Exercise 8.5.)

Given $X = (X_1, \ldots, X_n) \in \mathbf{Nom}^n$, define

$$P_{fs}^n X \triangleq P_{fs} X_1 \times \cdots \times P_{fs} X_n. \tag{8.48}$$

If Σ is a nominal algebraic signature with a single name-sort N and n data-sorts $D_1, \ldots, D_n$, then we get a sort-indexed family of equivariant functions

$$\Diamond_S : P_{fs}^n X \to P_{fs} (\llbracket S \rrbracket X) \tag{8.49}$$

defined by recursion on the structure of the sort S as follows:

$$\begin{aligned}
\Diamond_N P &= \mathbb{A}, \\
\Diamond_{D_i} P &= P_i, \\
\Diamond_1 P &= 1, \\
\Diamond_{S_1, S_2} P &= \{(d_1, d_2) \mid d_1 \in \Diamond_{S_1} P \wedge d_2 \in \Diamond_{S_2} P\}, \\
\Diamond_{N.S} P &= \{\langle a \rangle d \mid a \# P \wedge d \in \Diamond_S P\}.
\end{aligned} \tag{8.50}$$

Theorem 8.21 (α-Structural induction for nominal algebraic data types)
Let Σ be a nominal algebraic signature with a single name-sort N, with n data-sorts $D_1, \ldots, D_n$, and with operations as shown in (8.13). The initial algebra

$$D = (\Sigma_\alpha(D_1), \ldots, \Sigma_\alpha(D_n))$$

for the associated nominal algebraic functor $T : \mathbf{Nom}^n \to \mathbf{Nom}^n$ has the following induction property: for any $P = (P_1, \ldots, P_n) \in P_{fs}^n D$, to show that $P_i = \Sigma_\alpha(D_i)$ for each $i = 1, \ldots, n$ it suffices to show for each of the signature's operations $\mathrm{op}_{i,j} : S_{i,j} \to D_i$ that

$$(\forall d \in \llbracket S_{i,j} \rrbracket D) \, d \in \Diamond_{S_{i,j}} P \Rightarrow \mathrm{op}_{i,j}(I_{S_{i,j}} d) \in P_i, \tag{8.51}$$

where $I_{S_{i,j}} : \llbracket S_{i,j} \rrbracket D \to \Sigma_\alpha(S_{i,j})$ is as in (8.21).

Proof Given $P \in P_{fs}^n D$ satisfying (8.51) for all $i = 1, \ldots, n$ and $j = 1, \ldots, m_i$, we will show that the sort-indexed family of subsets

$$H_S \triangleq \{t \in \Sigma(S) \mid (\forall \pi \in \mathrm{Perm}\,\mathbb{A})(\exists d \in \Diamond_S P) \, I_S \, d = [\pi \cdot t]_{=_\alpha}\}$$

is closed under the rules in Definition 8.2 inductively defining the sets $\Sigma(S)$

of raw terms of each sort, and hence that $H_S = \Sigma(S)$. (The quantification over all finite permutations $\pi \in \mathrm{Perm}\,\mathbb{A}$ in the definition of H_S is there to ensure that these subsets are equivariant, despite the fact that P may have non-empty support; indeed, it is easy to see from the definition that we have $t \in H_S \Rightarrow \pi \cdot t \in H_S$.). We get $P_i = \Sigma_\alpha(D_i)$ from $H_S = \Sigma(S)$ in case $S = D_i$, since $\Sigma_\alpha(D_i) = \Sigma(D_i)/{=_\alpha}$, $\Diamond_{D_i} P = P_i$ and $I_{D_i} = \mathrm{id}_{\Sigma_\alpha(D_i)}$.

Closure of H_S under the rules in Definition 8.2 for atomic name, unit and pair raw terms is straightforward. Closure under the rule for raw terms of the form $\mathrm{op}\,t$ follows directly from the assumption (8.51). So it just remains to show closure under the rule for raw terms of the form $a \,.\, t$. So suppose $t \in H_S$, $a \in \mathbb{A}$ and $\pi \in \mathrm{Perm}\,\mathbb{A}$. We have to find $d \in \Diamond_{\mathtt{N}.S} P$ with $I_{\mathtt{N}.S}\, d = [\pi \cdot (a \,.\, t)]_{=_\alpha}$. Use the Choose-a-Fresh-Name Principle to pick $a'\,\#\,(a, \pi, t, P)$. Since $t \in H_S$, there exists $d' \in \Diamond_S P$ with $I_S\, d' = [(\pi\,a\,a') \cdot \pi \cdot t]_{=_\alpha}$. Since $a'\,\#\,P$, by definition of $\Diamond_{\mathtt{N}.S} P$ it contains $\langle a'\rangle d'$; and by definition of $I_{\mathtt{N}.S}$, we have $I_{\mathtt{N}.S}(\langle a'\rangle d') = a' \,.\, (I_S\, d') = [a' \,.\, ((\pi\,a\,a') \cdot \pi \cdot t)]_{=_\alpha} = [(\pi\,a) \,.\, (\pi \cdot t)]_{=_\alpha}$, since $a'\,\#\,(\pi\,a, \pi \cdot t)$. So we can take $d = \langle a'\rangle d'$. $\qquad\qquad\square$

We saw by example in Section 8.5 that the structure needed for a T-algebra is equivalent to giving some functions not directly involving the name abstraction construct, together with a 'freshness condition for binders'. Similarly, the induction hypothesis (8.51) in the α-structural induction theorem is equivalent to a more elementary, albeit more involved condition involving the freshness relation. See Pitts (2006, theorem 5.2) for the general case. Here we just illustrate this for the signature from Example 8.4. In this case $D = \Sigma_\alpha(\mathrm{Term})$ is the nominal set of λ-terms modulo α-equivalence. The induction hypothesis (8.51) for the signature's three operations, V, L and A is equivalent to asserting of a finitely supported subset $P \in P_{\mathrm{fs}}(\Sigma_\alpha(\mathrm{Term}))$ that it satisfies

$$
\begin{aligned}
&(\forall a \in \mathbb{A})\,\mathrm{V}\,a \in P \\
&\wedge\ (\mathsf{И}a)(\forall e \in \Sigma_\alpha(\mathrm{Term}))\ e \in P \Rightarrow \mathrm{L}\,a \,.\, e \in P \qquad\qquad (8.52)\\
&\wedge\ (\forall e_1, e_2 \in \Sigma_\alpha(\mathrm{Term}))\ e_1 \in P \wedge e_2 \in P \Rightarrow \mathrm{A}(e_1\,,\,e_2) \in P.
\end{aligned}
$$

(In the case of L we use the equivalence of

$$
(\forall a \in \mathbb{A})(\forall e \in \Sigma_\alpha(\mathrm{Term}))\ a \,\#\, P \wedge e \in P \Rightarrow \mathrm{L}\,a \,.\, e \in P,
$$

with

$$
(\mathsf{И}a)(\forall e \in \Sigma_\alpha(\mathrm{Term}))\ e \in P \Rightarrow \mathrm{L}\,a \,.\, e \in P,
$$

which follows from the 'some/any' theorem.) So we get the following corollary of Theorem 8.21.

Corollary 8.22 (α-**structural induction principle for** λ-**terms**) *With Σ as in Example 8.4, for any finitely supported subset $P \in P_{fs}(\Sigma_\alpha(\text{Term}))$, if (8.52) holds, then $(\forall e \in \Sigma_\alpha(\text{Term}))\ e \in P$.*

Example 8.23 Consider the definition (8.27) in Example 8.14 of capture-avoiding substitution $[a := e]e'$ of e for free occurrences of the variable $V\,a$ in e'. We saw above that $[a := e] : \Sigma_\alpha(\text{Term}) \to \Sigma_\alpha(\text{Term})$ is the function $\hat{F}$ in Theorem 8.17 when F_1, F_2, F_3 are defined as in Example 8.19. We illustrate the α-structural induction principle for λ-terms by using Corollary 8.22 to prove

$$a \# e_1 \Rightarrow [a := e]e_1 = e_1.$$

Given $a \in \mathbb{A}$ and $e \in \Sigma_\alpha(\text{Term})$, define

$$P \triangleq \{e_1 \in \Sigma_\alpha(\text{Term}) \mid a \# e_1 \Rightarrow [a := e]e_1 = e_1\}.$$

Thus $P \in P_{fs}(\Sigma_\alpha(\text{Term}))$ is supported by $\{a\} \cup \text{supp}\,e$. To see that P is the whole of $\Sigma_\alpha(\text{Term})$ we need to check that it satisfies (8.52).

Proof of $(\forall a_1 \in \mathbb{A})\ V\,a_1 \in P$.
For any $a_1 \in \mathbb{A}$, if $a \# V\,a_1$ then $a \neq a_1$ and hence $[a := e](V\,a_1) = F_1\,a_1 = V\,a_1$; so $V\,a_1 \in P$. □

Proof of $(\text{\rotatebox{180}{V}}a_1)(\forall e_1 \in \Sigma_\alpha(\text{Term}))\ e_1 \in P \Rightarrow L\,a_1\,.\,e_1 \in P$.
Since P is supported by $\{a\} \cup \text{supp}\,e$, by the 'some/any' theorem it suffices to prove

$$(\exists a_1 \in \mathbb{A})\ a_1 \# (a, e) \wedge (\forall e_1 \in \Sigma_\alpha(\text{Term}))\ e_1 \in P \Rightarrow L\,a_1\,.\,e_1 \in P.$$

Use the Choose-a-Fresh-Name Principle to pick $a_1 \in \mathbb{A}$ with $a_1 \# (a, e)$. For any $e_1 \in P$, if $a \# L\,a_1\,.\,e_1$, then since $a \neq a_1$ we must have $a \# e_1$ and therefore

$$
\begin{aligned}
&[a := e](L\,a_1\,.\,e_1) \\
={}& \{\text{since } [a := e] \text{ is } \hat{F} \text{ and } a_1 \# (a, e)\} \\
&F_2(a_1, e_1, [a := e]e_1) \\
={}& \{\text{by definition of } F_2\} \\
&L\,a_1\,.\,[a := e]e_1 \\
={}& \{\text{since } e_1 \in P \text{ and } a \# e_1\} \\
&L\,a_1\,.\,e_1.
\end{aligned}
$$

So $L\,a_1\,.\,e_1 \in P$. □

Proof of $(\forall e_1, e_2 \in \Sigma_\alpha(\text{Term}))\ e_1 \in P \wedge e_2 \in P \Rightarrow A(e_1, e_2) \in P$.
Suppose that $e_1 \in P$ and $e_2 \in P$. If $a \# A(e_1, e_2)$, then $a \# e_1 \wedge a \# e_2$ and hence $[a := e]e_i = e_i$ for $i = 1, 2$. Therefore $[a := e](A(e_1, e_2)) =$

$F_3(e_1, e_2, [a := e]e_1, [a := e]e_2) = A([a := e]e_1, [a := e]e_2) = A(e_1, e_2)$. Thus $A(e_1, e_2) \in P$. □

Exercises

8.1 Show that nominal algebraic functors preserve countable colimits of chains in **Nom**.

8.2 A *generalized* nominal algebraic signature has sorts constructed as in (8.2) except that N . S is replaced by S . S in that grammar. The intended meaning of a sort S_1 . S_2 is given by the generalized form of name abstraction considered in Section 4.6:

$$[\![S_1 . S_2]\!]X \triangleq [[\![S_1]\!]X]([\![S_2]\!]X).$$

Investigate whether the results in this chapter, and in particular the initial algebra theorem (Theorem 8.15), extend to this generalized form of signature.

8.3 (a) If $x \in (A \rightarrow_{\text{fs}} N) \rightarrow_{\text{fs}} N$, $\rho \in A \rightarrow_{\text{fs}} N$ and $\pi \in \text{Perm} A$, show that $\pi \cdot \rho = \rho \circ \pi^{-1}$ and $(\pi \cdot x)\rho = x(\rho \circ \pi)$.

   (b) If $\rho \in A \rightarrow_{\text{fs}} N$ and $a \in A$, define

$$\rho[a \mapsto 1] \triangleq \lambda b \in A \rightarrow \text{if } b = a \text{ then } 1 \text{ else } \rho b.$$

   Note that by the Finite Support Principle, $\rho[a \mapsto 1] \in A \rightarrow_{\text{fs}} N$; and similarly $\lambda\rho \in (A \rightarrow_{\text{fs}} N) \rightarrow x(\rho[a \mapsto 1])$ is in $(A \rightarrow_{\text{fs}} N) \rightarrow_{\text{fs}} N$. Given $a \in A$, show that there exists $x \in (A \rightarrow_{\text{fs}} N) \rightarrow_{\text{fs}} N$ such that a is in the support of $\lambda\rho \in (A \rightarrow_{\text{fs}} N) \rightarrow x(\rho[a \mapsto 1])$. [Hint: consider the equivariant function mapping each $\rho \in A \rightarrow_{\text{fs}} N$ to the cardinality of $\{b \in A \mid \rho b = 1\}$ if that set is finite and to 0 otherwise.]

8.4 Prove the category-theoretic induction principle mentioned at the beginning of Section 8.6.

8.5 If $T : \textbf{Nom}^n \rightarrow \textbf{Nom}^n$ is the nominal algebraic functor associated with a signature Σ as in Definition 8.12, then from (8.49) we get equivariant functions

$$\Diamond_T : P_{\text{fs}}^n X \rightarrow P_{\text{fs}}^n (TX)$$

mapping each $P \in P_{\text{fs}}^n X$ to $\Diamond_T P = (\Diamond_{T_1} P, \ldots, \Diamond_{T_n} P)$, where

$$\Diamond_{T_i} P \triangleq \bigcup_{j=1,\ldots,m_i} \{\text{inj}_j d \mid d \in \Diamond_{S_{i,j}} P\} \in P_{\text{fs}} (T_i X).$$

Show that these functions agree with the functorial action of T in the following sense: if $P_i \subseteq X_i$ ($i = 1, \ldots, n$) are equivariant subsets and we write $M_i : P_i \to X_i$ for the inclusion functions, prove that $TM : TP \to TX$ is again a monomorphism in $\mathbf{Nom}^n$ and that the corresponding element of $P^n_{fs} X$ is $\diamondsuit_T P$.

8.6 Use the α-structural induction principle for λ-terms to show that capture-avoiding substitution satisfies

$$a_2 \,\#\, (a_1, e_1)$$
$$\Rightarrow [a_1 := e_1]([a_2 := e_2]e) = [a_2 := [a_1 := e_1]e_2]([a_1 := e_1]e).$$

9

Locally scoped names

This chapter uses nominal sets to model language constructs for hiding the identity of a name outside a given scope. Such locally scoped names are a ubiquitous feature of programming languages, because of the need for constructs to control 'name spaces' and enable the modular construction of code without having to worry about accidental clashes of names between different constituent pieces. We consider nominal sets equipped with an operation of *name restriction* and use them to give semantics for two simple examples of languages with locally scoped names: the functional theory of local names of Odersky (1994) and the *v*-calculus of Pitts and Stark (1993).

9.1 The category of nominal restriction sets

We focus on three characteristic properties of locally scoped names that define what we mean by 'name restriction'. The first property is that the name restriction operation should be a binder: occurrences of the name within its scope can be consistently renamed without changing the overall meaning of the scoped expression. Assuming language expressions are modelled by the elements of a nominal set X, then in view of the results in Chapter 4, we require the name restriction operation to be given by an equivariant function $r : [\mathbb{A}]X \to X$ on the nominal set of name abstractions.

The second property is that if a sequence of names is hidden, then the order in which they are scoped is immaterial. So in particular for two names a_1 and a_2 we should have

$$r\langle a_1\rangle(r\langle a_2\rangle x) = r\langle a_2\rangle(r\langle a_1\rangle x). \qquad (9.1)$$

The third property is that if there are no free occurrences of a name within a particular scope, then hiding it should have no effect on the meaning of the expression. In view of the results in Chapter 3, we model 'no free occurrence' by the freshness relation of nominal sets and require

$$a \mathrel{\#} x \Rightarrow r\langle a\rangle x = x. \tag{9.2}$$

The conditions (9.1) and (9.2) on r can be expressed neatly by commutative diagrams in **Nom** using the following morphisms.

Definition 9.1 For each $X \in$ **Nom**, applying the freshness theorem (Theorem 3.11) to the fact that $a \mathrel{\#} \langle a\rangle x$ (Proposition 4.5), we get an equivariant function

$$\kappa_X : X \to [\mathbb{A}]X, \tag{9.3}$$

$$\kappa_X \triangleq \lambda x \in X \to \text{fresh } a \text{ in } \langle a\rangle x.$$

Similarly, applying Corollary 4.17 twice to the equivariant function $\mathbb{A} \times \mathbb{A} \times X \to [\mathbb{A}][\mathbb{A}]X$ that maps (a_1, a_2, x) to $\langle a_2\rangle(\langle a_1\rangle x)$, we get an equivariant function

$$\delta_X : [\mathbb{A}][\mathbb{A}]X \to [\mathbb{A}][\mathbb{A}]X$$

satisfying for all $a_1, a_2 \in \mathbb{A}$ and $x \in X$

$$a_1 \neq a_2 \Rightarrow \delta_X\langle a_1\rangle(\langle a_2\rangle x) = \langle a_2\rangle(\langle a_1\rangle x). \tag{9.4}$$

It is not hard to see that condition (9.2) on r is equivalent to requiring the following diagram to commute in **Nom**:

$$\begin{array}{ccc}
X & \xrightarrow{\ \kappa_X\ } & [\mathbb{A}]X \\
& \mathrlap{\text{id}_X} \searrow & \ \downarrow{r} \\
& & X\,.
\end{array} \tag{9.5}$$

Note that (9.1) is trivially equivalent to the restricted property $a_1 \neq a_2 \Rightarrow r\langle a_1\rangle(r\langle a_2\rangle x) = r\langle a_2\rangle(r\langle a_1\rangle x)$ and this is equivalent to the following commutative diagram, which uses the functoriality of name abstraction (Section 4.4):

$$\begin{array}{ccc}
[\mathbb{A}][\mathbb{A}]X & \xrightarrow{\ \ \delta_X\ \ } & [\mathbb{A}][\mathbb{A}]X \\
\downarrow{[\mathbb{A}]r} & & \downarrow{[\mathbb{A}]r} \\
[\mathbb{A}]X & & [\mathbb{A}]X\,. \\
& \mathrlap{r} \searrow \quad \swarrow \mathrlap{r} & \\
& X &
\end{array} \tag{9.6}$$

(Note that property (9.4) cannot be strengthened by dropping the condition $a_1 \neq a_2$; see Exercise 9.1.)

Definition 9.2 A *name restriction operation* on a nominal set X is a morphism $r \in \mathbf{Nom}([\mathbb{A}]X, X)$ making the diagrams in (9.5) and (9.6) commute. A nominal set equipped with such an operation is called a *nominal restriction set*. We write **Res** for the category whose objects are nominal restriction sets (X, r) and whose morphisms $(X, r) \to (X', r')$ are equivariant functions $f : X \to X'$ that commute with the name restriction operations:

$$
\begin{array}{ccc}
[\mathbb{A}]X & \xrightarrow{\;[\mathbb{A}]f\;} & [\mathbb{A}]X' \\
{\scriptstyle r}\downarrow & & \downarrow{\scriptstyle r'} \\
X & \xrightarrow[\;f\;]{} & X' .
\end{array}
\qquad (9.7)
$$

Remark 9.3 A nominal set can support several different name restriction operations (see Example 9.5). Nevertheless we will usually refer to a nominal restriction set (X, r) via its underlying nominal set X and use a single notation for the restriction operation: given $a \in \mathbb{A}$ and $x \in X$, we write $a \backslash x$ for $r\langle a \rangle x$. With this notation (9.2) and (9.1) become

$$(\forall a \in \mathbb{A}, x \in X)\; a \# x \Rightarrow a \backslash x = x, \qquad (9.8)$$

$$(\forall a_1, a_2 \in \mathbb{A}, x \in X)\; a_1 \backslash (a_2 \backslash x) = a_2 \backslash (a_1 \backslash x) . \qquad (9.9)$$

By (2.7) and Proposition 4.5 we have $a \notin \mathrm{supp}\langle a \rangle x \supseteq \mathrm{supp}\, r(\langle a \rangle x)$; and hence we also have

$$(\forall a \in \mathbb{A}, x \in X)\; a \# a \backslash x . \qquad (9.10)$$

Conversely, if an equivariant function $\_\backslash\_ : \mathbb{A} \times X \to X$ satisfies (9.8)–(9.10) then it induces an equivariant function $[\mathbb{A}]X \to X$ (by Corollary 4.17) that makes (9.5) and (9.6) commute. This formulation of name restriction operations is sometimes more convenient than the one in Definition 9.2 (and is the one used in Pitts, 2011).

Here are two examples of name restriction operations. Even though they are rather simple, when combined with the constructions in Sections 9.2 and 9.3 they can result in non-trivial examples of nominal restriction sets (Exercise 9.2).

Example 9.4 The discrete nominal set on a set X (Example 2.5) has a unique name restriction operation, necessarily satisfying $a \backslash x = x$.

Example 9.5   Suppose given a nominal set X and an element $x_0 \in X$ with supp $x_0 = \emptyset$. Such elements correspond to global sections of X in **Nom**, that is, elements of **Nom**$(1, X)$; see Exercise 2.1. Then there is a name restriction operation on X satisfying for all $a \in \mathbb{A}$ and $x \in X$

$$a \backslash x = \begin{cases} x & \text{if } a \, \# \, x, \\ x_0 & \text{otherwise.} \end{cases} \tag{9.11}$$

To see this one can apply Remark 9.3 and easily check that the equivariant function $\mathbb{A} \times X \to X$ given by (9.11) satisfies (9.8)–(9.10).

One way to obtain a nominal set with a global section is to start with any nominal set X and form the coproduct $X + 1$. The monad $\_ + 1 : \textbf{Nom} \to \textbf{Nom}$ is the 'notion of computation' (Moggi, 1991) consisting of a single global exception. Recall from Section 2.2 that coproducts in **Nom** are given by disjoint union. Identifying X with a subset of $X + 1$ and writing $\perp \in X + 1$ for the element corresponding to the unique element of 1, the above name restriction operation gives

$$a \backslash x = \begin{cases} x & \text{if } a \, \# \, x, \\ \perp & \text{otherwise,} \end{cases}$$

$$a \backslash \perp = \perp .$$

So this is a form of local scoping for names that tries to stick as close as it can to the common informal practice when manipulating syntax with binders of using locally scoped names in a trivial way, raising a global exception when the use turns out to be non-trivial, that is, when the scoped name does actually occur in the support of the expression.

9.2 Products and coproducts

Given a set-indexed family of nominal restriction sets $(X_i \mid i \in I)$, we saw in Section 2.2 that the disjoint union $\sum_{i \in I} X_i$ gives the coproduct in **Nom**. It is not hard to see that it also gives the coproduct in **Res** once we endow it with the name restriction operation satisfying $a \backslash (i, x) = (i, a \backslash x)$ for each $a \in \mathbb{A}$, $i \in I$ and $x \in X_i$.

The product of the X_i in **Nom** is given by finitely supported elements of the cartesian product, $(\prod_{i \in I} X_i)_{\text{fs}}$ (Corollary 2.16). Given such an element $(x_i \mid i \in I)$, then $(a \backslash x_i \mid i \in I)$ is another such. It is easy to see that this gives a name restriction operation on the product satisfying $a \backslash (x_i \mid i \in I) = (a \backslash x_i \mid i \in I)$; and this makes $(\prod_{i \in I} X_i)_{fs}$ into the product in **Res**. In particular, for finite products we get the following result.

Theorem 9.6 *Given* $X, X' \in$ **Res**, *the nominal set* $X \times X'$ *of ordered pairs possesses a name restriction operation satisfying for all* $a \in \mathbb{A}$, $x \in X$ *and* $x' \in X'$

$$a \backslash (x, x') = (a \backslash x, a \backslash x') . \tag{9.12}$$

This gives the product of X *and* X' *in the category* **Res**.

Proof It is easy to see that the equivariant function $\mathbb{A} \times (X \times X') \to (X \times X')$ given by (9.12) satisfies (9.8)–(9.10) and hence determines a name restriction operation on the cartesian product. Note that the projection functions commute with name restriction, so we get

$$X \overset{\pi_1}{\leftarrow} X \times X' \overset{\pi_2}{\to} X' \tag{9.13}$$

in **Res**. Furthermore, if we have $f \in$ **Res**(Y, X) and $f' \in$ **Res**(Y, X'), then the equivariant function $\langle f, f' \rangle \triangleq \lambda y \in Y \to (f y, f' y)$ also commutes with name restriction. It follows that (9.13) is indeed the product of X and X' in the category **Res**. $\square$

9.3 Functions

Theorem 9.7 *For each* $X \in$ **Nom** *and* $Y \in$ **Res**, *the nominal set* $X \to_{fs} Y$ *of finitely supported functions possesses a name restriction operation satisfying for all* $f \in X \to_{fs} Y$, $x \in X$ *and* $a \in \mathbb{A}$

$$(a \backslash f) x = \text{fresh } a' \text{ in } a' \backslash (((a \, a') \cdot f) x) \tag{9.14}$$

and hence also

$$a \# x \Rightarrow (a \backslash f) x = a \backslash (f x) . \tag{9.15}$$

Proof We lift the name restriction operation $r : [\mathbb{A}]Y \to Y$ on Y to one on $X \to_{fs} Y$ using the isomorphism $i : [\mathbb{A}](X \to_{fs} Y) \cong [\mathbb{A}]X \to_{fs} [\mathbb{A}]Y$ from Proposition 4.14. Define

$$r' \triangleq [\mathbb{A}](X \to_{fs} Y) \overset{i}{\cong} ([\mathbb{A}]X \to_{fs} [\mathbb{A}]Y) \overset{\kappa_X}{\to} (X \to_{fs} [\mathbb{A}]Y) \overset{r_*}{\to} (X \to_{fs} Y), \tag{9.16}$$

where κ_X is pre-composition with the morphism from (9.3) and r_* is post-composition with the name restriction operation r. Thus for any $f \in X \to_{fs} Y$,

$x \in X$ and $a \in \mathbb{A}$ we have

$$(a \backslash f) x$$
$= \quad$ {by defintion of the notation $\_\backslash\_$}
$$r'(\langle a \rangle f) x$$
$= \quad$ {by definition of r'}
$$r(i(\langle a \rangle f)(\kappa_X x))$$
$= \quad$ {by definition of i in (4.29)}
$$r(\text{fresh } a' \text{ in } \langle a' \rangle (((a \; a') \cdot f) x))$$
$= \quad$ {since r is equivariant}
$$\text{fresh } a' \text{ in } r \langle a' \rangle (((a \; a') \cdot f) x),$$

as required for (9.14). In particular, if $a \# x$, then

$$(a \backslash f) x$$
$= \quad$ {by (9.14), picking some/any $a' \# (f, x)$}
$$r \langle a' \rangle (((a \; a') \cdot f) x)$$
$= \quad$ {since $a, a' \# x$}
$$r \langle a' \rangle (((a \; a') \cdot (f \; x))$$
$= \quad$ {by Lemma 4.3, since $a' \# (a, f \; x)$}
$$r \langle a \rangle (f \; x)$$
$= \quad$ {by definition of the notation $\_\backslash\_$}
$$a \backslash (f \; x),$$

so that r' also satisfies (9.15). So it remains to prove that r' satisfies the properties (9.1) and (9.2) required of a name restriction operation. For the latter, if $a \# f$, then for all $x \in X$

$$(a \backslash f) x$$
$= \quad$ {by (9.14), picking some/any $a' \# (f, x)$}
$$r \langle a' \rangle (((a \; a') \cdot f) x)$$
$= \quad$ {since $a, a' \# f$}
$$r \langle a' \rangle (f \; x)$$
$= \quad$ {by (9.5) for r, since $a' \# f \; x$}
$$f \; x,$$

so that $a \backslash f = f$. Finally, for property (9.1) it suffices to check that $a_1 \backslash (a_2 \backslash f) =$

$a_2 \backslash (a_1 \backslash f)$ when $a_1 \neq a_2$; but in that case we have for any $x \in X$

$(a_1 \backslash (a_2 \backslash f)) \, x$
$= \{$by (9.14), picking some/any $a_1' \# (a_1, a_2, f, x)\}$
$r\langle a_1' \rangle (((a_1 \; a_1') \cdot (r'\langle a_2 \rangle f)) \, x)$
$= \{$since r' is equivariant and $a_2 \# (a_1, a_1')\}$
$r\langle a_1' \rangle ((r'\langle a_2 \rangle ((a_1 \; a_1') \cdot f)) \, x)$
$= \{$by (9.14), picking some/any $a_2' \# (a_1, a_1', a_2, f, x)\}$
$r\langle a_1' \rangle (r\langle a_2' \rangle (((a_2 \; a_2')(a_1 \; a_1') \cdot f) \, x))$
$= \{$since $a_2 \# (a_1, a_1') \# a_2'\}$
$r\langle a_1' \rangle (r\langle a_2' \rangle (((a_1 \; a_1')(a_2 \; a_2') \cdot f) \, x))$
$= \{$by (9.1) for $r\}$
$r\langle a_2' \rangle (r\langle a_1' \rangle (((a_1 \; a_1')(a_2 \; a_2') \cdot f) \, x))$
$= \{$by a symmetric argument$\}$
$(a_2 \backslash (a_1 \backslash f)) \, x$. $\qquad \square$

Supposing both X and Y are nominal restriction sets, $X \to_{\mathrm{fs}} Y$ equipped with the above name restriction operation does not in general give the exponential of Y by X in the category **Res**. We can get such an exponential by cutting down to a suitable equivariant subset of $X \to_{\mathrm{fs}} Y$.

Corollary 9.8 **Res** *is a cartesian closed category.*

Proof We noted in Section 9.2 that **Res** has finite products; so it just remains to show that it has exponentials. Given $X, Y \in$ **Res**, define

$$X \to_{\mathrm{res}} Y \triangleq \{f \in X \to_{\mathrm{fs}} Y \mid (\forall a \in \mathbb{A}, x \in X) \; a \backslash (f \, x) = a \backslash (f \, (a \backslash x))\}. \quad (9.17)$$

Since this is an equivariant subset of $X \to_{\mathrm{fs}} Y$, it determines a nominal set as in Lemma 2.22. Let $r' : [\mathbb{A}](X \to_{\mathrm{fs}} Y) \to (X \to_{\mathrm{fs}} Y)$ be the name restriction operation from Theorem 9.7. We claim that it induces one for the nominal set $X \to_{\mathrm{res}} Y$. For if $f \in X \to_{\mathrm{res}} Y$ and $a \in \mathbb{A}$, then for all $a' \in \mathbb{A}$ and $x \in X$

$a' \backslash (r'(\langle a \rangle f) \, x)$
$= \{$by (9.14), picking some/any $a'' \# (a, a', f, x)\}$
$a' \backslash a'' \backslash (((a \; a'') \cdot f) \, x)$
$= \{$by (9.9)$\}$
$a'' \backslash a' \backslash (((a \; a'') \cdot f) \, x)$
$= \{$since $(a \; a'') \cdot f \in X \to_{\mathrm{res}} Y\}$
$a'' \backslash a' \backslash (((a \; a'') \cdot f) \, (a' \backslash x))$
$= \{$by a symmetric argument$\}$
$a' \backslash (r'(\langle a \rangle f)(a' \backslash x))$

and hence $r'(\langle a \rangle f) \in X \to_{\text{res}} Y$. So r' restricts to give a morphism $[\mathbb{A}](X \to_{\text{res}} Y) \to (X \to_{\text{res}} Y)$; and this has properties (9.1) and (9.2) because r' does.

If $f \in X \to_{\text{fs}} Y$, $x \in X$ and $a \in \mathbb{A}$, then since $a \mathbin{\#} a \backslash x$ (9.10), from property (9.15) we have $(a \backslash f)(a \backslash x) = a \backslash (f(a \backslash x))$. So if f is in the subset $X \to_{\text{res}} Y$, then we have $(a \backslash f)(a \backslash x) = a \backslash (f(a \backslash x)) = a \backslash (f\,x)$. Therefore the application function app : $(X \to_{\text{fs}} Y) \times X \to Y$ from (2.13), when restricted to the subset $X \to_{\text{res}} Y \subseteq X \to_{\text{fs}} Y$, gives a morphism $(X \to_{\text{res}} Y) \times X \to Y$ in **Res**. This inherits from app the universal property needed to make $X \to_{\text{res}} Y$ the exponential in **Res**. To see this, it suffices to show that for any $f \in \mathbf{Res}(Z \times X, Y)$ that the curried function curry $f \in \mathbf{Nom}(Z, X \to_{\text{fs}} Y)$ (2.14) factors through the inclusion $X \to_{\text{res}} Y \subseteq X \to_{\text{fs}} Y$ to give a morphism $Z \to (X \to_{\text{res}} Y)$ in **Res**. For any $a \in \mathbb{A}$, $z \in Z$ and $x \in X$ we have

$$a \backslash (\text{curry } f\,z\,x)$$
$$= \quad \{\text{by definition of curry } f\}$$
$$a \backslash (f(z, x))$$
$$= \quad \{\text{since } f \text{ is a morphism in } \mathbf{Res}\}$$
$$f(a \backslash z, a \backslash x)$$
$$= \quad \{\text{by (9.8) and (9.10)}\}$$
$$f(a \backslash z, a \backslash (a \backslash x))$$
$$= \quad \{\text{since } f \text{ is a morphism in } \mathbf{Res}\}$$
$$a \backslash (f(z, a \backslash x))$$
$$= \quad \{\text{by definition of curry } f\}$$
$$a \backslash (\text{curry } f\,z\,(a \backslash x),$$

so that curry $f\,z \in X \to_{\text{res}} Y$; and

$$(a \backslash (\text{curry } f\,z))\,x$$
$$= \quad \{\text{by (9.14), picking some/any } a' \mathbin{\#} (a, f, z, x)\}$$
$$a' \backslash (((a\,a') \cdot (\text{curry } f\,z))\,x)$$
$$= \quad \{\text{by definition of curry } f\}$$
$$a' \backslash (f((a\,a') \cdot z, x))$$
$$= \quad \{\text{since } f \text{ is a morphism in } \mathbf{Res}\}$$
$$f(a' \backslash ((a\,a') \cdot z), a' \backslash x))$$
$$= \quad \{\text{by (9.8), since } a' \mathbin{\#} x\}$$
$$f(a' \backslash ((a\,a') \cdot z), x)$$
$$= \quad \{\text{since } a' \mathbin{\#} (a, z)\}$$
$$f(a \backslash z, x)$$
$$= \quad \{\text{by definition of curry } f\}$$
$$\text{curry } f\,(a \backslash z)\,x,$$

so that curry f is indeed a morphism $Z \to (X \to_{\text{res}} Y)$ in **Res**. $\qquad\square$

Remark 9.9 **Res** is not only a cartesian closed category, it is in fact a Grothendieck topos (Johnstone, 2002). This is a consequence of an unpublished observation by S. Staton that **Res** is equivalent to the functor category [**pInj**, **Set**]. Here **pInj** is the category whose objects are finite ordinals and whose morphisms are injective partial functions; see Exercise 9.7. This result should be compared with the better known equivalence of **Nom** with the Schanuel topos, described in Section 6.3.

9.4 *λv*-Calculus

It turns out that the way name restriction operations are defined on pairs and functions in Theorems 9.6 and 9.7 corresponds to an existing, if somewhat neglected, notion of locally scoped names in the presence of higher-order functions due to Odersky (1994). Odersky's *λv-calculus* adds to the *λ*-calculus (with pairs and booleans) names and expressions *va. e* for localizing the identity of a name *a* to an expression *e*. The usual reduction relation $e \to e'$ for *λ*-calculus is extended with new reductions that explain how the binder *va. _* interacts with booleans, names, pairs and functions:

$$va.\, \texttt{true} \to \texttt{true}, \tag{9.18}$$

$$va.\, \texttt{false} \to \texttt{false}, \tag{9.19}$$

$$va.\, a' \to a' \quad \text{if } a \neq a', \tag{9.20}$$

$$va.\, (e_1, e_2) \to (va.\, e_1, va.\, e_2), \tag{9.21}$$

$$va.\, \lambda x.\, e \to \lambda x.\, va.\, e. \tag{9.22}$$

Note that scopes are pushed inwards through the various data constructs as reduction proceeds. This is in contrast to the more common form of locally scoped name involving dynamic allocation of fresh names that we discuss in Section 9.6, where scopes of local names extrude during evaluation. The relationship between the reduction (9.21) and the way we defined name restriction for pairs in Theorem 9.6 is clear. Not so clear is the precise relationship between the name restriction operation for functions in Theorem 9.7 and the reduction (9.22). To explain it, we extract from Pitts (2011, section 3.2) the nominal sets semantics for a simply typed version of the *λv*-calculus. The language's syntax is given in Figure 9.1.

The calculus contains two sorts of identifier, variables $x \in Var$ and names $a \in \mathbb{A}$. We assume the countably infinite set of variables Var is disjoint from $\mathbb{A}$ and is partitioned into countably infinite subsets $Var(T)$, where T ranges over the set *Type* of types; the elements of each $Var(T)$ are the variables of type T.

Types
$T \in Type$ ::=   Name   type of names
                     Bool   type of booleans
                     1   unit type
                     $T \times T$ product type
                     $T \to T$ function type

Expressions
$e \in Expr$ ::= x variable ($x \in Var$)
                     a atomic name ($a \in \mathbb{A}$)
                     $va.\, e$ locally scoped name
                     true   boolean true
                     false   boolean false
                     if e then e else e conditional
                     $e = e$ name equality test
                     $()$ unit value
                     (e, e) pair
                     fst e first projection
                     snd e second projection
                     $\lambda x.\, e$ function abstraction
                     $e\, e$ function application

$$\frac{x \in Var(T)}{x \in Expr(T)} \qquad \frac{a \in \mathbb{A}}{a \in Expr(\text{Name})} \qquad \frac{a \in \mathbb{A} \qquad e \in Expr(T)}{va.\, e \in Expr(T)}$$

$$\frac{b \in \{\text{true, false}\}}{b \in Expr(\text{Bool})} \qquad \frac{e_1 \in Expr(\text{Bool}) \qquad e_2 \in Expr(T) \qquad e_3 \in Expr(T)}{\text{if}\, e_1 \text{ then } e_2 \text{ else } e_3 \in Expr(T)}$$

$$\frac{e_1 \in Expr(\text{Name}) \qquad e_2 \in Expr(\text{Name})}{e_1 = e_2 \in Expr(\text{Bool})} \qquad \frac{}{() \in Expr(1)}$$

$$\frac{e_1 \in Expr(T_1) \qquad e_2 \in Expr(T_2)}{(e_1, e_2) \in Expr(T_1 \times T_2)} \qquad \frac{e \in Expr(T_1 \times T_2)}{\text{fst}\, e \in Expr(T_1)} \qquad \frac{e \in Expr(T_1 \times T_2)}{\text{snd}\, e \in Expr(T_2)}$$

$$\frac{x \in Var(T) \qquad e \in Expr(T')}{\lambda x.\, e \in Expr(T \to T')} \qquad \frac{e_1 \in Expr(T \to T') \qquad e_2 \in Expr(T)}{e_1\, e_2 \in Expr(T')}$$

Figure 9.1 Simply typed λ-calculus with locally scoped names.

Among all the expressions given by the grammar in Figure 9.1 we are only interested in the ones that are *well-typed*; the sets $Expr(T)$ of expressions of type T are inductively defined by the rules in the lower half of the figure.

Remark 9.10   Each $Expr(T)$ can be made into a nominal set as in Example 2.6, so that supp e is the finite set of atomic names occurring anywhere in the syntax tree e. Note that although $va.\, \_$ and $\lambda x.\, \_$ are binding operations, for the purposes of this section we do not bother to identify expressions up to α-equivalence of bound atomic names and bound variables. So in the terminology of Chapter 8 we are using the 'raw' terms of the λv-calculus (see Remark 8.3).

Simply typed λ-calculus can be interpreted in any cartesian closed category; see Lambek and Scott (1986), or Crole (1993), for example. So one might expect to use the cartesian closed category **Res** to model the λv-calculus. This does not work because some of its syntactic forms do not commute with $va. \_$ and hence do not denote morphisms of nominal restriction sets; for example, in the λv-calculus, a locally scoped function application $va.(e_1\ e_2)$ is not in general convertible with $(va.e_1)(va.e_2)$. In fact we interpret the calculus in a full subcategory of **Nom** whose objects are (the underlying nominal sets of) nominal restriction sets.

Each type $T \in Type$ determines a nominal set $[\![T]\!]_{\lambda v} \in$ **Nom** as follows:

$$[\![\text{Name}]\!]_{\lambda v} = \mathbb{A} \uplus \{\bot\} \qquad \text{nominal set of atomic names} \qquad (9.23)$$
with a global section adjoined,

$$[\![\text{Bool}]\!]_{\lambda v} = \mathbb{B} = \{\text{true}, \text{false}\} \quad \text{discrete nominal set}, \qquad (9.24)$$

$$[\![1]\!]_{\lambda v} = 1 = \{()\} \qquad \text{discrete nominal set}, \qquad (9.25)$$

$$[\![T_1 \times T_2]\!]_{\lambda v} = [\![T_1]\!]_{\lambda v} \times [\![T_2]\!]_{\lambda v} \quad \text{cartesian product}, \qquad (9.26)$$

$$[\![T_1 \to T_2]\!]_{\lambda v} = [\![T_1]\!]_{\lambda v} \to_{\text{fs}} [\![T_2]\!]_{\lambda v} \quad \text{finitely supported functions}. \qquad (9.27)$$

These each carry a nominal restriction operation: the one for $[\![\text{Name}]\!]_{\lambda v}$ is as in Example 9.5; the ones for $[\![\text{Bool}]\!]_{\lambda v}$ and $[\![1]\!]_{\lambda v}$ are as in Example 9.4; the one for $[\![T_1 \times T_2]\!]_{\lambda v}$ is inherited from those for $[\![T_1]\!]_{\lambda v}$ and $[\![T_2]\!]_{\lambda v}$ as in Theorem 9.6; and the one for $[\![T_1 \to T_2]\!]_{\lambda v}$ is inherited from the one for $[\![T_2]\!]_{\lambda v}$ as in Theorem 9.7.

The nominal set of λv-*environments* consists of finitely supported functions mapping variables of type T to elements of $[\![T]\!]_{\lambda v}$ for each $T \in Type$:

$$Env_{\lambda v} \triangleq \left(\prod_{T \in Type} Var(T) \to_{\text{fs}} [\![T]\!]_{\lambda v} \right)_{\text{fs}}. \qquad (9.28)$$

We can define equivariant functions

$$[\![\_]\!] : Expr(T) \to (Env_{\lambda v} \to_{\text{fs}} [\![T]\!]_{\lambda v}) \qquad (T \in Type) \qquad (9.29)$$

that give the meaning $[\![e]\!]\rho \in [\![T]\!]_{\lambda v}$ of an expression $e \in Expr(T)$ as a finitely supported function of environments $\rho \in Env_{\lambda v}$ supplying meanings for its free variables. The definition of $[\![e]\!]$ is by induction on the structure of e and gives the denotation functions the properties listed in Figure 9.2. Nearly all of these

$$\llbracket x \rrbracket \rho = \rho\, x$$

$$\llbracket a \rrbracket \rho = a$$

$$\llbracket va.\, e \rrbracket \rho = a \backslash (\llbracket e \rrbracket \rho) \quad \text{if } a \mathbin{\#} \rho$$

$$\llbracket \texttt{true} \rrbracket \rho = \text{true}$$

$$\llbracket \texttt{false} \rrbracket \rho = \text{false}$$

$$\llbracket \texttt{if } e_1 \texttt{ then } e_2 \texttt{ else } e_3 \rrbracket \rho = \text{if } \llbracket e_1 \rrbracket \rho \text{ then } \llbracket e_2 \rrbracket \rho \text{ else } \llbracket e_3 \rrbracket \rho$$

$$\llbracket e_1 = e_2 \rrbracket \rho = (\llbracket e_1 \rrbracket \rho = \llbracket e_2 \rrbracket \rho)$$

$$\llbracket () \rrbracket \rho = ()$$

$$\llbracket (e_1, e_2) \rrbracket \rho = (\llbracket e_1 \rrbracket \rho, \llbracket e_2 \rrbracket \rho)$$

$$\llbracket \texttt{fst } e \rrbracket \rho = \pi_1(\llbracket e \rrbracket \rho)$$

$$\llbracket \texttt{snd } e \rrbracket \rho = \pi_2(\llbracket e \rrbracket \rho)$$

$$\llbracket \lambda x.\, e \rrbracket \rho = \lambda d \in \llbracket T \rrbracket_{\lambda v} \to \llbracket e \rrbracket (\rho[x \mapsto d]) \quad \text{if } x \in Var(T)$$

$$\llbracket e_1\, e_2 \rrbracket \rho = \llbracket e_1 \rrbracket \rho (\llbracket e_2 \rrbracket \rho)$$

Figure 9.2 Denotational semantics of the λv-calculus.

properties are quite standard for an environment-style semantics of simply-typed λ-calculus; in particular the meaning of a function abstraction makes use of the operation updating an environment ρ to one $\rho[x \mapsto d]$ that maps x to d and otherwise acts like ρ. The only subtlety is for locally scoped names, where the clause in Figure 9.2 only specifies the value of $\llbracket va.\, e \rrbracket \rho$ in case $a \mathbin{\#} \rho$. In fact this is enough to define $\llbracket va.\, e \rrbracket$ as a total function: we use the name restriction operation on $\llbracket T \rrbracket_{\lambda v}$ to define one on $Env_{\lambda v} \to_{\text{fs}} \llbracket T \rrbracket_{\lambda v}$ as in Theorem 9.7 and define

$$\llbracket va.\, e \rrbracket \triangleq a \backslash \llbracket e \rrbracket . \tag{9.30}$$

Then as in (9.15) we have that $a \mathbin{\#} \rho$ implies $\llbracket va.\, e \rrbracket \rho = a \backslash (\llbracket e \rrbracket \rho)$.

This denotational semantics of λv-calculus expressions is sound for reduction: reducible expressions have equal denotations. We just show this for the reduction (9.22).

Proposition 9.11 *For all* $T, T' \in Type$, $a \in \mathbb{A}$, $x \in Var(T)$ *and* $e \in Expr(T')$, $\llbracket va.\, \lambda x.\, e \rrbracket = \llbracket \lambda x.\, va.\, e \rrbracket \in Env_{\lambda v} \to_{\text{fs}} \llbracket T \to T' \rrbracket_{\lambda v}$.

Proof For all $\rho \in Env_{\lambda v}$ we have

$$[\![va.\,\lambda x.\,e]\!]\rho$$
$$= \quad \{\text{by (9.30)}\}$$
$$(a\backslash[\![\lambda x.\,e]\!])\rho$$
$$= \quad \{\text{by (9.14), picking some/any } a' \, \# \, (a, e, \rho)\}$$
$$a'\backslash(((a\;a')\cdot[\![\lambda x.\,e]\!])\rho)$$
$$= \quad \{\text{since } [\![\_]\!] \text{ is equivariant}\}$$
$$a'\backslash((([\![\lambda x.\,(a\;a')\cdot e]\!])\rho).$$

Hence for any $d \in [\![T]\!]_{\lambda v}$

$$[\![va.\,\lambda x.\,e]\!]\rho\,d$$
$$=$$
$$(a'\backslash((([\![\lambda x.\,(a\;a')\cdot e]\!])\rho))\,d$$
$$= \quad \{\text{by (9.14), picking some/any } a'' \, \# \, (a, a', e, \rho, d)\}$$
$$a''\backslash(((a'\;a'')\cdot([\![\lambda x.\,(a\;a')\cdot e]\!])\rho)\,d)$$
$$= \quad \{\text{by equivariance and since } a', a'' \, \# \, (e, \rho)\}$$
$$a''\backslash([\![\lambda x.\,(a\;a'')\cdot e]\!]\rho\,d)$$
$$= \quad \{\text{by Figure 9.2}\}$$
$$a''\backslash([\![(a\;a'')\cdot e]\!]\,(\rho[x \mapsto d]))$$
$$= \quad \{\text{since } [\![\_]\!] \text{ is equivariant}\}$$
$$a''\backslash(((a\;a'')\cdot[\![e]\!])\,(\rho[x \mapsto d]))$$
$$= \quad \{\text{by (9.14), since } a'' \, \# \, ([\![e]\!], \rho[x \mapsto d])\}$$
$$(a\backslash[\![e]\!])\,(\rho[x \mapsto d])$$
$$= \quad \{\text{by (9.30)}\}$$
$$[\![va.\,e]\!]\,(\rho[x \mapsto d])$$
$$= \quad \{\text{by Figure 9.2}\}$$
$$[\![\lambda x.\,va.\,e]\!]\rho\,d. \qquad\qquad \square$$

9.5 Free nominal restriction sets

For each nominal set X there is a freely generated nominal restriction set Frs X. In other words the forgetful functor **Res** $\rightarrow$ **Nom** has a left adjoint Frs : **Nom** $\rightarrow$ **Res**. This can be deduced from the fact that **Res** is a category of algebras for a suitable generalization of universal algebra with the notions of freshness and name abstraction. There are several, related versions of 'nominal universal algebra': by Gabbay and Mathijssen (2009), by Clouston and Pitts (2007) and as a special case of the very general framework of Fiore and Hur (2008a). Here we give an explicit construction of Frs X and verify its universal property.

Definition 9.12   Given $X \in \mathbf{Nom}$, $(x, A), (x', A') \in X \times P_f \mathbb{A}$ and $\pi \in \operatorname{Perm} \mathbb{A}$, define

$$\pi : (x, A) \sim_\nu (x', A') \tag{9.31}$$

to mean $\pi \cdot x = x'$ and $\pi \, \# \, (\operatorname{supp} x - A) = (\operatorname{supp} x' - A')$. Here we regard $\operatorname{Perm} \mathbb{A}$ as a nominal set as in Lemma 2.21; so $\pi \, \# \, (\operatorname{supp} x - A)$ means $(\forall a \in \operatorname{supp} x - A) \, \pi a = a$. Write

$$(x, A) \sim_\nu (x', A')$$

to mean that $\pi : (x, A) \sim_\nu (x', A')$ holds for some $\pi \in \operatorname{Perm} \mathbb{A}$. The following properties are easily verified:

$$\operatorname{id} : (x, A) \sim_\nu (x, A), \tag{9.32}$$

$$\pi : (x, A) \sim_\nu (x', A') \Rightarrow \pi^{-1} : (x', A') \sim_\nu (x, A), \tag{9.33}$$

$$\pi : (x, A) \sim_\nu (x', A') \land \pi' : (x', A') \sim_\nu (x'', A'')$$
$$\Rightarrow \pi' \circ \pi : (x, A) \sim_\nu (x'', A''), \tag{9.34}$$

$$\pi : (x, A) \sim_\nu (x', A')$$
$$\Rightarrow \pi' \circ \pi \circ (\pi')^{-1} : (\pi' \cdot x, \pi' \cdot A) \sim_\nu (\pi' \cdot x', \pi' \cdot A'). \tag{9.35}$$

Therefore $\sim$ is an equivariant equivalence relation on $X \times P_f \mathbb{A}$. We write $\operatorname{Frs} X$ for the quotient nominal set $(X \times P_f \mathbb{A})/\sim$ and $x \backslash_A$ for the equivalence class of $(x, A) \in X \times P_f \mathbb{A}$.

Lemma 9.13   *If $\pi : (x, A) \sim_\nu (x, , A')$, then $\pi \cdot (\operatorname{supp} x \cap A) = \operatorname{supp} x' \cap A'$.*

Proof   Suppose $\pi : (x, A) \sim_\nu (x, , A')$. Then we have

$$(\operatorname{supp} x' - A') \uplus (\operatorname{supp} x' \cap A')$$
$$=$$
$$\operatorname{supp} x'$$
$$= \quad \{\text{since } \pi \cdot x = x'\}$$
$$\operatorname{supp} (\pi \cdot x)$$
$$= \quad \{\text{by Proposition 2.11}\}$$
$$\pi \cdot (\operatorname{supp} x)$$
$$=$$
$$\pi \cdot (\operatorname{supp} x - A) \uplus \pi \cdot (\operatorname{supp} x \cap A)$$
$$= \quad \{\text{since } \pi \, \# \, (\operatorname{supp} x - A)\}$$
$$(\operatorname{supp} x - A) \uplus \pi \cdot (\operatorname{supp} x \cap A)$$
$$= \quad \{\text{since } \operatorname{supp} x - A = \operatorname{supp} x' - A'\}$$
$$(\operatorname{supp} x' - A') \uplus \pi \cdot (\operatorname{supp} x \cap A),$$

and therefore $\operatorname{supp} x' \cap A' = \pi \cdot (\operatorname{supp} x \cap A)$.   □

Lemma 9.14 *For all $X \in \mathbf{Nom}$, $x \in X$ and $A \in P_f \, \mathbb{A}$, $\mathrm{supp}(x \backslash_A) = \mathrm{supp}\, x - A$.*

Proof Note that by definition of $\sim$, there is an equivariant function $s : \mathrm{Frs}\, X \to$ $P_f \, \mathbb{A}$ satisfying $s(x \backslash_A) = \mathrm{supp}\, x - A$. So for any $x \in X$ and $A \in P_f \, \mathbb{A}$

$$
\begin{aligned}
&\mathrm{supp}\, x - A \\
=\ &\{\text{by Example 2.10}\} \\
&\mathrm{supp}\,(\mathrm{supp}\, x - A) \\
=\ &\{\text{by defintion of } s : \mathrm{Frs}\, X \to P_f \, \mathbb{A}\} \\
&\mathrm{supp}\, s(x \backslash_A) \\
\subseteq\ &\{\text{Lemma 2.12}\} \\
&\mathrm{supp}\, x \backslash_A \,.
\end{aligned}
$$

For the reverse inclusion, just note that if $a, a' \notin \mathrm{supp}\, x - A$, then $(a\ a') :$ $(x, A) \sim_v ((a\ a') \cdot x, (a\ a') \cdot A)$; and hence $x \backslash_A = ((a\ a') \cdot x) \backslash_{(a\ a') \cdot A} = (a\ a') \cdot (x \backslash_A)$. Therefore by Proposition 2.1, $\mathrm{supp}\, x - A$ supports $x \backslash_A$ and therefore contains the least supporting set, $\mathrm{supp}\, x \backslash_A$. $\square$

Theorem 9.15 *For each nominal set X, there is a name restriction operation on $\mathrm{Frs}\, X$ that makes it the value at X of a left adjoint $\mathrm{Frs} : \mathbf{Nom} \to \mathbf{Res}$ for the forgetful functor $\mathbf{Res} \to \mathbf{Nom}$, with unit $\eta_X : X \to \mathrm{Frs}\, X$ given by*

$$\eta_X \, x = x \backslash_\emptyset \,. \tag{9.36}$$

In other words, given any $Y \in \mathbf{Res}$ and $f \in \mathbf{Nom}(X, Y)$, there is a unique morphism $\hat{f} \in \mathbf{Res}(\mathrm{Frs}\, X, Y)$ making the following diagram in $\mathbf{Nom}$ commute:

$$
\begin{array}{ccc}
X & \xrightarrow{\ \eta_X\ } & \mathrm{Frs}\, X \\
 & {\scriptstyle f} \searrow & \downarrow {\scriptstyle \hat{f}} \\
 & & Y \,.
\end{array}
\tag{9.37}
$$

Proof Note that the relations $\pi : \_ \sim_v \_$ satisfy

$$\pi : (x, A) \sim_v (x', A') \Rightarrow \pi : (x, A \cup A'') \sim_v (x', A' \cup A'') . \tag{9.38}$$

Hence there is an equivariant function $\_\backslash\_ : \mathbb{A} \times \mathrm{Frs}\, X \to \mathrm{Frs}\, X$ well defined by

$$a \backslash (x \backslash_A) = x \backslash_{\{a\} \cup A} \,. \tag{9.39}$$

In view of Lemma 9.14, this function satisfies property (9.10). If $a \,\#\, x \backslash_A$, then by that lemma $a \notin \mathrm{supp}\, x - A$ and hence $\mathrm{id} : (x, A) \sim_v (x, A \cup \{a\})$; therefore we also have property (9.8). Finally, property (9.9) is immediate from (9.39). So we do indeed have a name restriction operation on $\mathrm{Frs}\, X$.

Given $Y \in \mathbf{Res}$, note that in view of property (9.9) its binary operation of name restriction $\_\backslash\_$ extends to an equivariant function $\_\backslash\_ : P_f\, \mathbb{A} \times Y \rightarrow Y$ satisfying for all $A \in P_f\, \mathbb{A}$ and $y \in Y$

$$A\backslash y = a_1\backslash(a_2\backslash \cdots (a_n\backslash y)\cdots) \quad \text{if } A = \{a_1, a_2, \ldots, a_n\}, \qquad (9.40)$$

where in case $A = \emptyset$ and hence $n = 0$, the right-hand side is just y. Given $f \in \mathbf{Nom}(X, Y)$, we claim that

$$\hat{f}(x\backslash_A) = A\backslash(f\, x) \qquad (9.41)$$

gives a well defined equivariant function $\hat{f} : \mathrm{Frs}\, X \rightarrow Y$. To see this, note that if $\pi : (x, A) \sim_v (x', A')$, then $\pi\ \#\ (\operatorname{supp} x - A) \supseteq (\operatorname{supp}(f\, x) - A)$; and by (9.10) and equivariance of $\_\backslash\_$ and f we have $\operatorname{supp}(A\backslash(f\, x)) \subseteq \operatorname{supp}(f\, x) - A$. Therefore $\pi \cdot (A\backslash(f\, x)) = A\backslash f\, x$. Hence

$$A\backslash(f\, x)$$
$$=$$
$$\pi \cdot (A\backslash(f\, x))$$
$$= \quad \{\text{by (9.8), since } a \notin \operatorname{supp} x \Rightarrow a\ \#\ f\, x\}$$
$$\pi \cdot ((A \cap \operatorname{supp} x)\backslash(f\, x))$$
$$= \quad \{\text{by equivariance of } f \text{ and } \_\backslash\_\}$$
$$\pi \cdot (A \cap \operatorname{supp} x)\backslash(f\,(\pi \cdot x))$$
$$= \quad \{\text{by Lemmma 9.13 and since } x' = \pi \cdot x\}$$
$$(A' \cap \operatorname{supp} x')\backslash(f\, x')$$
$$= \quad \{\text{by (9.8), since } a \notin \operatorname{supp} x' \Rightarrow a\ \#\ f\, x'\}$$
$$A'\backslash(f\, x').$$

So we get $\hat{f} \in \mathbf{Nom}(\mathrm{Frs}\, x, Y)$ satisfying (9.41) and hence in particular $\hat{f}(\eta_X\, x) = \hat{f}(x\backslash_\emptyset) = \emptyset\backslash(f\, x) = f\, x$, so that $\hat{f} \circ \eta_X = f$. So it remains to prove that $\hat{f}$ is a morphism of nominal restriction sets and is the unique one making (9.37) commute.

To see that $\hat{f}$ commutes with name restriction, note that

$$\hat{f}(a\backslash(x\backslash_A))$$
$$= \quad \{\text{by (9.39)}\}$$
$$\hat{f}(x\backslash_{\{a\}\cup A})$$
$$= \quad \{\text{by (9.41)}\}$$
$$(\{a\} \cup A)\backslash(f\, x)$$
$$= \quad \{\text{by (9.9)}\}$$
$$a\backslash(A\backslash(f\, x))$$
$$= \quad \{\text{by (9.41)}\}$$
$$a\backslash(\hat{f}(x\backslash_A)).$$

Finally, for uniqueness, suppose $g \in \mathbf{Res}(\mathrm{Frs}\, X, Y)$ also satisfies $g \circ \eta_X = f$. For all $x \in X$ and $A = \{a_1, \ldots, a_n\} \in P_f \mathbb{A}$, note that $x\backslash_A = a_1\backslash(\cdots a_n\backslash(\eta_X x)\cdots)$ in Frs X. So since g commutes with restriction

$$g(x\backslash_A) = a_1\backslash(\cdots a_n\backslash(g(\eta_X x))\cdots) = a_1\backslash(\cdots a_n\backslash(f x)\cdots) = A\backslash(f x) = \hat{f}(x\backslash_A).$$

So $g = \hat{f}$. $\qquad\square$

Remark 9.16 (Restriction monad) As for any adjunction, composing the forgetful function **Res** → **Nom** with its left adjoint Frs : **Nom** → **Res**, we get a monad Frs : **Nom** → **Nom** on **Nom** (see MacLane, 1971, chapter VI). The unit of the monad $\eta_X : X \to$ Frs X is given by (9.36); the multiplication $\mu_X : $ Frs(Frs X) → Frs X is $(\mathrm{id}_{\mathrm{Frs}\,X})\hat{}$ and satisfies

$$\mu_X((x\backslash_A)\backslash_{A'}) = x\backslash_{A\cup A'}. \qquad (9.42)$$

In the next section we need to use a form of Kleisli lifting operation associated with this monad: given $f \in \mathbf{Nom}(X \times Z, Y)$ with $Y \in \mathbf{Res}$, we get lift $f \in \mathbf{Nom}(\mathrm{Frs}\,X \times Z, Y)$ by first currying f (2.14) to get curry $f \in \mathbf{Nom}(X, Z \to_{\mathrm{fs}} Y)$, then applying Theorem 9.15 to get (curry $f)\hat{} \in \mathbf{Res}(\mathrm{Frs}\,X, Z \to_{\mathrm{fs}} Y)$ (using the name restriction operation on $Z \to_{\mathrm{fs}} Y$ from Theorem 9.7) and then passing back over the exponential adjunction to get

$$\mathrm{lift}\, f \triangleq \mathrm{app} \circ ((\mathrm{curry}\, f)\hat{} \times \mathrm{id}_Z) : \mathrm{Frs}\,X \times Z \to Y.$$

From properties (9.15) and (9.41) we get for all $x \in X$, $A \in P_f \mathbb{A}$ and $z \in Z$

$$\mathrm{lift}\, f(x\backslash_A, z) = A\backslash(f(x, z)) \quad \text{if } A \mathbin{\#} z. \qquad (9.43)$$

If $\lambda(x, z) \in X \times Z \to \varphi(x, z)$ is some description of f, then we will use the notation

$$\mathrm{let}_{\mathrm{Frs}}\, x = u \text{ in } \varphi(x, z) \qquad (9.44)$$

to stand for lift $f(u, z)$.

Remark 9.17 (Restriction versus abstraction) Comparing $\pi : \_ \sim_v \_$ in Definition 9.12 with the definition of $\pi : \_ \sim_\alpha \_$ in Section 4.6, evidently there is a connection between Frs X and the nominal set $[P_f \mathbb{A}]X$ of $P_f \mathbb{A}$-abstractions of elements of X. Note that Lemma 9.13 implies

$$\pi : (x, A) \sim_v (x', A') \Rightarrow \pi : (\mathrm{supp}\, x \cap A, x) \sim_\alpha (\mathrm{supp}\, x' \cap A', x'). \qquad (9.45)$$

So we get an equivariant function $i : \mathrm{Frs}\,X \to [P_f \mathbb{A}]X$ satisfying

$$i(x\backslash_A) = \langle \mathrm{supp}\, x \cap A \rangle x.$$

It is not hard to see that the converse of (9.45) is valid and hence that i is a monomorphism. Therefore Frs X is isomorphic in **Nom** to the image of i:

$$\text{Frs}\, X \cong \{\langle A\rangle x \in [\text{P}_{\text{f}}\, \mathbb{A}]X \mid A \subseteq \text{supp}\, x\}. \tag{9.46}$$

Thus one could avoid $\pi : \_\sim_\nu\_$ and just define Frs X using $\pi : \_\sim_\alpha\_$. The reason we did not do this, and in particular considered representatives (x, A) for $x\backslash_A$ not necessarily satisfying $A \subseteq \text{supp}\, x$, is that it makes the definition of the restriction operation on Frs X a bit simpler.

Going in the other direction, nominal sets of name abstractions can be recovered from free nominal restriction sets; see Exercise 9.5.

9.6 ν-Calculus

The operational semantics of locally scoped names is commonly specified in terms of *dynamically allocated* fresh names, also known as *generative* names. This is a state-based explanation of the meaning of the scoping construct: to evaluate an expression $\nu a.\, e$ with a locally scoped name, the current state is augmented with a fresh name and the body e of the scope is evaluated with the scoped name a bound to the fresh one. The combination of this simple mechanism with other features, especially higher-order functions as occurs in the ML family of languages, can result in programs with very complicated behaviour. The ν-calculus (Pitts and Stark, 1993) was intended to make this point, taking the measure of behaviour to be *contextual equivalence*, the relation between two expressions of being interchangeable in the context of any program without affecting the observable behaviour of the program. Syntactically, the ν-calculus is the same simply-typed λ-calculus with locally scoped names that we used for Odersky's $\lambda\nu$-calculus (Figure 9.1). Unlike Odersky's calculus, the ν-calculus is given an operational semantics that makes it a fragment of Standard ML (Milner *et al.*, 1997) by interpreting the type Name as the ML type unit ref of references to the unit value and taking $\nu a.\, e$ to be let $a = \text{ref}()$ in e. The properties of contextual equivalence for the ν-calculus turn out to be remarkably complex, despite the simplicity of the language. See Benton and Koutavas (2007) for a survey of the literature on the ν-calculus.

Here we will use free nominal restriction sets to give a version of Stark's denotational semantics for the ν-calculus (Stark, 1994, section 3.7). In particular, we follow the monadic style of denotational semantics of Moggi (1991), using the monad Frs mentioned in Remark 9.16. For each type T in the set *Type* of types defined in Figure 9.1 we define a nominal set $[\![T]\!]_v \in \mathbf{Nom}$ as follows:

$$[\![\texttt{Name}]\!]_v = \mathbb{A} \qquad\qquad \text{nominal set of atomic names,} \qquad (9.47)$$

$$[\![\texttt{Bool}]\!]_v = \mathbb{B} = \{\text{true, false}\} \qquad \text{discrete nominal set,} \qquad (9.48)$$

$$[\![\texttt{1}]\!]_v = 1 = \{()\} \qquad\qquad \text{discrete nominal set,} \qquad (9.49)$$

$$[\![T_1 \times T_2]\!]_v = [\![T_1]\!]_v \times [\![T_2]\!]_v \qquad \text{cartesian product,} \qquad (9.50)$$

$$[\![T_1 \to T_2]\!]_v = [\![T_1]\!]_v \to_{\text{fs}} \text{Frs}\,[\![T_2]\!]_v \qquad \text{finitely supported functions to} \qquad (9.51)$$
$$\text{a free nominal restriction set.}$$

The elements of $[\![T]\!]_v$ will be used to denote v-calculus *values* of type T; by definition these are the elements of the (equivariant) subset $Val(T) \subseteq Expr(T)$ determined by the grammar

$$v ::= x \mid a \mid \texttt{true} \mid \texttt{false} \mid () \mid (v, v) \mid \lambda x.\, e . \qquad (9.52)$$

In contrast to values, arbitrary expressions of type T are denoted by elements of the free nominal restriction set $\text{Frs}\,[\![T]\!]_v$. Variables in the v-calculus stand for unknown values, so we use a nominal set of v-*environments* consisting of finitely supported functions mapping variables of type T to elements of $[\![T]\!]_v$ for each $T \in Type$:

$$Env_v \triangleq \left(\prod_{T \in Type} Var(T) \to_{\text{fs}} [\![T]\!]_v \right)_{\text{fs}} . \qquad (9.53)$$

We define equivariant functions

$$|\_| : Val(T) \to (Env_v \to_{\text{fs}} [\![T]\!]_v), \qquad (9.54)$$

$$[\![\_]\!] : Expr(T) \to (Env_v \to_{\text{fs}} \text{Frs}\,[\![T]\!]_v), \qquad (9.55)$$

which give the meaning $|v|\rho \in [\![T]\!]_v$ of values $v \in Val((T)$ and the meaning $[\![e]\!]\rho \in \text{Frs}\,[\![T]\!]_v$ of expressions $e \in Expr(T)$ as finitely supported functions of environments $\rho \in Env_v$ supplying meanings for their free variables. The definition of $|v|$ and $[\![e]\!]$ is by induction on the structure of v and e and gives the denotation functions the properties listed in Figure 9.3. In that figure we make use of the 'let_{Frs}' notation described in Remark 9.16 – a version of Moggi's computational λ-calculus notation (Moggi, 1991) specialized to the monad Frs on **Nom**. The definition of the denotation of locally scoped names is $[\![va.\, e]\!] \triangleq a \backslash [\![e]\!]$. This is the same as for the λv-calculus except that here the name restriction operation is the one for $Env_v \to_{\text{fs}} \text{Frs}\,[\![T]\!]_v$, obtained by applying Theorem 9.7 to the free nominal restriction set $\text{Frs}\,[\![T]\!]_v$.

Although we will not prove it here, this denotational semantics of the v-calculus is in fact adequate for contextual equivalence, but not fully abstract; which is to say that equality of denotation implies contextual equivalence, but that the reverse is not true in general.

$$|x|\rho = \rho\,x$$
$$|a|\rho = a$$
$$|\mathtt{true}|\rho = \mathrm{true}$$
$$|\mathtt{false}|\rho = \mathrm{false}$$
$$|()|\rho = ()$$
$$|(v_1, v_2)|\rho = (|v_1|\rho, |v_2|\rho)$$
$$|\lambda x.\,e|\rho = \lambda d \in [\![T]\!]_\nu \to [\![e]\!]\,(\rho[x \mapsto d]) \quad \text{if } x \in Var(T)$$

$$[\![\nu a.\,e]\!]\rho = a\backslash([\![e]\!]\rho) \quad \text{if } a \,\#\, \rho$$
$$[\![\mathtt{if}\,e_1\,\mathtt{then}\,e_2\,\mathtt{else}\,e_3]\!]\rho = \mathrm{let}_{\mathrm{Frs}}\,b = [\![e_1]\!]\rho \text{ in if } b \text{ then } [\![e_2]\!]\rho \text{ else } [\![e_3]\!]\rho$$
$$[\![e_1 = e_2]\!]\rho = \mathrm{let}_{\mathrm{Frs}}\,a_1 = [\![e_1]\!]\rho \text{ in } \mathrm{let}_{\mathrm{Frs}}\,a_2 = [\![e_2]\!]\rho \text{ in } (a_1 = a_2)\backslash_\emptyset$$
$$[\![\mathtt{fst}\,e]\!]\rho = \mathrm{let}_{\mathrm{Frs}}\,p = [\![e]\!]\rho \text{ in } (\pi_1\,p)\backslash_\emptyset$$
$$[\![\mathtt{snd}\,e]\!]\rho = \mathrm{let}_{\mathrm{Frs}}\,p = [\![e]\!]\rho \text{ in } (\pi_2\,p)\backslash_\emptyset$$
$$[\![e_1\,e_2]\!]\rho = \mathrm{let}_{\mathrm{Frs}}\,f = [\![e_1]\!]\rho \text{ in } \mathrm{let}_{\mathrm{Frs}}\,d = [\![e_2]\!]\rho \text{ in } f\,d$$

Figure 9.3 Denotational semantics of the ν-calculus.

9.7 Total concretion

We saw in Section 4.3 that the nominal set $[\mathbb{A}]X$ of name abstractions on a nominal set X is a subobject of the nominal set $\mathbb{A} \to_{\mathrm{fs}} X$ of finitely supported partial functions: each name abstraction determines a partial function from $\mathbb{A}$ to X given by concretion and whose domain of definition is determined by a freshness condition (Lemma 4.7). This partiality complicates calculations with name abstractions, since one has to check freshness side conditions to ensure that concretions are well defined. If X is a nominal restriction set, then we will see that it is possible to extend concretion to a totally defined operation with nice properties. In particular, $[\mathbb{A}]X$ becomes a retract of the nominal restriction set $\mathbb{A} \to_{\mathrm{fs}} X$ of total, finitely supported functions. This was used by Pitts (2011) to design a calculus of total functions featuring name abstraction and concretion.

Theorem 9.18 *For each $X \in \mathbf{Res}$, the nominal set $[\mathbb{A}]X$ of name abstractions possesses a name restriction operation satisfying for all $a, a' \in \mathbb{A}$ and $x \in X$*

$$a \neq a' \Rightarrow a\backslash(\langle a'\rangle x) = \langle a'\rangle(a\backslash x). \tag{9.56}$$

Regarding $[\mathbb{A}]X$ as an object of $\mathbf{Res}$ in this way, it is a retract of the nominal restriction set $\mathbb{A} \to_{\mathrm{fs}} X$ of finitely supported functions (which uses the name restriction operation from Theorem 9.7). In other words, there are morphisms

$\operatorname{conc}_X \in \mathbf{Res}([\mathbb{A}]X, (\mathbb{A} \to_{fs} X))$ *and* $e_X \in \mathbf{Res}((\mathbb{A} \to_{fs} X), [\mathbb{A}]X)$ *satisfying* $e_X \circ \operatorname{conc}_X = \operatorname{id}_{[\mathbb{A}]X}$.

Proof If $r : [\mathbb{A}]X \to X$ is the name restriction operation for X, define

$$r' \triangleq [\mathbb{A}][\mathbb{A}]X \xrightarrow{\delta_X} [\mathbb{A}][\mathbb{A}]X \xrightarrow{[\mathbb{A}]r} [\mathbb{A}]X. \tag{9.57}$$

Thus r' satisfies for all $a, a' \in \mathbb{A}$ and $x \in X$

$$a \neq a' \Rightarrow r'\langle a\rangle(\langle a'\rangle x) = \langle a'\rangle(r\langle a\rangle x),$$

as required for property (9.56). If $a \# y \in [\mathbb{A}]X$, then we can pick a representative $y = \langle a'\rangle x$ with $a \# (a', x)$ and apply property (9.2) of r to get $r'\langle a\rangle y = \langle a'\rangle(r\langle a\rangle x) = \langle a'\rangle x = y$; therefore r' also satisfies property (9.2). Similarly, given $a_1, a_2 \in \mathbb{A}$ and $y \in [\mathbb{A}]X$, we can pick a representative $y = \langle a\rangle x$ with $a \neq a_1, a_2$ and deduce from property (9.1) for r that r' also has this property: $r'\langle a_1\rangle(r'\langle a_2\rangle y) = \langle a\rangle(r\langle a_1\rangle(r\langle a_2\rangle x)) = \langle a\rangle(r\langle a_2\rangle(r\langle a_1\rangle x)) = r'\langle a_2\rangle(r'\langle a_1\rangle y)$. Thus r' is indeed a name restriction operation on $[\mathbb{A}]X$ satisfying (9.56).

Using the freshness theorem (Theorem 3.11) we get an equivariant function

$$e_X : (\mathbb{A} \to_{fs} X) \to [\mathbb{A}]X, \tag{9.58}$$

$$e_X \triangleq \lambda f \in (\mathbb{A} \to_{fs} X) \to \text{fresh } a \text{ in } \langle a\rangle(f\, a).$$

It commutes with name restriction because for all $a \in \mathbb{A}$ and $f \in \mathbb{A} \to_{fs} X$

$$\begin{aligned}
&e_X(a\backslash f)\\
=\ & \{\text{by (9.58), picking some/any } a' \# (a, f)\}\\
&\langle a'\rangle((a\backslash f)\, a')\\
=\ & \{\text{by (9.15)}\}\\
&\langle a'\rangle(a\backslash(f\, a'))\\
=\ & \{\text{by (9.56)}\}\\
&a\backslash(\langle a'\rangle(f\, a'))\\
=\ & \{\text{by (9.58), since } a' \# f\}\\
&a\backslash(e_X\, f),
\end{aligned}$$

and hence gives a morphism $e_X \in \mathbf{Res}(\mathbb{A} \to_{fs} X, [\mathbb{A}]X)$.

In the other direction, we get an equivariant function $(\mathbb{A} \times X) \to (\mathbb{A} \to_{fs} X)$ mapping each (a, x) to the finitely supported function $a\backslash(\lambda a' \in \mathbb{A} \to (a\, a')\cdot x) \in \mathbb{A} \to_{fs} X$. By Corollary 4.17 this induces an equivariant function

$$\operatorname{conc}_X : [\mathbb{A}]X \to (\mathbb{A} \to_{fs} X),$$

satisfying for all $a \in \mathbb{A}$ and $x \in X$

$$\operatorname{conc}_X \langle a\rangle x = a\backslash(\lambda a' \in \mathbb{A} \to (a\, a')\cdot x). \tag{9.59}$$

It is not hard to see that conc_X commutes with name restriction and so gives a morphism $\mathrm{conc}_X \in \mathbf{Res}([\mathbb{A}]X, \mathbb{A} \to_{\mathrm{fs}} X)$ (Exercise 9.6). Finally, we have $e_X \circ \mathrm{conc}_X = \mathrm{id}_{[\mathbb{A}]X}$ in $\mathbf{Res}$, because for all $a \in \mathbb{A}$ and $x \in X$

$$
\begin{aligned}
& e_X\,(\mathrm{conc}_X(\langle a\rangle x)) \\
=\ & \{\text{by (9.58), picking some/any } a' \,\#\, (a, x)\} \\
& \langle a'\rangle(\mathrm{conc}_X(\langle a\rangle x)\,a') \\
=\ & \{\text{by (9.59) and (9.15), since } a \neq a'\} \\
& \langle a'\rangle(a\backslash((a\ a')\cdot x)) \\
=\ & \{\text{by (9.56)}\} \\
& a\backslash((\langle a'\rangle((a\ a')\cdot x)) \\
=\ & \{\text{by Lemma 4.3, since } a' \,\#\, (a, x)\} \\
& a\backslash((\langle a\rangle x) \\
=\ & \{\text{by (9.8), since } a \,\#\, \langle a\rangle x\} \\
& \langle a\rangle x\,. \qquad\qquad\qquad\qquad\qquad\qquad\qquad\qquad \square
\end{aligned}
$$

As its name suggests, the morphism conc_X defined in (9.59) extends the partial operation of concretion from Section 4.3 to a total function.

Corollary 9.19 *For each nominal restriction set X, the partial operation of concretion (Definition 4.8) extends to a total equivariant function $[\mathbb{A}]X \times \mathbb{A} \to X$ that corresponds to function application under the monomorphism from $[\mathbb{A}]X$ to $\mathbb{A} \to_{\mathrm{fs}} X$ from Theorem 9.18.*

Proof Consider

$$
\begin{aligned}
& [\mathbb{A}]X \times \mathbb{A} \to X\,, \\
& (y, a) \mapsto \mathrm{conc}_x\, y\, a\,.
\end{aligned}
$$

If $y \in [\mathbb{A}]X$, $a \in \mathbb{A}$ and $a \,\#\, y$, picking a representative $y = \langle a'\rangle x$ with $a \,\#\, (a', x)$, we have $y \,@\, a = (a'\ a) \cdot x$ and

$$
\begin{aligned}
& \mathrm{conc}_X\, y\, a \\
=\ & \{\text{since } y = \langle a'\rangle x\} \\
& \mathrm{conc}_X\,(\langle a'\rangle x)\, a \\
=\ & \{\text{by (9.59) and (9.15), since } a \neq a'\} \\
& a'\backslash((a'\ a) \cdot x) \\
=\ & \{\text{by (9.8), since } a' \,\#\, (a'\ a) \cdot x\} \\
& (a'\ a) \cdot x\,,
\end{aligned}
$$

so that $y \,@\, a = \mathrm{conc}_X\, y\, a$. $\qquad\qquad\qquad\qquad\qquad\qquad\qquad \square$

Remark 9.20 Note that from the above proof we have for all $X \in \mathbf{Res}$, $x \in X$

and $a, a' \in \mathbb{A}$

$$a \neq a' \implies \mathrm{conc}_X(\langle a' \rangle x) a = a' \backslash ((a'\ a) \cdot x), \qquad (9.60)$$

whether or not $a \# x$ holds. This property validates the conversion

$$(\alpha a' . e) @ a \to \nu a' . (a' \rightleftharpoons a) e$$

in the nominal sets semantics of the $\lambda \alpha \nu$-calculus from Pitts (2011); this is a calculus that extends Odersky's $\lambda \nu$-calculus with name-swapping expressions $(a \rightleftharpoons a') e$, name abstraction expressions $\alpha a. e$ and concretion expressions $e @ a$ (or, equivalently, a form of unbinding via matching name abstraction patterns). We consider a similar extension of the ν-calculus in Section 10.8.

Example 9.21 Consider the nominal restriction set $\mathbb{A} + 1$ as in Example 9.5. We regard $\mathbb{A}$ as a subset of $\mathbb{A} + 1$ and write $\bot \in \mathbb{A} + 1$ for the element corresponding to the unique element of 1. If $a \neq a'$, then the concretion of $\langle a' \rangle a \in [\mathbb{A}](\mathbb{A} + 1)$ at a is undefined (because a is in the support of $\langle a' \rangle a$). On the other hand, from (9.60) we get $\mathrm{conc}_x(\langle a' \rangle a) a = a' \backslash ((a'\ a) \cdot a) = a' \backslash a' = \bot$.

Exercises

9.1 Give an example of a nominal set X for which the equivariant function $\delta_X : [\mathbb{A}][\mathbb{A}]X \to [\mathbb{A}][\mathbb{A}]X$ satisfies $\delta_X(\langle a \rangle(\langle a \rangle x)) \neq \langle a \rangle(\langle a \rangle x)$ for some $a \in \mathbb{A}$ and $x \in X$. [Hint: recall Exercise 4.1.]

9.2 Given $X \in$ **Nom**, recall from Section 2.5 that there is an isomorphism $\mathrm{P}_{\mathrm{fs}} X \cong X \to_{\mathrm{fs}} \mathbb{B}$, where $\mathbb{B}$ is a two-element discrete nominal set. By combining Theorem 9.7 with Example 9.4 we get a name restriction operation on $X \to_{\mathrm{fs}} \mathbb{B}$. Show that the corresponding name restriction operation on $\mathrm{P}_{\mathrm{fs}} X$ satisfies for all $a \in \mathbb{A}$ and $S \in \mathrm{P}_{\mathrm{fs}} X$

$$a \backslash S = \{ x \in X \mid (\text{И} a') \ x \in (a\ a') \cdot S \}. \qquad (9.61)$$

When $X = \mathbb{A}$, recall that $\mathrm{P}_{\mathrm{fs}} \mathbb{A}$ consists of the finite and the cofinite subsets of $\mathbb{A}$ (Proposition 2.9). In this case show that if $S \in \mathrm{P}_{\mathrm{fs}} \mathbb{A}$ is finite then $a \backslash S = S - \{a\}$; whereas if S is cofinite, then $a \backslash S = S \cup \{a\}$.

9.3 Making $\mathbb{A} + 1$ into a nominal restriction set as in Example 9.5, show that it is isomorphic in **Res** to Frs $\mathbb{A}$, the free nominal restriction set on the nominal set of atomic names.

9.4 Show that the elements of the free nominal restriction set Frs X can be expressed in terms of the orbit-finite hull construct from Definition 5.20:

$$x \backslash_A = \mathrm{hull}_{\mathrm{supp}\, x - A} \{ (x, \mathrm{supp}\, x \cap A) \} \quad (x \in X, A \in \mathrm{P}_{\mathrm{f}} \mathbb{A}). \qquad (9.62)$$

9.5 For each $X \in$ **Nom** show that the nominal set of name abstractions $[\mathbb{A}]X$ is isomorphic in the category **Nom** to the following equivariant subset of $\text{Frs}(\mathbb{A} \times X)$:

$$\{(a, x)\backslash_{\{a\}} \mid a \in \mathbb{A} \wedge x \in X\}. \tag{9.63}$$

9.6 Show that the equivariant function m defined by (9.59) is a morphism of nominal restriction sets from $[\mathbb{A}]X$ to $\mathbb{A} \to_{\text{fs}} X$ (see Pitts, 2011, appendix B).

9.7 (**The Staton topos, [pI, Set]**) Let **pI** be the category whose objects are the finite subsets of $\mathbb{A}$ and whose morphisms are injective partial functions. Thus given $A, B \in P_f \mathbb{A}$, the morphisms $i \in$ **pI**(A, B) are subsets $i \subseteq A \times B$ satisfying $(\forall (a, b), (a', b') \in i)\, a = a' \Leftrightarrow b = b'$. So i gives a bijection $\text{Dom}\, i \cong \text{Img}\, i$. Composition in **pI** is the usual composition of partial functions; and identities are given by identity functions. Show that the functor category **[pI, Set]** is equivalent to the category **Res** of nominal restriction sets (*cf.* Remark 9.9).

[Hint: show that if $X \in$ **Res**, then (6.14) can be extended to a functor $I_* X \in$ **[pI, Set]**, where for each $i \in$ **pI**(A, B), the function $I_* X i :$ $I_* X A \to I_* X B$ is well defined by

$$I_* X i \triangleq \lambda x \in (I_* X A) \to \pi \cdot ((A - \text{Dom}\, i)\backslash x)$$

where $\pi \in \text{Perm}\, \mathbb{A}$ is any finite permutation satisfying $i \subseteq \pi$. (The homogeneity lemma (Lemma 1.14) guarantees that there is such a π.) In this definition we use the extension of restriction from single atomic names $a\backslash_-$ to finite sets of them $A\backslash_-$, as in (9.40). Extending I_* to a functor **Res** $\to$ **[pI, Set]** as in (6.16), show that it is full, faithful and essentially surjective.]

10

Functional programming

A very useful feature of functional programming languages such as OCaml (http://caml.inria.fr/ocaml) or Haskell (http://www.haskell.org) is the facility for programmers to declare their own algebraic data types and to specify functions on that data using pattern-matching. This makes them especially useful for *metaprogramming*, that is, writing programs that manipulate programs, or more generally, expressions in formal languages. In this context the functional programming language is often called the *meta-level* language, while the language whose expressions appear as data in the functional programs is called the *object-level* language. We already noted at the beginning of Chapter 8 that object-level languages often involve name binding operations. In this case we may well want meta-level programs to operate not on object-level parse trees, but on their α-equivalence classes. OCaml or Haskell programmers have to deal with this issue on a case-by-case basis, according to the nature of the object-level language being implemented, using a self-imposed discipline. For example, they might work out some 'nameless' representation of α-equivalence classes for their object-level language, in the style of de Bruijn (1972). When designing extensions of OCaml or Haskell that deal more systematically with this issue, three desirable properties come to mind:

- *Expressivity.* Informal algorithms for manipulating syntactic data very often make explicit use of the names of bound entities; when representing α-equivalence classes of object-level expressions as meta-level data, one would still like programmers to have access to object-level bound names. Furthermore, one would like the wide variety of scoping and binding operations that occur 'in the wild' to be representable in the meta-level programming language with reasonable ease.
- *Abstractness.* Issues to do with object-level α-equivalence should be dealt with automatically by the meta-level language, not by the programmer. It

177

should be a property of the whole meta-level programming language that its programs respect object-level α-equivalence (up to a suitable notion of equivalence for meta-level programs).

- *Purity*. One should aim to write programs whose correctness is easy to verify. Functional programming has aspirations in this direction, especially in the case of Haskell, with its use of monads in the type system to encapsulate 'impure' computational effects (Peyton Jones, 2001). It is certainly desirable that new features for computing with names and name-binding should reside within the effect-free, or 'pure', core of functional programming.

It is not clear to what extent these criteria can be satisfied simultaneously. This chapter describes work on this problem inspired by the theory of nominal sets and which gave rise to the FreshML family of languages (Pitts and Gabbay, 2000; Shinwell *et al.*, 2003; Pottier, 2005, 2007; Shinwell, 2005b). If one thinks of the type and function expressions of a conventional functional programming language as describing various sets of values and functions on those sets, then types and expressions of the languages in the FreshML family instead describe nominal sets and finitely supported functions.

We will concentrate on Shinwell's Fresh OCaml (Shinwell, 2005a,b; Shinwell and Pitts, 2005a). It addresses the criterion of *Expressivity* by extending OCaml version 3.8 with the language features described in sections 10.1–10.7, illustrated by the sample code in Figure 10.1. Sections 10.8–10.12 discuss how Fresh OCaml addresses the *Abstractness* criterion; to do so we use a small subset of the full language, formulated as a typed λ-calculus with names, called λFML. Finally, Section 10.13 discusses the shortcomings of Fresh OCaml with respect to the *Purity* criterion and what alternatives have been developed in the literature.

10.1 Types of names

Fresh OCaml programmers can declare as many different sorts of atomic name as they need using a built-in polymorphic family ' *a name* of equality types, whose instances correspond to the sets of sorted atomic names considered in Section 4.7. For example, line 1 of Figure 10.1 declares a new type t and then instantiates the family a' *name* at this type to get a type called var. Values of type var are atomic names that can be generated as needed (line 4), tested for equality (line 5) and used in name abstraction expressions (Section 10.6).

```
type t and var = t name ;;                                                    1
type term = (* untyped λ-terms modulo α-equivalence, cf. Example 8.4 *)       2
     V of var | L of <<var>>term | A of term * term;;                          3
let x, y, z = fresh, fresh, fresh;;                                            4
x = y;;  (* false *)                                                           5
let tm1 = L(<<x>>(A(V x, V z )));;  (* λx. x z *)                              6
let tm2 = L(<<y>>(A(V y, V z )));;  (* λy. y z *)                              7
let tm3 = L(<<y>>(A(V y, V x )));;  (* λy. y x *)                              8
tm1 = tm2;;  (* true *)                                                        9
tm2 = tm3;;  (* false *)                                                       10
x freshfor tm1;; (* true *)                                                    11
z freshfor tm1;; (* false *)                                                   12
let sub (x : var)(t : term) : term -> term =                                   13
     (*  capture-avoiding substitution, cf. Example 8.19 *)                    14
     let rec f (t1 : term) : term =                                            15
       match t1 with V x1 -> if x = x1 then t else t1                          16
                  | L(<<x2>> t2) -> L(<<x2>>(f t2))                            17
                  | A(t2,t3) -> A(f t2,  f t3)                                 18
     in f;;                                                                    19
let tm4 = sub z (V x) tm1;;  (* [z := x](λx. x z) *)                          20
tm4 = tm3;;  (* true *)                                                        21
x freshfor sub;; (* raises an exception *)                                     22
let i (z : <<var>>term * <<var>>term) : <<var>>(term * term) =                 23
     (* an instance of the isomorphism in Exercise 4.4 *)                      24
     match z with (<<x1>>t1, <<x2>>t2) ->                                      25
     let x = fresh in <<x>>(swap x and x1 in t1, swap x and x2 in t2);;       26
type sem =  F of ((unit -> sem) -> sem) | T of term;; (* semantic domain *)    27
type env = var -> sem;; (* environments *)                                     28
let up : env = function x -> T(V x);;  (* initial  environment *)             29
let update (x : var) (v : unit -> sem) (e : env) : env =                       30
     (* updating an environment *)                                            31
     function y -> if y = x then v() else e y;;                               32
let rec down (d : sem) : term = (* reification *)                              33
     match d with F f -> let x = fresh                                         34
                    in L(<<x>>(down(f(function u -> up x))))                   35
                  | T t -> t;;                                                 36
let rec eval (t : term) (e : env) : sem  = (* evaluation *)                    37
     match t with V x -> e x                                                   38
     | L(<<x1>>t1) -> F(function v -> eval t1 (update x1 v e))                 39
     | A(t1,t2) -> (match eval t1 e with F f -> f(function () -> eval t2 e)    40
                  | T t3 -> T(A(t3, down(eval t2 e ))));;                      41
(* normalization-by-evaluation, cf. Filinski and Korsholm Rohde (2004) *)      42
let norm (t : term) : term = down (eval t up);;                               43
```

Figure 10.1 Example Fresh OCaml code.

10.2 Name abstraction types

If the Fresh OCaml types `ty1` and `ty2` describe elements of nominal sets X_1 and X_2, then values of type `<<ty1>>ty2` describe elements of the nominal set $[X_1]X_2$ from Section 4.6. This is subject to the restriction that the support of values of type `ty1` can be calculated accurately; Fresh OCaml can only do this for certain values (typically, those not involving function closures) and raises an exception otherwise. In particular, if `ty1` is a type of names in the sense of the previous paragraph, then `<<ty1>>ty2` corresponds to the nominal set $[\mathbb{A}]X_2$ of name abstractions from Chapter 4. Just as for nominal algebraic signatures, name abstraction types are used in data type declarations to get constructors involving name binding. For example, lines 2–3 of Figure 10.1 declare a type `term` corresponding to the nominal algebraic signature for λ-terms from Example 8.4. The design of Fresh OCaml ensures that the values of type `term` do indeed correspond to α-equivalence classes of raw λ-terms (Section 4.1). In particular, the boolean valued expression `e1 = e2` at type `term` tests for α-equivalence. For example, lines 6–8 declare three values of type `term` corresponding to the λ-terms mentioned in the comments; the first two are equal up to α-equivalence and thus the boolean expression at line 9 evaluates to `true`.

Fresh OCaml data type declarations go beyond nominal algebraic signatures, because name abstraction types `<<ty1>>ty2` can be mixed with the use of function types, `ty1 -> ty2`. For example, line 27 of Figure 10.1 declares a data type `sem` whose definition mixes functions (in the argument of the F constructor) with name abstractions (since the constructor T refers to `term`, which involves name abstraction in its L constructor).

10.3 Dynamically allocated names

The Fresh OCaml expression `fresh` is of polymorphic type `'a name` and dynamically allocates a fresh atomic name when evaluated (in the same way that `ref` expressions dynamically allocate named storage locations; *cf.* Example 7.7). It is used in line 4 of Figure 10.1 to generate three names of variables. A more subtle use occurs at lines 34–35, where a fresh name is used while 'reifying' a function as a λ-term. The code in this figure implements the simple, 'tentative' algorithm from Filinski and Korsholm Rohde (2004, section 1.4) for computing the β-normal form of an untyped λ-term (if it exists) using the method of *normalization by evaluation*. It is a good example of how well Fresh OCaml meets the *Expressivity* criterion mentioned at the start of this chapter.

10.4 Name swapping

Since Fresh OCaml expressions are intended to denote elements of nominal sets and the action of name permutations is a key aspect of nominal sets, it is not surprising that the language provides the means to express this action. It does so via expressions of the form swap *e1* and *e2* in *e3*, which has the same type as *e3* provided *e1* and *e2* have the same type and one that is an instance of 'a name. The expression evaluates by evaluating the three subexpressions and then transposing the atomic names obtained from the first two in the value obtained from the third. For example, such expressions occur at line 26 of Figure 10.1 in the definition of the function for converting a pair of name abstractions into a name-abstracted pair.

10.5 Freshness relation

Apart from permutation actions, the other characteristic feature of nominal sets is the notion of finite support and the complementary relation of freshness (Section 3.1). Fresh OCaml provides an infix, boolean-valued operation *e1* freshfor *e2* that attempts to compute whether the atomic name denoted by *e1* is not in the support of the value denoted by *e2*. This is subject to the same caveats as for the general form of name abstraction type <<*ty1*>>*ty2*: since support is not a computable notion at higher types (involving as it does extensional equality of functions), Fresh OCaml raises an exception if the operation freshfor is invoked on values for which it cannot accurately compute support, typically function closures. For example, the expression at line 22 of Figure 10.1 raises an exception even though the meaning of *sub* is a mathematical function with empty support; whereas it can compute supports for values of data types like *term* and the expressions at lines 11 and 12 evaluate as expected.

10.6 Name abstraction expressions

Fresh OCaml expressions of type <<*ty1*>>*ty2* are introduced using the syntax <<*e1*>>*e2*, where *e1* has type *ty1* and *e2* has type *ty2*. For example, in line 17 of Figure 10.1, the expression <<*x2*>>(*f t2*) has type <<*var*>>*term* provided its free identifiers *x2*, *f* and *t2* and have types *var*, *term* –> *term* and *term* respectively. Expressions of the form <<*e1*>>*e2* are used to compute bindings in object-level languages, but are not themselves binding forms in Fresh OCaml (see also Note 10.2). For example, the occurrence of $x2$ in the expression $<<x2>>(f\ t2)$ is free to be bound by some enclosing meta-level binding construct; in line 17 it is bound to the occurrence of this identifier in the pattern $L(<<x2>>t2)$ to the left of $->$. We discuss such patterns next.

10.7 Name abstraction patterns

A crucial aspect of Fresh OCaml from the point of view of usability is that it extends the use of patterns for defining functions on data to encompass name abstraction types. If $pat1$ and $pat2$ are patterns describing values of types $ty1$ and $ty2$, then

$$<<pat1>>pat2 \qquad\qquad (10.1)$$

is a pattern for values of type $<<ty1>>ty2$. Such patterns occur in the `match` expressions in Figure 10.1 at lines 17, 25 and 39. Although (10.1) is formed from a pair of patterns, the behaviour under matching is quite different from a pair pattern ($pat1$, $pat2$). We will define that behaviour formally below (see Figure 10.7). Informally, matching a value against (10.1) involves transposing names that match $pat1$ with fresh names in values that match $pat2$. For this reason we claim that the function sub declared at lines 13–19 of Figure 10.1 implements capture-avoiding rather than naive substitution – despite the simplicity of line 17 defining the behaviour of substitution on a λ-abstraction. For example, line 20 uses sub to compute $[z := x](\lambda x.\ x\,z)$; and line 21 shows that we get $\lambda y.\ y\,x$ and not $\lambda x.\ x\,x$, as we would with a naive, possibly capturing substitution. We prove that sub implements capture-avoiding substitution in Section 10.12 (Example 10.30).

10.8 λFML

We wish to prove properties of the Fresh OCaml language to do with the *Abstractness* criterion mentioned at the beginning of this chapter. To do so we use a small subset of the language formulated as a typed λ-calculus with names, called λFML. It is designed to illustrate the main novel feature of Fresh OCaml, namely the mechanism for matching name-abstraction patterns using swapping with dynamically allocated fresh names.

Figure 10.2 gives the grammar of λFML types and expressions. We have used

Types
$T \in Type$ ::=

	N	name-sort ($N \in Nsort$)
	D	data-sort ($D \in Dsort$)
	Bool	type of booleans
	1	unit type
	$T \times T$	product type
	$《N》T$	name abstraction type
	$T \to T$	function type

Expressions
$e \in Expr$ ::=

	x	value identifier ($x \in Vid$)
	a	atomic name ($a \in \mathbb{A}$)
	$va.\,e$	locally scoped fresh name
	$(e \rightleftharpoons e)\,e$	name swapping
	$C\,e$	data value ($C \in Oper$)
	match e with $branch$	data inversion
	true	boolean true
	false	boolean false
	if e then e else e	conditional
	$e = e$	name equality test
	$()$	unit value
	$(e\,,e)$	pair
	let $(x\,,x) = e$ in e	unpairing
	$《e》e$	name abstraction
	let $《a》x = e$ in e	unbinding
	$\lambda x\,x = e$	recursively defined function
	$e\,e$	function application

where
$branch$ ::=

	$C\,x \to e$	
	$branch \mid C\,x \to e$	

Figure 10.2 λFML syntax.

slightly more compact syntax for some Fresh Objective Caml forms:

λFML	Fresh OCaml,
$va.\,e$	let a = fresh in e,
$va.\,a$	fresh,
$(e_1 \rightleftharpoons e_2)\,e_3$	swap $e1$ and $e2$ in $e3$,
$\lambda f\,x = e$	let rec $f\,x = e$ in f.

Instead of using a polymorphic family 'a name of types of names, the grammar is implicitly parameterized by a finite set *Nsort* of name-sorts together with a sorting $s : \mathbb{A} \to Nsort$ for the set $\mathbb{A}$ of atomic names (see Section 4.7); it is also parameterized by a finite set *Dsort* of data-sorts standing for recursively defined data types and a finite set *Oper* of data constructors. Also we fix once and for all a countably infinite set *Vid* of value identifiers which we assume is disjoint from $\mathbb{A}$. This division of identifiers into value identifiers and atomic names is not made in the syntax of Fresh OCaml programs; but it is useful for developing the theoretical properties of the language, since these properties are invariant under arbitrary (value) substitutions for value identifiers, but only invariant under permutations for the atomic names. Several of λFML's constructs involve binding identifiers of these two sorts:

- locally scoped fresh name expressions bind an atomic name;
- unpairing-expressions involve binding two value identifiers in their continuation;
- unbinding-expressions involve binding an atomic name and a value identifier in their continuation expression;
- recursively defined function expressions bind the two value identifiers in their body;
- and each branch of a data inversion expression involves binding a value identifier in its continuation expression.

We identify expressions up to α-conversion of bound value identifiers and bound atomic names. The author, together with some more experienced readers no doubt, understands precisely what he means by the preceding sentence. For the rest, we digress into the details, using the machinery of Chapter 8.

Remark 10.1 ('We identify expressions up to α-equivalence') Figure 10.3 gives a nominal algebraic signature ΣFML for λFML expressions that specifies precisely what are the binding constructs. Using $Vid \cup \mathbb{A}$ as the set of atomic names, with the evident sorting function

$$Vid \cup \mathbb{A} \to \{\mathtt{Vid}, \mathtt{Atom}\}, \tag{10.2}$$

we can generate the raw terms over ΣFML of sort $\mathtt{Expr}$ as in Definition 8.2. Quotienting by the associated relation of α-equivalence (Definition 8.6) we get a nominal algebraic data type

$$Expr \triangleq \Sigma\mathrm{FML}_\alpha(\mathtt{Expr}), \tag{10.3}$$

whose elements are what we mean by λFML *expressions*. Much as in Definition 8.11, we use the concrete notation from Figure 10.2 to denote these α-equivalence classes. *Expr* is a *s*-sorted nominal set (Definition 4.27) for the sorting *s* in (10.2). Just as in Proposition 8.10, the support of an λFML expression is the finite set of free value identifiers and free atomic names of any representative raw term in the α-equivalence class.

Note 10.2 (Abstraction and concretion) Note that even though name abstraction expressions $\langle\!\langle e_1 \rangle\!\rangle e_2$ are used to represent object-level binding, they

Name-sorts	Vid Atom
Data-sorts	Expr Branch
Operations	$V : \text{Vid} \to \text{Expr}$
	$A : \text{Atom} \to \text{Expr}$
	$Nu : \text{Atom . Expr} \to \text{Expr}$
	$Swap : \text{Expr , Expr , Expr} \to \text{Expr}$
	$C : \text{Expr} \to \text{Expr} \quad (C \in Oper)$
	$Match : \text{Expr , Branch} \to \text{Expr}$
	$True : 1 \to \text{Expr}$
	$False : 1 \to \text{Expr}$
	$If : \text{Expr , Expr , Expr} \to \text{Expr}$
	$Eq : \text{Expr , Expr} \to \text{Expr}$
	$Unit : 1 \to \text{Expr}$
	$Pair : \text{Expr , Expr} \to \text{Expr}$
	$Unpair : \text{Expr , (Vid . Vid . Expr)} \to \text{Expr}$
	$Bind : \text{Expr , Expr} \to \text{Expr}$
	$Unbind : \text{Expr , (Atom . Vid . Expr)} \to \text{Expr}$
	$Fun : \text{Vid . Vid . Expr} \to \text{Expr}$
	$App : \text{Expr , Expr} \to \text{Expr}$
	$Arm : \text{Vid . Expr} \to \text{Branch}$
	$Arms : \text{Branch , (Vid . Expr)} \to \text{Branch}$

Figure 10.3 ΣFML: a nominal algebraic signature for λFML expressions.

are not themselves binding constructs in λFML. It is possible to define a binding form of name abstraction by using a locally scoped name:

$$\alpha a. e \triangleq \nu a. \langle\!\langle a \rangle\!\rangle e. \tag{10.4}$$

The non-binding form $\langle\!\langle e_1 \rangle\!\rangle e_2$ can be recovered from this up to contextual equivalence via a use of name-swapping expressions, as $\alpha a. (e_1 \rightleftharpoons a) e_2$ (where $a \,\#\, (e_1, e_2)$); see Exercise 10.4. One can also use name-swapping together with unbinding to define an analogue of the concretion operation from Section 4.3:

$$e_1 \,@\, e_2 \triangleq \text{let } \langle\!\langle a \rangle\!\rangle x = e_1 \text{ in } (e_2 \rightleftharpoons a) x \quad \text{(where } a, x \,\#\, e_2).$$

Definition 10.3 A λFML *data type declaration* Δ consists of a (possibly mutually recursive) definition for each of the data-sorts $D_1, \ldots, D_n$ in *Dsort*. This takes the form

$$D_1 = C_{1,1} \text{ of } T_{1,1} \mid \cdots \mid C_{1,m_1} \text{ of } T_{1,m_1}$$

$$\vdots$$

$$D_n = C_{n,1} \text{ of } T_{n,1} \mid \cdots \mid C_{n,m_n} \text{ of } T_{n,m_n}$$

where the $C_{i,j} \in Oper$ are distinct.

Example 10.4 Assuming $Nsort = \{Var\}$, $Dsort = \{Term\}$ and $Oper = \{V, L, A\}$, then

$$\text{Term} = \text{V of Var} \mid \text{L of } \langle\!\langle Var \rangle\!\rangle \text{Term} \mid \text{A of Term} \times \text{Term}$$

is a λFML data type declaration corresponding to the Fresh OCaml declaration of `term` in Figure 10.1. The function *sub* declared in that figure in λFML would be given by the expression

$$sub \triangleq \lambda x. \lambda t. \tag{10.5}$$
$$\lambda f\, t_1 = \text{match}\, t_1 \text{ with}$$
$$V\, x_1 \rightarrow \text{if } x = x_1 \text{ then } t \text{ else } V\, x_1$$
$$\mid\ L\, x_1 \rightarrow \text{let } \langle\!\langle a_2 \rangle\!\rangle t_2 = x_1 \text{ in } L(\langle\!\langle a_2 \rangle\!\rangle (f\, t_2))$$
$$\mid\ A\, x_1 \rightarrow \text{let } (t_2, t_3) = x_1 \text{ in } A(f\, t_2, f\, t_3),$$

where in general we define ordinary (non-recursive) function abstractions by

$$\lambda x. e \triangleq \lambda f\, x = e \quad \text{where } f \,\#\, (x, e). \tag{10.6}$$

This example illustrates the fact that compared with Fresh OCaml, λFML only uses shallow patterns. We have sacrificed readability, but not expressiveness, in order to simplify the theoretical development.

10.9 Type assignment

We only consider well-typed λFML expressions. To do so we use a λFML *typing relation*

$$\Gamma \vdash e : T \tag{10.7}$$

that is inductively defined by the rule schemes in Figure 10.4, which are implicitly parameterized by a fixed data type declaration Δ. The typing relation uses *type environments* Γ that are finite partial functions in $Vid \rightarrow_f Type$. Some of the rules use the notation $\Gamma(x : T)$ for the typing environment that maps x to T and otherwise maps like Γ.

The definition in the figure is quite standard (see Pierce, 2002, for example),

$$\frac{(x,T) \in \Gamma}{\Gamma \vdash x : T} \qquad \frac{a \in A_N}{\Gamma \vdash a : N} \qquad \frac{\Gamma \vdash e : T \quad a \in A}{\Gamma \vdash va.\, e : T} \qquad \frac{\Gamma \vdash e_1 : N \quad \Gamma \vdash e_2 : N \\ \Gamma \vdash e_3 : T}{\Gamma \vdash (e_1 \rightleftharpoons e_2)\, e_3 : T}$$

$$\frac{\Gamma \vdash e : T \\ (D = \cdots \mid \mathsf{C}\, \mathsf{of}\, T \mid \cdots) \in \Delta}{\Gamma \vdash \mathsf{C}\, e : D} \qquad \frac{\Gamma \vdash e : D \\ \Gamma(x_1 : T_1) \vdash e_1 : T \;\cdots\; \Gamma(x_n : T_n) \vdash e_n : T \\ (D = \mathsf{C}_1\, \mathsf{of}\, T_1 \mid \cdots \mid \mathsf{C}_n\, \mathsf{of}\, T_n) \in \Delta \\ x_1, \ldots, x_n \notin \mathrm{Dom}\, \Gamma}{\Gamma \vdash \mathsf{match}\, e\, \mathsf{with}\, \mathsf{C}_1\, x_1 \to e_1 \mid \cdots \mid \mathsf{C}_n\, x_n \to e_n : T}$$

$$\frac{}{\Gamma \vdash \mathsf{true} : \mathsf{Bool}} \qquad \frac{}{\Gamma \vdash \mathsf{false} : \mathsf{Bool}} \qquad \frac{\Gamma \vdash e_1 : \mathsf{Bool} \\ \Gamma \vdash e_2 : T \quad \Gamma \vdash e_3 : T}{\Gamma \vdash \mathsf{if}\, e_1\, \mathsf{then}\, e_2\, \mathsf{else}\, e_3 : T}$$

$$\frac{\Gamma \vdash e_1 : N \quad \Gamma \vdash e_2 : N}{\Gamma \vdash e_1 = e_2 : \mathsf{Bool}} \qquad \frac{}{\Gamma \vdash () : 1}$$

$$\frac{\Gamma \vdash e_1 : T_1 \quad \Gamma \vdash e_2 : T_2}{\Gamma \vdash (e_1, e_2) : T_1 \times T_2} \qquad \frac{\Gamma \vdash e : T_1 \times T_2 \quad \Gamma(x_1 : T_1, x_2 : T_2) \vdash e' : T_3 \\ x_1, x_2 \notin \mathrm{Dom}\, \Gamma \quad x_1 \neq x_2}{\Gamma \vdash \mathsf{let}\, (x_1, x_2) = e\, \mathsf{in}\, e' : T_3}$$

$$\frac{\Gamma \vdash e_1 : N \quad \Gamma \vdash e_2 : T}{\Gamma \vdash \langle\!\langle e_1 \rangle\!\rangle e_2 : \langle\!\langle N \rangle\!\rangle T} \qquad \frac{\Gamma \vdash e : \langle\!\langle N \rangle\!\rangle T_1 \quad \Gamma(x : T_1) \vdash e' : T_2 \\ x \notin \mathrm{Dom}\, \Gamma \quad a \in A_N}{\Gamma \vdash \mathsf{let}\, \langle\!\langle a \rangle\!\rangle x = e\, \mathsf{in}\, e' : T_2}$$

$$\frac{\Gamma(f : T_1 \to T_2)(x : T_1) \vdash e : T_2 \\ f, x \notin \mathrm{Dom}\, \Gamma \quad f \neq x}{\Gamma \vdash \lambda f\, x = e : T_1 \to T_2} \qquad \frac{\Gamma \vdash e : T_1 \to T_2 \quad \Gamma \vdash e' : T_1}{\Gamma \vdash e\, e' : T_2}$$

Figure 10.4 λFML typing relation.

apart from the fact that typing environments do not contain a component assigning sorts to atomic names; this is because we have chosen to use explicitly sorted atomic names (and because there is no dependence of type expressions upon atomic names). The sets of atomic names A_N mentioned in some of the rules in Figure 10.4 are those associated with the given sorting $s : A \to Nsort$ as in (4.43). Recall from (4.44) that $\mathrm{Perm}_s\, A$ is the group of finite permutations of A that respect s. The many-sorted version of Theorem 7.3 implies that the typing relation is equivariant with respect to the action of $\mathrm{Perm}_s\, A$:

$$(\forall \pi \in \mathrm{Perm}_s\, A)\, \Gamma \vdash e : T \;\Rightarrow\; \Gamma \vdash \pi \cdot e : T. \tag{10.8}$$

Hence for each $T \in Type$ we get an equivariant subset of the many-sorted nominal set of expressions $Expr \in \mathbf{Nom}_s$, given by

$$Expr(T) \triangleq \{e \in Expr \mid \emptyset \vdash e : T\}. \qquad (10.9)$$

It is not hard to see that in general, if $\Gamma \vdash e : T$ holds, then the free value identifiers of e all lie in $\mathrm{Dom}\,\Gamma$. Therefore each $Expr(T)$ consists of *closed* expressions, that is, ones having no free value identifiers. They may have free atomic names and indeed the least support of an element $e \in Expr(T)$ is its finite set of free atomic names.

Example 10.5 The expression *sub* in (10.5) is in $Expr(\mathtt{Var} \rightarrow \mathtt{Term} \rightarrow \mathtt{Term} \rightarrow \mathtt{Term})$.

Definition 10.6 (λFML **values**) The subset $Val \subseteq Expr$ consisting of λFML *values* is given by the following grammar:

$$
\begin{array}{lll}
v \in Val \quad ::= & x & (x \in Vid) \\
& a & (a \in \mathbb{A}) \\
& C\,v & (C \in Oper) \\
& \mathtt{true} & \\
& \mathtt{false} & \\
& () & \\
& (v\,,v) & \\
& \langle\!\langle v \rangle\!\rangle v & \\
& \lambda x\, x = e & (e \in Expr).
\end{array}
$$

Values are the possible results of evaluating λFML expressions. Note that *Val* is an equivariant subset of *Expr*. As for expressions, we single out the values that are well-typed and have no free value identifiers; so we define for each $T \in Type$

$$Val(T) \triangleq \{v \in Val \mid \emptyset \vdash v : T\}. \qquad (10.10)$$

As well as actions of permutations $\pi \in \mathrm{Perm}_s\,\mathbb{A}$ on expressions and values, we need to consider the operation of capture-avoiding substitution. Its definition for λFML expressions is a straightforward extension to the case of many sorts of names (Section 4.7) of the definition for λ-terms in Example 8.19. We write

$$[x := v]e \qquad (10.11)$$

for the result of capture-avoiding substitution of a value v for all free occurrences of the value identifier x in the expression e. It is not hard to see that this operation preserves typing:

$$\Gamma \vdash v : T_1 \ \wedge \ \Gamma(x : T_1) \vdash e : T_2 \ \Rightarrow \ \Gamma \vdash [x := v]e : T_2. \qquad (10.12)$$

10.10 Contextual equivalence

The *Abstractness* criterion mentioned at the beginning of this chapter asks of a meta-level programming language that its programs respect object-level α-equivalence up to a suitable notion of equivalence for meta-level programs. We use *contextual equivalence* of λFML expressions as the notion of program equivalence. In general, two phrases in a programming language are contextually equivalent if the observable results of executing any program involving a use of the first phrase are unaffected by replacing the occurrence with the second phrase. Thus there is a range of potentially different notions of equivalence depending upon what are the 'observable results of executing a program'. Here we take programs to be closed, well-typed λFML expressions $e \in Expr(T)$, and just observe whether or not their evaluation terminates, written $e{\downarrow}$. The precise definition of termination is given below (10.20). Other reasonable choices of observation (such as the outermost form of the value resulting from evaluating e, if any) would not change the notion of λFML contextual equivalence. This is a consequence of using a strict, or 'call-by-value', evaluation strategy (Plotkin, 1975); it is also a consequence of the fact that λFML does not involve any concurrency features – the latter complicate the range of properties one might wish to observe of program execution.

Traditionally, contextual equivalence is defined by quantifying over program contexts, which are syntax trees in which one leaf has been replaced by a 'hole', • (Milner, 1977). Filling the hole with an expression gives a contextual use of the expression. Since this is a form of potentially-capturing substitution, program contexts cannot be identified up to α-equivalence. For example, $\lambda x.$ • is not the same program context as $\lambda y.$ •, since filling the hole with x gives different expressions up to α-equivalence. Here we will use a more abstract, 'relational' approach to defining contextual equivalence due to Lassen (1998) that does not require one to descend below the level of α-equivalence.

Definition 10.7 (λFML **congruence relations**) A *type-respecting binary relation* between λFML expressions is specified by a set $\mathcal{R}$ of quadruples (Γ, e, e', T) where $\Gamma \vdash e : T$ and $\Gamma \vdash e' : T$. (We assume given some fixed data type declaration Δ.) We write

$$\Gamma \vdash e \, \mathcal{R} \, e' : T \qquad (10.13)$$

instead of $(\Gamma, e, e', T) \in \mathcal{R}$. We say that $\mathcal{R}$ is *compatible* if it is respected by the various ways of constructing λFML expressions, that is, if it is closed under the rules in Figure 10.5. Note that compatibility implies *reflexivity*: $\Gamma \vdash e : T \Rightarrow \Gamma \vdash e \, \mathcal{R} \, e : T$. If $\mathcal{R}$ is also *symmetric* ($\Gamma \vdash e \, \mathcal{R} \, e' : T \Rightarrow \Gamma \vdash e' \, \mathcal{R} \, e : T$) and

$$\frac{(x,T) \in \Gamma}{\Gamma \vdash x \,\mathcal{R}\, x : T} \qquad \frac{a \in \mathbb{A}_\mathbb{N}}{\Gamma \vdash a \,\mathcal{R}\, a : \mathbb{N}} \qquad \frac{\Gamma \vdash e \,\mathcal{R}\, e' : T \qquad a \in \mathbb{A}}{\Gamma \vdash va.\, e \,\mathcal{R}\, va.\, e' : T}$$

$$\frac{\Gamma \vdash e_1 \,\mathcal{R}\, e_1' : \mathbb{N} \quad \Gamma \vdash e_2 \,\mathcal{R}\, e_2' : \mathbb{N}}{\Gamma \vdash e_3 \,\mathcal{R}\, e_3' : T} \qquad \frac{\Gamma \vdash e \,\mathcal{R}\, e' : T}{(D = \cdots \mid \mathsf{C} \,\mathsf{of}\, T \mid \cdots) \in \Delta}$$
$$\frac{}{\Gamma \vdash (e_1 \Rightarrow e_2)\, e_3 \,\mathcal{R}\, (e_1' \Rightarrow e_2')\, e_3' : T} \qquad \frac{}{\Gamma \vdash \mathsf{C}\, e \,\mathcal{R}\, \mathsf{C}\, e' : D}$$

$$\frac{\Gamma \vdash e \,\mathcal{R}\, e' : D \quad \Gamma(x_1 : T_1) \vdash e_1 \,\mathcal{R}\, e_1' : T \;\cdots\; \Gamma(x_n : T_n) \vdash e_n \,\mathcal{R}\, e_n' : T}{(D = \mathsf{C}_1 \,\mathsf{of}\, T_1 \mid \cdots \mid \mathsf{C}_n \,\mathsf{of}\, T_n) \in \Delta \qquad x_1, \ldots, x_n \notin \mathrm{Dom}\,\Gamma}$$
$$\frac{}{\begin{array}{c}\Gamma \vdash \mathsf{match}\, e \,\mathsf{with}\, \mathsf{C}_1\, x_1 \to e_1 \mid \cdots \mid \mathsf{C}_n\, x_n \to e_n \,\mathcal{R} \\ \mathsf{match}\, e' \,\mathsf{with}\, \mathsf{C}_1\, x_1 \to e_1' \mid \cdots \mid \mathsf{C}_n\, x_n \to e_n' : T\end{array}}$$

$$\frac{}{\Gamma \vdash \mathsf{true} \,\mathcal{R}\, \mathsf{true} : \mathsf{Bool}} \qquad \frac{}{\Gamma \vdash \mathsf{false} \,\mathcal{R}\, \mathsf{false} : \mathsf{Bool}}$$

$$\frac{\Gamma \vdash e_1 \,\mathcal{R}\, e_1' : \mathsf{Bool} \quad \Gamma \vdash e_2 \,\mathcal{R}\, e_2' : T \quad \Gamma \vdash e_3 \,\mathcal{R}\, e_3' : T}{\Gamma \vdash \mathsf{if}\, e_1 \,\mathsf{then}\, e_2 \,\mathsf{else}\, e_3 \,\mathcal{R}\, \mathsf{if}\, e_1' \,\mathsf{then}\, e_2' \,\mathsf{else}\, e_3' : T}$$

$$\frac{\Gamma \vdash e_1 \,\mathcal{R}\, e_1' : \mathbb{N} \quad \Gamma \vdash e_2 \,\mathcal{R}\, e_2' : \mathbb{N}}{\Gamma \vdash e_1 = e_2 \,\mathcal{R}\, e_1' = e_2' : \mathsf{Bool}} \qquad \frac{}{\Gamma \vdash () \,\mathcal{R}\, () : 1}$$

$$\frac{\Gamma \vdash e_1 \,\mathcal{R}\, e_1' : T_1 \quad \Gamma \vdash e_2 \,\mathcal{R}\, e_2' : T_2}{\Gamma \vdash (e_1, e_2) \,\mathcal{R}\, (e_1', e_2') : T_1 \times T_2}$$

$$\frac{\Gamma \vdash e_1 \,\mathcal{R}\, e_1' : T_1 \times T_2 \quad \Gamma(x_1 : T_1, x_2 : T_2) \vdash e_2 \,\mathcal{R}\, e_2' : T_3}{x_1, x_2 \notin \mathrm{Dom}\,\Gamma \qquad x_1 \neq x_2}$$
$$\frac{}{\Gamma \vdash \mathsf{let}\,(x_1, x_2) = e_1 \,\mathsf{in}\, e_2 \,\mathcal{R}\, \mathsf{let}\,(x_1, x_2) = e_1' \,\mathsf{in}\, e_2' : T_3}$$

$$\frac{\Gamma \vdash e_1 \,\mathcal{R}\, e_1' : \mathbb{N} \quad \Gamma \vdash e_2 \,\mathcal{R}\, e_2' : T}{\Gamma \vdash \langle\!\langle e_1 \rangle\!\rangle e_2 \,\mathcal{R}\, \langle\!\langle e_1' \rangle\!\rangle e_2' : \langle\!\langle \mathbb{N} \rangle\!\rangle T}$$

$$\frac{\Gamma \vdash e_1 \,\mathcal{R}\, e_1' : \langle\!\langle \mathbb{N} \rangle\!\rangle T_1 \quad \Gamma(x : T_1) \vdash e_2 \,\mathcal{R}\, e_2' : T_2 \quad x \notin \mathrm{Dom}\,\Gamma \quad a \in \mathbb{A}_\mathbb{N}}{\Gamma \vdash \mathsf{let}\, \langle\!\langle a \rangle\!\rangle x = e_1 \,\mathsf{in}\, e_2 \,\mathcal{R}\, \mathsf{let}\, \langle\!\langle a \rangle\!\rangle x = e_1' \,\mathsf{in}\, e_2' : T_2}$$

$$\frac{\Gamma(f : T_1 \to T_2)(x : T_1) \vdash e \,\mathcal{R}\, e' : T_2}{f, x \notin \mathrm{Dom}\,\Gamma \qquad f \neq x} \qquad \frac{\Gamma \vdash e_1 \,\mathcal{R}\, e_1' : T_1 \to T_2}{\Gamma \vdash e_2 \,\mathcal{R}\, e_2' : T_1}$$
$$\frac{}{\Gamma \vdash \lambda f\, x = e \,\mathcal{R}\, \lambda f\, x = e' : T_1 \to T_2} \qquad \frac{}{\Gamma \vdash e_1\, e_2 \,\mathcal{R}\, e_1'\, e_2' : T_2}$$

Figure 10.5 λFML compatibility conditions.

transitive ($\Gamma \vdash e \,\mathcal{R}\, e' : T \,\wedge\, \Gamma \vdash e' \,\mathcal{R}\, e'' : T \Rightarrow \Gamma \vdash e \,\mathcal{R}\, e'' : T$), then we call $\mathcal{R}$ a λFML *congruence relation*.

We define λFML contextual equivalence so that it is the largest λFML congruence relation that relates closed expressions with the same termination behaviour (see Proposition 10.12). So first we have to define the termination relation for λFML. The operational semantics of languages in the ML family were originally specified via a 'big-step' evaluation relation (Milner *et al.*, 1997). For λFML this takes the form

$$A, e \Downarrow A', v. \tag{10.14}$$

Here $e \in Expr$ is required to have no free value identifiers and free atomic names contained in $A \in P_f\,\mathbb{A}$; and $v \in Val$ must have no free value identifiers and free atomic names contained in $A' \in P_f\,\mathbb{A}$. For example, using this form of operational semantics, evaluation of unbinding expressions is given by the following rule:

$$\frac{A, e_1 \Downarrow A', \langle\!\langle a' \rangle\!\rangle v_1 \qquad a \notin A'}{A, \texttt{let } \langle\!\langle a \rangle\!\rangle x = e_1 \texttt{ in } e_2 \Downarrow A'', v_2} \tag{10.15}$$

Given a full definition of the evaluation relation (10.14), the termination relation $e{\downarrow}$ holds iff $(\exists A', v)\, A, e \Downarrow A', v$, where $A = \operatorname{supp} e$ is the set of free atomic names of e.

However, experience shows that proving properties of contextual equivalence in higher-order functional programming languages is more easily done starting from a characterization of termination based on a 'small-step' semantics formulated in the style of Felleisen and Hieb (1992) using evaluation contexts; and to make proofs about evaluation contexts easier to formalize, it pays to write them 'inside out' as a *stack* (that is, an ordered list) of basic contexts, or evaluation *frames* (see Pitts, 2002, for example). Figure 10.6 gives the definition of λFML evaluation frames and frame stacks.

Regarding the 'hole' $\bullet$ in an evaluation frame as a distinguished value identifier, one can regard evaluation frames as particular expressions; and like expressions, we identify them up to α-equivalence. (Unlike more general forms of program context, the hole of an evaluation frame is not within the scope of any binder, so this identification up to α-equivalence is not problematic from the point of view of substituting expressions for $\bullet$.) Thus we type evaluation frames by asking that

$$\Gamma(\bullet : T) \vdash E : T'$$

be derivable from the rules in Figure 10.4; and then we extend the typing rela-

Frame stacks $F \in Stack$ ::=   Id   empty
                                        $F \circ E$ non-empty

Evaluation frames E ::= $(\bullet \rightleftharpoons e)\, e$
                                   $(v \rightleftharpoons \bullet)\, e$
                                   $(v \rightleftharpoons v)\, \bullet$
                                   C $\bullet$
                                   match $\bullet$ with *branch*
                                   if $\bullet$ then e else e
                                   $\bullet = e$
                                   $v = \bullet$
                                   $(\bullet, e)$
                                   $(v, \bullet)$
                                   let $(x, x) = \bullet$ in e
                                   $\langle\!\langle \bullet \rangle\!\rangle e$
                                   $\langle\!\langle v \rangle\!\rangle \bullet$
                                   let $\langle\!\langle a \rangle\!\rangle x = \bullet$ in e
                                   $\bullet\, e$
                                   $v\, \bullet$

Figure 10.6 λFML evaluation frame stacks.

tion to frame stacks using the following two rules:

$$\frac{}{\Gamma \vdash \mathrm{Id} : T \to T} \qquad \frac{\Gamma \vdash F : T_2 \to T_3 \qquad \Gamma(\bullet : T_1) \vdash E : T_2}{\Gamma \vdash F \circ E : T_1 \to T_3}.$$

We define

$$Stack(T) \triangleq \{F \in Stack \mid (\exists T' \in Type)\ \emptyset \vdash F : T \to T'\} \qquad (10.16)$$

to be the set of closed, well-typed frame stacks whose argument type is $T \in$ *Type*. As for expressions and values, $Stack(T)$ is an object of **Nom**$_s$ with the Perm$_s$ $\mathbb{A}$-action inherited from that on evaluation frames (regarded as expressions containing a special value identifier $\bullet$):

$$\pi \cdot \mathrm{Id} = \mathrm{Id},$$
$$\pi \cdot (F \circ E) = (\pi \cdot F) \circ (\pi \cdot E).$$

With respect to this action, the least support of $F \in Stack(T)$ is the finite set of atomic names that occur free in some evaluation frame in F.

We specify how λFML expressions evaluate in terms of an abstract machine whose λFML abstract machine *configurations* are pairs (F, e) consisting of a frame stack F and an expression e, both of which are closed, that is, have no free value identifiers (but which may have free atomic names). Terminal configurations for the abstract machine take the form (Id, v) where Id denotes the

$$(F, va.\, e) \to (F, e) \qquad\qquad 1$$
$$\text{if } a \mathrel{\#} F$$
$$(F, (e_1 \mathrel{\Rightarrow} e_2)\, e_3) \to (F \circ ((\bullet \mathrel{\Rightarrow} e_2)\, e_3), e_1) \qquad 2$$
$$(F, C\, e) \to (F \circ (C \bullet), e) \qquad\qquad 3$$
$$\text{if } e \notin Val$$
$$(F, \text{match}\, e \text{ with } branch) \to (F \circ (\text{match} \bullet \text{ with } branch), e) \qquad 4$$
$$(F, \text{if } e_1 \text{ then } e_2 \text{ else } e_3) \to (F \circ (\text{if} \bullet \text{ then } e_2 \text{ else } e_3), e_1) \qquad 5$$
$$(F, e_1 = e_2) \to (F \circ (\bullet = e_2), e_1) \qquad\qquad 6$$
$$(F, (e_1, e_2)) \to (F \circ (\bullet, e_2), e_1) \qquad\qquad 7$$
$$\text{if } (e_1, e_2) \notin Val$$
$$(F, \text{let } (x_1, x_2) = e_1 \text{ in } e_2) \to (F \circ (\text{let } (x_1, x_2) = \bullet \text{ in } e_2), e_1) \qquad 8$$
$$(F, \langle\!\langle e_1 \rangle\!\rangle e_2) \to (F \circ (\langle\!\langle \bullet \rangle\!\rangle e_2), e_1) \qquad\qquad 9$$
$$\text{if } \langle\!\langle e_1 \rangle\!\rangle e_2 \notin Val$$
$$(F, \text{let } \langle\!\langle a \rangle\!\rangle x = e_1 \text{ in } e_2) \to (F \circ (\text{let } \langle\!\langle a \rangle\!\rangle x = \bullet \text{ in } e_2), e_1) \qquad 10$$
$$(F, e_1\, e_2) \to (F \circ (\bullet\, e_2), e_1) \qquad\qquad 11$$
$$(F \circ ((\bullet \mathrel{\Rightarrow} e_1)\, e_2), a) \to (F \circ ((a \mathrel{\Rightarrow} \bullet)\, e_2), e_1) \qquad 12$$
$$(F \circ ((a_1 \mathrel{\Rightarrow} \bullet)\, e), a_2) \to (F \circ ((a_1 \mathrel{\Rightarrow} a_2)\, \bullet), e) \qquad 13$$
$$(F \circ ((a_1 \mathrel{\Rightarrow} a_2)\, \bullet), v) \to (F, (a_1\, a_2) \cdot v) \qquad\qquad 14$$
$$(F \circ (C \bullet), v) \to (F, C\, v) \qquad\qquad 15$$
$$(F \circ (\text{match} \bullet \text{ with } \cdots \mid C\, x \to e \mid \cdots), C\, v) \to (F, [x := v]e) \qquad 16$$
$$(F \circ (\text{if} \bullet \text{ then } e_1 \text{ else } e_2), \text{true}) \to (F, e_1) \qquad\qquad 17$$
$$(F \circ (\text{if} \bullet \text{ then } e_1 \text{ else } e_2), \text{false}) \to (F, e_2) \qquad\qquad 18$$
$$(F \circ (\bullet = e), a) \to (F \circ (a = \bullet), e) \qquad\qquad 19$$
$$(F \circ (a = \bullet), a) \to (F, \text{true}) \qquad\qquad 20$$
$$(F \circ (a = \bullet), a') \to (F, \text{false}) \qquad\qquad 21$$
$$\text{if } a \neq a'$$
$$(F \circ (\bullet, e), v) \to (F \circ (v, \bullet), e) \qquad\qquad 22$$
$$(F \circ (v_1, \bullet), v_2) \to (F, (v_1, v_2)) \qquad\qquad 23$$
$$(F \circ (\text{let } (x_1, x_2) = \bullet \text{ in } e), (v_1, v_2)) \to (F, [x_1 := v_1][x_2 := v_2]e) \qquad 24$$
$$(F \circ (\langle\!\langle \bullet \rangle\!\rangle e), a) \to (F \circ (\langle\!\langle a \rangle\!\rangle \bullet), e) \qquad\qquad 25$$
$$(F \circ (\langle\!\langle a \rangle\!\rangle \bullet), v) \to (F, \langle\!\langle a \rangle\!\rangle v) \qquad\qquad 26$$
$$(F \circ (\text{let } \langle\!\langle a \rangle\!\rangle x = \bullet \text{ in } e), \langle\!\langle a' \rangle\!\rangle v) \to (F, [x := (a\, a') \cdot v]e) \qquad 27$$
$$\text{if } a \mathrel{\#} (F, a', v)$$
$$(F \circ (\bullet\, e), v) \to (F \circ (v \bullet), e) \qquad\qquad 28$$
$$(F \circ (v_1 \bullet), v_2) \to (F, [f := v_1][x := v_2]e) \qquad\qquad 29$$
$$\text{if } v_1 = (\lambda f\, x = e)$$

Figure 10.7 λFML abstract machine transitions.

empty stack and v is a closed value. The possible *transitions* between configurations

$$(F, e) \to (F', e') \qquad\qquad (10.17)$$

are given in Figure 10.7, by cases according to the structure first of the expression e and secondly of the frame stack F.

Remark 10.8 (Dynamic allocation and matching) Transition 1 in Figure 10.7 appears simpler than it really is, because we identify expressions up to

α-equivalence. Although it may not seem so at first sight, it embodies the interpretation of locally scoped names in terms of dynamically allocated fresh names (*cf.* Example 7.7). The finite set of atomic names supp$(F, e) = \text{supp } F \cup$ supp e plays the role of the current state of dynamically allocated names, or at least that part of it relevant to the rest of the computation as embodied by F. Thus for a configuration of the form $(F, va. e)$, the state is supp $F \cup (\text{supp } e - \{a\})$; and so if $a \# F$, then a is not in this set. In this case Figure 10.7 gives $(F, va. e) \rightarrow (F, e)$. On the other hand, if $a \# F$ does not hold, then we can always choose some $a' \# (F, a, e)$ and for this we have $(F, va. e) = (F, va'. (a\ a') \cdot e) \rightarrow (F, (a\ a') \cdot e)$. In particular, the λFML version of the Fresh OCaml expression `fresh`,

$$fresh \triangleq va. a, \qquad\qquad (10.18)$$

satisfies $(F, fresh) \rightarrow (F, a)$ for any $a \# F$.

The other part of Figure 10.7 involving dynamic allocation is transition 27, for matching a name abstraction value $\langle\!\langle a' \rangle\!\rangle v$ against a name abstraction pattern $\langle\!\langle a \rangle\!\rangle x$. As for the first transition, up to α-conversion of the evaluation frame `let` $\langle\!\langle a \rangle\!\rangle x = \bullet$ `in` e, the condition $a \# (F, a', v)$ can always be satisfied. Thus the matching executes by unbinding $\langle\!\langle a' \rangle\!\rangle v$ using a fresh name a to obtain $(a\ a') \cdot v$ and then executing the continuation expression with x substituted by that value. (Compare this with the rule in (10.15).)

For each type $T \in Type$ the set of well-typed configurations is

$$Config(T) \triangleq Stack(T) \times Expr(T).$$

Proposition 10.9 (λFML **type soundness**)   *Suppose* $(F, e) \in Config(T)$.

(i) *Preservation: if* $(F, e) \rightarrow (F', e')$, *then* $(F', e') \in Config(T)$.
(ii) *Progress: either* (F, e) *is terminal, that is,* $F = \text{Id}$ *and* $e \in Val(T)$, *or there exist* F' *and* e' *with* $(F, e) \rightarrow (F', e')$.

Proof   The preservation property uses (10.12); and the progress property relies upon the above remarks about dynamic allocation and matching. The details are left as an exercise (Exercise 10.1). $\square$

We write $(F, e)\!\downarrow_n$ to mean that there exists a chain of transitions from the configuration (F, e) to a terminal configuration (Id, v) of length less than or equal to $n \in \mathbb{N}$. This relation can be inductively defined by the two rule schemes:

$$\frac{}{(\text{Id}, v)\!\downarrow_n} \qquad \frac{(F', e')\!\downarrow_n \quad (F, e) \rightarrow (F', e')}{(F, e)\!\downarrow_{n+1}}. \qquad (10.19)$$

We then define *termination* as follows:

$$(F, e)\!\downarrow \triangleq (\exists n \in \mathbb{N})\, (F, e)\!\downarrow_n,$$
$$e\!\downarrow \triangleq (\mathtt{Id}, e)\!\downarrow. \tag{10.20}$$

Example 10.10 (Divergence) Define

$$\Omega \triangleq (\lambda f\, x = f\, x)\, ().$$

Thus $\Omega \in Expr(T)$ for all $T \in Type$. It is a diverging expression, since it follows from the definition of $\downarrow$ that the only transitions from the configuration (F, Ω) are

$$(F, \Omega) \to (F \circ (\bullet\, ()), \lambda f\, x = f\, x)$$
$$\to (F \circ (\lambda f\, x = f\, x)\, \bullet, ())$$
$$\to (F, (\lambda f\, x = f\, x)\, ())$$
$$= (F, \Omega) \to \cdots,$$

and hence $(F, \Omega)\!\downarrow$ cannot hold.

Definition 10.11 (λFML contextual equivalence) A type-respecting binary relation $\mathcal{R}$ is said to be *adequate* for termination if it satisfies for all $e, e' \in Expr$ and $T \in Type$

$$\emptyset \vdash e\, \mathcal{R}\, e' : T \;\Rightarrow\; (e\!\downarrow \Leftrightarrow e'\!\downarrow).$$

Let $=_{\text{ctx}}$ be the union of all adequate and compatible type-respecting relations (with respect to the fixed data type declaration Δ). We call it λFML *contextual equivalence*. When e and e' have no free value identifiers we abbreviate $\emptyset \vdash e =_{\text{ctx}} e' : T$ to

$$e =_{\text{ctx}} e' : T. \tag{10.21}$$

Proposition 10.12 $=_{\text{ctx}}$ *is the largest adequate congruence relation.*

Proof It suffices to show that $=_{\text{ctx}}$ is both adequate and a congruence relation; for any other such relation is adequate and compatible and hence contained in $=_{\text{ctx}}$ by definition.

Note that from the definition of adequacy, such relations are closed under taking unions and therefore $=_{\text{ctx}}$ is adequate.

The identity relation

$$Id \triangleq \{(\Gamma, e, e, T) \mid \Gamma \vdash e : T\}$$

is clearly adequate and compatible; so it is contained in $=_{\text{ctx}}$, which therefore is reflexive. If $\mathcal{R}$ and $\mathcal{R}'$ are adequate, then clearly so are

$$\mathcal{R}^{op} \triangleq \{(\Gamma, e', e, T) \mid (\Gamma, e, e', T) \in \mathcal{R}\},$$

$$\mathcal{R}' \circ \mathcal{R} \triangleq \{(\Gamma, e, e'', T) \mid (\exists e') \, (\Gamma, e, e', T) \in \mathcal{R} \wedge (\Gamma, e', e'', T) \in \mathcal{R}'\}.$$

Similarly, if $\mathcal{R}$ and $\mathcal{R}'$ are closed under the rules in Figure 10.5, then so are $\mathcal{R}^{op}$ and $\mathcal{R}' \circ \mathcal{R}$. From this it follows that $=^{op}_{ctx} \subseteq \,=_{ctx}$ and $=_{ctx} \circ =_{ctx} \subseteq \,=_{ctx}$. Therefore $=_{ctx}$ is also symmetric and transitive.

It remains to show that $=_{ctx}$ is compatible. Note that because some of the rules in Figure 10.5 have hypotheses with more than one instance of the relation, the union of compatible relations is not necessarily compatible. However, we can use the transitivity of $=_{ctx}$ to side-step this problem. We show closure of $=_{ctx}$ under the rule

$$\frac{\Gamma \vdash e_1 =_{ctx} e_1' : T_1 \qquad \Gamma \vdash e_2 =_{ctx} e_2' : T_2}{\Gamma \vdash (e_1, e_2) =_{ctx} (e_1', e_2') : T_1 \times T_2}.$$

The proof of closure under the other rules in Figure 10.5 is similar. So suppose $\Gamma \vdash e_1 =_{ctx} e_1' : T_1$ and $\Gamma \vdash e_2 =_{ctx} e_2' : T_2$. Thus $\Gamma \vdash e_1 \, \mathcal{R}_1 \, e_1' : T_1$ and $\Gamma \vdash e_2 \, \mathcal{R}_2 \, e_2' : T_2$ hold for some adequate and compatible relations $\mathcal{R}_1$ and $\mathcal{R}_2$. We noted above that compatible relations are necessarily reflexive. So we have $\Gamma \vdash e_1 \, \mathcal{R}_1 \, e_1' : T_1 \,\wedge\, \Gamma \vdash e_2 \, \mathcal{R}_1 \, e_2 : T_2$ and hence also $\Gamma \vdash (e_1, e_2) \, \mathcal{R}_1 \, (e_1', e_2) : T_1 \times T_2$ by compatibility of $\mathcal{R}_1$; and therefore $\Gamma \vdash (e_1, e_2) =_{ctx} (e_1', e_2) : T_1 \times T_2$. Similarly, we get $\Gamma \vdash (e_1', e_2) =_{ctx} (e_1', e_2') : T_1 \times T_2$. Therefore by transitivity of $=_{ctx}$, we have $\Gamma \vdash (e_1, e_2) \, \mathcal{R} \, (e_1', e_2') : T_1 \times T_2$, as required. $\qquad \square$

The following result will eventually be proved in the next section.

Theorem 10.13 (Extensionality) λ_{FML} *contextual equivalence has the following properties for closed values:*

(i) $a =_{ctx} a' : N \Leftrightarrow a = a' \in \mathbb{A}_N$.

(ii) $C\,v =_{ctx} C'v' : D \Leftrightarrow C = C' \,\wedge\, v =_{ctx} v' : T$ *(where the fixed data type declaration* Δ *contains* $D = \cdots \mid C \,\text{of}\, T \mid \cdots$*)*.

(iii) $b =_{ctx} b' : \text{Bool} \Leftrightarrow b = b' \in \{\text{true}, \text{false}\}$.

(iv) $() =_{ctx} () : 1$.

(v) $(v_1, v_2) =_{ctx} (v_1', v_2') : T_1 \times T_2 \Leftrightarrow v_1 =_{ctx} v_1' : T_1 \,\wedge\, v_2 =_{ctx} v_2' : T_2$.

(vi) $\langle\!\langle a \rangle\!\rangle v =_{ctx} \langle\!\langle a' \rangle\!\rangle v' : \langle\!\langle N \rangle\!\rangle T \Leftrightarrow (\mathcal{V}a'' : N) \, (a \, a'') \cdot v =_{ctx} (a' \, a'') \cdot v' : T$.

(vii) $v =_{ctx} v' : T_1 \to T_2 \Leftrightarrow (\forall v_1, v_1') \, v_1 =_{ctx} v_1' : T_1 \Rightarrow [f := v][x := v_1]e =_{ctx} [f := v'][x := v_1']e' : T_2$, *where* $v = (\lambda f \, x = e)$ *and* $v' = (\lambda f \, x = e')$.

Remark 10.14 The restriction to closed *values* rather than arbitrary closed expressions is important for the validity of some of the above properties of $=_{ctx}$, because λFML is an impure language. In particular, it is known that a function extensionality property such as

$$((\forall v \in Val(T_1))\, e\, v =_{\text{ctx}} e'v : T_2) \Rightarrow e =_{\text{ctx}} e' : T_1 \to T_2$$

fails to hold for all expressions $e, e' \in Expr(T_1 \to T_2)$; see Pitts and Stark (1998, example 1.2).

How does one prove the properties in Theorem 10.13? From the definition of $=_{\text{ctx}}$, to prove that two expressions are contextually equivalent it suffices to find an adequate and compatible relation that contains them. However, in any particular case that can be quite hard, since the compatibility property tells us that various pairs must be in the relation besides the pair of expressions of interest and this makes checking the adequacy property difficult. The next section develops a technique for proving properties of $=_{\text{ctx}}$, including those in the theorem.

Property (vi) in Theorem 10.13 is the one we need in order to show that λFML respects object-level α-equivalence up to contextual equivalence (Theorem 10.28). It is stated using the many-sorted (Section 4.7) version of the freshness quantifier (Section 3.2). In view of the following lemma, the 'some/any' theorem (Theorem 3.9) implies that $\langle\!\langle a \rangle\!\rangle v =_{\text{ctx}} \langle\!\langle a' \rangle\!\rangle v' : \langle\!\langle N \rangle\!\rangle T$ holds iff

$$(\exists a'' \in A_N)\, a'' \,\#\, \text{supp}(a, v, a,', v') \,\wedge\, (a\, a'') \cdot v =_{\text{ctx}} (a'\, a'') \cdot v' : T,$$

or equivalently, iff

$$(\forall a'' \in A_N)\, a'' \,\#\, (a, v, a,', v') \Rightarrow (a\, a'') \cdot v =_{\text{ctx}} (a'\, a'') \cdot v' : T.$$

Lemma 10.15 *λFML contextual equivalence is equivariant:*

$$(\forall \pi \in \text{Perm}_s A)\, \Gamma \vdash e =_{\text{ctx}} e' : T \Rightarrow \Gamma \vdash \pi \cdot e =_{\text{ctx}} \pi \cdot e' : T.$$

Proof In view of Definition 10.11, it suffices to show that if $\mathcal{R}$ is an adequate and compatible type-respecting relation, then so is

$$\pi \cdot \mathcal{R} = \{(\Gamma, \pi \cdot e, \pi \cdot e', T) \mid \Gamma \vdash e\, \mathcal{R}\, e' : T\}.$$

Since $\mathcal{R}$ is closed under the rules in Figure 10.5, it is easy to see that $\pi \cdot \mathcal{R}$ is as well, so $\pi \cdot \mathcal{R}$ is compatible. For adequacy, we just need to know that termination is equivariant: $(\forall \pi \in \text{Perm}_s A)\, e{\downarrow} \Rightarrow (\pi \cdot e){\downarrow}$. In view of definitions (10.19)–(10.20), this follows from the equivariance of the abstract machine transitions

$$(\forall \pi \in \text{Perm}_s A)\, (F, e) \to (F', e') \Rightarrow (\pi \cdot F, \pi \cdot e) \to (\pi \cdot F', \pi \cdot e'),$$

which is a consequence of the Equivariance Principle applied to the definition of $\to$ in Figure 10.7. $\qquad\square$

10.11 Step-indexed logical relation

'Logical relations' were originally used in the denotational semantics of languages based on typed λ-calculus (Plotkin, 1973; Statman, 1985). Subsequently they have proved useful for proving properties of operationally defined notions of program equivalence in higher-order typed programming languages; see Pitts (2005), for example. Although there are many different flavours of logical relation, their common feature is that at function types two functions are related iff they send related arguments to related results. This feature means that the relation being defined occurs both positively and negatively in the recursive specification of its desired properties. This creates a difficulty when trying to construct them. For example, a naive application of Tarski's fixed-point theorem (Theorem 7.12) will not suffice, because even though the specification of the logical relation is in the form of a fixed-point of a function on relations, that function is not monotone. This difficulty did not arise in the original work on logical relations for simply typed languages, where a definition by recursion on the structure of types is possible. However, it was a block on the application of the method of logical relations in more complicated cases, such as for languages involving recursively defined data types (such as λFML). Recently the difficulty has been overcome by using certain kinds of indexed families of relations where the indices relate to steps of computation in the language's operational semantics. A well-founded relation between the indices allows a definition of the entire logical relation by well-founded recursion. This is the notion of *step-indexed logical relation* introduced by Appel and McAllester (2001) and adapted to the kind of contextual equivalence with which we are concerned here by Ahmed (2006). The notion is even more effective when combined with the use of *bi-orthogonal closure* of relations (Pitts, 2000); see Dreyer *et al.* (2010), for example. Using this combination we obtain a proof of properties of λFML related to the *Abstractness* criterion (Theorem 10.13) that is somewhat simpler than other ones in the literature. For example, compare the proof of extensionality for name abstraction types in (Pitts and Shinwell, 2008, appendix B) with its proof here as a corollary of the way the logical relation is defined (proof of property (vi) in Theorem 10.13). Even so, the development in this section is rather long and tedious. The reader more interested in the application of Theorem 10.13 may consider skipping to the next section.

Figure 10.8 specifies step-indexed logical relations for closed values, expressions and frame stacks in λFML. Bi-orthogonality features in the way that the relation for expressions ($\mathcal{E}$) is defined in terms of the relation for frame stacks ($\mathcal{F}$) and the way in which the latter is defined in terms of the relation for values ($\mathcal{V}$). Step-indexing features through the use of indices $(n, T) \in \mathbb{N} \times Type$

$\_ \, \mathcal{V}_n \, \_ : T \subseteq Val(T) \times Val(T) \quad (n \in \mathbb{N}, T \in Type)$:

$$a \, \mathcal{V}_n \, a' : \mathbb{N} \Leftrightarrow a = a' \in \mathbb{A_N} \tag{10.22}$$

$$C v \, \mathcal{V}_n \, C'v' : D \Leftrightarrow C = C' \wedge (\forall m < n) \, v \, \mathcal{V}_m \, v' : T \tag{10.23}$$
$$\text{where } (D = \cdots \mid C \text{ of } T \mid \cdots) \in \Delta$$

$$b \, \mathcal{V}_n \, b' : \texttt{Bool} \Leftrightarrow b = b' \in \{\texttt{true}, \texttt{false}\} \tag{10.24}$$

$$() \, \mathcal{V}_n \, () : 1 \tag{10.25}$$

$$(v_1, v_2) \, \mathcal{V}_n \, (v_1', v_2') : T_1 \times T_2 \Leftrightarrow v_1 \, \mathcal{V}_n \, v_1' : T_1 \wedge v_2 \, \mathcal{V}_n \, v_2' : T_2 \tag{10.26}$$

$$\langle\!\langle a \rangle\!\rangle v \, \mathcal{V}_n \, \langle\!\langle a' \rangle\!\rangle v' : \langle\!\langle \mathbb{N} \rangle\!\rangle T \Leftrightarrow (\forall a'' : \mathbb{N}) \, (a \, a'') \cdot v \, \mathcal{V}_n \, (a' \, a'') \cdot v' : T \tag{10.27}$$

$$v \, \mathcal{V}_n \, v' : T_1 \rightarrow T_2 \Leftrightarrow (\forall m < n)(\forall v_1, v_1') \, v_1 \, \mathcal{V}_m \, v_1' : T_1 \tag{10.28}$$
$$\Rightarrow [f := v][x := v_1]e \, \mathcal{E}_m \, [f := v'][x := v_1']e' : T_2$$
$$\text{where } v = (\lambda f \, x = e) \text{ and } v' = (\lambda f \, x = e')$$

$\_ \, \mathcal{E}_n \, \_ : T \subseteq Expr(T) \times Expr(T) \quad (n \in \mathbb{N}, T \in Type)$:

$$e \, \mathcal{E}_n \, e' : T \Leftrightarrow (\forall m \leq n)(\forall F, F') \, F \, \mathcal{F}_m \, F' : T \tag{10.29}$$
$$\Rightarrow ((F, e){\downarrow}_m \Rightarrow (F', e'){\downarrow})$$
$$\wedge ((F', e'){\downarrow}_m \Rightarrow (F, e){\downarrow})$$

$\_ \, \mathcal{F}_n \, \_ : T \subseteq Stack(T) \times Stack(T) \quad (n \in \mathbb{N}, T \in Type)$:

$$F \, \mathcal{F}_n \, F' : T \Leftrightarrow (\forall m \leq n)(\forall v, v') \, v \, \mathcal{V}_m \, v' : T \tag{10.30}$$
$$\Rightarrow ((F, v){\downarrow}_m \Rightarrow (F', v'){\downarrow})$$
$$\wedge ((F', v'){\downarrow}_m \Rightarrow (F, v){\downarrow})$$

Figure 10.8 λFML step-indexed logical relations.

that in their first component relate to the number of steps until the abstract machine terminates, via (10.29) and (10.30). The value relations $\_ \, \mathcal{V}_n \, \_ : T$ are defined by recursion over the well-founded relation $\prec$ between indices given by a lexicographic order

$$(n, T) \prec (n', T') \triangleq n < n' \ \vee \ (n = n' \wedge size \, T < size \, T'),$$

where $size \, T$ counts the number of symbols in a type T. Note that there are two places in the definition in Figure 10.8 where the order $\prec$ goes down because the first component of an index is strictly smaller: (10.23), where the recursive definition of a data-sort is unrolled; and (10.28), where the recursive definition of a function is unrolled. The first is needed for a well-founded definition of $\mathcal{V}$, since the size of the type of v may well be bigger than the size of the type of $C v$. The second obviates the need to prove 'unwinding theorems' for recursive function values (such as theorem 7.4.4 of Pitts, 2005) in order to prove the fundamental property of the logical relation (Lemma 10.21); see also Exercise 10.6.

Lemma 10.16   *The step-indexed logical relations are equivariant:*

$$v \, \mathcal{V}_n \, v' : T \Rightarrow \pi \cdot v \, \mathcal{V}_n \, \pi \cdot v' : T, \tag{10.31}$$

$$e \, \mathcal{E}_n \, e' : T \Rightarrow \pi \cdot e \, \mathcal{E}_n \, \pi \cdot e' : T,$$

$$F \, \mathcal{F}_n \, F' : T \Rightarrow \pi \cdot F \, \mathcal{F}_n \, \pi \cdot F' : T.$$

Proof   Apply the Equivariance Principle to the definition in Figure 10.8 using the fact, noted in the proof of Lemma 10.15, that $\rightarrow$, $\downarrow_n$ and $\downarrow$ are equivariant. □

Remark 10.17   In view of this lemma, the use of the freshness quantifier in (10.27) is equivalent to requiring that $(a \, a'') \cdot v \, \mathcal{V}_n \, (a' \, a'') \cdot v' : T$ hold for some $a'' \in \mathbb{A}_\mathbb{N} - \text{supp}(a, v, a', v')$, or indeed for any such a'' (see Theorem 3.9).

Lemma 10.18   *For all* $n \in \mathbb{N}$, $\mathcal{V}_{n+1} \subseteq \mathcal{V}_n \subseteq \mathcal{E}_n$, $\mathcal{E}_{n+1} \subseteq \mathcal{E}_n$ *and* $\mathcal{F}_{n+1} \subseteq \mathcal{F}_n$.

Proof   The fact that $\mathcal{V}_n$, $\mathcal{E}_n$ and $\mathcal{F}_n$ are decreasing in $n \in \mathbb{N}$ is immediate from their definition in Figure 10.8. Then $\mathcal{V}_n \subseteq \mathcal{E}_n$ follows from this and the way $\mathcal{E}$ is defined in terms of $\mathcal{V}$ in (10.29) and (10.30). □

We are aiming to show that $e =_{\text{ctx}} e' : T$ holds iff $(\forall n \in \mathbb{N}) \, e \, \mathcal{E}_n \, e' : T$. The following rather long list of properties takes us toward that goal.

Lemma 10.19   (i) $\text{Id} \, \mathcal{F}_n \, \text{Id} : T$.
(ii) *For all* $a \in \mathbb{A}_\mathbb{N}$, $a \, \mathcal{E}_n \, a : \mathbb{N}$.
(iii) *If* $e \, \mathcal{E}_n \, e' : T$, *then* $va. e \, \mathcal{E}_n \, va. e' : T$.
(iv) *If* $F \, \mathcal{F}_n \, F' : T$, $a_1, a_2 \in \mathbb{A}_\mathbb{N}$, $e_1 \, \mathcal{E}_n \, e'_1 : \mathbb{N}$, $e_2 \, \mathcal{E}_n \, e'_2 : \mathbb{N}$ *and* $e_3 \, \mathcal{E}_n \, e'_3 : T$, *then*

$$(F \circ (a_1 \rightleftharpoons a_2) \bullet) \, \mathcal{F}_{n+1} \, (F' \circ (a_1 \rightleftharpoons a_2) \bullet) : T,$$

$$(F \circ (a_1 \rightleftharpoons \bullet) e_3) \, \mathcal{F}_{n+1} \, (F' \circ (a_1 \rightleftharpoons \bullet) e'_3) : \mathbb{N},$$

$$(F \circ (\bullet \rightleftharpoons e_2) e_3) \, \mathcal{F}_{n+1} \, (F \circ (\bullet \rightleftharpoons e'_2) e'_3) : \mathbb{N},$$

$$(e_1 \rightleftharpoons e_2) e_3 \, \mathcal{E}_n \, (e'_1 \rightleftharpoons e'_2) e'_3 : T.$$

(v) *If* $(\mathsf{D} = \cdots \mid \mathsf{C} \, \text{of} \, T \mid \cdots) \in \Delta$, $F \, \mathcal{F}_n \, F' : \mathsf{D}$ *and* $e \, \mathcal{E}_n \, e' : T$, *then*

$$(F \circ \mathsf{C} \bullet) \, \mathcal{F}_{n+1} \, (F' \circ \mathsf{C} \bullet) : T,$$

$$\mathsf{C} \, e \, \mathcal{E}_n \, \mathsf{C} \, e' : \mathsf{D}.$$

(vi) *Suppose* $(D = C_1 \text{ of } T_1 \mid \cdots \mid C_k \text{ of } T_k) \in \Delta$, $e \, \mathcal{E}_n \, e' : D$, $F \, \mathcal{F}_n \, F' : T$ and
for $i = 1, \ldots, k$, $(\lambda x_i. e_i), (\lambda x_i. e_i') \in Val(T_i \to T)$ *satisfy*

$$(\forall m \le n)(\forall v, v') \, v \, \mathcal{V}_m \, v' : T_i \Rightarrow [x_i := v]e_i \, \mathcal{E}_m \, [x_i := v']e_i' : T .$$

Then writing

$$branch \triangleq C_1 \, x_1 \to e_1 \mid \cdots \mid C_k \, x_k \to e_k ,$$
$$branch' \triangleq C_1 \, x_1 \to e_1' \mid \cdots \mid C_k \, x_k \to e_k' ,$$

we have

$$(F \circ \text{match} \bullet \text{ with } branch) \, \mathcal{F}_{n+1} \, (F' \circ \text{match} \bullet \text{ with } branch') : D ,$$
$$(\text{match } e \text{ with } branch) \, \mathcal{E}_n \, (\text{match } e' \text{ with } branch') : T .$$

(vii) $\text{true} \, \mathcal{E}_n \, \text{true} : \text{Bool}$ *and* $\text{false} \, \mathcal{E}_n \, \text{false} : \text{Bool}$.

(viii) *If* $F \, \mathcal{F}_n \, F' : T$, $e_1 \, \mathcal{E}_n \, e_1' : \text{Bool}$, $e_2 \, \mathcal{E}_n \, e_2' : T$ and $e_3 \, \mathcal{E}_n \, e_3' : T$, *then*

$$(F \circ \text{if} \bullet \text{ then } e_2 \text{ else } e_3) \, \mathcal{F}_{n+1} \, (F' \circ \text{if} \bullet \text{ then } e_2' \text{ else } e_3') : \text{Bool} ,$$
$$(\text{if } e_1 \text{ then } e_2 \text{ else } e_3) \, \mathcal{E}_n \, (\text{if } e_1' \text{ then } e_2' \text{ else } e_3') : T .$$

(ix) *If* $F \, \mathcal{F}_n \, F' : \text{Bool}$, $e_1 \, \mathcal{E}_n \, e_1' : N$ and $e_2 \, \mathcal{E}_n \, e_2' : N$, *then*

$$F \circ (a = \bullet) \, \mathcal{F}_{n+1} \, F' \circ (a = \bullet) : N ,$$
$$F \circ (\bullet = e_2) \, \mathcal{F}_{n+1} \, F' \circ (\bullet = e_2') : N ,$$
$$(e_1 = e_2) \, \mathcal{E}_n \, (e_1' = e_2') : \text{Bool} .$$

(x) $() \, \mathcal{E}_n \, () : 1$.

(xi) *If* $F \, \mathcal{F}_n \, F' : T_1 \times T_2$, $v_1 \, \mathcal{V}_n \, v_1' : T_1$, $e_1 \, \mathcal{E}_n \, e_1' : T_1$ and $e_2 \, \mathcal{E}_n \, e_2' : T_2$, *then*

$$F \circ (v_1 , \bullet) \, \mathcal{F}_{n+1} \, F' \circ (v_1' , \bullet) : T_2 ,$$
$$F \circ (\bullet , e_2) \, \mathcal{F}_{n+1} \, F' \circ (\bullet , e_2') : T_1 ,$$
$$(e_1 , e_2) \, \mathcal{E}_n \, (e_1' , e_2') : T_1 \times T_2 .$$

(xii) *Suppose* $(\lambda x_1. \lambda x_2. e_2), (\lambda x_1. \lambda x_2. e_2') \in Val(T_1 \to T_2 \to T)$ *satisfy*

$$(\forall m \le n)(\forall v_1, v_2, v_1', v_2') \, v_1 \, \mathcal{V}_m \, v_1' : T_1 \wedge v_2 \, \mathcal{V}_m \, v_2' : T_2$$
$$\Rightarrow [x_1 := v_1][x_2 := v_2]e_2 \, \mathcal{E}_m \, [x_1 := v_1'][x_2 := v_2']e_2' : T .$$

If $F \, \mathcal{F}_n \, F' : T$ and $e_1 \, \mathcal{E}_n \, e_1' : T_1 \times T_2$, *then*

$$(F \circ \text{let } (x_1 , x_2) = \bullet \text{ in } e_2) \, \mathcal{F}_{n+1} \, (F' \circ \text{let } (x_1 , x_2) = \bullet \text{ in } e_2') : T_1 \times T_2 ,$$
$$(\text{let } (x_1 , x_2) = e_1 \text{ in } e_2) \, \mathcal{E}_n \, (\text{let } (x_1 , x_2) = e_1' \text{ in } e_2') : T .$$

(xiii) *If $F \, \mathcal{F}_n \, F' : \langle\!\langle N \rangle\!\rangle T$, $a \in \mathbb{A}_N$, $e_1 \, \mathcal{E}_n \, e_1' : N$ and $e_2 \, \mathcal{E}_n \, e_2' : T$, then*

$$(F \circ \langle\!\langle a \rangle\!\rangle \bullet) \, \mathcal{F}_{n+1} \, (F' \circ \langle\!\langle a \rangle\!\rangle \bullet) : T \,,$$

$$(F \circ \langle\!\langle \bullet \rangle\!\rangle e_2) \, \mathcal{F}_{n+1} \, (F' \circ \langle\!\langle \bullet \rangle\!\rangle e_2') : N \,,$$

$$\langle\!\langle e_1 \rangle\!\rangle e_2 \, \mathcal{E}_n \, \langle\!\langle e_1' \rangle\!\rangle e_2' : \langle\!\langle N \rangle\!\rangle T \,.$$

(xiv) *Suppose $(\lambda x. \, e_2), (\lambda x. \, e_2') \in Val(T_1 \to T_2)$ satisfy*

$$(\forall m \le n)(\forall v_1, v_1') \, v_1 \, \mathcal{V}_m \, v_1' : T_1 \Rightarrow [x := v_1]e_2 \, \mathcal{E}_m \, [x := v_1']e_2' : T_2 \,.$$

If $F \, \mathcal{F}_n \, F' : T_2$, $a \in \mathbb{A}_N$ and $e_1 \, \mathcal{E}_n \, e_1' : \langle\!\langle N \rangle\!\rangle T_1$, then

$$(F \circ \text{let } \langle\!\langle a \rangle\!\rangle x = \bullet \text{ in } e_2) \, \mathcal{F}_{n+1} \, (F' \circ \text{let } \langle\!\langle a \rangle\!\rangle x = \bullet \text{ in } e_2') : \langle\!\langle N \rangle\!\rangle T_1 \,,$$

$$(\text{let } \langle\!\langle a \rangle\!\rangle x = e_1 \text{ in } e_2) \, \mathcal{E}_n \, (\text{let } \langle\!\langle a \rangle\!\rangle x = e_1' \text{ in } e_2') : T_2 \,.$$

(xv) *If $F \, \mathcal{F}_n \, F' : T_2$, $v_1 \, \mathcal{V}_{n+1} \, v_1' : T_1 \to T_2$, $e_1 \, \mathcal{E}_n \, e_1' : T_1 \to T_2$ and $e_2 \, \mathcal{E}_n \, e_2' : T_1$, then*

$$(F \circ (v_1 \, \bullet)) \, \mathcal{F}_{n+1} \, (F' \circ (v_1' \, \bullet)) : T_1 \,,$$

$$(F \circ (\bullet \, e_2)) \, \mathcal{F}_{n+1} \, (F' \circ (\bullet \, e_2')) : T_1 \to T_2 \,,$$

$$e_1 \, e_2 \, \mathcal{E}_n \, e_1' \, e_2' : T_2 \,.$$

Proof The properties follow from the definitions in Figures 10.7 and 10.8, together with Lemmas 10.16 and 10.18. We give the argument for properties (xiii) and (xiv) (since those cases illustrate the use of equivariant techniques) and for property (xv) (which, like property (vi), depends delicately upon the use of $<$ rather than $\le$ at certain places in Figure 10.8); proof of the remaining properties is left as an exercise (Exercise 10.2).

For property (xiii), suppose

$$F \, \mathcal{F}_n \, F' : \langle\!\langle N \rangle\!\rangle T \,, \tag{10.32}$$

$$e_1 \, \mathcal{E}_n \, e_1' : N \,, \tag{10.33}$$

$$e_2 \, \mathcal{E}_n \, e_2' : T \,, \tag{10.34}$$

and that $a \in \mathbb{A}_N$. To prove $(F \circ \langle\!\langle a \rangle\!\rangle \bullet) \, \mathcal{F}_{n+1} \, (F' \circ \langle\!\langle a \rangle\!\rangle \bullet) : T$, by (10.30) it suffices to show for any $m \le n + 1$ that

$$v \, \mathcal{V}_m \, v' : T \,, \tag{10.35}$$

$$(F \circ \langle\!\langle a \rangle\!\rangle \bullet , v) \!\downarrow_m \tag{10.36}$$

imply $(F' \circ \langle\!\langle a \rangle\!\rangle \bullet , v') \!\downarrow$ (and a symmetric property with F and F' reversed). Applying the Rule Inversion Principle to the inductive definition of termination, it must be the case that (10.36) is the conclusion of the second of the two rules in (10.19); furthermore, by inspection of Figure 10.7, the only transition from $(F \circ \langle\!\langle a \rangle\!\rangle\bullet, v)$ is to $(F, \langle\!\langle a \rangle\!\rangle v)$. Therefore $m > 0$ and

$$(F, \langle\!\langle a \rangle\!\rangle v)\!\downarrow_{m-1}. \tag{10.37}$$

By the equivariance property (10.31), from (10.35) we get $(a\, a') \cdot v\, \mathcal{V}_m\, (a\, a') \cdot v' : T$ for any $a' \# (a, v, v')$ and hence by (10.27) that $\langle\!\langle a \rangle\!\rangle v\, \mathcal{V}_m\, \langle\!\langle a \rangle\!\rangle v' : \langle\!\langle \mathrm{N} \rangle\!\rangle T$. So by Lemma 10.18 we have

$$\langle\!\langle a \rangle\!\rangle v\, \mathcal{V}_{m-1}\, \langle\!\langle a \rangle\!\rangle v' : \langle\!\langle \mathrm{N} \rangle\!\rangle T. \tag{10.38}$$

Since $m - 1 \le n$ we can apply definition (10.30) to (10.32), (10.37) and (10.38) to get $(F', \langle\!\langle a \rangle\!\rangle v')\!\downarrow$; and since $(F \circ \langle\!\langle a \rangle\!\rangle\bullet, v') \to (F', \langle\!\langle a \rangle\!\rangle v')$ it follows that $(F' \circ \langle\!\langle a \rangle\!\rangle\bullet, v')\!\downarrow$, as required. Having now established the first of the three relations in (xiii), the second one follows from it by examining the termination behaviour of $(F \circ \langle\!\langle \bullet \rangle\!\rangle e_2, v)$; and then the third one follows from the second, by examining the termination behaviour of $(F, \langle\!\langle e_1 \rangle\!\rangle e_2)$.

For property (xiv), suppose

$$F\, \mathcal{F}_n\, F' : T_2, \tag{10.39}$$

$$e_1\, \mathcal{E}_n\, e_1' : \langle\!\langle \mathrm{N} \rangle\!\rangle T_1, \tag{10.40}$$

$$(\forall m \le n)(\forall v_1, v_1')\, v_1\, \mathcal{V}_m\, v_1' : T_1 \Rightarrow [x := v_1]e_2\, \mathcal{E}_m\, [x := v_1']e_2' : T_2, \tag{10.41}$$

and that $a \in \mathbb{A}_\mathrm{N}$. To prove $(F \circ \mathtt{let}\, \langle\!\langle a \rangle\!\rangle x = \bullet\, \mathtt{in}\, e_2)\, \mathcal{F}_{n+1}\, (F' \circ \mathtt{let}\, \langle\!\langle a \rangle\!\rangle x = \bullet\, \mathtt{in}\, e_2') : \langle\!\langle \mathrm{N} \rangle\!\rangle T_1$, it suffices to show for any $m \le n + 1$ that

$$\langle\!\langle a_1 \rangle\!\rangle v_1\, \mathcal{V}_m\, \langle\!\langle a_1' \rangle\!\rangle v_1' : \langle\!\langle \mathrm{N} \rangle\!\rangle T_1, \tag{10.42}$$

$$(F \circ \mathtt{let}\, \langle\!\langle a \rangle\!\rangle x = \bullet\, \mathtt{in}\, e_2, \langle\!\langle a_1 \rangle\!\rangle v_1)\!\downarrow_m \tag{10.43}$$

imply $(F' \circ \mathtt{let}\, \langle\!\langle a \rangle\!\rangle x = \bullet\, \mathtt{in}\, e_2', \langle\!\langle a_1' \rangle\!\rangle v_1')\!\downarrow$ (and symmetrically). Note that if we change the representative bound atomic name a in $(\mathtt{let}\, \langle\!\langle a \rangle\!\rangle x = \bullet\, \mathtt{in}\, e_2)$ and $(\mathtt{let}\, \langle\!\langle a \rangle\!\rangle x = \bullet\, \mathtt{in}\, e_2')$, then by Lemma 10.16, property (10.41) will continue to hold for the renamed e_2 and e_2'. So we can assume a is sufficiently fresh, that is, $a \# (F, F', e_2, e_2', a_1, a_1', v_1, v_1')$. Arguing as for the case of property (xiii), (10.43) must have been deduced by an application of the second rule in (10.19), $m > 0$ and

$$(F, [x := (a\, a_1) \cdot v_1]e_2)\!\downarrow_{m-1}. \tag{10.44}$$

Since $a \# (a_1, v_1, a_1', v_1')$, from (10.27), (10.42) and Lemma 10.18 we get $(a\, a_1) \cdot v_1\, \mathcal{V}_{m-1}\, (a\, a_1') \cdot v_1' : T_1$; and then (10.41) gives

$$[x := (a\, a_1) \cdot v_1]e_2\, \mathcal{E}_{m-1}\, [x := (a\, a_1') \cdot v_1']e_2' : T_2. \tag{10.45}$$

Since $m - 1 \leq n$ we can apply definition (10.29) to (10.39), (10.44) and (10.45) to get $(F', [x := (a\, a_1') \cdot v_1'] e_2') \downarrow$; and since $a \,\#\, (F', a_1', v_1')$ we have

$$(F' \circ \mathtt{let}\ \langle\!\langle a \rangle\!\rangle x = \bullet\ \mathtt{in}\ e_2', \langle\!\langle a_1' \rangle\!\rangle v_1') \to (F', [x := (a\, a_1') \cdot v_1'] e_2').$$

So we do indeed have $(F' \circ \mathtt{let}\ \langle\!\langle a \rangle\!\rangle x = \bullet\ \mathtt{in}\ e_2', \langle\!\langle a_1' \rangle\!\rangle v_1') \downarrow$, as required. Having now established the first of the two properties in (xiv), the second one follows from it by examining the termination behaviour of $(F, \mathtt{let}\ \langle\!\langle a \rangle\!\rangle x = e_1\ \mathtt{in}\ e_2)$.

For property (xv), suppose

$$F\ \mathcal{F}_n\ F' : T_2, \tag{10.46}$$

$$v_1\ \mathcal{V}_{n+1}\ v_1' : T_1 \to T_2, \tag{10.47}$$

with $v_1 = (\lambda f\, x = e)$ and $v_1' = (\lambda f\, x = e')$, say. To prove $F \circ (v_1 \bullet)\ \mathcal{F}_{n+1}$ $F' \circ (v_1' \bullet) : T_1$, it suffices to show for any $m \leq n + 1$ that

$$v_2\ \mathcal{V}_m\ v_2' : T_1, \tag{10.48}$$

$$(F \circ (v_1 \bullet), v_2) \downarrow_m \tag{10.49}$$

imply $(F' \circ (v_1' \bullet), v_2') \downarrow$ (and symmetrically). As for the previous cases, (10.49) must have been deduced by an application of the second rule in (10.19), $m > 0$ and

$$(F, [f := v_1][x := v_2] e) \downarrow_{m-1}. \tag{10.50}$$

Since $m - 1 < n + 1$ and from (10.48) we have $v_2\ \mathcal{V}_{m-1}\ v_2' : T_1$, by definition (10.28) applied to (10.47) we get

$$[f := v_1][x := v_2] e\ \mathcal{E}_{m-1}\ [f := v_1'][x := v_2'] e' : T_2. \tag{10.51}$$

Since $m - 1 \leq n$ we can apply definition (10.29) to (10.46), (10.50) and (10.51) to get $(F', [f := v_1'][x := v_2'] e') \downarrow$; and since $(F' \circ (v_1' \bullet), v_2') \to (F', [f := v_1'][x := v_2'] e')$, we do indeed have $(F' \circ (v_1' \bullet), v_2') \downarrow$, as required. Having now established the first of the three properties in (xv), the second one follows from it by examining the termination behaviour of $(F \circ (\bullet e_2), v)$; and then the third one follows from the second, by examining the termination behaviour of $(F, e_1 e_2)$. □

Definition 10.20 Given a type environment $\Gamma \in \mathit{Vid} \to_f \mathit{Type}$, the set of *closed-value substitutions* associated with Γ is

$$Sub\,\Gamma \triangleq \{\sigma \in \mathit{Vid} \to_f \mathit{Val} \mid \mathrm{Dom}\,\sigma = \mathrm{Dom}\,\Gamma \,\wedge\, (\forall x \in \mathrm{Dom}\,\Gamma)\, \emptyset \vdash \sigma x : \Gamma x\}.$$

We write $[\sigma]e$ for the result of carrying out on an expression e the substitution specified by σ; thus if σ maps x_i to v_i for $i = 1, \ldots, n$, then

$$[\sigma]e \triangleq [x_1 := v_1] \cdots [x_n := v_n]e.$$

Similarly for values $[\sigma]v$ and frame stacks $[\sigma]F$. We extend the logical relation to closed-value substitutions by defining

$$\sigma \, \mathcal{V}_n \, \sigma' : \Gamma \triangleq (\forall x \in \mathrm{Dom}\,\Gamma) \, \sigma x \, \mathcal{V}_n \, \sigma' x : \Gamma x.$$

Then we extend the logical relation to open values, expressions and frame stacks as follows:

$$\Gamma \vdash v \, \mathcal{V} \, v' : T$$
$$\triangleq (\forall \sigma, \sigma' \in Sub\,\Gamma)(\forall n \in \mathbb{N}) \, \sigma \, \mathcal{V}_n \, \sigma' : \Gamma \Rightarrow [\sigma]v \, \mathcal{V}_n \, [\sigma']v' : T,$$

$$\Gamma \vdash e \, \mathcal{E} \, e' : T$$
$$\triangleq (\forall \sigma, \sigma' \in Sub\,\Gamma)(\forall n \in \mathbb{N}) \, \sigma \, \mathcal{V}_n \, \sigma' : \Gamma \Rightarrow [\sigma]e \, \mathcal{E}_n \, [\sigma']e' : T,$$

$$\Gamma \vdash F \, \mathcal{F} \, F' : T$$
$$\triangleq (\forall \sigma, \sigma' \in Sub\,\Gamma)(\forall n \in \mathbb{N}) \, \sigma \, \mathcal{V}_n \, \sigma' : \Gamma \Rightarrow [\sigma]F \, \mathcal{F}_n \, [\sigma']F' : T.$$

Lemma 10.21 $\mathcal{E}$ *is an adequate and compatible type-respecting relation. Hence it is in particular a reflexive relation:*

$$\Gamma \vdash e : T \Rightarrow \Gamma \vdash e \, \mathcal{E} \, e : T. \tag{10.52}$$

Proof Adequacy of $\mathcal{E}$ is a consequence of part (i) of Lemma 10.19 together with (10.29). For compatibility, first note that if $(x, T) \in \Gamma$, then $\Gamma \vdash x \, \mathcal{E} \, x : T$ holds because $\mathcal{V}_n \subseteq \mathcal{E}_n$ (Lemma 10.18). Closure of $\mathcal{E}$ under all the other rules in Figure 10.5, except one, follows from the properties listed in Lemma 10.19. The missing case is the rule for recursive function expressions, which requires a more involved proof. So suppose

$$\Gamma(f : T_1 \to T_2)(x : T_1) \vdash e \, \mathcal{E} \, e' : T_2, \tag{10.53}$$

where $f, x \notin \mathrm{Dom}\,\Gamma$ and $f \neq x$. We have to prove $\Gamma \vdash (\lambda f \, x = e) \, \mathcal{E} \, (\lambda f \, x = e') : T_1 \to T_2$. Since $\mathcal{V}_n \subseteq \mathcal{E}_n$ (Lemma 10.18), it suffices to show for all $m \in \mathbb{N}$

$$(\forall \sigma, \sigma' \in Sub\,\Gamma) \, \sigma \, \mathcal{V}_m \, \sigma' : \Gamma$$
$$\Rightarrow (\lambda f \, x = [\sigma]e) \, \mathcal{V}_m \, (\lambda f \, x = [\sigma']e') : T_1 \to T_2. \tag{10.54}$$

(Note that since $f, x \notin \mathrm{Dom}\,\sigma$ and the latter substitutes *closed* values, we have $[\sigma](\lambda f \, x = e) = (\lambda f \, x = [\sigma]e)$; and similarly for σ'.)

We prove (10.54) by well-founded induction for $<$. Given $n \in \mathbb{N}$, suppose (10.54) holds for all $m < n$ and that $\sigma \, \mathcal{V}_n \, \sigma' : \Gamma$. Defining $v \triangleq (\lambda f \, x = [\sigma]e)$ and $v' \triangleq (\lambda f \, x = [\sigma]e')$, for the induction step, we need to show that $v \, \mathcal{V}_n \, v' : T_1 \to T_2$. By definition (10.28), this means that we have to prove for all $m < n$

and $v_1 \; \mathcal{V}_m \; v_1' : T_1$ that $[f := v][x := v_1][\sigma]e \; \mathcal{E}_m \; [f := v'][x := v_1'][\sigma']e' : T_2$. But since $\sigma \; \mathcal{V}_n \; \sigma' : \Gamma$, by Lemma 10.18 we have $\sigma \; \mathcal{V}_m \; \sigma' : \Gamma$; and since by induction hypothesis (10.54) holds, this gives us $v \; \mathcal{V}_m \; v' : T_1 \to T_2$. Hence the closed-value substitutions $\sigma(f := v)(x := v_1), \sigma'(f := v')(x := v_1') \in Sub \, \Gamma(f : T_1 \to T_2)(x : T_1)$ are related by $\mathcal{V}_m$. Therefore (10.53) gives $[f := v][x := v_1][\sigma]e \; \mathcal{E}_m \; [f := v'][x := v_1'][\sigma']e' : T_2$, as required for the induction step. $\square$

Since contextual equivalence is by definition the union of all adequate and compatible type-respecting relations, the lemma gives the following result.

Corollary 10.22 *If* $\Gamma \vdash e \, \mathcal{E} \, e' : T$, *then* $\Gamma \vdash e =_{\text{ctx}} e' : T$. $\square$

It is useful to introduce an appropriate version of the *CIU equivalence* of Mason and Talcott (1991), defined as follows.

Definition 10.23 ('CIU' equivalence)   The type-respecting relation $=_{\text{ciu}}$ is given by:

$$\Gamma \vdash e =_{\text{ciu}} e' : T \triangleq (\forall \sigma \in Sub \, \Gamma)(\forall F \in Stack(T)) \; (F, [\sigma]e)\downarrow \; \Leftrightarrow \; (F, [\sigma]e')\downarrow.$$

Lemma 10.24   *If* $\Gamma \vdash e =_{\text{ciu}} e' : T$, *then* $\Gamma \vdash e \, \mathcal{E} \, e' : T$.

Proof   Suppose $\Gamma \vdash e =_{\text{ciu}} e' : T$. Given any $\sigma, \sigma' \in Sub \, \Gamma$ and $n \in \mathbb{N}$ satisfying $\sigma \; \mathcal{V}_n \; \sigma' : \Gamma$, we have to show that $[\sigma]e \; \mathcal{E}_n \; [\sigma']e' : T$. We do so using the defining property (10.29).

From (10.52) we have $[\sigma]e \; \mathcal{E}_n \; [\sigma']e : T$ and $[\sigma]e' \; \mathcal{E}_n \; [\sigma']e' : T$. So for any $m \leq n$ and $F \; \mathcal{F}_m \; F' : T$ by (10.29) we have

$$(F, [\sigma]e)\downarrow_m \; \Rightarrow \; (F', [\sigma]e)\downarrow$$
$$(F', [\sigma']e')\downarrow_m \; \Rightarrow \; (F, [\sigma]e')\downarrow.$$

Since $\Gamma \vdash e =_{\text{ciu}} e' : T$, we also have

$$(F', [\sigma']e)\downarrow \; \Rightarrow \; (F', [\sigma']e')\downarrow$$
$$(F, [\sigma]e')\downarrow \; \Rightarrow \; (F, [\sigma]e)\downarrow.$$

So $(F, [\sigma]e)\downarrow_m \; \Rightarrow \; (F', [\sigma']e')\downarrow$ and $(F', [\sigma']e')\downarrow_m \; \Rightarrow \; (F, [\sigma]e)\downarrow$. Therefore by (10.29) we do indeed have $[\sigma]e \; \mathcal{E}_n \; [\sigma']e' : T$. $\square$

Lemma 10.25 λFML *contextual equivalence is* value substitutive*:*

$$\Gamma(x : T_1) \vdash e =_{\text{ctx}} e' : T_2 \; \wedge \; \Gamma \vdash v =_{\text{ctx}} v' : T_1$$
$$\Rightarrow \; \Gamma \vdash [x := v]e =_{\text{ctx}} [x := v']e' : T_2.$$

$$\Gamma \vdash va.\, e =_{\text{ctx}} e : T \quad \text{if } a \,\#\, e \tag{10.55}$$

$$\Gamma \vdash va.\, va'.\, e =_{\text{ctx}} va'.\, va.\, e : T$$

$$\Gamma \vdash \text{match } C\,v \text{ with } \cdots \mid C\,x \to e \mid \cdots =_{\text{ctx}} [x := v]e : T$$

$$\Gamma \vdash \text{if true then } e \text{ else } e' =_{\text{ctx}} e : T$$

$$\Gamma \vdash \text{if false then } e \text{ else } e' =_{\text{ctx}} e' : T$$

$$\emptyset \vdash (a_1 \doteq a_2)v =_{\text{ctx}} (a_1\ a_2)\cdot v : T \tag{10.56}$$

$$\emptyset \vdash (a \doteq a) =_{\text{ctx}} \text{true} : \text{Bool}$$

$$\emptyset \vdash (a \doteq a') =_{\text{ctx}} \text{false} : \text{Bool} \quad \text{if } a \ne a'$$

$$\Gamma \vdash \text{let } (x_1\,, x_2) = (v_1\,, v_2) \text{ in } e =_{\text{ctx}} [x_1 := v_1][x_2 := v_2]e : T$$

$$\Gamma \vdash \text{let } \langle\!\langle a \rangle\!\rangle x = \langle\!\langle a_1 \rangle\!\rangle v_1 \text{ in } e =_{\text{ctx}} va.\, [x := (a \doteq a_1)\,v]e : T \quad \text{if } a \,\#\, (a_1, v) \tag{10.57}$$

$$\Gamma \vdash v_1\, v_2 =_{\text{ctx}} [f := v_1][x := v_2]e : T \quad \text{if } v_1 = (\lambda f\, x = e) \tag{10.58}$$

Figure 10.9 Properties of λFML contextual equivalence.

In particular, if $\Gamma \vdash e =_{\text{ctx}} e' : T$ and $\sigma \in Sub\,\Gamma$, then $\emptyset \vdash [\sigma]e =_{\text{ctx}} [\sigma]e' : T$.

Proof If $\Gamma(x : T_1) \vdash e =_{\text{ctx}} e' : T_2$ and $\Gamma \vdash v =_{\text{ctx}} v' : T_1$, then by the compatibility property of $=_{\text{ctx}}$ we have $\Gamma \vdash (\lambda x.\, e)v =_{\text{ctx}} (\lambda x.\, e')v' : T_2$. So the result follows by transitivity of $=_{\text{ctx}}$ once we know that

$$\Gamma \vdash [x := v]e =_{\text{ctx}} (\lambda x.\, e)v : T_2 \quad \text{and} \quad \Gamma \vdash (\lambda x.\, e')v' =_{\text{ctx}} [x := v']e' : T_2\,.$$

It is easy to see from the definition of CIU equivalence that these identities hold for $=_{\text{ciu}}$; so we can apply Corollary 10.22 and Lemma 10.24 to deduce that they also hold for $=_{\text{ctx}}$. □

Proposition 10.26 *The type-respecting relations $=_{\text{ctx}}$, $\mathcal{E}$ and $=_{\text{ciu}}$ are all equal.*

Proof In view of Corollary 10.22 and Lemma 10.24, it just remains to show that $\Gamma \vdash e =_{\text{ctx}} e' : T$ implies $\Gamma \vdash e =_{\text{ciu}} e' : T$. By Lemma 10.25, it suffices to prove the implication for closed expressions, that is, when $\Gamma = \emptyset$; and for this it suffices to show by induction on the length of the list of evaluation frames in a stack F that

$$(F, e)\!\downarrow \;\land\; \emptyset \vdash e =_{\text{ctx}} e' : T \;\Rightarrow\; (F, e')\!\downarrow.$$

The base case when $F = \text{Id}$ follows from the adequacy property of $=_{\text{ctx}}$; and each induction step makes use of the compatibility property of $=_{\text{ctx}}$ together with the definition of $\to$. □

The CIU equivalence $\Gamma \vdash (\lambda x.\, e)v =_{\text{ciu}} [x := v]e : T_2$ used in the proof of Lemma 10.25 is an immediate consequence of the definition of the transition relation in Figure 10.7. Figure 10.9 gives some properties that hold for the same reason; it is not hard to see that these identities hold up to $=_{\mathrm{ciu}}$ and hence are valid contextual equivalences. Note that identities (10.56) and (10.57) take account of the fact that for open expressions there can be a difference between the name swapping expression $(a_1 \rightleftharpoons a_2) v$ and the value $(a_1 \; a_2) \cdot v$ obtained from v by actually transposing occurrences of a_1 and a_2; see Exercise 10.3. For closed values we also have that $=_{\mathrm{ctx}}$ coincides with $\mathcal{V}$:

Lemma 10.27 $\emptyset \vdash v \; \mathcal{V} \; v' : T$ iff $\emptyset \vdash v =_{\mathrm{ctx}} v' : T$.

Proof   In view of Proposition 10.26, we just have to show that $\emptyset \vdash v \; \mathcal{V} \; v' : T$ holds iff $\emptyset \vdash v \; \mathcal{E} \; v' : T$. We already have from Lemma 10.18 that $\mathcal{V}_n \subseteq \mathcal{E}_n$. So it suffices to show for all $T \in Type$ and $v, v' \in Val(T)$ that $\emptyset \vdash v \; \mathcal{E} \; v' : T \Rightarrow \emptyset \vdash v \; \mathcal{V} \; v' : T$. We do this by induction on the size of the values $v, v' \in Val(T)$.

(i) *Case* $\emptyset \vdash a \; \mathcal{E} \; a' : \mathrm{N}$, where $a, a' \in \mathbb{A}_{\mathrm{N}}$. With Ω is as in Example 10.10, the frame stack

$$F_a \triangleq \mathrm{Id} \circ (\texttt{if} \bullet \texttt{then} \; () \; \texttt{else} \; \Omega) \circ (a = \bullet)$$

satisfies $(\forall a'') \; (F_a , a'') \!\downarrow \; \Leftrightarrow \; a = a''$. So since $\emptyset \vdash a \; \mathcal{E} \; a' : \mathrm{N}$, $\emptyset \vdash F_a \; \mathcal{F} \; F_a : \mathrm{N}$ (by (10.52) and Lemma 10.19) and $(F_a , a) \!\downarrow$, it follows that $(F_a , a') \!\downarrow$; so $a = a'$ and hence $\emptyset \vdash a \; \mathcal{V} \; a' : \mathrm{N}$.

(ii) *Case* $\emptyset \vdash \mathsf{C}_i \; v \; \mathcal{E} \; \mathsf{C}_j \; v' : \mathrm{D}$, where $(\mathrm{D} = \mathsf{C}_1 \; \texttt{of} \; T_1 \mid \cdots \mid \mathsf{C}_n \; \texttt{of} \; T_n) \in \Delta$, say. Consider the frame stack

$$F_i \triangleq \mathrm{Id} \circ (\texttt{match} \bullet \texttt{with} \; \mathsf{C}_1 \, x_1 \to \Omega \mid \cdots \mid \mathsf{C}_i \, x_i \to () \mid \cdots \mid \mathsf{C}_n \, x_n \to \Omega).$$

Since for $(\forall v'') \; (F_i , \mathsf{C}_j \, v'') \!\downarrow \; \Leftrightarrow \; i = j$, arguing as above we get that $\mathsf{C}_i = \mathsf{C}_j$. So it just remains to show that $\emptyset \vdash v \; \mathcal{V} \; v' : T_i$ and by induction hypothesis, for this it suffices to show $\emptyset \vdash v \; \mathcal{E} \; v' : T_i$. For any $n \in \mathbb{N}$ and $F \; \mathcal{F}_n \; F' : T_i$ define $F_1 \triangleq F \circ E$ and $F_1' \triangleq F' \circ E$, where

$$E \triangleq \texttt{match} \bullet \texttt{with} \; \mathsf{C}_1 \, x_1 \to \Omega \mid \cdots \mid \mathsf{C}_i \, x_i \to x_i \mid \cdots \mid \mathsf{C}_n \, x_n \to \Omega.$$

Then by part (vi) of Lemma 10.19 (and reflexivity of $\mathcal{E}$) we have $F_1 \; \mathcal{F}_{n+1} \; F_1' : \mathrm{D}$. So if $(F , v) \!\downarrow_n$, then $(F_1 , \mathsf{C}_i \, v) \!\downarrow_{n+1}$ and hence $(F_1' , \mathsf{C}_i \, v') \!\downarrow$ (by (10.29), since by assumption $\mathsf{C}_i \, v \; \mathcal{E}_{n+1} \; \mathsf{C}_j \, v' : \mathrm{D}$), which implies that $(F' , v') \!\downarrow$. Similarly, $(F' , v') \!\downarrow_n \Rightarrow (F , v) \!\downarrow$. Therefore by (10.29) we do indeed have $(\forall n \in \mathbb{N}) \; v \; \mathcal{E}_n \; v' : T_i$, as required.

(iii) *Case* $\emptyset \vdash b \; \mathcal{E} \; b' : \mathrm{Bool}$, where $b, b' \in \{\texttt{true}, \texttt{false}\}$. This is similar to case (i), but using the frame stacks $\mathrm{Id} \circ (\texttt{if} \bullet \texttt{then} \; () \; \texttt{else} \; \Omega)$ if $b = \texttt{true}$, and $\mathrm{Id} \circ (\texttt{if} \bullet \texttt{then} \; \Omega \; \texttt{else} \; ())$ if $b = \texttt{false}$.

(iv) *Case* $\emptyset \vdash () \; \mathcal{E} \; () : 1$ is trivial.

(v) *Case* $\emptyset \vdash (v_1, v_2) \; \mathcal{E} \; (v_1', v_2') : T_1 \times T_2$. We have to show $\emptyset \vdash v_i \; \mathcal{V} \; v_i' : T_i$ for $i = 1, 2$; by induction hypothesis, for this it suffices to show $\emptyset \vdash v_i \; \mathcal{E} \; v_i' : T_i$. For any $n \in \mathbb{N}$ and $F \; \mathcal{F}_n \; F' : T_1$ define $F_1 \triangleq F \circ E$ and $F_1' \triangleq F' \circ E$ where

$$E \triangleq \mathsf{let}\,(x_1, x_2) = \bullet \;\mathsf{in}\; x_1 \,.$$

By part (xii) of Lemma 10.19 we have $F_1 \; \mathcal{F}_{n+1} \; F_1' : T_1 \times T_2$. So if $(F, v_1)\!\downarrow_n$, then $(F_1, (v_1, v_2))\!\downarrow_{n+1}$, hence $(F_1', (v_1', v_2'))\!\downarrow$ and therefore $(F', v_1')\!\downarrow$. Similarly $(F', v_1')\!\downarrow_n \Rightarrow (F, v_1)\!\downarrow$. Thus $\emptyset \vdash v_1 \; \mathcal{E} \; v_1' : T_1$; and a similar argument shows $\emptyset \vdash v_2 \; \mathcal{E} \; v_2' : T_2$.

(vi) *Case* $\emptyset \vdash \langle\!\langle a \rangle\!\rangle v \; \mathcal{E} \; \langle\!\langle a' \rangle\!\rangle v' : \langle\!\langle N \rangle\!\rangle T$. We have to show for some $a'' \;\#\; (a, v, a', v')$ that $\emptyset \vdash (a \; a'') \cdot v \; \mathcal{V} \; (a' \; a'') \cdot v' : T$; and by induction hypothesis, for the latter it suffices to show $\emptyset \vdash (a \; a'') \cdot v \; \mathcal{E} \; (a' \; a'') \cdot v' : T$. For any $n \in \mathbb{N}$ and $F \; \mathcal{F}_n \; F' : T$, pick any $a'' \;\#\; (F, F', a, v, a', v'')$ and define $F_1 \triangleq F \circ E$ and $F_1' \triangleq F' \circ E$ where

$$E \triangleq \mathsf{let}\, \langle\!\langle a'' \rangle\!\rangle x = \bullet \;\mathsf{in}\; x \,.$$

By part (i) of Lemma 10.19 we have $F_1 \; \mathcal{F}_{n+1} \; F_1' : \langle\!\langle N \rangle\!\rangle T$. If $(F, (a \; a'') \cdot v)\!\downarrow_n$, then $(F_1, \langle\!\langle a \rangle\!\rangle v)\!\downarrow_{n+1}$, hence $(F_1', \langle\!\langle a' \rangle\!\rangle v')\!\downarrow$ and therefore $(F', (a' \; a'') \cdot v')\!\downarrow$. Similarly $(F', (a' \; a'') \cdot v')\!\downarrow_n \Rightarrow (F, (a \; a'') \cdot v)\!\downarrow$. Thus $\emptyset \vdash (a \; a'') \cdot v \; \mathcal{E} \; (a' \; a'') \cdot v' : T$.

(vii) *Case* $\emptyset \vdash v \; \mathcal{E} \; v' : T_1 \to T_2$, where $v = (\lambda f \, x = e)$ and $v' = (\lambda f \, x = e')$, say. To prove $\emptyset \vdash v \; \mathcal{V} \; v' : T_1 \to T_2$ we have to show for all $n \in \mathbb{N}$ and $v_1 \; \mathcal{V}_n \; v_1' : T_1$ that $[f := v][x := v_1]e \; \mathcal{E}_n \; [f := v'][x := v_1']e' : T_2$. We use a slight sharpening of the second property in part (xv) of Lemma 10.19, which can be proved in the same way as in that lemma:

$$(\forall m, F, F', v_1, v_1') \; F \; \mathcal{F}_m \; F' : T_2 \;\wedge\; v_1 \; \mathcal{V}_m \; v_1' : T_1$$
$$\Rightarrow \; F \circ (\bullet v_1) \; \mathcal{F}_{m+2} \; F' \circ (\bullet v_1') : T_1 \to T_2 \,.$$

So for all $m \leq n$ and $F \; \mathcal{F}_m \; F' : T_2$, since $v_1 \; \mathcal{V}_m \; v_1' : T_1$ we have $F \circ (\bullet v_1) \; \mathcal{F}_{m+2} \; F' \circ (\bullet v_1') : T_1 \to T_2$. Therefore if $(F, [f := v][x := v_1]e)\!\downarrow_m$, then $(F \circ (\bullet v_1), v)\!\downarrow_{m+2}$ and hence $(F' \circ (\bullet v_1'), v')\!\downarrow$ (since $v \; \mathcal{E}_{m+2} \; v' : T_1 \to T_2$ by assumption) and thus $(F', [f := v'][x := v_1']e')\!\downarrow$. Similarly $(F', [f := v'][x := v_1']e')\!\downarrow_m \Rightarrow (F, [f := v][x := v_1]e)\!\downarrow$. So by definition (10.29) we do indeed have $[f := v][x := v_1]e \; \mathcal{E}_n \; [f := v'][x := v_1']e' : T_2$, as required.

$\square$

We are now in a position to prove the theorem from the previous section.

Proof of Theorem 10.13   In view of Lemma 10.27, properties (i)–(vi) in the theorem follow directly from the definition of $\mathcal{V}$ in Figure 10.8. For property (vii), the left-to-right implication follows from (10.58). For the converse, if

$$(\forall v_1, v_1')\ v_1 =_{\mathrm{ctx}} v_1' : T_1 \Rightarrow [f := v][x := v_1]e =_{\mathrm{ctx}} [f := v'][x := v_1']e' : T_2$$

then by the coincidence of $=_{\mathrm{ctx}}$ with $=_{\mathrm{ciu}}$ (Proposition 10.26) we have

$$\{x : T_1\} \vdash [f := v]e =_{\mathrm{ctx}} [f := v']e' : T_2$$

and hence by compatibility, $\lambda x.\,[f := v]e =_{\mathrm{ctx}} \lambda x.\,[f := v]e : T_1 \rightarrow T_2$. So the desired conclusion follows from the 'η-value' law for $v = (\lambda f\, x = e) \in Val(T_1 \rightarrow T_2)$:

$$v =_{\mathrm{ctx}} \lambda x.\,[f := v]e : T_1 \rightarrow T_2. \tag{10.59}$$

To prove this, note that since $(\forall n \in \mathbb{N})\ v\ \mathcal{V}_n\ v : T_1 \rightarrow T_2$ (by Lemma 10.27, since $=_{\mathrm{ctx}}$ is reflexive), from definition (10.28) we get $v\ \mathcal{V}_n\ \lambda x.\,[f := v]e : T_1 \rightarrow T_2$ for all n. Thus (10.59) holds by Lemma 10.27. $\square$

10.12 Abstractness

Object-level languages that can be specified by a nominal algebraic signature (Definition 8.2) can be very simply represented as closed values in the meta-level language λFML. In this section we show that λFML programs respect object-level α-equivalence by proving that α-equivalence between the raw terms over a signature coincides with contextual equivalence between the corresponding closed values. We also show that α-structural recursion (Section 8.5) can be programmed in λFML.

Suppose Σ is a nominal algebraic signature. Each of its sorts S denotes a λFML type S° once we interpret sorts of pairs and sorts of name abstraction by product and name abstraction types:

$$
\begin{aligned}
\mathtt{N}^{\circ} &= \mathtt{N},\\
\mathtt{D}^{\circ} &= \mathtt{D},\\
\mathtt{1}^{\circ} &= \mathtt{1},\\
(\mathtt{S_1}\,,\,\mathtt{S_2})^{\circ} &= \mathtt{S_1^{\circ}} \times \mathtt{S_2^{\circ}},\\
(\mathtt{N}\,.\,\mathtt{S})^{\circ} &= \langle\!\langle \mathtt{N} \rangle\!\rangle \mathtt{S}^{\circ}.
\end{aligned}
$$

The typing information for the operations in Σ gives rise to a λFML data type declaration (Definition 10.3) Δ_Σ. For example, if Σ is the signature in Example 8.4, then Δ_Σ is the data type declaration in Example 10.4. In general the declaration for each $\mathtt{D} \in Dsort$ contains clauses 'C of $\mathtt{S}^{\circ}$' for each operation

C : S → D with result sort equal to D. Comparing the formation rules for raw terms over a signature in Definition 8.2 with the typing rules in Figure 10.4 and the definition of λFML values (Definition 10.6), it is clear that we can translate raw terms $t \in \Sigma(S)$ into λFML closed values $t° \in Val(S°)$ over the data type declaration Δ_Σ:

$$
\begin{aligned}
a° &= a, \\
(C\,t)° &= C\,t°, \\
\cdot\; ()° &= (), \\
(t_1, t_2)° &= (t_1°, t_2°), \\
(a \cdot t)° &= \langle\!\langle a \rangle\!\rangle t° .
\end{aligned}
\tag{10.60}
$$

Theorem 10.28 (Correctness of representation) *The above translation from a nominal algebraic signature into λFML induces a bijection between each nominal algebraic data type $\Sigma_\alpha(S)$ (Definition 8.9) and the set $Val(S°)/=_{ctx}$ of equivalence classes for contextual equivalence of closed values of type $S°$.*

Proof It is easy to see, by induction on the structure of values, that (10.60) induces a bijection between raw terms of each sort S and closed values of type $S°$. So we just have to see that under this bijection α-equivalence (Definition 8.6) corresponds to contextual equivalence:

$$
t =_\alpha t' \Leftrightarrow t° =_{ctx} t'° : S° .
$$

This follows from the extensionality properties of $=_{ctx}$ in Theorem 10.13, once we note that the bijection $\_°$ is equivariant:

$$
\pi \cdot t° = (\pi \cdot t)° ,
$$

and hence that $\operatorname{supp} t° = \operatorname{supp} t$. □

   This theorem is the basis for representing functions on nominal algebraic data types by λFML function expressions. We illustrate this for the data type of untyped λ-terms, $\Sigma_\alpha(Term)$, where Σ is the signature from Example 8.4. For any λFML type $T \in Type$, consider the nominal set

$$
X \triangleq Val(T)/=_{ctx} = \{[v]_{=_{ctx}} \mid v \in Val(T)\}
$$

of closed expressions of type T modulo contextual equivalence. Suppose we are given finitely supported functions

$$
\begin{aligned}
&F_1 \in A \to_{fs} X , \\
&F_2 \in A \times \Sigma_\alpha(Term) \times X \to_{fs} X , \\
&F_3 \in \Sigma_\alpha(Term) \times \Sigma_\alpha(Term) \times X \times X \to_{fs} X ,
\end{aligned}
$$

and that F_2 satisfies the 'freshness condition for binders' (8.40). Let $\hat{F} \in$

$\Sigma_\alpha(\text{Term}) \to_{\text{fs}} X$ be the function defined from F_1, F_2 and F_3 by α-structural primitive recursion as in Theorem 8.17. We will show that if F_1, F_2 and F_3 can be programmed in λFML in a suitable sense, then so can $\hat{F}$. To do so we make use of the following notation: if $e \in Expr(T)$ and $x \in X = Val(T)/=_{\text{ctx}}$ define

$$e \Downarrow_{\text{ctx}} x \triangleq (\exists v \in Val(T)) \, e =_{\text{ctx}} v : T \,\wedge\, v \in x.$$

Note that because $=_{\text{ctx}}$ is equivariant, so is $\Downarrow_{\text{ctx}}$.

Theorem 10.29 (Representation of α-structural primitive recursion for λ-terms) *Let X, F_1, F_2 and F_3 be as above. Suppose that the closed λFML values*

$$v_1 \in Val(\text{Var} \to T),$$
$$v_2 \in Val(\text{Var} \to \text{Term} \to T \to T),$$
$$v_3 \in Val(\text{Term} \to \text{Term} \to T \to T \to T),$$

satisfy

$$
\begin{aligned}
&(\forall a) \, v_1 \, a \Downarrow_{\text{ctx}} F_1 \, a \\
&\wedge \;\; (\text{M}a)(\forall t)(\forall v) \, v_2 \, a \, t^\circ \, v \Downarrow_{\text{ctx}} F_2(a, [t]_{=_\alpha}, [v]_{=_{\text{ctx}}}) \\
&\wedge \;\; (\forall t_1, t_2)(\forall v_1, v_2) \, v_3 \, t_1^\circ \, t_2^\circ \, v_1 \, v_2 \Downarrow_{\text{ctx}} F_3([t_1]_{=_\alpha}, [t_2]_{=_\alpha}, [v_1]_{=_{\text{ctx}}}, [v_2]_{=_{\text{ctx}}}).
\end{aligned}
\tag{10.61}
$$

Define the λFML function value $\hat{v} \in Val(\text{Term} \to T)$ to be

$$
\begin{aligned}
\hat{v} \triangleq \lambda f \, t = &\,\text{match } t \text{ with} \\
&\text{V} \, x \to v_1 \, x \\
\mid &\;\text{L} \, x \to \text{let } \langle\!\langle a \rangle\!\rangle x_1 = x \text{ in } v_2 \, a \, x_1 \, (f \, x_1) \\
\mid &\;\text{A} \, x \to \text{let } (x_1, x_2) = x \text{ in } v_3 \, x_1 \, x_2 \, (f \, x_1) \, (f \, x_2).
\end{aligned}
$$

Then the finitely supported function $\hat{F} \in \Sigma_\alpha(\text{Term}) \to_{\text{fs}} X$ defined by α-structural primitive recursion from (F_1, F_2, F_3) is represented by $\hat{v}$ in the sense that

$$(\forall t \in \Sigma(\text{Term})) \; \hat{v} \, t^\circ \Downarrow_{\text{ctx}} \hat{F}[t]_{=_\alpha}.$$

Proof Note that by Theorem 10.28, if $t_1 =_\alpha t_2$ then $t_1^\circ =_{\text{ctx}} t_2^\circ : \text{Term}$ and so for any $x \in X$, $\hat{v} \, t_1^\circ \Downarrow_{\text{ctx}} x \Rightarrow \hat{v} \, t_2^\circ \Downarrow_{\text{ctx}} x$. Therefore it suffices to show that subset

$$P \triangleq \{[t]_{=_\alpha} \mid \hat{v} \, t^\circ \Downarrow_{\text{ctx}} \hat{F}[t]_{=_\alpha}\} \in P_{\text{fs}}(\Sigma_\alpha(\text{Term}))$$

(finitely supported by $\text{supp}(\hat{v}, \hat{F})$) is the whole of $\Sigma_\alpha(\text{Term})$. We can do so using the α-structural induction principle for λ-terms (Corollary 8.22), verifying that P satisfies the three clauses in (8.52). We give the argument for the second clause, the other two cases being simpler. So we have to prove

$$(\text{M}a)(\forall t) \, \hat{v} \, t^\circ \Downarrow_{\text{ctx}} \hat{F}[t]_{=_\alpha} \Rightarrow \hat{v} \, (\text{L}a \,.\, t)^\circ \Downarrow_{\text{ctx}} \hat{F}[\text{L}a \,.\, t]_{=_\alpha}.$$

Suppose $a \,\#\, (\hat{v}, \hat{F})$ and $\hat{v}\,t^\circ \Downarrow_{ctx} \hat{F}[t]_{=_\alpha}$, that is, $\hat{v}\,t^\circ =_{ctx} v : T$ for some v with $[v]_{=_{ctx}} = \hat{F}[t]_{=_\alpha}$. The properties of $=_{ctx}$ in Figure 10.9 together with the definition of $\hat{v}$ give

$$\hat{v}\,(La \,.\, t)^\circ =_{ctx} va.\,v_2\,a\,t^\circ\,(\hat{v}\,t^\circ) =_{ctx} va.\,v_2\,a\,t^\circ\,v : T.$$

By definition of $\hat{F}$ and (10.61) we have

$$\hat{F}[La \,.\, t]_{=_\alpha} = F_2(a, [t]_{=_\alpha}, \hat{F}\,[t]_{=_\alpha}) = F_2(a, [t]_{=_\alpha}, [v]_{=_{ctx}}) = [v']_{=_{ctx}}$$

for some v' with $v_2\,a\,t^\circ\,v =_{ctx} v' : T$. So we will have the desired conclusion $\hat{v}\,(La \,.\, t)^\circ \Downarrow_{ctx} \hat{F}[La \,.\, t]_{=_\alpha}$ provided we can show that $va.\,v_2\,a\,t^\circ\,v =_{ctx} v_2\,a\,t^\circ\,v : T$. This follows from the fact that v_2 represents F_2 and the latter satisfies the 'freshness condition for binders' (8.40) and hence

$$a \,\#\, F_2(a, [t]_{=_\alpha}, [v]_{=_{ctx}}) = [v']_{=_{ctx}}.$$

Pick some $a' \,\#\, (v_2, a, t, v, v')$. Since neither a nor a' are in the support of $[v']_{=_{ctx}}$ we have $(a\,a') \cdot [v']_{=_{ctx}} = [v']_{=_{ctx}}$ and therefore $(a\,a') \cdot v' =_{ctx} v' : T$. So

$$va.\,v_2\,a\,t^\circ\,v =_{ctx} va.\,v' = va'.\,(a\,a') \cdot v' =_{ctx} va'.\,v' =_{ctx} v' =_{ctx} v_2\,a\,t^\circ\,v : T$$

with the penultimate step using property (10.55) from Figure 10.9, since $a' \,\#\, v'$. □

Example 10.30 We can use Theorem 10.29 to verify that the function expression *sub* in Example 10.4 correctly implements capture-avoiding substitution (Example 8.19). Given $a \in \mathbb{A}$ and $t \in \Sigma(\text{Term})$, consider $\hat{v}$ when

$$v_1 \triangleq \lambda x.\,\text{if}\,a = x\,\text{then}\,t^\circ\,\text{else}\,V\,x,$$
$$v_2 \triangleq \lambda x.\,\lambda y.\,\lambda z.\,L(\langle\!\langle x\rangle\!\rangle z),$$
$$v_3 \triangleq \lambda y_1.\,\lambda y_2.\,\lambda z_1.\,\lambda z_2.\,A(z_1, z_2).$$

Using the properties of $=_{ctx}$ in Figure 10.9 we have on the one hand that *sub* $a\,t^\circ =_{ctx} \hat{v} : \text{Term} \to \text{Term}$ and on the other that the representations properties (10.61) hold for the functions (F_1, F_2, F_3) used in Example 8.19 to define capture-avoiding substitution by α-structural recursion. Thus the theorem gives for all $t_1 \in \Sigma(\text{Term})$ that

$$sub\,a\,t^\circ\,t_1^\circ =_{ctx} \hat{v}\,t_1^\circ \Downarrow_{ctx} [a := [t]_{=_\alpha}]\,[t_1]_{=_\alpha}.$$

So given λ-terms $e, e_1 \in \Sigma_\alpha(\text{Term})$, if t and t_1 and t_2 are raw terms representing e, e_1 and the capture-avoiding substitution $[a := e]e_1$ respectively, it is the case that *sub* $a\,t^\circ\,t_1^\circ =_{ctx} t_2^\circ : \text{Term}$.

10.13 Purity

Informal algorithms that compute with syntactical data involving binders very often make use of the operation of choosing a fresh name. Here 'fresh' means 'avoiding some finite set of bad names that is implicit from the context'. Such computations are *impure*, in the sense that they involve side-effects: there is a state given by a finite set of names and it changes as fresh names are chosen and added to it. However, it seems that for the kind of computations that arise in practice, these state changes are unobservable and hence ignorable, because the value of final result is independent of the fresh names chosen during the computation. The nominal sets notion of freshness (Chapter 3) provides a very good mathematical model for this kind of independence of values from (freshly chosen) names. For example, in an α-structural primitive recursion (Section 8.5), the 'freshness condition on binders' is exactly this kind of independence condition and guarantees that we get a well defined mathematical function of α-equivalence classes from the functions specifying the recursion. We have just seen that such structural recursions can be computed correctly by Fresh OCaml's method for eliminating name-abstractions using dynamic allocation of fresh names. However, the language makes no attempt to enforce the property that final values of computations are independent of choices of fresh name. For example, we cannot apply Theorem 8.17 to

$X \triangleq \mathbb{A}^*$ (finite lists of atomic names),

$F_1 \in \mathbb{A} \to_{\text{fs}} X \triangleq \lambda a \to []$,

$F_2 \in \mathbb{A} \times \Sigma_\alpha(\text{Term}) \times X \to_{\text{fs}} X \triangleq \lambda(a, e, \ell) \to a :: \ell$,

$F_3 \in \Sigma_\alpha(\text{Term}) \times \Sigma_\alpha(\text{Term}) \times X \times X \to_{\text{fs}} X \triangleq \lambda(e_1, e_2, \ell_1, \ell_2) \to \ell_1 \mathbin{+\!\!+} \ell_2,$,

where [] is the empty list, $\_ :: \_$ is list append and $\_ \mathbin{+\!\!+} \_$ is list concatenation, to deduce the existence of a function $\hat{F} \in \Sigma_\alpha(\text{Term}) \to_{\text{fs}} \mathbb{A}^*$ satisfying

$$\hat{F}(\text{V}\,a) = [],$$
$$\hat{F}(\text{L}a \,.\, e) = a :: (\hat{F}\,e), \qquad\qquad (10.62)$$
$$\hat{F}(\text{A}(e_1 \,,\, e_2)) = (\hat{F}\,e_1) \mathbin{+\!\!+} (\hat{F}\,e_2).$$

Such a function attempts to list the bound variables occurring in a λ-term and since the latter is by definition an α-equivalence class of raw terms, no such function exists. (For example, if there were such a function then for any pair of distinct atomic names, $[a] = \hat{F}(\text{L}a \,.\, \text{V}\,a) = \hat{F}(\text{L}a' \,.\, \text{V}\,a') = [a']$, contradicting $a \neq a'$.) Theorem 8.17 is not applicable because the above function F_2 does not satisfy the 'freshness condition on binders' (8.40), since $a \in \text{supp}(a :: \ell)$. However, there is nothing to stop the Fresh OCaml programmer from trying to mimic (10.62) by declaring the following function bvs : $term \rightarrow var\ list$ (following on from the declarations in Figure 10.1):

```
let rec bvs (t : term) : var list =
  match t with
    V x -> []
    | L(<<x1>>t1) -> x1 :: bvs t1
    | A(t1,t2) -> bvs t1 @ bvs t2;;
```

When bvs is applied to the representation of a λ-term and evaluated it does not return its list of bound variables (that would contradict Theorem 10.28); rather, the effect is to create as many fresh names as there are λ-abstractions in the term and to return that list of names. So two applications of bvs to the same expression return different lists; for example $bvs\ tm1 = bvs\ tm1$ evaluates to `false` (creating two fresh names as it does so). Such behaviour is no different from that for other features of OCaml involving dynamic allocation, such as `ref` expressions. Nevertheless, it is reasonable to ask whether there is a *pure* version of FreshML that does not allow declarations like the one above in which names obtained from evaluating a name abstraction against an unbinding (in this case $L(<<x1>>t1) \rightarrow x1 :: bvs\ t1$) remain in the support of the value of the continuation expression (which in this case is $x1 :: bvs\ t1$).

The original version of FreshML (Pitts and Gabbay, 2000) enforced such purity by building a certain amount of inference about the freshness relation into its type system. Its typing judgements take the form

$$(A_1 \# x_1 : T_1, \ldots, A_n \# x_n : T_n) \vdash A \# e : T . \tag{10.63}$$

Here $A_1, \ldots, A_n, A$ are finite sets of atomic names. The intended meaning of the judgement is: 'if for $i = 1, \ldots, n$, the value identifier x_i stands for an element of the nominal set denoted by the type T_i and that element has support disjoint from A_i, then e describes an element of the nominal set denoted by T whose support is disjoint from A. The rules for generating valid typing judgements combine ordinary rules for typing (such as in Figure 10.4) with basic properties of freshness for various types of value.

Remark 10.31 The form of the context to the left of $\vdash$ in (10.63) is more general than necessary. Cheney (2009) uses a form of bunched context (Pym, 2002) generated by the two operations $\Gamma \mapsto \Gamma(x : T)$ (add a typing hypothesis) and $\Gamma \mapsto a \# \Gamma$ (add a freshness hypothesis).

Whatever the precise form of the judgement, a design criterion of the type system is that the 'type-and-freshness' relation be decidable, so that it can be checked at compile-time, rather than at run-time. However, the semantic notion of freshness is not in general decidable and the type system in Pitts and Gabbay (2000) provides a sound, but far from complete approximation for the 'independence from freshly chosen names' property. For example, it rejects the above declaration of *bvs*, but also rejects many semantically pure uses of fresh names. For this reason freshness inference was dropped from the type system for later versions of FreshML (Shinwell *et al.*, 2003), including Fresh OCaml.

There are at least two sources of difficulty when devising systems for inferring freshness properties:

(i) Freshness for recursively defined data in general involves proof by induction.

(ii) As we remarked in Note 3.6, freshness for functions in general involves comparing functions for (extensional) equality.

The *Pure FreshML* of Pottier (2007) neatly overcomes the first difficulty by combining a conventional type system with an expressive proof system for Hoare-style assertions with pre- and post-constraints on expressions. The constraints are Boolean combinations of facts about finite sets of atoms, equations between values and a primitive for support. Pottier gives a conservative decision procedure for constraint entailment. The design of Pure FreshML seems to deal rather well with difficulty (i), but as far as I am aware has not been extended to deal with functions as first-class values (function closures) where difficulty (ii) has to be avoided in some pragmatic way.

In order to formulate its correctness properties (Pottier, 2007, section 4.2), Pure FreshML uses a statically scoped local name construct, like λFML's *va. e*, rather than an expression like `fresh` in Fresh OCaml that dynamically generates a fresh name when evaluated. Using the former rather than the latter allows one to give a version of the operational semantics that attempts to deallocate fresh names upon leaving their scope. Thus, in terms of the λFML language, Pottier replaces lines 1 and 27 in Figure 10.7 with

$$(F, va. e) \rightarrow (F \circ va, e)$$
$$\text{if } a \# F$$
$$(F \circ (\text{let } \langle\!\langle a \rangle\!\rangle x = \bullet \text{ in } e), \langle\!\langle a' \rangle\!\rangle v) \rightarrow (F \circ va, [x := (a\ a') \cdot v]e)$$
$$\text{if } a \# (F, a', v)$$

using a new form of evaluation frame, *va*, that marks the entry into a local scope. One then has to give rules for transitions from configurations of the form $(F \circ va, v)$ when evaluation of the scoped expression has finished and we are ready to leave the local scope. For Pure FreshML, since the syntactic value

v does not involve unevaluated expressions (there are no function closures, for example), it is possible to give a finite set of atomic names fn v by recursion on the structure of v that coincides with the support of the semantic value it denotes. So one can use the transition

$$(F \circ va , v) \rightarrow (F , v) \quad \text{if } a \notin \text{fn } v \qquad (10.64)$$

and declare that configurations $(F \circ va, v)$ with $a \in \text{fn } v$ are stuck. Pottier shows that configurations that are valid in his proof system cannot get stuck in this way.

Remark 10.32 (Odersky-style locally scoped names) An alternative possibility, one that has yet to be investigated in this context of ML-like functional programming languages, is to interpret the local scoping construct $va. e$ in the style of Odersky (1994); see Section 9.4. Using this one could replace (10.64) with

$$(F \circ va , v) \rightarrow (F , a\backslash v),$$

where $v \mapsto a\backslash v$ is an Odersky-style name restriction operation on values: for example, at product types one has $a\backslash(v_1,v_2) = (a\backslash v_1, a\backslash v_2)$ and at function types one has $a\backslash(\lambda f\, x = e) = (\lambda f\, x = va. e)$. When it comes to name-abstraction types it seems best to use closed values of the form $\alpha a. v$ rather than $\langle\!\langle a \rangle\!\rangle v$ (see Note 10.2) and define $a\backslash \alpha a'. v = \alpha a'. a\backslash v$ (where $a \neq a'$); see Pitts (2011).

Exercises

10.1 Prove the type soundness properties of λFML stated in Proposition 10.9.

10.2 Complete the proof of Lemma 10.19. A more exciting and challenging exercise would be to create fully formal proofs for the material in Sections 10.8–10.12 in a interactive theorem prover such as Nominal Isabelle/HOL (http://isabelle.in.tum.de/nominal) or Coq (http://coq.inria.fr).

10.3 Show that if a_1 and a_2 are distinct elements of A_N, then $\{x : N\} \vdash (a_1 \rightleftharpoons a_2)\, x =_{\text{ctx}} x : N$ does not hold. [Hint: use Proposition 10.26 and (10.56).]

10.4 Use part (vi) of Theorem 10.13 to show that if $a, a' \in A_N$, $v \in \text{Val}(T)$ and $a' \# (a, v)$, then $\langle\!\langle a \rangle\!\rangle v =_{\text{ctx}} \langle\!\langle a' \rangle\!\rangle (a\, a') \cdot v : \langle\!\langle N \rangle\!\rangle T$. Use this together with Proposition 10.26 to show that the binding form of name abstraction defined in (10.4) satisfies

$$\Gamma \vdash \langle\!\langle e_1 \rangle\!\rangle e_2 =_{\text{ctx}} \alpha a. (e_1 \rightleftharpoons a)\, e_2 : \langle\!\langle N \rangle\!\rangle T \quad (\text{where } a \# (e_1, e_2)).$$

10.5 Show that the operations defined in Note 10.2 satisfy

$$\Gamma \vdash (\alpha a. e) @ a' =_{ctx} \nu a. (a \rightleftharpoons a') e : T \quad \text{(where } a \neq a').$$

10.6 The λFML *contextual preorder* $\leq_{ctx}$ is the union of all type-respecting relations that are compatible and satisfy a one-sided version of adequacy from Definition 10.11: if $\emptyset \vdash e \mathcal{R} e' : T$, then $e{\downarrow} \Rightarrow e'{\downarrow}$. By removing one of the implications in (10.29) and in (10.30), develop a step-indexed logical relation satisfying for $\leq_{ctx}$ the analogue of Proposition 10.26 for $=_{ctx}$. Use this logical relation to show that recursive function expressions $\lambda f \, x = e \in Val(T_1 \rightarrow T_2)$ have a *least pre-fixed-point* property (*cf.* Theorem 7.12) with respect to the contextual preorder:

$$(\lambda x. [f := v]e) \leq_{ctx} v : T_1 \rightarrow T_2 \quad \Leftrightarrow \quad (\lambda f \, x = e) \leq_{ctx} v : T_1 \rightarrow T_2.$$

[Hint: see Schwinghammer and Birkedal, 2011, section 6.]

11

Domain theory

Chapter 10 considered functional programming with data involving names and name abstractions. The new language features introduced in that chapter were motivated by the theory of nominal sets introduced in Part One of the book. We encouraged the reader to think of the type and function expressions of the FreshML functional programming language as describing nominal sets and finitely supported functions between them. However, just as for conventional functional programming, the sets-and-functions viewpoint is too naive, because of the facilities these languages provide for making recursive definitions. Giving a compositional semantics for such language features requires solving fixed-point equations both at the level of types (for recursively defined data types) and the level of expressions of some type (for recursively defined functions). As is well known, solutions to these fixed-point equations cannot always be found within the world of sets and totally defined functions; and this led the founders of denotational semantics to construct mathematical models of partially defined objects, functions, functionals, etc., based on a fascinating mixture of partial order, topology and computation theory that has come to be known as *domain theory*. For an introduction to domain theory we refer the reader to Abramsky and Jung (1994).

In this chapter we consider merging domain theory with the concepts from nominal sets – names, permutations, support and freshness. As a result we gain new forms of domain, in particular domains of name abstractions. These can be used with more familiar domain-theoretic constructs (such as lifting and various function spaces) when constructing the solutions for recursive domain equations. Such solutions are useful for the denotational semantics of languages in the FreshML family (Shinwell and Pitts, 2005b) and more generally, for programming language features involving local scoping and abstraction of names of various kinds (Benton and Leperchey, 2005; Birkedal and Yang, 2008; Turner and Winskel, 2009). However, to get well-behaved domains for name abstraction it turns out that nominal domain theory has to be something more than just 'doing conventional domain theory in the higher-order logic of nominal sets'. We discuss why this is the case in Section 11.2, having first set up the underlying framework of nominal posets in the next section.

Domain theory is not the only part of denotational semantics where the theory of nominal sets has been applied. *Game semantics* (Abramsky, 1997) has the desirable compositionality properties of traditional, domain-based denotational semantics, but also has the algorithmic content usually associated with an operational approach to program semantics. Game semantics within nominal sets (Abramsky *et al.*, 2004; Tzevelekos, 2008) has provided computationally useful, fully abstract models of generative local state; see Murawski and Tzevelekos (2012), for example.

11.1 Nominal posets

We briefly reviewed the notions of partially ordered set (poset), meet and join in Section 7.4. A *nominal poset* is a nominal set D equipped with a partial order $\sqsubseteq$ that is equivariant:

$$(\forall d, d' \in D)(\forall \pi \in \text{Perm } \mathbb{A}) \, d \sqsubseteq d' \Rightarrow \pi \cdot d \sqsubseteq \pi \cdot d'.$$

If D is a nominal poset, then for each $\pi \in \text{Perm } \mathbb{A}$ the functions $\lambda d \in D \to \pi \cdot d$ and $\lambda d \in D \to \pi^{-1} \cdot d$ are monotone and mutually inverse. Therefore they preserve any joins or meets that happen to exist in D:

$$\pi \cdot (\bigsqcup S) = \bigsqcup \{\pi \cdot d \mid d \in S\} \qquad \pi \cdot (\bigsqcap S) = \bigsqcap \{\pi \cdot d \mid d \in S\}. \qquad (11.1)$$

In particular, if D has a least element $\bot$, then

$$\pi \cdot \bot = \bot. \qquad (11.2)$$

Note also that we have

$$(d \sqsubseteq \pi \cdot d \vee \pi \cdot d \sqsubseteq d) \Rightarrow \pi \cdot d = d. \qquad (11.3)$$

For if $d \sqsubseteq \pi \cdot d$, then $d \sqsubseteq \pi \cdot d \sqsubseteq \pi^2 \cdot d \sqsubseteq \pi^3 \cdot d \sqsubseteq \cdots$. Since π is a finite permutation $\pi^n = \text{id}$ for some $n \in \mathbb{N}$ (Exercise 1.10). Hence $d \sqsubseteq \pi \cdot d \sqsubseteq \pi^n \cdot d = \text{id} \cdot d = d$ and so by anti-symmetry of $\sqsubseteq$ we have $d = \pi \cdot d$. Similarly if $\pi \cdot d \sqsubseteq d$, then $d = \pi \cdot d$.

Example 11.1 If $X \in \textbf{Nom}$, then the nominal powerset $P_{\text{fs}} X$ (Definition 2.26) is a nominal poset when equipped with the partial order given by subset inclusion. It possesses joins and meets of all finitely supported subsets. The join of $S \in P_{fs}(P_{fs}X)$ is its union $\bigcup S$, since this is a finitely supported subset of X (by the Finite Support Principle of Section 2.5). Similarly, the meet of $S \in P_{fs}(P_{fs}X)$ is its intersection $\bigcap S$.

Remark 11.2 There is no connection in general between the partial order on a nominal poset and the support of its elements: if $d \sqsubseteq d'$, it is not necessarily the case that $\text{supp}\,d \subseteq \text{supp}\,d'$ or $\text{supp}\,d' \subseteq \text{supp}\,d$. For example, in the nominal poset $P_{fs}\,\mathbb{A}$, we have $\{a\} \subseteq \mathbb{A} - \{a'\}$ (assuming a and a' are distinct atomic names); but $\text{supp}\{a\} = \{a\}$ and $\text{supp}\,\mathbb{A} - \{a'\} = \{a'\}$ are incomparable.

11.2 Discontinuity of name abstraction

Two ideas motivate the development of domain theory:

- *Approximation*: the denotation of a program with potentially infinite behaviour should be the limit of approximations that are finite in some suitable sense.
- *Compositionality*: the denotation of a compound program should be a function of the denotations of the programs of which it is compounded; moreover these functions should be *continuous*, that is, preserve limits of approximations.

For domain theory based on approximation via a partial ordering (rather than via a metric), limits are given by taking joins of directed subsets; and continuity means preservation of joins of directed subsets. Therefore one might expect the 'nominal' version of domain theory to use nominal posets D possessing joins for finitely supported subsets $S \in P_{fs}\,D$ that are *directed*

$$(\forall F \in P_f\,S)(\exists d \in S)(\forall d' \in F)\, d' \sqsubseteq d. \tag{11.4}$$

Then the denotations of program constructions would need to be equivariant monotone functions that preserve such joins. Unfortunately, Turner and Winskel (2009) have shown by example that a key notion provided by the nominal approach, the operation of name abstraction, does not necessarily preserve joins of finitely supported directed subsets. We give their example (Proposition 11.5) and discuss how to get around the problem, having first extended the name-abstraction construct from nominal sets to nominal posets.

Definition 11.3 Given a nominal poset D, we make the nominal set of name abstractions $[\mathbb{A}]D$ (Definition 4.4) into a nominal poset via the operation of concretion at a fresh name. Thus we define for all $e, e' \in [\mathbb{A}]D$

$$e \sqsubseteq e' \triangleq (\mathsf{N}a)\, e @ a \sqsubseteq e' @ a. \tag{11.5}$$

In other words, given $a, a' \in \mathbb{A}$ and $d, d' \in D$, we have $\langle a \rangle d \sqsubseteq \langle a' \rangle d'$ in $[\mathbb{A}]D$ iff for some/any $a'' \# (a, a', d, d')$ we have $(a \; a'') \cdot d \sqsubseteq (a' \; a'') \cdot d'$ in D. (Reflexivity, transitivity and anti-symmetry of this relation on $[\mathbb{A}]D$ follow from the corresponding properties of $\sqsubseteq$ on D together with the properties of name abstraction and concretion developed in Chapter 4.) Note that the operation of name abstraction is monotone:

$$d \sqsubseteq d' \Rightarrow \langle a \rangle d \sqsubseteq \langle a \rangle d' . \tag{11.6}$$

To see this, note that if $d \sqsubseteq d'$, then by (4.14) $(\langle a \rangle d) @ a = d \sqsubseteq d' = (\langle a \rangle d') @ a$, so that $\langle a \rangle d \sqsubseteq \langle a \rangle d'$ by (11.5).

Proposition 11.4 *Suppose that D is a nominal poset. For any $S \in P_{fs} ([\mathbb{A}]D)$, picking $a \# S$, if the finitely supported subset $\{d \in D \mid \langle a \rangle d \in S\}$ possesses a join in D, then the join of S in $[\mathbb{A}]D$ is $\langle a \rangle (\bigsqcup \{d \in D \mid \langle a \rangle d \in S\})$.*

Proof We have to show that $e_S \triangleq \langle a \rangle (\bigsqcup \{d \in D \mid \langle a \rangle d \in S\})$ is the least upper bound of S in $[\mathbb{A}]D$. First note that we can apply the freshness theorem (Theorem 3.11) to the finitely supported partial function $F_S \in \mathbb{A} \rightharpoonup_{fs} [\mathbb{A}]D$ given by $F_S \, a \equiv \langle a \rangle (\bigsqcup \{d \in D \mid \langle a \rangle d \in S\})$ to deduce that

$$(\forall a' \# S) \, e_S \equiv \langle a' \rangle (\bigsqcup \{d \in D \mid \langle a' \rangle d \in S\}) \tag{11.7}$$

(and in particular that the join of $\{d \in D \mid \langle a' \rangle d \in S\}$ exists in D for each $a' \# S$).

If $e \in S$, then picking any $a' \# (S, e)$, by Proposition 4.9 we have $\langle a' \rangle (e @ a') = e \in S$; so $e @ a' \in \{d \in D \mid \langle a' \rangle d \in S\}$ and hence $e @ a' \sqsubseteq \bigsqcup \{d \in D \mid \langle a' \rangle d \in S\}$. Thus by (11.6) and (11.7), we have $e = \langle a' \rangle (e @ a') \sqsubseteq e_S$. Therefore e_S is an upper bound for S. To see that it is the least upper bound, suppose that $e' \in [\mathbb{A}]D$ satisfies $(\forall e \in S) \, e \sqsubseteq e'$. Then picking any $a' \# (S, e')$ we have for all $d \in D$

$$\langle a' \rangle d \in S \Rightarrow \langle a' \rangle d \sqsubseteq e' \Rightarrow d = ((\langle a' \rangle d) @ a' \sqsubseteq e' @ a' .$$

Therefore $\bigsqcup \{d \mid \langle a' \rangle d \in S\} \sqsubseteq e' @ a'$ and hence by (11.6) and (11.7) we have $e_S \sqsubseteq \langle a' \rangle (e' @ a') = e'$.   □

Combining Example 11.1 with Proposition 11.4, for each nominal set X the nominal poset $[\mathbb{A}](P_{fs} X)$ has joins for all finitely supported subsets and in particular for all finitely supported, directed subsets. We show by example that the name abstraction functions $\langle a \rangle_- : P_{fs} X \rightarrow [\mathbb{A}](P_{fs} X)$ do not always preserve these joins.

Proposition 11.5 (Turner and Winskel, 2009, section 3.1) *For each $a \in \mathbb{A}$, the function $\langle a \rangle_- \in P_{fs} \mathbb{A} \rightharpoonup_{fs} [\mathbb{A}](P_{fs} \mathbb{A})$ that maps each $S \in P_{fs} \mathbb{A}$ to $\langle a \rangle S \in$*

[A]$(P_{fs} A)$, *does not preserve all joins of directed, finitely supported subsets of* $P_{fs} A$.

Proof Consider the (equivariant) directed subset $P_f A \subseteq P_{fs} A$ of all finite subsets. Its join in $P_{fs} A$ is the union $\bigcup P_f A = A$. Choosing some $a' \neq a$, for each $F \in P_f A$ we have

$$\langle a \rangle F$$
$$= \quad \{\text{picking any } b \,\#\, (a, a', F)\}$$
$$\langle b \rangle ((a\ b) \cdot F)$$
$$\sqsubseteq \quad \{\text{since } F \subseteq A - \{b\}, \text{ so that } (a\ b) \cdot F \subseteq A - \{a\}\}$$
$$\langle b \rangle (A - \{a\})$$
$$= \quad \{\text{since } a', b \,\#\, A - \{a\}\}$$
$$\langle a' \rangle (A - \{a\}),$$

so that $\bigsqcup \{\langle a \rangle F \mid F \in P_f A\} \sqsubseteq \langle a' \rangle (A - \{a\})$; and $\langle a' \rangle A \not\sqsubseteq \langle a' \rangle (A - \{a\})$. Therefore $\langle a \rangle (\bigsqcup P_f A) = \langle a \rangle A = \langle a' \rangle A \neq \bigsqcup \{\langle a \rangle F \mid F \in P_f A\}$.   □

Remark 11.6 In Proposition 11.4, if S is not just finitely supported, but is a uniformly supported (Definition 5.27) subset of [A]D, then from $a \,\#\, S$ we can infer by Lemma 5.28 that $a \,\#\, e$ for each $e \in S$; and hence $\{d \in D \mid \langle a \rangle d \in S\} = \{e \,@\, a \mid e \in S\}$. So for uniformly supported subsets of [A]D, Proposition 11.4 gives

$$\bigsqcup S = \langle a \rangle (\bigsqcup \{e \,@\, a \mid e \in S\}) \qquad \text{for some/any } a \,\#\, S \qquad (11.8)$$

provided $\{e \,@\, a \mid e \in S\}$ has a join in D.

If S' is a uniformly supported subset of a nominal poset D and S' possesses a join, then for any $a \in A$, applying the above remark to $S \triangleq \{\langle a \rangle d \mid d \in S'\}$, we get $\bigsqcup S = \langle a' \rangle (\bigsqcup \{(a\ a') \cdot d \mid d \in S'\})$ for any $a' \,\#\, (a, S')$; and since $\langle a' \rangle (\bigsqcup \{(a\ a') \cdot d \mid d \in S'\}) = \langle a' \rangle ((a\ a') \cdot \bigsqcup S') = \langle a \rangle (\bigsqcup S')$, altogether we get

$$\langle a \rangle (\bigsqcup S') = \bigsqcup \{\langle a \rangle d \mid d \in S'\}. \qquad (11.9)$$

So despite Proposition 11.5, $\langle a \rangle_- : D \rightarrow$ [A]D preserves any joins of *uniformly supported* subsets that happen to exist. This observation prompted Turner and Winskel (2009) to develop a nominal domain theory based upon joins of uniformly supported and directed subsets, which we develop in the rest of this chapter. There is a good reason why the use of uniform support in this context is not too restrictive, which we discuss in the next section (Proposition 11.9).

However, while the use of joins of uniformly supported, directed subsets yields a well-behaved name abstraction operation, there is still a problem with the partial operation of name concretion: *it is not monotone*. When considering *partial* functions $F : D \rightharpoonup E$ between posets, the natural definition of monotonicity is the following one (see Plotkin, 1985):

$$(d, e) \in F \wedge d \sqsubseteq d' \Rightarrow (\exists e' \in E)\, e \sqsubseteq e' \wedge (d', e') \in F. \tag{11.10}$$

For this condition is equivalent to requiring the corresponding total function $\hat{F} : D \to E_\perp$ to be monotone in the usual sense. Here $E_\perp$ is the lift of E, the poset obtained from E by adjoining a distinct least element $\perp$; and $\hat{F}$ is the total function satisfying for all $d \in D$

$$\hat{F}\, d = \begin{cases} e & \text{if } (d, e) \in F, \\ \perp & \text{if } \neg(\exists e \in E)\, (d, e) \in F. \end{cases}$$

Example 11.7 Consider the nominal poset $P_{fs}\, \mathbb{A}$ (Example 11.1) and its nominal poset of name abstractions $[\mathbb{A}](P_{fs}\, \mathbb{A})$ (Definition 11.3). For each $a \in \mathbb{A}$, the partial function $\_ @ a : [\mathbb{A}](P_{fs}\, \mathbb{A}) \rightharpoonup_{fs} P_{fs}\, \mathbb{A}$ given by concretion (Definition 4.8) does not satisfy the monotonicity property (11.10), because of the lack of any connection in nominal posets between support and partial order noted in Remark 11.2. For example, if $a' \neq a$, then $\{a'\} \sqsubseteq \mathbb{A} - \{a\}$ in $P_{fs}\, \mathbb{A}$, so $\langle a'\rangle\{a'\} \sqsubseteq \langle a'\rangle(\mathbb{A} - \{a\})$ in $[\mathbb{A}](P_{fs}\, \mathbb{A})$. According to (4.14), $(\langle a'\rangle\{a'\}) @ a$ is defined (and equal to a), whereas $(\langle a'\rangle(\mathbb{A} - \{a\})) @ a$ is undefined.

Remark 11.8 This difficulty with name concretion is avoided if one moves to a setting where nominal posets D come with monotone operations $a \backslash \_ : D \to_{fs} D$ of name restriction in the sense of Chapter 9. For then one can use the extension of concretion to a total function $\operatorname{conc} \_ a : [\mathbb{A}]D \to_{fs} D$ discussed in Section 9.7. For each $a \in \mathbb{A}$ and $e \in [\mathbb{A}]D$, from (9.59) we have that this satisfies

$$\operatorname{conc} e\, a = a' \backslash ((a\ a') \cdot (e @ a')) \qquad \text{some/any } a' \# (e, a). \tag{11.11}$$

So if $e_1 \sqsubseteq e_2$ in $[\mathbb{A}]D$, then choosing $a' \# (e_1, e_2, a)$, by (11.5) we have $e_1 @ a' \sqsubseteq e_2 @ a'$ in D and hence also $(a\ a') \cdot (e_1 @ a') \sqsubseteq (a\ a') \cdot (e_2 @ a')$. Therefore since $a' \backslash \_$ is monotone, from (11.11) we get $\operatorname{conc} e_1\, a \sqsubseteq \operatorname{conc} e_2\, a$. Thus $\operatorname{conc} \_ a$ is indeed monotone (and turns out to be continuous, in the sense of preserving joins of uniformly supported directed subsets, provided restriction is continuous). Fortunately, many nominal domains do come with a continuous operation of name restriction; see Lösch and Pitts (2013).

11.3 Uniform directed complete posets

Recall that a *chain* in a poset D is a non-empty subset $C \subseteq D$ for which the partial order on D restricts to a total order:

$$(\forall d, d' \in C)\ d \sqsubseteq d' \vee d' \sqsubseteq d. \qquad (11.12)$$

Clearly every chain is a directed subset (11.4). So long as one considers chains of arbitrary size, a poset possesses joins of directed subsets iff it possesses joins of chains (see Markowsky, 1976). However, this equivalence relies on the Axiom of Choice and, as we noted in Section 2.7, that fails to hold for nominal sets. Therefore, in a 'nominal' version of domain theory, formulating limits in terms of joins of chains is more restrictive than using joins of arbitrary directed subsets. (Of course, both the chains and the directed subsets should be finitely supported, to make sense nominally.) However, in view of the following proposition one can use the classical result about chains and directed subsets to deduce that a nominal poset has joins for all finitely supported chains iff it has joins for all uniformly supported directed subsets. So a domain theory based upon joins of uniformly supported directed subsets is in effect the development of domain theory based upon chain-completeness within the higher-order logic of nominal sets.

Proposition 11.9 (Turner, 2009, lemma 3.4.2.1) *In a nominal poset D, every finitely supported chain C is necessarily a uniformly supported subset.*

Proof Suppose $A \in P_f \mathbb{A}$ supports C in $P_{fs} D$. So for any $a_1, a_2 \in \mathbb{A} - A$ we have $(a_1\ a_2) \cdot C = C$. Thus if $x \in C$, then $(a_1\ a_2) \cdot x \in C$ and since C is a chain, this implies that either $x \sqsubseteq (a_1\ a_2) \cdot x$, or $(a_1\ a_2) \cdot x \sqsubseteq x$; hence by (11.3) $(a_1\ a_2) \cdot x = x$. So for all $a_1, a_2 \in \mathbb{A} - A$ we have $(a_1\ a_2) \cdot x = x$. Therefore by Proposition 2.1, A supports each $x \in C$. $\qquad\square$

Definition 11.10 A *uniform directed complete poset* (*udcpo*) is a nominal poset D for which every uniformly supported directed subset has a join. If D also has a *least element* $\bot_D \in D$ then we call it a *pointed* udcpo. (When D is understood from the context, we just write $\bot_D$ as $\bot$.) If E is another udcpo, we say that a function $f : D \to E$ is *uniform-continuous* if it is monotone and preserves joins of all uniformly supported directed subsets. Of course we will be interested in uniform-continuous functions that are also equivariant (or more generally, finitely supported). We write **Udcppo** for the category whose objects are pointed udcpos and whose morphisms are equivariant, uniform-continuous functions; identities and composition are as for ordinary functions.

A morphism $f \in$ **Udcppo**(D, E) is called *strict* if it preserves the least element: $f \perp_D = \perp_E$. We write **Udcppo**₁ for the subcategory of **Udcppo** given by strict morphisms.

Example 11.11 The *discrete udcpo* on a nominal set X is given by taking the (equivariant) partial order on X to be equality; the only directed subsets are singletons, which trivially have joins. The *lift* of a udcpo D is the pointed udcpo

$$D_\perp \triangleq D \cup \{\perp\},$$

where we assume $\perp$ is some element not in D and define the partial order on $D_\perp$ to be $\{(d, d') \in D \times D \mid d \sqsubseteq d'\} \cup \{(\perp, d) \mid d \in D\}$. Clearly $\perp$ is the least element of $D_\perp$; and $D_\perp$ has joins for all uniformly supported directed subsets, because D does. A pointed udcpo is called *flat* if it is of the form $X_\perp$ for some discrete udcpo X.

Example 11.12 The above examples are directed-complete in the usual sense. However this is not generally the case. Consider for example the nominal set $P_f \, \mathbb{A}$ of finite subsets of the nominal set of atomic names (Example 2.10). The partial order of subset inclusion makes it into a (pointed) udcpo; indeed $P_f \, \mathbb{A}$ possesses joins of all uniformly supported subsets. For if $S \subseteq P_f \, \mathbb{A}$ is uniformly supported then by Lemma 5.28 for all $A \in S$ we have $A = \operatorname{supp} A \subseteq \operatorname{supp} S$; so $\bigcup S \subseteq \operatorname{supp} S$, hence $\bigcup S \in P_f \, \mathbb{A}$ and it is necessarily the join of S. However, $P_f \, \mathbb{A}$ certainly contains chains with no join, such as $\emptyset \subseteq \{a_0\} \subseteq \{a_0, a_1\} \subseteq \cdots$, where $a_0, a_1, a_2, \ldots$ is some enumeration of the countably infinite set $\mathbb{A}$.

Proposition 11.13 *If D is a udcpo, then so is its nominal poset of name abstractions $[\mathbb{A}]D$ (Definition 11.3). If D is pointed, then so is $[\mathbb{A}]D$.*

Proof Suppose S is a uniformly supported and directed subset of $[\mathbb{A}]D$. Picking any $a \,\#\, S$, then by Lemma 5.28, $a \,\#\, e$ holds for each $e \in S$. So we can form the subset $\{e @ a \mid e \in S\} \subseteq D$. It is uniformly supported by $\operatorname{supp} S \cup \{a\}$; and it is directed, because of the way $\sqsubseteq$ is defined on $[\mathbb{A}]D$ in (11.5). So the subset has a join in D. Then as in Remark 11.6 we have that S has a join in $[\mathbb{A}]D$, namely $\bigsqcup S = \langle a \rangle (\bigsqcup \{e @ a \mid e \in S\})$.

Finally, if D has a least element $\perp$, then clearly $\langle a \rangle \perp$ is the least element of $[\mathbb{A}]D$, for some/any $a \in \mathbb{A}$. □

Proposition 11.14 **Udcppo** *is a cartesian closed category.*

Proof The terminal object in **Udcppo** is the trivial pointed udcpo with a single element, $\{\perp\}$. The binary product $D_1 \times D_2$ of pointed udcpos $D_1, D_2 \in$ **Ndom** is given by their product in **Nom** equipped with the equivariant partial order

$$(d_1, d_2) \sqsubseteq (d_1', d_2') \triangleq d_1 \sqsubseteq d_1' \wedge d_2 \sqsubseteq d_2'. \tag{11.13}$$

To see this, note that if $S \subseteq D_1 \times D_2$ is a uniformly supported and directed subset, then $\{d_1 \in D_1 \mid (\exists d_2 \in D_2)\,(d_1, d_2) \in S\}$ and $\{d_2 \in D_2 \mid (\exists d_1 \in D_1)\,(d_1, d_2) \in S\}$ are each directed and uniformly supported by $\mathrm{supp}\,S$; so we can form their joins in D_1 and D_2. It follows that

$$(\bigsqcup\{d_1 \in D_1 \mid (\exists d_2 \in D_2)\,(d_1, d_2) \in S\}, \bigsqcup\{d_2 \in D_2 \mid (\exists d_1 \in D_1)\,(d_1, d_2) \in S\})$$

is the join of S in $D_1 \times D_2$. Furthermore, $D_1 \times D_2$ has a least element, namely $(\bot, \bot)$.

Turning to exponentials in **Udcppo**, suppose D and E are pointed udcpos and that $f \in D \to_{\mathrm{fs}} E$ is a finitely supported function. In view of (11.1), if f is uniform-continuous then so is $\pi \cdot f$ for any $\pi \in \mathrm{Perm}\,\mathbb{A}$. Therefore

$$D \to E \triangleq \{f \in D \to_{\mathrm{fs}} E \mid f \text{ is uniform-continuous}\} \tag{11.14}$$

is an equivariant subset of $D \to_{\mathrm{fs}} E$ and hence is itself a nominal set. We get an equivariant partial order on this nominal set by defining

$$f \sqsubseteq f' \triangleq (\forall d \in D)\, f\,d \sqsubseteq f'\,d. \tag{11.15}$$

This makes $D \to E$ into a pointed udcpo, called the *udcpo of uniform-continuous functions* from D to E. To see this, note that if $S \subseteq D \to E$ is a uniformly supported directed set, then $\{f\,d \mid f \in S\}$ is directed and uniformly supported by $\mathrm{supp}\,S \cup \mathrm{supp}\,d$. So we can take its join and define

$$(\bigsqcup S)d \triangleq \bigsqcup\{f\,d \mid f \in S\}.$$

In this way we get a function $\bigsqcup S$ which is easily seen to be supported by $\mathrm{supp}\,S$, uniform-continuous and a least upper bound for S in $D \to E$. Furthermore, $\lambda d \in D \to \bot_E$ is in $D \to E$ and is a least element with respect to the partial order on $D \to E$. The pointed udcpo $D \to E$ is the exponential of E by D in **Udcppo** since one can easily check that function application gives a morphism $(D \to E) \times D \to E$ in **Udcppo** and that currying a morphism $f \in \mathbf{Udcppo}(D' \times D, E)$ gives a morphism in $\mathbf{Udcppo}(D', D \to E)$. □

In view of Proposition 11.9, every finitely supported ω-chain in a nominal poset is uniformly supported. Thus nominal domain theory based on joins of finitely supported ω-chains, such as developed by Shinwell and Pitts (2005b) and Shinwell's thesis (2005a), is subsumed by one based on joins of uniformly directed subsets. A case in point is the existence of least fixed-points.

Proposition 11.15   *Let D be a pointed udcpo. Every finitely supported, uniform-continuous function $f \in D \to D$ has a least fixed-point* lfp $f \in D$, *given by*

$$\text{lfp}\, f = \bigsqcup \{ f^n \bot \mid n \in \mathbb{N} \}. \tag{11.16}$$

Furthermore, the assignment $f \mapsto \text{lfp}\, f$ gives a morphism lfp $\in$ **Udcppo**$(D \to D, D)$.

Proof   Note that $\{ f^n \bot \mid n \in \mathbb{N} \}$ is an ω-chain supported by supp f. So by Proposition 11.9 we can take its join in D. Thus (11.16) well-defines lfp f; and given that, the rest of the proof follows exactly as for the classic case of directed complete posets (see Abramsky and Jung, 1994, theorem 2.1.19).   □

The existence of least fixed-points in individual objects of **Udcppo** allows one to model some recursive and iterative features of programs. To go further, one needs to solve recursive equations at the level of the objects themselves. We pursue this in the next section.

11.4 Recursive domain equations

The denotational approach to programming language semantics seeks to find mathematical structures together with operations on them that can be used to model programming language constructs in a compositional fashion, that is, so that the meaning of a phrase is obtained from the meaning of its sub-phrases by applying one of the operations (see for example Mosses, 1990). The requirements on a structure for such a semantics to exist can often be expressed as a series of fixed-point equations at the level of structures. An early example was the search by Scott for denotational semantics for the untyped λ-calculus, which throws up the need for a structure D isomorphic to its own function space $D \to D$. Although non-trivial sets satisfying $X \cong X^X$ do not exist for cardinality reasons, famously Scott showed that the equation $X = X \to X$ has non-trivial solutions if one restricts $X \to X$ to be a space of continuous functions. From these beginnings Scott, Plotkin and others have developed a rich theory of denotational semantics based on the use of domains recursively defined by equations of the form

$$X \cong \Psi X. \tag{11.17}$$

Here '$\cong$' indicates isomorphism of domains and $X \mapsto \Psi X$ is a construction built up from some of the domain-forming constructs needed for the denotational semantics of programming languages. These include standard ones such as various kinds of product, sum, function space, lifting, etc.; to which in the nominal setting we can add a construct for name-abstraction.

In general there may be many non-isomorphic solutions to (11.17). Usually one is interested in a particular solution that is minimal in a suitable sense, in order to adequately represent operational behaviour of programs. Although there are several ways to express a minimality property, the most convenient one is the so-called 'minimal invariant' property. To express it one has to examine the functorial properties of the construction $X \mapsto \Psi X$. Since Ψ may well contain uses of function spaces in which X occurs both positively and negatively (the classic example being when ΨX is simply $X \to X$), Ψ is not necessarily the object-part of a co- or contra-variant functor for continuous functions between domains. However, one can usually see that $\Psi X = \Phi X X$, where $(X, Y) \mapsto \Phi X Y$ is a construction that is contravariantly functorial in X and covariantly functorial in Y. We refer the reader to Abramsky and Jung (1994, section 5) and Pitts (1996) for accounts of modern techniques for solving recursive domain equations in classical domain theory, based upon the construction of minimal invariants for such mixed variance, locally continuous functors. We will develop a version of this construction for uniform directed complete posets.

Recall from Definition 11.10 that $\mathbf{Udcppo}_!$ is the category whose objects are pointed udcpos and whose morphisms are functions that are equivariant, uniform-continuous and strict. Given $D, E \in \mathbf{Udcppo}_!$, the subset

$$D \multimap E \triangleq \{ f \in D \to E \mid f \perp_D = \perp_E \} \tag{11.18}$$

of strict functions is equivariant by (11.2), is closed under joins of uniformly supported directed subsets and contains the least element. So it is an object of $\mathbf{Udcppo}_!$, called the pointed *udcpo of strict uniform-continuous functions* from D to E.

Definition 11.16 A (mixed variance) *locally uniform continuous functor*

$$\Phi : \mathbf{Udcppo}_!^{op} \times \mathbf{Udcppo}_! \to \mathbf{Udcppo}_! \tag{11.19}$$

is specified by the following data:

- For each $D, E \in \mathbf{Udcppo}_!$, an object $\Phi D E \in \mathbf{Udcppo}_!$.
- For each $D, D', E, E' \in \mathbf{Udcppo}_!$, an equivariant, uniform continuous function

$$(D' \multimap D) \times (E \multimap E') \to (\Phi D E \multimap \Phi D' E'), \tag{11.20}$$

$$(f, g) \mapsto \Phi f g$$

satisfying

$$\Phi \, \mathrm{id}_D \, \mathrm{id}_D = \mathrm{id}_{\Phi D D}, \tag{11.21}$$

$$\Phi \, (f' \circ f)(g \circ g') = (\Phi \, f \, g) \circ (\Phi \, f' g'). \tag{11.22}$$

Note that since each function is equivariant and uniform-continuous, we also have

$$\pi \cdot (\Phi \, f \, g) = \Phi \, (\pi \cdot f)(\pi \cdot g), \tag{11.23}$$

$$f \sqsubseteq f' \wedge g \sqsubseteq g' \Rightarrow \Phi \, f \, g \sqsubseteq \Phi \, f' g', \tag{11.24}$$

$$\Phi \, (\bigsqcup S)(\bigsqcup T) = \bigsqcup \{\Phi \, f \, g \mid f \in S \wedge g \in T\} \tag{11.25}$$

$$(S, T \text{ uniformly supported and directed}).$$

An *invariant* object for such a Φ is a pointed udcpo D together with an isomorphism $i : \Phi D D \cong D$ in **Udcppo**$_!$. It is a *minimal invariant* if the identity $\mathrm{id}_D \in D \multimap D$ is the least fixed-point of the equivariant, uniform-continuous function

$$\delta_\Phi : (D \multimap D) \to (D \multimap D), \tag{11.26}$$

$$\delta_\Phi \triangleq \lambda f \in (D \multimap D) \to i \circ (\Phi \, f \, f) \circ i^{-1}.$$

From Proposition 11.15, this means that $\mathrm{id}_D = \bigsqcup \{p_n \mid n \in \mathbb{N}\}$, where

$$\begin{cases} p_0 = \bot_{D \multimap D}, \\ p_{n+1} = i \circ (\Phi \, p_n \, p_n) \circ i^{-1}. \end{cases} \tag{11.27}$$

Example 11.17 Both (11.14) and (11.18) are the object parts of locally uniform-continuous functors, with (11.20) being given by function composition.

Remark 11.18 We gave the above definition for mixed variance functors of two arguments, since that is the form needed for minimal invariant objects. However, the definition should be clear for 'locally uniform-continuous' functors of other arities, such as **Udcppo**$_! \to$ **Udcppo**$_!$, **Udcppo**$_!^{op} \to$ **Udcppo**$_!$, **Udcppo**$_! \times$ **Udcppo**$_! \to$ **Udcppo**$_!$, etc., and such functors can be composed together. This allows one to build up a rich collection of locally uniform-continuous functors, starting from some basic ones: as well as Example 11.17, other constructs from classical domain theory give rise to locally uniform-continuous functors on **Udcppo**$_!$ – such as lifting, cartesian and smashed product, and coalesced sum. In addition we gain access to names, via the flat pointed udcpo $\mathbb{A}_\bot$ (Example 11.11), and name abstraction $D \mapsto [\mathbb{A}]D$ (Proposition 11.13). The latter gives a locally uniform-continuous functor $[\mathbb{A}]\_ :$ **Udcppo**$_! \to$ **Udcppo**$_!$. To see this, first note that the equivariant functions

$f \mapsto [\mathbb{A}]f$ from Remark 4.11 preserve joins of uniformly supported directed subsets:

$$[\mathbb{A}]f(\bigsqcup S)$$
$$= \quad \{\text{by (11.8), where } a \,\#\, (f, S)\}$$
$$[\mathbb{A}]f(\langle a\rangle \bigsqcup \{e @ a \mid e \in S\})$$
$$= \quad \{\text{by (4.17)}\}$$
$$\langle a\rangle(f(\bigsqcup \{e @ a \mid e \in S\}))$$
$$= \quad \{\text{since } f \text{ is uniform-continuous}\}$$
$$\langle a\rangle(\bigsqcup \{f(e @ a) \mid e \in S\})$$
$$= \quad \{\text{by (11.9), since } S \text{ is uniformly supported}\}$$
$$\bigsqcup \{\langle a\rangle(f(e @ a)) \mid e \in S\}$$
$$= \quad \{\text{by (4.17)}\}$$
$$\bigsqcup \{[\mathbb{A}]f e \mid e \in S\}.$$

Furthermore, if f is strict, then picking any $a \,\#\, f$ we have

$$[\mathbb{A}]f \perp = [\mathbb{A}]f(\langle a\rangle\perp) = \langle a\rangle(f \perp) = \langle a\rangle\perp = \perp$$

so that $[\mathbb{A}]f$ is also strict. Thus we get equivariant functions

$$
\begin{array}{lll}
(D \multimap E) & \to & ([\mathbb{A}]D \multimap [\mathbb{A}]E), \\
f \in D \multimap E & \mapsto & [\mathbb{A}]f
\end{array}
\qquad (D, E \in \mathbf{Udcppo}_!), \qquad (11.28)
$$

with the required functoriality properties (Lemma 4.10). Calculations similar to the ones above show that $f \mapsto [\mathbb{A}]f$ is uniform-continuous (Exercise 11.2).

Theorem 11.19 *Every locally uniform-continuous functor* $\Phi : \mathbf{Udcppo}_!^{op} \times \mathbf{Udcppo}_! \to \mathbf{Udcppo}_!$ *possesses a minimal invariant object.*

Proof Just as in the classical case, the minimal invariant is constructed by iterating the operation $D \mapsto \Phi D D$ on pointed udcpos, staring with the trivial one $\{\perp\}$, and taking a 'bilimit'. We give a slightly more elementary description of the bilimit than can be found in the existing literature.

Define $(D_n \in \mathbf{Udcppo}_! \mid n \in \mathbb{N})$ and $(f_{m,n} \in (D_m \multimap D_n) \mid m, n \in \mathbb{N})$ as follows:

$$
\begin{cases}
D_0 = \{\perp\}, \\
D_{n+1} = \Phi D_n D_n
\end{cases}
\qquad
\begin{cases}
f_{0,n} = \perp = f_{m,0}, \\
f_{m+1,n+1} = \Phi f_{n,m} f_{m,n}.
\end{cases}
\qquad (11.29)
$$

We noted in the proof of Proposition 11.14 that binary products in $\mathbf{Udcppo}$ are given by taking products in $\mathbf{Nom}$ and using the equivariant partial order induced from the partial order in each component (11.13). The same is true for infinite products. Thus we get a pointed udcpo from the objects D_n by taking their product $(\prod_{n \in \mathbb{N}} D_n)_{\text{fs}}$ in $\mathbf{Nom}$ (Corollary 2.16) and using the equivariant partial order $(d_n \mid n \in \mathbb{N}) \sqsubseteq (d'_n \mid n \in \mathbb{N}) \triangleq (\forall n \in \mathbb{N}) \, d_n \sqsubseteq d'_n$. Given a uniformly supported and directed subset $S \subseteq (\prod_{n\in\mathbb{N}} D_n)_{\mathrm{fs}}$ its join satisfies

$$(\bigsqcup S)_n = \bigsqcup\{d_n \mid d \in S\} \qquad (n \in \mathbb{N}).$$

From this and the fact that because of (11.23) each function $f_{n,m}$ has empty support, in other words is equivariant, it follows that the subset

$$D \triangleq \{d \in (\textstyle\prod_{n\in\mathbb{N}} D_n)_{\mathrm{fs}} \mid (\forall m,n) \, f_{m,n} \, d_m \sqsubseteq d_n\} \tag{11.30}$$

is equivariant and closed under taking joins of uniformly supported directed subsets; and D contains $\bot$, since each $f_{m,n}$ is strict. Therefore D determines a pointed udcpo. We will show that it is a minimal invariant object for Φ.

The following three properties of the functions $f_{m,n}$ follow easily from their definition in (11.29), where in the third one we write $k \wedge n$ for the minimum of two natural numbers $k, n \in \mathbb{N}$:

$$f_{m,n} \circ f_{k,m} \sqsubseteq f_{k,n}, \tag{11.31}$$

$$f_{n,n} = \mathrm{id}_{D_n}, \tag{11.32}$$

$$m > k \wedge n \Rightarrow f_{m,n} \circ f_{k,m} = f_{k,n}. \tag{11.33}$$

It follows from (11.31) that for each $m \in \mathbb{N}$ and $d \in D_m$

$$i_m \, d \triangleq (f_{m,n} \, d \mid n \in \mathbb{N}) \tag{11.34}$$

defines an element of D; and then that $i_m \in D_m \multimap D$. We also have functions $r_m \in D \multimap D_m$ given by projection:

$$r_m \, d \triangleq d_m. \tag{11.35}$$

From these definitions, (11.31) and (11.32) we get for all $m, n \in \mathbb{N}$

$$r_n \circ i_m = f_{m,n}, \tag{11.36}$$

$$f_{m,n} \circ r_m \sqsubseteq r_n, \tag{11.37}$$

$$i_m \circ f_{n,m} \sqsubseteq i_n, \tag{11.38}$$

$$r_n \circ i_n = \mathrm{id}_{D_n}. \tag{11.39}$$

Note that by (11.32) and (11.33)

$$m < n \Rightarrow f_{n,m} \circ f_{m,n} = f_{m,m} = \mathrm{id}_{D_m}, \tag{11.40}$$

and hence $i_m \circ r_m = i_m \circ f_{n,m} \circ f_{m,n} \circ r_m \sqsubseteq i_n \circ r_n$, by (11.37) and (11.38). So $\{i_n \circ r_n \mid n \in \mathbb{N}\}$ is a chain in $D \multimap D$; and it is finitely supported since in fact all the functions $f_{m,n}$, i_n and r_n have empty support, because of property (11.23) of Φ. So we can form the join $\bigsqcup\{i_n \circ r_n \mid n \in \mathbb{N}\}$. We claim that it is equal to id_D. To see this, first note that from (11.32) and (11.33) we have

$m > n \Rightarrow f_{m,n} \circ f_{n,m} = f_{n,n} = \mathrm{id}_{D_n}$. So for all $d \in D$, if $m > n$ then by definition of D, $d_n = f_{m,n}(f_{n,m}\,d_n) \sqsubseteq f_{m,n}\,d_m \sqsubseteq d_n$ and hence $f_{m,n}d_m = d_n$. Thus for each $d \in D$ and $n \in \mathbb{N}$

$$((\bigsqcup\{i_m \circ r_m \mid m \in \mathbb{N}\})\,d)_n = \bigsqcup\{((i_m \circ r_m)\,d)_n \mid m \in \mathbb{N}\}$$
$$= \bigsqcup\{f_{m,n}\,d_m \mid m \in \mathbb{N}\} = \bigsqcup\{f_{m,n}\,d_m \mid m > n\} = d_n = r_n\,d\,.$$

Therefore we have

$$\bigsqcup\{f_{m,n} \circ r_m \mid m \in \mathbb{N}\} = r_n\,, \tag{11.41}$$
$$\bigsqcup\{i_n \circ r_n \mid n \in \mathbb{N}\} = \mathrm{id}_D\,. \tag{11.42}$$

Furthermore, by (11.33)

$$((\bigsqcup\{i_m \circ f_{n,m} \mid m \in \mathbb{N}\})\,d)_k = \bigsqcup\{((i_m(f_{n,m}\,d))_k \mid m \in \mathbb{N}\}$$
$$= \bigsqcup\{f_{m,k}(f_{n,m}\,d) \mid m \in \mathbb{N}\} = \bigsqcup\{f_{m,k}(f_{n,m}\,d) \mid m > k \wedge n\} = f_{n,k}\,d = (i_n\,d)_k\,,$$

so that we also have

$$\bigsqcup\{i_m \circ f_{n,m} \mid m \in \mathbb{N}\} = i_n\,. \tag{11.43}$$

Next we construct an isomorphism $i : \Phi D D \cong D$. Note that if $m < n$, then

$$i_{m+1} \circ (\Phi\,i_m\,r_m)$$
$$= \quad \{\text{by (11.40)}\}$$
$$i_{m+1} \circ f_{n+1,m+1} \circ f_{m+1,n+1} \circ (\Phi\,i_m\,r_m)$$
$$= \quad \{\text{by (11.29)}\}$$
$$i_{m+1} \circ (\Phi\,f_{m,n}\,f_{n,m}) \circ (\Phi\,f_{n,m}\,f_{m,n}) \circ (\Phi\,i_m\,r_m)$$
$$= \quad \{\text{by (11.22)}\}$$
$$i_{m+1} \circ (\Phi\,(i_m \circ f_{n,m} \circ f_{m,n})\,(f_{n,m} \circ f_{m,n} \circ r_m))$$
$$\sqsubseteq \quad \{\text{by (11.37), (11.38) and (11.24)}\}$$
$$i_{m+1} \circ (\Phi\,(i_n \circ f_{m,n})\,(f_{n,m} \circ r_n))$$
$$= \quad \{\text{by (11.22)}\}$$
$$i_{m+1} \circ (\Phi\,f_{m,n}\,f_{n,m}) \circ (\Phi\,i_n\,r_n)$$
$$= \quad \{\text{by (11.29)}\}$$
$$i_{m+1} \circ f_{n+1,m+1} \circ (\Phi\,i_n\,r_n)$$
$$\sqsubseteq \quad \{\text{by (11.38)}\}$$
$$i_{n+1} \circ (\Phi\,i_n\,r_n)\,,$$

and similarly $m < n \Rightarrow (\Phi\,r_m\,i_m) \circ r_{m+1} \sqsubseteq (\Phi\,r_n\,i_n) \circ r_{n+1}$. So we get chains

$$\{i_{n+1} \circ (\Phi\,i_n\,r_n) \in (\Phi D D) \multimap D \mid n \in \mathbb{N}\}\,,$$
$$\{(\Phi\,r_n\,i_n) \circ r_{n+1} \in D \multimap (\Phi D D) \mid n \in \mathbb{N}\}\,,$$

both with empty support. Taking their joins we define

$$i \triangleq \bigsqcup \{i_{n+1} \circ (\Phi \, i_n \, r_n) \mid n \in \mathbb{N}\} \in (\Phi \, D \, D) \multimap D, \tag{11.44}$$

$$i' \triangleq \bigsqcup \{(\Phi \, r_n \, i_n) \circ r_{n+1} \mid n \in \mathbb{N}\} \in D \multimap (\Phi \, D \, D). \tag{11.45}$$

A calculation using (11.39), (11.22), (11.25), (11.42) and (11.21) shows that $i' \circ i = \mathrm{id}_{\Phi \, D \, D}$ and $i \circ i' = \mathrm{id}_D$. So i is indeed an isomorphism, with inverse i'.

Finally, the minimal invariant property $\mathrm{id}_D = \bigsqcup \{p_n \mid n \in \mathbb{N}\}$, where the p_n are as in (11.27), follows from (11.42) using the fact that $(\forall n) \, p_n = i_n \circ r_n$. The latter can be proved by induction on n, using (11.36), (11.41) and (11.43). $\qquad \square$

Remark 11.20 A minimal invariant object for a locally uniform-continuous functor is unique up to isomorphism: if $i : \Phi \, D \, D \cong D$ and $j : \Phi \, E \, E \cong E$ are both minimal invariants for $\Phi : \mathbf{Udcppo}_!^{op} \times \mathbf{Udcppo}_! \to \mathbf{Udcppo}_!$, then there is an isomorphism $f : D \cong E$ making the following square commute in $\mathbf{Udcppo}_!$:

$$
\begin{array}{ccc}
\Phi \, D \, D & \xrightarrow{\ i\ } & D \\
{\scriptstyle \Phi f^{-1} f} \downarrow & & \downarrow {\scriptstyle f} \\
\Phi \, E \, E & \xrightarrow[\ j\ ]{} & E.
\end{array}
$$

The proof of this fact is the same as in the classical case and is part of the more general fact, due to Freyd (1992), that a minimal invariant $i : \Phi \, D \, D \cong D$ is a 'free mixed variance algebra': for all $f \in E \multimap \Phi \, E' E$ and $f' \in \Phi \, E \, E' \multimap E'$, there exists unique $g \in E \multimap D$ and $g' \in D \multimap E'$ making the following two squares commute in $\mathbf{Udcppo}_!$:

$$
\begin{array}{ccc}
\Phi \, E' E & \xrightarrow{\ \Phi g' g\ } & \Phi \, D \, D \\
{\scriptstyle f} \uparrow & & \uparrow {\scriptstyle i^{-1}} \\
E & \xrightarrow[\ g\ ]{} & D
\end{array}
\qquad
\begin{array}{ccc}
\Phi \, D \, D & \xrightarrow{\ \Phi g g'\ } & \Phi \, E \, E' \\
{\scriptstyle i} \downarrow & & \downarrow {\scriptstyle f'} \\
D & \xrightarrow[\ g'\ ]{} & E'.
\end{array}
$$

See Abramsky and Jung (1994, theorem 5.3.9) for a proof of this.

11.5 Nominal Scott domains

An important feature of domain theory is that the denotation of a program with potentially infinite behaviour is given as the limit of finite approximations. We have discussed an appropriate notion of limit for nominal domain theory, namely joins of directed subsets that are uniformly supported. But we have yet to discuss *finiteness* of approximations, which in conventional domain theory is modelled by the property of being compact; see Abramsky and Jung (1994, definition 2.2.1). Here the obvious modification is to specialize from the use of directed subsets in the definition of compactness to directed subsets that are also uniformly supported. Doing so, one finds that the role of 'finite subset' has to be replaced by the more liberal notion of 'orbit-finite subset' from Section 5.4.

Definition 11.21   An element $u \in D$ of a udcpo D is *uniform-compact* if for all uniformly supported directed subsets $S \subseteq D$

$$u \sqsubseteq \bigsqcup S \Rightarrow (\exists d \in S)\, u \sqsubseteq d. \tag{11.46}$$

We write KD for the set of uniform-compact elements of D; note that it is an equivariant subset of D and hence is a nominal poset when equipped with the partial order from D. We say that D is an *algebraic* udcpo if each of its elements is the join of a uniformly supported directed subset of KD; it is ω-*algebraic* if the underlying set of KD is countable.

Example 11.22   We saw in Theorem 5.31 that if X is a nominal set, then $(P_{\mathrm{fs}} X, \subseteq)$ is an algebraic udcpo with $K(P_{\mathrm{fs}} X) = P_{\mathrm{of}} X$, the nominal poset of orbit-finite subsets of X. In view of Proposition 5.25, if X is countable then so is $P_{\mathrm{of}} X$ and hence $P_{\mathrm{fs}} X$ is ω-algebraic.

Remark 11.23   Recall that a subset $S \subseteq D$ of a (nominal) poset is directed if every finite subset of S has an upper bound in S. The theme of this section is that for a useful nominal domain theory, one should replace 'finite' by 'orbit-finite'. So one might wonder why we did not use a stricter form of directedness in Definition 11.21, one for which orbit-finite subsets have upper bounds. In fact this coincides with the usual notion of being directed, so long as S is uniformly supported; see Exercise 11.4.

   In order to get a cartesian closed category of domains and continuous functions from algebraic dcpos one needs to impose some extra conditions, such as existence of joins for all subsets with an upper bound – which gives the notion of a Scott domain (Abramsky and Jung, 1994, p. 56). In the current setting this gives the following notion of nominal domain.

Definition 11.24   A *nominal Scott domain* is by definition an ω-algebraic udcpo D with a least element and joins for all finitely supported subsets that have upper bounds. The category **Nsd** is the full subcategory of **Udcppo** that has nominal Scott domains for its objects.

Remark 11.25 Theorem 5.31 implies that a pointed ω-algebraic udcpo is a nominal Scott domain if it has joins for all orbit-finite subsets with upper bounds.

Proposition 11.26 *If D is a nominal Scott domain, then so is its nominal poset of name abstractions $[\mathbb{A}]D$ and*

$$K([\mathbb{A}]D) = \{\langle a \rangle u \mid a \in \mathbb{A} \wedge u \in KD\}. \tag{11.47}$$

Proof Suppose D is a nominal Scott domain. We know from Proposition 11.13 that $[\mathbb{A}]D$ is a pointed udcpo. To see that it has joins for all finitely supported subsets that have upper bounds, note that if $S \in P_{fs}([\mathbb{A}]D)$ is bounded above by $e \in [\mathbb{A}]D$, then picking $a \# (S, e)$, it is the case that $\{d \in D \mid \langle a \rangle d \in S\} \in P_{fs}D$ is bounded above by $e @ a \in D$; so we can apply Proposition 11.4.

Since every element of $[\mathbb{A}]D$ is of the form $\langle a \rangle d$ for some $a \in \mathbb{A}$ and $d \in D$, and since from Remark 11.6 $\langle a \rangle_- : D \to [\mathbb{A}]D$ is uniform-continuous, to see that $[\mathbb{A}]D$ is algebraic, it suffices to show that $\langle a \rangle_-$ preserves the property of being uniform-compact. But if $u \in KD$ and $\langle a \rangle u \sqsubseteq \bigsqcup S$ with S a uniformly supported directed subset of $[\mathbb{A}]D$, picking any $a' \# (a, d, S)$, then by (11.8)

$$(a\,a') \cdot u \sqsubseteq (\bigsqcup S) @ a' = \bigsqcup\{e @ a' \mid e \in S\}.$$

Since KD is an equivariant subset of D, $(a\,a') \cdot u$ is uniform-compact and hence for some $e \in S$ we have $(a\,a') \cdot u \sqsubseteq e @ a'$ and hence also

$$\langle a \rangle u = \langle a' \rangle (a\,a') \cdot u \sqsubseteq \langle a' \rangle (e @ a') = e.$$

Hence we do indeed have $\langle a \rangle u \in K([\mathbb{A}]D)$ when $u \in KD$.

So $[\mathbb{A}]D$ is an algebraic udcpo and $\{\langle a \rangle d \mid a \in \mathbb{A} \wedge d \in KD\} \subseteq K([\mathbb{A}]D)$. To see that $\{\langle a \rangle d \mid a \in \mathbb{A} \wedge d \in KD\}$ is the whole of $K([\mathbb{A}]D)$, it suffices to show that

$$e \in K([\mathbb{A}]D) \wedge a \# e \Rightarrow e @ a \in KD \tag{11.48}$$

and then apply Proposition 4.9. To prove (11.48), suppose $v \in K([\mathbb{A}]D)$, $a \# v$ and $v @ a \sqsubseteq \bigsqcup S$ with S uniformly supported and directed. Then by Proposition 4.9 and uniform-continuity of $\langle a \rangle_-$, we have $v = \langle a \rangle (v @ a) \sqsubseteq \langle a \rangle (\bigsqcup S) = \bigsqcup\{\langle a \rangle u \mid u \in S\}$; so since v is uniform-compact, $v \sqsubseteq \langle a \rangle u$ for some $u \in S$ and therefore $v @ a \sqsubseteq u$. So $v @ a$ is indeed uniform-compact.

Finally, note that (11.47) implies that $K([\mathbb{A}]D)$ is countable, because $\mathbb{A}$ and KD are. $\square$

Lemma 11.27 *Let D be a udcpo. If an orbit-finite subset of KD possesses a join in D, then that join is also uniform-compact.*

Proof Suppose $K \in P_{of}(KD)$ possesses a join and that $\bigsqcup K \sqsubseteq \bigsqcup S$ for some uniformly supported directed subset $S \subseteq D$. We have to show that $\bigsqcup K \sqsubseteq d$ holds for some $d \in S$. By Lemma 5.24 and Proposition 5.25, $K = \text{hull}_A F$ for some $A \in P_f \mathbb{A}$ with $\text{supp}\, S \subseteq A$ and some $F \in P_f(KD)$. Since $F \subseteq \text{hull}_A F = K$ we have $(\forall u \in F)\, u \sqsubseteq \bigsqcup K \sqsubseteq \bigsqcup S$; so since F is finite and S is directed, there exists $d \in S$ with

$$(\forall u \in F)\, u \sqsubseteq d. \tag{11.49}$$

By Lemma 5.28, $\text{supp}\, d \subseteq \text{supp}\, S$ and hence d is supported by A. From this and (11.49) it follows that every $u \in \text{hull}_A F$ satisfies $u \sqsubseteq d$ and hence that $\bigsqcup K = \bigsqcup \text{hull}_A F \sqsubseteq d$, as required. □

Proposition 11.28 **Nsd** *is a cartesian closed category.*

Proof In view of the fact that **Nsd** is a full subcategory of **Udcppo**, which is cartesian closed (Proposition 11.14), it suffices to show that nominal Scott domains are closed under finite products and exponentials in that category. Closure under finite products is straightforward (Exercise 11.6). So we concentrate on exponentials and show that if D and E are nominal Scott domains, then so is the udcpo $D \to E$ from (11.14).

First note that since E has joins of all finitely supported subsets with upper bounds, then so does $D \to E$. For if $S \in P_{fs}(D \to E)$ is bounded above by f, then for each $d \in D$, $\{s\, d \mid s \in S\}$ is bounded above by $f\, d$; hence the join of S is given by

$$\bigsqcup S = \lambda d \in D \to \bigsqcup \{s\, d \mid s \in S\}$$

which is indeed an element of $D \to E$. Note also that $D \to E$ has a least element, namely $\lambda x \in D \to \bot$. So it just remains to show that the pointed udcpo $D \to E$ is ω-algebraic.

We wish to show that each $f \in D \to E$ is the join of a uniformly supported directed set of uniform-compact elements of $D \to E$. As for ordinary Scott function domains, to describe the uniform-compact elements of $D \to E$, we make use of *step-functions* (see Abramsky and Jung, 1994, section 4, for example). For each $u \in KD$, $v \in KE$ and $d \in D$ define

$$(u \searrow v)\, d \triangleq \begin{cases} v & \text{if } u \sqsubseteq d, \\ \bot & \text{otherwise.} \end{cases} \tag{11.50}$$

It is not hard to see that $(u \searrow v) \in D \to E$ and that

$$(\forall f \in D \to E)\, (u \searrow v) \sqsubseteq f \Leftrightarrow v \sqsubseteq f\, u. \tag{11.51}$$

From this and the uniform-compactness of v it follows that $(u \searrow v) \in \mathrm{K}(D \to E)$. Given $f \in D \to E$, define

$$S_f \triangleq \{(u \searrow v) \mid u \in \mathrm{K}D \wedge v \in \mathrm{K}E \wedge (u \searrow v) \sqsubseteq f\} \subseteq \mathrm{K}(D \to E). \quad (11.52)$$

Any $F \in \mathrm{P}_{\mathrm{of}}(\mathrm{K}(D \to E))$ satisfying $F \subseteq S_f$ is bounded above by f and hence has a join; and by Lemma 11.27 that join is uniform-compact. So

$$S'_f \triangleq \{\bigsqcup F \mid F \in \mathrm{P}_{\mathrm{of}}(\mathrm{K}(D \to E)) \wedge F \subseteq S_f \wedge \operatorname{supp} F \subseteq \operatorname{supp} f\} \quad (11.53)$$

is a subset of $\mathrm{K}(D \to E)$ that is uniformly supported by $\operatorname{supp} f$ and is directed (since the union of finitely many orbit-finite subsets is again orbit-finite). Therefore it suffices to show that $f = \bigsqcup S'_f$. Clearly $\bigsqcup S'_f \sqsubseteq f$, by definition of S_f. So it suffices to show that $f \sqsubseteq \bigsqcup S'_f$, that is, $(\forall d \in D)\, f\, d \sqsubseteq (\bigsqcup S'_f)\, d$; and since D is algebraic, for this it suffices to show $(\forall u \in \mathrm{K}D)\, f\, u \sqsubseteq (\bigsqcup S'_f)\, u$. For any $u \in \mathrm{K}D$, since E is algebraic we have $f\, u = \bigsqcup V$ for some uniformly supported directed subset of $\mathrm{K}E$. So for each $v \in V$, by (11.51) $(u \searrow v) \in S_f$; hence $\operatorname{hull}_{\operatorname{supp} f}\{(u \searrow v)\} \subseteq S_f$ (since S_f is supported by $\operatorname{supp} f$) and thus $(u \searrow v) \sqsubseteq \bigsqcup \operatorname{hull}_{\operatorname{supp} f}\{(u \searrow v)\} \in S'_f$. Therefore $(u \searrow v) \sqsubseteq \bigsqcup S'_f$ and hence $v = (u \searrow v)\, u \sqsubseteq (\bigsqcup S'_f)\, u$. Since this is true for each $v \in V$, we get $f\, u = \bigsqcup V \sqsubseteq (\bigsqcup S'_f)\, u$, as required.

We have shown that $D \to E$ is an algebraic udcpo. So it only remains to show that it is actually ω-algebraic. Note that if we apply the proof in the above paragraph when f is actually uniform-compact, then we can conclude from $f = \bigsqcup S'_f$ that $f \in S'_f$ and hence (by Proposition 5.25) that $f = \bigsqcup \operatorname{hull}_A F$ with $A \in \mathrm{P}_f \mathbb{A}$ and F a finite subset of $\{(u \searrow v) \mid u \in \mathrm{K}D \wedge v \in \mathrm{K}E\}$. It follows from this that since $\mathrm{K}D$ and $\mathrm{K}E$ are countable, so is $\mathrm{K}(D \to E)$. $\qquad\square$

Example 11.29 If $X \in \mathbf{Nom}$ has a countable underlying set, then the flat udcpo $X_\perp$ (Example 11.11) is a nominal Scott domain. In particular we have nominal Scott domains of booleans $\mathbb{B}_\perp$, numbers $\mathbb{N}_\perp$ and names $\mathbb{A}_\perp$. The latter has interesting compactness properties that are exploited by Lösch and Pitts (2013) to get an analogue for nominal Scott domains of the classic full abstraction result of of Plotkin (1977). For example, for each $f \in \mathbb{A}_\perp \to \mathbb{B}_\perp$ consider the following form of existential quantification:

$$exists_\mathbb{A} f \triangleq \begin{cases} \text{true} & \text{if } (\exists a \in \mathbb{A})\, f\, a = \text{true}, \\ \text{false} & \text{if } (\forall a \in \mathbb{A})\, f\, a = \text{false}, \\ \perp & \text{otherwise}. \end{cases} \quad (11.54)$$

Picking any $a \in \mathbb{A}$, one can show that $exists_\mathbb{A}$ is equal to

$$\bigsqcup \operatorname{hull}_\emptyset\{((a \searrow \text{true}) \searrow \text{true}), (\bigsqcup \operatorname{hull}_\emptyset\{(a \searrow \text{false})\} \searrow \text{false})\}.$$

Hence as in the proof of Proposition 11.28 we have that *exists*$_\mathbb{A}$ is not only uniform-continuous, but is also a uniform-compact element of $(\mathbb{A}_\perp \to \mathbb{B}_\perp) \to \mathbb{B}_\perp$. Note that the corresponding functional for $\mathbb{N}_\perp$ is not even continuous.

The topic of nominal Scott domains is a relatively recent one and much of their theory remains to be investigated. For example, there should be a nominal version of the 'information systems' of Scott (1982), with the role of finiteness replaced by orbit-finiteness; and, more generally, a 'nominal domain theory in logical form' extending the work of Abramsky (1991).

Exercises

11.1 Show that for udcpos, the operations of lifting (Example 11.11) and name abstraction (Proposition 11.13) commute up to isomorphism:

$$[\mathbb{A}](D_\perp) \cong ([\mathbb{A}]D)_\perp.$$

11.2 Prove that the functions $f \mapsto [\mathbb{A}]f$ in (11.28) are uniform-continuous.

11.3 Investigate whether the separated product of nominal sets (Section 3.4) extends to a construction on uniform directed complete posets.

11.4 Suppose D is a nominal poset and $S \subseteq D$ is a uniformly supported and directed subset. Show that every orbit-finite subset of S has an upper bound in S. [Hint: use Proposition 5.25 and Lemma 5.28.]

11.5 Show that a nominal Scott domain possesses meets of all non-empty, finitely supported subsets (*cf.* Exercise 7.1).

11.6 Show that if $D, E \in$ **Udcppo** are nominal Scott domains, then so is their product $D \times E$ and that $K(D \times E) = (KD) \times (KE)$.

11.7 For each atomic name $a \in \mathbb{A}$, consider the function $eq_a : \mathbb{A}_\perp \to \mathbb{B}_\perp$ given by

$$eq_a\, d \triangleq \begin{cases} \text{true} & \text{if } d = a, \\ \text{false} & \text{if } d \in \mathbb{A} - \{a\}, \\ \perp & \text{if } d = \perp, \end{cases}$$

for each $d \in \mathbb{A}_\perp$. Show that $eq_a = \bigsqcup \text{hull}_{\{a\}}\{(a \searrow \text{true}), (a' \searrow \text{false})\}$, where a' is any atomic name not equal to a. Deduce that eq_a is a uniform-compact element of the nominal Scott domain $\mathbb{A}_\perp \to \mathbb{B}_\perp$.

12

Computational logic

The development of the mathematical properties of nominal sets has from the outset gone hand-in-hand with axiomatizing the properties of the key notions – permutation action, support, freshness and name abstraction – within various kinds of logic. Table 12.1 gives some pointers to the literature on nominal logics. In this chapter we concentrate on computational aspects of these logics. More specifically, we take a brief look at algorithms for solving equations over nominal algebraic data types. This has led to various forms of term rewriting and logic programming with syntactic data involving binders.

Table 12.1 Nominal logics.

Set theory	Gabbay (2000); Gabbay and Pitts (2002).
Higher-order logic	Gabbay (2002); Urban (2008).
First-order logic	Pitts (2003); Gabbay and Cheney (2004); Cheney (2005b); Gabbay and Mathijssen (2008).
Equational logic	Clouston and Pitts (2007); Mathijssen (2007); Fiore and Hur (2008b); Clouston (2009); Gabbay and Mathijssen (2009); Kurz *et al.* (2010).
Constructive type theory	Schöpp and Stark (2004); Schöpp (2006); Westbrook (2008); Westbrook *et al.* (2009); Cheney (2012).

12.1 Unification

Unification is the process of finding a substitution of terms for variables that satisfies a given set of equations involving those variables; see Baader and Nipkow (1998), for example. Making precise what are the terms and what it means for a substitution to satisfy an equation leads to many different notions

240

of unification. The classic example (Robinson, 1965) is for terms over an algebraic signature and where satisfaction means syntactic identity. Here we look at an extension of this to the nominal algebraic signatures of Section 8.1, called *nominal unification* by Urban *et al.* (2004).

Example 12.1 (Urban *et al.*, 2004, section 1.2) Consider the following equational problems over the nominal algebraic signature for untyped λ-terms from Example 8.4, where $x, y \in \mathbb{A}_{\mathtt{Var}}$ are distinct atomic names of name-sort $\mathtt{Var}$:

$$L(x . L(y . A(t_1 , V y))) =_\alpha L(y . L(x . A(V x , t_1))), \qquad (12.1)$$

$$L(x . L(y . A(t_2 , V y))) =_\alpha L(y . L(x . A(V x , t_3))), \qquad (12.2)$$

$$L(x . L(y . A(V y , t_4))) =_\alpha L(y . L(x . A(V x , t_5))), \qquad (12.3)$$

$$L(x . L(y . A(V y , t_6))) =_\alpha L(x . L(x . A(V x , t_7))). \qquad (12.4)$$

In the first case the problem is to find a raw term t_1 that makes the left- and right-hand sides of (12.1) α-equivalent (Definition 8.6). In fact there is no such t_1, because if there were, then from (12.1) and the definition of $=_\alpha$ we deduce that

$$A((w\,y)(z\,x) \cdot t_1 , V w) =_\alpha A(V w , (w\,x)(z\,y) \cdot t_1),$$

where $z, w \mathbin{\#} (x, y, t_1)$ and $z \neq w$; hence we would have to have

$$(w\,y)(z\,x) \cdot t_1 =_\alpha V w \;\wedge\; V w =_\alpha (w\,x)(z\,y) \cdot t_1,$$

which implies

$$V y = (x\,z)(y\,w) \cdot V w =_\alpha t_1 =_\alpha (y\,z)(x\,w) \cdot V w = V x,$$

contradicting the assumption that $y \neq x$.

The second problem above asks whether there are raw terms t_2 and t_3 that make (12.2) a valid α-equivalence. In this case, applying the same kind of reasoning about $=_\alpha$ as above, one finds that there is a unique solution, namely $t_2 = V y$ and $t_3 = V x$.

The third problem (12.3) can be solved by taking t_4 to be $(x\,y) \cdot t_5$, for any raw term t_5. And the fourth problem (12.4) can be solved by taking t_6 to be $(x\,y) \cdot t_7$, for any raw term t_7 satisfying $y \notin \mathrm{fn}\, t_7$.

We will see that it is always possible to decide whether or not such 'equations modulo α-equivalence' over a nominal algebraic signature can be solved. In the case that such a problem can be solved, one would like also to have an explicit description of all solutions. To get that, we extend the language of raw terms from Definition 8.2 to include variables X ranging over unknown terms (of each data-sort). However, as the solution to problems (12.3) and (12.4)

$$\frac{a \in \mathbb{A_N}}{a : N} \qquad \frac{t : S \qquad op : S \to D}{op\, t : D} \qquad \frac{}{() : 1} \qquad \frac{t_1 : S_1 \qquad t_2 : S_2}{t_1 , t_2 : S_1 , S_2}$$

$$\frac{a \in \mathbb{A_N} \qquad t : S}{a \,.\, t : N \,.\, S} \qquad \frac{\pi \in \text{Perm}_s \, \mathbb{A} \qquad X \in Var_D}{\pi * X : D}$$

Figure 12.1 Nominal terms.

suggests, we also need to include syntax for explicitly permuting some atomic names in a yet-to-be-determined solution term. This leads to the following definition of nominal terms with variables.

Definition 12.2 Let Σ be a nominal algebraic signature (Definition 8.2). We fix a sorting $s : \mathbb{A} \to Nsort$ (Section 4.7) of the set $\mathbb{A}$ of atomic names that partitions it into disjoint, countably infinite subsets $\mathbb{A_N}$ as N ranges over the signature's name-sorts. We also fix a countably infinite set *Var* of *variables*, partitioned into disjoint, countably infinite subsets Var_D as D ranges over the signature's data-sorts.[1] The (open) *nominal terms* over Σ are inductively defined by the rules in Figure 12.1, where we write $t : S$ to indicate that t is a nominal term of sort S. (Recall from (8.2) how the sorts of Σ are defined.)

Nominal terms of the form $\pi * X$ are called *suspensions*, to indicate that the effect of the permutation π is suspended until we know more about the unknown X, for example by making a substitution for X. A *substitution* σ is defined to be a function from variables to nominal terms that is sort-respecting ($\sigma X : D$, if $X \in Var_D$) and finitely supported in the sense that σX is equal to the suspension id $* X$ for all but finitely many variables X. The result of applying a substitution σ to a nominal term t is denoted by σt and defined in Figure 12.2. This makes use of an auxiliary definition of an action $\pi * t$ of a (well-sorted, finite) permutation $\pi \in \text{Perm}_s \, \mathbb{A}$ on a nominal term t. It is not hard to see that if $t : S$, then $\sigma t : S$ and $\pi * t : S$. There is another permutation action on nominal terms that we need to use, written $\pi, t \mapsto \pi \cdot t$; see (12.8).

Notation 12.3 We will usually write the trivial suspension id $* X$ just as X. With that notation, the *domain* of a substitution σ is by definition the finite set

$$\text{dom}\, \sigma \triangleq \{X \in Var \mid \sigma X \neq X\}. \tag{12.5}$$

If it consists of the distinct variables $X_1, \ldots, X_n$ and $\sigma X_i = t_i$ for $i = 1, \ldots, n$, then we sometimes write σ as $[X_1 := t_1, \ldots, X_n := t_n]$.

---

[1] The use of variables of name- as well as data-sort is discussed below in Remark 12.15.

$$\sigma\, a = a$$
$$\sigma\,(\mathrm{op}\, t) = \mathrm{op}\,(\sigma\, t)$$
$$\sigma\,() = ()$$
$$\sigma\,(t_1\,,\, t_2) = (\sigma\, t_1)\,,\, (\sigma\, t_2)$$
$$\sigma\,(a\,.\, t) = a\,.\, (\sigma\, t)$$
$$\sigma\,(\pi X) = \pi * (\sigma\, t)$$

$$\pi * a = \pi\, a$$
$$\pi * (\mathrm{op}\, t) = \mathrm{op}\,(\pi * t)$$
$$\pi * () = ()$$
$$\pi * (t_1\,,\, t_2) = (\pi * t_1)\,,\, (t_2 * t_2)$$
$$\pi * (a\,.\, t) = (\pi\, a)\,.\, (\pi * t)$$
$$\pi * (\pi' * X) = (\pi \circ \pi') * X$$

Figure 12.2 Substitution and permutation action for nominal terms.

Remark 12.4 The finite set $\mathrm{var}\, t$ of variables occurring in a nominal term is defined as expected:

$$
\begin{aligned}
&\mathrm{var}\, a = \mathrm{var}\,() = \emptyset,\\
&\mathrm{var}\,(\mathrm{op}\, t) = \mathrm{var}\,(a\,.\, t) = \mathrm{var}\, t,\\
&\mathrm{var}\,(t_1\,,\, t_2) = \mathrm{var}\, t_1 \cup \mathrm{var}\, t_2,\\
&\mathrm{var}\,(\pi * X) = \{X\}.
\end{aligned}
\tag{12.6}
$$

What is the finite set of atomic names occurring in a nominal term? Nominal terms are 'raw', that is, not quotiented by any notion of α-equivalence associated with the binding construct $a, t \mapsto a\,.\, t$. So we should collect both a and the names in t when collecting the names occurring in $a\,.\, t$; *cf.* (8.4). However, the notion of 'name occurrence' is not entirely trivial, because we have used a slightly more abstract definition of 'nominal term' than occurs in the literature (Urban *et al.*, 2004). Specifically, in Definition 12.2 we used finite permutations (which are infinite sets with a certain finiteness property), rather than some finite representation of them. We know from Theorem 1.15 that every finite permutation can be represented by a list of pairs of atomic names whose corresponding transpositions compose to give the permutation. So we get a more conventional syntax for nominal terms if we define suspensions u by

$$u ::= X \mid (a\, b) * u, \tag{12.7}$$

where a and b range over atomic names of the same sort; and for this syntax the notion of an occurrence of an atomic name is straightforward. As it stands, from all that we have seen so far in this book, it makes sense to take 'a occurs in $\pi * X$' to mean a is in supp π, where Perm$_s$ A is regarded as a nominal set as in Lemma 2.21, so that supp $\pi = \{a \in \mathbb{A} \mid \pi a \neq a\}$.

Note that nominal terms t that are *closed* in the sense that var $t = \emptyset$ holds, are the same thing as the raw terms over a nominal algebraic signature used in Chapter 8. In that chapter we made use of the fact that raw terms are the elements of a nominal set, once one endows them with a permutation action as in (8.3). There are two ways (at least) to extend this permutation action to open nominal terms. The first way uses the conjugation action for permutations (Example 1.6): we define $\pi \cdot t$ as follows:

$$
\begin{aligned}
\pi \cdot a &= \pi a, \\
\pi \cdot (\text{op } t) &= \text{op} (\pi \cdot t), \\
\pi \cdot () &= () \\
\pi \cdot (t_1 , t_2) &= (\pi \cdot t_1) , (\pi \cdot t_2), \\
\pi \cdot (a . t) &= (\pi a) . (\pi \cdot t), \\
\pi \cdot (\pi' * X) &= (\pi \circ \pi' \circ \pi^{-1}) * X.
\end{aligned}
\tag{12.8}
$$

We have seen that the conjugation action on permutations makes Perm$_s$ A into a nominal set (Lemma 2.21); and from this it follows that the above action makes the collection of open nominal terms into a nominal set as well. Recalling the notational convention that X stands for the nominal term id $* X$, the $\pi' = $ id case of the last clause in (12.8) is $\pi \cdot X = X$. Therefore the use of this action implies that variables stand for nominal algebraic terms with empty support. This is not sufficiently general: we wish to substitute terms with free names (and with variables) for variables. Accordingly we make use of another action for permutations, given by composition, and take

$$
\pi * (\pi' * X) = (\pi \circ \pi') * X.
\tag{12.9}
$$

This is one of the base cases in the structurally recursive definition of the function $\pi, t \mapsto \pi * t$ in Figure 12.2. It is not hard to see that this does define a Perm$_s$ A-action. However, it does not make nominal terms into the elements of a nominal set – in general we do not have the finite support property with respect to this action (see Exercise 2.8). Nevertheless, as the solution to problem (12.4) indicates, we need to work with the complement of support, that is, freshness. We do so by making hypothetical freshness assumptions ∇ about variables and then deducing the consequent freshness properties of open nominal terms t.

$$\frac{a \neq a'}{\nabla \vdash a \mathrel{\#} a'} \qquad \frac{\nabla \vdash a \mathrel{\#} t}{\nabla \vdash a \mathrel{\#} \mathrm{op}\, t} \qquad \frac{}{\nabla \vdash a \mathrel{\#} ()} \qquad \frac{\nabla \vdash a \mathrel{\#} t_1 \qquad \nabla \vdash a \mathrel{\#} t_2}{\nabla \vdash a \mathrel{\#} t_1 , t_2}$$

$$\frac{}{\nabla \vdash a \mathrel{\#} a . t} \qquad \frac{\nabla \vdash a \mathrel{\#} t \qquad a \neq a'}{\nabla \vdash a \mathrel{\#} a' . t} \qquad \frac{(\pi^{-1}a, X) \in \nabla)}{\nabla \vdash a \mathrel{\#} \pi X}$$

Figure 12.3 Hypothetical freshness.

Definition 12.5 A *freshness environment* ∇ is a finite subset of $\mathbb{A} \times Var$. We think of its elements (a, X) as *freshness constraints* on what may be substituted for X, namely terms not containing a as a free atomic name. We sometimes write an element $(a, X) \in \nabla$ as $a \mathrel{\#} X$. The freshness constraints on variables that are present in a freshness environment generate freshness properties for nominal terms involving those variables. These are captured by judgements of the following form:

$$\nabla \vdash a \mathrel{\#} t, \tag{12.10}$$

which are inductively defined by the rules in Figure 12.3.

Next we extend the definition of $=_\alpha$ in Section 8.2 to a relation of α-equivalence for open nominal terms over a given nominal algebraic signature. Since α-equivalence depends upon freshness and we have seen that the latter may depend upon freshness constraints on variables, it is not surprising that α-equivalence does too. So we use a judgement of the form

$$\nabla \vdash t \approx t', \tag{12.11}$$

where ∇ is a freshness environment and t, t' are nominal terms of the same sort; it is inductively defined by the rules in Figure 12.4. Note that the last rule in the figure has only finitely many hypotheses, because π and π' are finite permutations and hence

$$\{a \in \mathbb{A} \mid \pi a \neq \pi' a\} = \{a \in \mathbb{A} \mid a \neq (\pi^{-1} \circ \pi') a\} = \mathrm{supp}\,(\pi^{-1} \circ \pi')$$

is a finite set of atomic names. (We regard $\mathrm{Perm}_s\, \mathbb{A}$ as a nominal set as in Lemma 2.21, generalized in the obvious way to the case of many sorts of names.)

Example 12.6 If a, b are distinct atomic names of the same sort, then $\{c \in \mathbb{A} \mid \mathrm{id}\, c = (a\, b)\, c\} = \{a, b\}$ and hence

$$\{(a, X), (b, X)\} \vdash X \approx (a\, b) * X$$

$$\frac{}{\nabla \vdash a \approx a} \qquad \frac{\nabla \vdash t \approx t'}{\nabla \vdash \mathsf{op}\, t \approx \mathsf{op}\, t'} \qquad \frac{}{\nabla \vdash () \approx ()} \qquad \frac{\nabla \vdash t_1 \approx t_1' \qquad \nabla \vdash t_2 \approx t_2'}{\nabla \vdash t_1, t_2 \approx t_1', t_2'}$$

$$\frac{\nabla \vdash t \approx t'}{\nabla \vdash a\,.\,t \approx a\,.\,t'} \qquad \frac{\nabla \vdash t \approx (a\,a') * t' \qquad \nabla \vdash a \not\approx t' \qquad a \neq a'}{\nabla \vdash a\,.\,t \approx a'\,.\,t'}$$

$$\frac{(\forall a \in \mathbb{A})\, \pi a \neq \pi'a \Rightarrow (a, X) \in \nabla}{\nabla \vdash \pi * X \approx \pi' * X}$$

Figure 12.4 Hypothetical α-equivalence.

is derivable. Since $\{(a, X), (b, X)\} \vdash a \not\approx X$ is derivable from Figure 12.3, we get

$$\{(a, X), (b, X)\} \vdash a\,.\,X \approx b\,.\,X$$

On the other hand, it is not hard to see that there is no proof of $\emptyset \vdash a\,.\,X \approx b\,.\,X$ from the rules in Figures 12.3 and 12.4.

Remark 12.7 The above definition of $\approx$ follows the characterization of name abstraction given in Lemma 4.3. If one followed its defining property (4.7), one would replace the two rules for name abstraction terms in Figure 12.4 by the rule

$$\frac{\nabla \uplus \{(a'', X)\} \vdash (a\,a'') * t \approx (a'\,a'') * t'}{\nabla \vdash a\,.\,t \approx a'\,.\,t'},$$

where a'' does not occur in ∇, a, t, a', t'. Compared with this rule, an advantage of the rules in Figures 12.3 and 12.4 is that the freshness environment on the left-hand side of judgements does not change from hypotheses to conclusion. So in the same way that variables have attached sorting information, one could dispense with the use of freshness environments entirely by attaching the freshness information directly to variables. This approach, and more, is taken in the *permissive nominal* theory of Dowek and Gabbay (2012); see Section 2.10. This has its own version of unification (Dowek *et al.*, 2010), which is somewhat closer in form to unification for first-order terms than the nominal unification described below.

Even though the presentation of $\approx$ differs from that of $=_\alpha$, it does extend that relation in the sense that if $t, t' \in \Sigma(\mathsf{S})$ are raw terms over Σ of the same sort S, then (they are nominal terms and) $\emptyset \vdash t \approx t'$ is derivable from the rules in Figure 12.4 iff $t =_\alpha t'$ holds (Definition 8.6). The proof of this can be found in Urban *et al.* (2004, proposition 2.16). We leave as an exercise the verification that $\approx$ is an equivalence relation, that $\#$ respects it, and that these relations are equivariant with respect to the $*$-action; see Exercise 12.1.

We can express the kind of problems illustrated by Example 12.1 in terms of the relations $\#$ and $\approx$ on open nominal terms. For example, (12.4) becomes the problem

$$L(a \cdot L(b \cdot A(\nabla b , X))) \; ?\!\approx_? \; L(a \cdot L(a \cdot A(\nabla a , Y)))$$

and it is solved by the substitution $[X := (b \; a) * Y]$ and the freshness environment $\{(b, Y)\}$, because

$$\{(b, Y)\} \vdash L(a \cdot L(b \cdot A(\nabla b , (b \; a) * Y))) \approx L(a \cdot L(a \cdot A(\nabla a , Y)))$$

is derivable. Note that solving such equational problems may involve solving freshness problems, because the rules in Figure 12.4 depend upon those in Figure 12.3. In building up a solution we may need to compose substitutions: $\sigma' \circ \sigma$ is the substitution that maps each $X \in Var$ to the result of applying the substitution σ' to the nominal term σX:

$$(\sigma' \circ \sigma) X \triangleq \sigma' (\sigma X). \tag{12.12}$$

We also extend the freshness and equality judgements from individual nominal terms to substitutions:

$$\nabla \vdash \sigma \nabla' \triangleq (\forall (a, X) \in \nabla') \, \nabla \vdash a \# \sigma X, \tag{12.13}$$

$$\nabla \vdash \sigma \approx \sigma' \triangleq (\forall X \in \mathrm{dom}\,\sigma \cup \mathrm{dom}\,\sigma') \, \nabla \vdash \sigma X \approx \sigma'X. \tag{12.14}$$

Definition 12.8 A *nominal unification problem P* over a nominal algebraic signature is a finite set of atomic problems, each of which is either an *equational problem*

$$t \; ?\!\approx_? \; t',$$

where t and t' are nominal terms of the same sort over the signature, or a *freshness problem*

$$a \; \#_? \; t,$$

where a is an atomic name and t a term over the signature. A *solution* for P consists of a pair (∇, σ) where ∇ is a freshness environment and σ is a substitution satisfying:

- $\nabla \vdash a \# \sigma t$ holds for each freshness problem $a \; \#_? \; t$ in P;
- $\nabla \vdash \sigma t \approx \sigma t'$ holds for each equational problem $t \; ?\!\approx_? \; t'$ in P.

$$\{a \;{}_?\!\approx_?\; a\} \uplus P \xrightarrow{\text{id}} P$$

$$\{\mathrm{op}\, t \;{}_?\!\approx_?\; \mathrm{op}\, t'\} \uplus P \xrightarrow{\text{id}} \{t \;{}_?\!\approx_?\; t'\} \cup P$$

$$\{() \;{}_?\!\approx_?\; ()\} \uplus P \xrightarrow{\text{id}} P$$

$$\{t_1 , t_2 \;{}_?\!\approx_?\; t'_1 , t'_2\} \uplus P \xrightarrow{\text{id}} \{t_1 \;{}_?\!\approx_?\; t'_1, t_2 \;{}_?\!\approx_?\; t'_2\} \cup P$$

$$\{a . t \;{}_?\!\approx_?\; a . t'\} \uplus P \xrightarrow{\text{id}} \{t \;{}_?\!\approx_?\; t'\} \cup P$$

$$\{a . t \;{}_?\!\approx_?\; a' . t'\} \uplus P \xrightarrow{\text{id}} \{t \;{}_?\!\approx_?\; (a\,a') * t', a \;\#_?\; t'\} \cup P \quad \text{if } a \neq a'$$

$$\{\pi * X \;{}_?\!\approx_?\; \pi' * X\} \uplus P \xrightarrow{\text{id}} \{a \;\#_?\; X \mid \pi a \neq \pi'a\} \cup P$$

$$\{\pi * X \;{}_?\!\approx_?\; t'\} \uplus P \xrightarrow{\sigma} \sigma P \quad \text{if } X \notin \mathrm{var}\, t', \text{ where } \sigma \triangleq [X := \pi^{-1} * t']$$

$$\{t \;{}_?\!\approx_?\; \pi' * X\} \uplus P \xrightarrow{\sigma} \sigma P \quad \text{if } X \notin \mathrm{var}\, t, \text{ where } \sigma \triangleq [X := \pi'^{-1} * t]$$

Figure 12.5 Transforming equality problems.

The pair (∇, σ) is a *most general* solution for P if given any other solution (∇', σ'), then there is a substitution σ'' satisfying $\nabla' \vdash \sigma'' \nabla$ and $\nabla' \vdash \sigma'' \circ \sigma \approx \sigma'$. A solution (∇, σ) for P is *idempotent* provided $\nabla \vdash \sigma \circ \sigma \approx \sigma$.

Theorem 12.9 *It is decidable whether or not a nominal unification problem P over any nominal algebraic signature Σ has a solution. Furthermore, if P does have a solution, then a most general and idempotent one exists.*

Proof Urban *et al.* (2004) prove the correctness of an algorithm for deciding nominal unification problems based upon the use of transitions between problems labelled with either substitutions or freshness environments: $P \xrightarrow{\sigma} P'$, $P \xrightarrow{\nabla} P'$. The algorithm either fails, when the problem has no solution, or produces a most general idempotent solution. We describe the algorithm and refer the reader to their paper for the proof of its correctness.

In a first phase, the algorithm simplifies the equational subproblems in a problem P by using repeatedly the transitions in Figure 12.5. (In the last two transitions, σP is the problem that results from applying the substitution σ to all nominal terms occurring in the problem P.) A simple measure on the size of problems (Urban *et al.*, 2004, lemma 3.2) shows that this process must terminate after a finite number of steps, resulting in a sequence of the form $P \xrightarrow{\sigma_1} \cdots \xrightarrow{\sigma_n} P'$, where no substitution-labelled transitions are possible from P'. If P' still contains equational subproblems, then the algorithm signals failure. Otherwise it enters a second phase in which the freshness problems in P' are simplified using as many of the transformations in Figure 12.6 as possible,

$$\{a \mathrel{\#_?} a'\} \uplus P \xrightarrow{\emptyset} P \quad \text{if } a \neq a'$$

$$\{a \mathrel{\#_?} \text{op } t\} \uplus P \xrightarrow{\emptyset} \{a \mathrel{\#_?} t\} \cup P$$

$$\{a \mathrel{\#_?} ()\} \uplus P \xrightarrow{\emptyset} P$$

$$\{a \mathrel{\#_?} t_1 , t_2\} \uplus P \xrightarrow{\emptyset} \{a \mathrel{\#_?} t_1, a \mathrel{\#_?} t_2\} \cup P$$

$$\{a \mathrel{\#_?} a . t\} \uplus P \xrightarrow{\emptyset} P$$

$$\{a \mathrel{\#_?} a' . t\} \uplus P \xrightarrow{\emptyset} \{a \mathrel{\#_?} t\} \cup P \quad \text{if } a \neq a'$$

$$\{a \mathrel{\#_?} \pi * X\} \uplus P \xrightarrow{\nabla} P \quad \text{where } \nabla \triangleq \{(\pi^{-1}a, X)\}$$

Figure 12.6 Transforming freshness problems.

in any order. Once again, this process must terminate after a finite number of steps, resulting in a sequence of the form $P' \xrightarrow{\nabla_1} \cdots \xrightarrow{\nabla_m} P''$, where no freshness-environment-labelled transitions are possible from P''. If P'' is not empty, then the algorithm signals failure. Otherwise it returns $(\nabla_1 \cup \cdots \cup \nabla_m, \sigma_n \circ \cdots \circ \sigma_1)$, which is provably an idempotent most general solution for the original problem P. $\qquad\qquad\qquad\qquad\qquad\qquad\qquad\qquad\qquad\qquad\qquad\qquad\qquad\qquad\Box$

Example 12.10 If we apply the above algorithm to the problem corresponding to (12.1), we get the following sequence of transitions:

$$\{L(a . L(b . A(X , V b))) \mathrel{?\approx_?} L(b . L(a . A(V a , X)))\}$$

$\xrightarrow{\text{id}}$

$$\{a . L(b . A(X , V b)) \mathrel{?\approx_?} b . L(a . A(V a , X))\}$$

$\xrightarrow{\text{id}}$

$$\{L(b . A(X , V b)) \mathrel{?\approx_?} L(b . A(V b , (a b) * X)),$$
$$a \mathrel{\#_?} L(a . A(V a , X))\}$$

$(\xrightarrow{\text{id}})^3$

$$\{X \mathrel{?\approx_?} V b, V b \mathrel{?\approx_?} (a b) * X, a \mathrel{\#_?} L(a . A(V a , X))\}$$

$\xrightarrow{[X := V b]}$

$$\{V b \mathrel{?\approx_?} V a, a \mathrel{\#_?} L(a . A(V a , V b))\}$$

$\xrightarrow{\text{id}}$

$$\{b \mathrel{?\approx_?} a, a \mathrel{\#_?} L(a . A(V a , V b))\}$$

FAIL ,

and indeed the problem has no solution. If we apply the algorithm to the problem corresponding to (12.4), we get the following sequence of transitions:

$$\{L(a \cdot L(b \cdot A(V b , X))) _? \approx_? L(a \cdot L(a \cdot A(V a , Y)))\}$$

$$(\overset{\text{id}}{\rightarrow})^3$$

$$\{b \cdot A(V b , X) _? \approx_? a \cdot A(V a , Y)\}$$

$$\overset{\text{id}}{\rightarrow}$$

$$\{A(V b , X) _? \approx_? A(V b , (b a) * Y), b \,\#_? A(V a , Y)\}$$

$$(\overset{\text{id}}{\rightarrow})^3$$

$$\{X _? \approx_? (b a) * Y, b \,\#_? A(V a , Y)\}$$

$$\overset{[X:=(b a)*Y]}{\rightarrow}$$

$$\{b \,\#_? A(V a , Y)\}$$

$$\overset{\emptyset}{\rightarrow}$$

$$\{b \,\#_? V a, b \,\#_? Y\}$$

$$(\overset{\emptyset}{\rightarrow})^2$$

$$\{b \,\#_? Y\}$$

$$\overset{\{(b,Y)\}}{\rightarrow}$$

$$\emptyset,$$

and indeed $(\{(b, Y)\}, [X := (b a) * Y])$ is an idempotent most general solution for the problem.

The naive algorithm given in the proof of Theorem 12.9 makes the proof of correctness (Urban *et al.*, 2004, theorem 3.7) relatively easy; but its running time can be exponential in the size of the problem. Calvès and Fernández (2008) describe a polynomial-time algorithm based on a graph representation of nominal terms with lazy propagation of action of permutations. Currently the best-known nominal unification algorithms are quadratic (Calvès, 2010; Levy and Villaret, 2010). There are also interesting connections between nominal unification and *higher-order pattern unification* (Miller, 1991; Nipkow, 1993). Cheney (2005a) reduces the latter to nominal unification and, more subtly, Levy and Villaret (2012) give a quadratic-time reduction in the other direction.

12.2 Term rewriting

The standard notion of term rewriting system for first-order terms (Terese, 2003) has been generalized to nominal terms by Fernández *et al.* (2004). Fixing a nominal algebraic signature, a *nominal rewrite rule* takes the form

$$\nabla \vdash l \rightarrow r, \tag{12.15}$$

where ∇ is a freshness environment (Definition 12.5), l, r are nominal terms over the signature, and we require that any variables occurring in ∇ or r already occur in l:

$$\text{var}(\nabla, t) \subseteq \text{var}\, l. \tag{12.16}$$

This requirement on variable occurrences is similar to the one imposed in ordinary term rewriting (var $r \subseteq$ var l), extended to accomodate the fact that equality of open nominal terms ($\approx$) in general involves hypothetical freshness constraints.

Example 12.11 Let Σ be the nominal algebraic signature obtained from the one for untyped λ-calculus in Example 8.4 by adding an operation symbol sub : Var . Term , Term $\to$ Term for explicit substitution. The intention is that a nominal term of the form $\text{sub}(a \,.\, t \,,\, t')$ should rewrite to one representing the untyped λ-term resulting from the capture-avoiding substitution of the λ-term represented by t' for all free occurrences of the variable $V\,a$ in the λ-term represented by t. Accordingly, following nominal rewrite rules express properties of β-reduction (12.17) and capture-avoiding substitution (12.18)–(12.21) for λ-terms:

$$\emptyset \vdash \text{A}(\text{L}(a \,.\, X) \,,\, Y) \to \text{sub}(a \,.\, X \,,\, Y), \tag{12.17}$$

$$\{a \mathbin{\#} X\} \vdash \text{sub}(a \,.\, X \,,\, Y) \to X, \tag{12.18}$$

$$\emptyset \vdash \text{sub}(a \,.\, V\,a \,,\, Y) \to Y, \tag{12.19}$$

$$\{b \mathbin{\#} Y\} \vdash \text{sub}(a \,.\, \text{L}(b \,.\, X) \,,\, Y) \to \text{L}(b \,.\, \text{sub}(a \,.\, X \,,\, Y)), \tag{12.20}$$

$$\emptyset \vdash \text{sub}(a \,.\, \text{A}(X \,,\, X') \,,\, Y) \to \text{A}(\text{sub}(a \,.\, X \,,\, Y) \,,\, \text{sub}(a \,.\, X' \,.\, ,\, Y)). \tag{12.21}$$

Nominal rewrite rules (12.15) are used to transform nominal terms t by replacing occurrences in t of the left-hand term l by the right-hand term r. However, this only makes sense if the freshness constraints in ∇ are respected. Therefore rewrites operate on terms with freshness constraints. To deal with occurrences of a term in another term, we can use a distinguished variable in *Var*, written '$\_$' and let C range over nominal terms containing one occurrence of that variable; we call C a nominal term *context* and write $C[t]$ for the result of applying the substitution $[\_ := t]$ to C. If R is a set of nominal rewrite rules, ∇ is a freshness environment and s, t are nominal terms (over a fixed nominal algebraic signature), then

$$\nabla \vdash t \to_R t' \tag{12.22}$$

is defined to hold if there exist a nominal rewrite rule $(\nabla' \vdash l' \to r') \in R$, a substitution σ, a nominal term l and a context C such that

$$\mathrm{var}\,(l') \cap \mathrm{var}\,(\nabla, t) = \emptyset, \tag{12.23}$$

$$C[l] = t, \tag{12.24}$$

$$\nabla \vdash \sigma\nabla' \quad \text{and} \quad \nabla \vdash \sigma l' \approx l, \tag{12.25}$$

$$\nabla \vdash C[\sigma r'] \approx t'. \tag{12.26}$$

In words: the variables in the rewrite rule do not clash with those in the subject (12.23); the subject term t contains an occurrence of a term (12.24) that can be matched (12.25) with the freshness contraints and left-hand side of a rewrite rule in R; and after replacing the subterm with the right-hand side of the matched rewrite, up to α-equivalence we obtain the term t' (12.26).

Definition 12.12 The definition of the rewriting relation (12.22) makes use of *nominal matching*, a special case of nominal unification where, roughly speaking, only variables on the left-hand sides of equational problems get instantiated. More precisely, in this setting a *matching problem* takes the form

$$(\nabla' \vdash t') \; {}_?\!\approx (\nabla \vdash t), \tag{12.27}$$

where ∇, ∇' are freshness environments and t, t' are nominal terms over the given signature. A substitution σ solves the matching problem if

$$(\forall X \in \mathrm{var}(\nabla, t))\, \sigma X = X, \tag{12.28}$$

$$\nabla \vdash \sigma\nabla' \quad \text{and} \quad \nabla \vdash \sigma t' \approx t. \tag{12.29}$$

Calvès and Fernández (2010) give efficient algorithms for nominal matching. Fernández and Gabbay (2007) and Fernández and Rubio (2012) explore the properties of term rewriting based upon nominal terms and nominal matching and compare it with notions of rewriting based upon the use of λ-calculus to represent binders.

Remark 12.13 For conventional rewriting on first-order terms, it is usual to restrict attention to finite sets of rewrite rules. This is because each rewrite is 'schematic', in the sense that it stands for a potentially infinite collection of identities via the substitution of terms for its variables that occurs during matching.

However, in addition to variables, nominal terms feature atomic names and these are not instantiated during nominal matching. Yet when one gives a particular nominal rewrite rule it is likely that some or all of the atomic names it involves are schematic. For example, the five rules (12.17)–(12.21) make use of two particular distinct atomic names a and b; but we also want rules of the same shape obtained by permuting a and b to any other pair of distinct names.

The mathematically simple way of ensuring that is to require that in the nominal rewriting relation (12.22), R is a set of the form $\text{hull}_\emptyset F$, where F is a finite set of nominal rewrite rules; in other words R is equivariant and generated by applying permutations to a finite set of rules. (More generally, one might consider arbitrary orbit-finite subsets of rules, $\text{hull}_A F$.) Here we are regarding nominal rewrite rules as the elements of a nominal set via the action of permutations on nominal terms given by (12.8) and on freshness environments given by $\pi \cdot \nabla = \{(\pi a, X) \mid (a, X) \in \nabla\}$. So, for example, applying the 3-cycle $(a\ b\ c)$ to (12.20) yields the nominal rewrite rule

$$\{c \mathbin{\#} Y\} \vdash \mathsf{sub}(b \mathbin. \mathsf{L}(c \mathbin. X)\,,\, Y) \to \mathsf{L}(c \mathbin. \mathsf{sub}(b \mathbin. X\,,\, Y)).$$

Although mathematically straightforward, requiring nominal rewrite systems to be orbit-finite rather than actually finite complicates the algorithmic aspects of nominal term rewriting. If we are trying to compute a right-hand side for $\nabla \vdash C[l] \to_R$? when $R = \text{hull}_\emptyset F$, then we can look at each of the finitely many rules $\nabla' \vdash l \to r$ in F in turn; but in each case we have to search for a permutation π and solve the matching problem $(\pi \cdot \nabla', \pi \cdot l') \mathbin{?\approx} (\nabla, l)$. This has been called the *equivariant matching problem*. Similarly one can consider the *equivariant unification problem*: given nominal terms t and t', find a permutation π such that the nominal unification problem $\pi \cdot t \mathbin{?\approx?} t'$ is solvable. Cheney (2010) gives exponential-time algorithms for deciding these problems, but also shows that they are NP-complete problems.

It seems that this computationally expensive form of 'rewriting up to permutation of atomic names' can very often be avoided in practice. Fernández and Gabbay (2007) identify a class of nominal rewrite systems called the *closed* ones, for which all rewrites can be generated by first freshening the atomic names in a rule in the same way that one freshens variables (12.23) and then using the quadratic-time nominal matching algorithm. Roughly speaking, closed rules are ones that preserve abstracted atoms during rewriting (and Example 12.11 is an example of a closed nominal rewrite system). Evidence for the expressivity of closed systems is provided by Fernández *et al.* (2004), who encode *combinatory reduction systems* (Klop *et al.*, 1993) using closed nominal rewrite rules.

12.3 Logic programming

Unification of first-order terms is the key ingredient of the resolution proof method for first-order logic and of logic programming languages that are based upon it; see Apt (1990), for example. Adding name abstraction and freshness to first-order logic (Pitts, 2003; Gabbay and Cheney, 2004), there are resolution proof methods based upon nominal and equivariant unification that have been used as the basis of a Prolog-like logic programming language (Cheney and Urban, 2008). The motivations for such a language are similar to those for functional programming: to obtain the expressivity, abstractness and purity properties discussed at the start of Chapter 10 for logic programs that deal with syntactic data involving bound names and α-equivalence.

As a simple example of nominal resolution, we consider resolution-based proof search for elements of inductively defined subsets of the terms of a nominal algebraic data type. Given a nominal algebraic signature Σ, let P range over a finite set of *predicate symbols* standing for subsets of the various sorts of data specified by Σ. So we assume each P comes with a designated sort and consider *formulas* P t, where t is a nominal term (Figure 12.1) of the same sort as P. (Since nominal terms include pairing (t_1, t_2), we need only use such unary predicate symbols, rather than n-ary ones.) A *nominal inductive definition* over Σ is given by a set R of rule schemes (Section 7.1) of the form

$$\frac{\Phi \qquad \nabla}{\mathsf{P}\,t}, \tag{12.30}$$

where Φ is a finite set of formulas, P t is a formula, and ∇ is a freshness environment that acts as a set of side conditions restricting applicability of the rule. The intended meaning of R is the subset $[\![R]\!]$ of raw terms over Σ (Definition 8.2) inductively defined in the sense of Chapter 7 by all the closed substitution instances of the rule schemes in R.

Example 12.14 Let Σ be the nominal algebraic signature for the untyped λ-calculus from Example 8.4. Taking a single predicate symbol Sub of sort Var . Term , Term , Term, consider the following nominal inductive definition:

$$\frac{a \mathbin{\#} X}{\mathsf{Sub}(a\,.\,X\,,\,Y\,,\,X)} \qquad \frac{}{\mathsf{Sub}(a\,.\,\mathsf{V}\,a\,,\,Y\,,\,Y)}$$

$$\frac{\mathsf{Sub}(a\,.\,X\,,\,Y\,,\,Z) \qquad b \mathbin{\#} Y}{\mathsf{Sub}(a\,.\,\mathsf{L}(b\,.\,X)\,,\,Y\,,\,\mathsf{L}(b\,.\,Z))}$$

$$\frac{\mathsf{Sub}(a\,.\,X\,,\,Y\,,\,Z) \qquad \mathsf{Sub}(a\,.\,X'\,,\,Y\,,\,Z')}{\mathsf{Sub}(a\,.\,\mathsf{A}(X\,,\,X')\,,\,Y\,,\,\mathsf{A}(Z\,,\,Z'))}\ .$$

The intention is that Sub(a . t , t' , t'') should be provable iff t'' represents the untyped λ-term resulting from the capture-avoiding substitution of the λ-

term represented by t' for all free occurrences of the variable V a in the λ-term represented by t (cf. Example 12.11).

Given a set R of rules of the form (12.30), resolution based upon nominal unification transforms a query of the form (Φ, ∇) by picking a formula P $t \in \Phi$, picking a rule

$$\frac{\Phi' \quad \nabla'}{\mathrm{P}\,t'}$$

in R whose conclusion concerns the predicate P (and whose variables do not clash with those of (Φ, ∇)), and using nominal unification to find a solution to the problem $\{t\ {}_?\approx_?\ t'\} \cup \nabla \cup \nabla'$ (where we regard freshness environments as freshness problems in the obvious way); if a solution is found, (∇'', σ) say, then the query is transformed by removing P t, applying σ and adding $\sigma\,\Phi'$ and ∇''. This resolution method is sound, in the sense that starting with a query $(\{\mathrm{P}\,t\}, \emptyset)$ where t is closed, iterated resolution will eventually succeed in removing all the formulas only if t is in $[\![R]\!]$. However, Cheney (2004) shows that it is not complete. The reason is the same as discussed in Remark 12.13 and can be solved in the same way, by replacing nominal unification by the computationally more expensive equivariant unification algorithm in the resolution method.

Cheney and Urban (2008) develop these ideas into a Prolog-like programming language for nominal first-order logic called αProlog. They also identify a syntactic condition on αProlog programs that ensures completeness for resolution based upon nominal unification and which seems to encompass programs that arise in practice.

Lakin and Pitts (2009) focus on nominal inductive definitions rather than nominal logic and develop a higher-order functional logic programming language called αML. The language extends FreshML with a type of semi-decidable propositions and existential quantification for types with decidable equality; these features allow inductive definitions to be expressed as recursive function declarations. The operational semantics of αML involves a constraint satisfaction problem closely related to equivariant unification and of similar complexity (NP-complete). As its name suggests, αML is by design a member of the ML family of strongly typed functional programming languages. By contrast, the αKanren language of Byrd and Friedman (2007) provides nominal logic programming features within the context of the untyped functional language Scheme.

Remark 12.15 (**Variables of name-sort**) The *nominal terms* used in this chapter feature 'data variables', that is, variables for each data-sort in the given nominal algebraic signature. It is natural to consider also adding 'name variables', that is, variables of name-sort. Cheney (2004) and later Cheney and Urban (2008) use a syntax for nominal terms that features variables of name-sort. Since such variables can be substituted for, this avoids the need for orbit-finite hulls of finite rule sets in nominal logic programs (without avoiding a computational expense equivalent to that for equivariant unification, unfortunately). Lakin and Pitts (2009) go one step further and eliminate atomic names from the syntax of αML programs, relying entirely on variables of name sort together with freshness constraints between them to enforce distinctions. Arguably this corresponds to what happens in the vernacular of mathematical texts. For example, in this book we fixed upon a countably infinite set $\mathbb{A}$ of atomic names. Which particular set did we mean? For definiteness, we could take $\mathbb{A}$ to be the set $\mathbb{N} = \{0, 1, 2, 3, \ldots\}$ of natural numbers, but we never made use of that choice. Instead, we referred to elements of $\mathbb{A}$ via metavariables called $a, b, c, \ldots$ and used the normal convention that statements involving such metavariables are implicitly universally quantified, with explicit conditions on the metavariables such as $a \neq b$ added as necessary. This corresponds to the use in αML (Lakin and Pitts, 2009) of variables of name sort instead of atomic names. By contrast, the use of atomic names in the syntax of nominal terms corresponds to a vernacular in which metavariables of name sort are implicitly quantified using Ⅵ rather than $\forall$; so distinct metavariables always refer to distinct atomic names – what Jamie Gabbay terms the 'permutative convention' (Gabbay, 2011, section 1.3).

Exercises

12.1 Show that the judgements (12.10) and (12.11) have the following properties:

$$\nabla \vdash a \mathbin{\#} t \Rightarrow \nabla \vdash \pi a \mathbin{\#} \pi * t,$$

$$((\forall a \in \mathbb{A})\, \pi a \neq \pi' a \Rightarrow \nabla \vdash a \mathbin{\#} t) \Rightarrow \nabla \vdash \pi * t \approx \pi' * t,$$

$$\nabla \vdash a \mathbin{\#} t \wedge \nabla \vdash t \approx t' \Rightarrow \nabla \vdash a \mathbin{\#} t',$$

$$\nabla \vdash t \approx t,$$

$$\nabla \vdash t \approx t' \Rightarrow \nabla \vdash t' \approx t,$$

$$\nabla \vdash t \approx t' \wedge \nabla \vdash t' \approx t'' \Rightarrow \nabla \vdash t \approx t'',$$

$$\nabla \vdash t \approx t' \Rightarrow \nabla \vdash \pi * t \approx \pi * t'.$$

12.2 Use the algorithm from the proof of Theorem 12.9 to calculate most general solutions to nominal unification problems corresponding to (12.2) and (12.3).

References

Abramsky, S. 1991. Domain theory in logical form. *Annals of Pure and Applied Logic*, **51**, 1–77.

Abramsky, S. 1997. Semantics of interaction: an introduction to game semantics. Pages 1–31 of: Pitts, A. M. and Dybjer, P. (eds), *Semantics and Logics of Computation*. Publications of the Newton Institute. Cambridge University Press.

Abramsky, S. and Jung, A. 1994. Domain theory. Chap. 1 of: Abramsky, S., Gabbay, D. M. and Maibaum, T. S. E. (eds), *Handbook of Logic in Computer Science, Volume 3. Semantic Structures*. Oxford University Press. Corrected and expanded version available via the second author's web pages.

Abramsky, S., Ghica, D. R., Murawski, A. S., Ong, C.-H. L. and Stark, I. D. B. 2004. Nominal games and full abstraction for the nu-calculus. Pages 150–159 of: *Nineteenth Annual Symposium on Logic in Computer Science, LICS 2004*. IEEE Computer Society Press.

Ahmed, A. 2006. Step-indexed syntactic logical relations for recursive and quantified types. Pages 69–83 of: Sestoft, P. (ed), *Programming Languages and Systems, 15th European Symposium on Programming, ESOP 2006, Vienna, Austria*. Lecture Notes in Computer Science, vol. 3924. Springer.

Andrews, P. B. 2002. *An Introduction to Mathematical Logic and Type Theory: To Truth Through Proof*. 2nd edn. Applied Logic Series, vol. 27. Kluwer.

Appel, A. and McAllester, D. 2001. An indexed model of recursive types for foundational proof-carrying code. *Transactions on Programming Languages and Systems*, **23**(5), 657–683.

Apt, K. R. 1990. Logic programming. Pages 493–574 of: van Leeuwen, J. (ed), *Handbook of Theoretical Computer Science, Volume B. Formal Methods and Semantics*. Elsevier.

Baader, F. and Nipkow, T. 1998. *Term Rewriting and All That*. Cambridge University Press.

Barendregt, H. P. 1984. *The Lambda Calculus: Its Syntax and Semantics*. 2nd edn. North-Holland.

Barr, M. and Diaconescu, R. 1980. Atomic toposes. *Journal of Pure and Applied Algebra*, **17**(1), 1–24.

Beardon, A. F. 2005. *Algebra and Geometry*. Cambridge University Press.

Bengtson, J. and Parrow, J. 2009. Psi-calculi in Isabelle. Pages 99–114 of: Berghofer, S., Nipkow, T., Urban, C. and Wenzel, M. (eds), *Theorem Proving in Higher Order Logics*. Lecture Notes in Computer Science, vol. 5674. Springer.

Benton, N. and Koutavas, V. 2007. *A Mechanized Bisimulation for the Nu-Calculus*. Tech. rept. MSR-TR-2008-129. Microsoft Research Cambridge.

Benton, P. N. and Leperchey, B. 2005. Relational reasoning in a nominal semantics for storage. Pages 86–101 of: Urzyczyn, P. (ed), *Typed Lambda Calculi and Applications*. Lecture Notes in Computer Science, vol. 3461. Springer.

Birkedal, L. and Yang, H. 2008. Relational parametricity and separation logic. *Logical Methods in Computer Science*, **4**(2:6), 1–27.

Bojańczyk, M. and Lasota, S. 2012. A machine-independent characterization of timed languages. Pages 92–103 of: Czumaj, A., Mehlhorn, K., Pitts, A. M. and Wattenhofer, R. (eds), *39th International Colloquium on Automata, Languages and Programming, ICALP 2012, Proceedings, Part II*. Lecture Notes in Computer Science, vol. 7392. Springer.

Bojańczyk, M. and Place, T. 2012. Towards model theory with data values. Pages 116–127 of: Czumaj, A., Mehlhorn, K., Pitts, A. M. and Wattenhofer, R. (eds), *39th International Colloquium on Automata, Languages and Programming, ICALP 2012, Proceedings, Part II*. Lecture Notes in Computer Science, vol. 7392. Springer.

Bojańczyk, M., Klin, B. and Lasota, S. 2011. Automata with group actions. Pages 355–364 of: *Twenty-Sixth Annual IEEE Symposium on Logic in Computer Science, LICS 2011*. IEEE Computer Society Press.

Bojańczyk, M., Braud, L., Klin, B. and Lasota, S. 2012. Towards nominal computation. Pages 401–412 of: Hicks, M. (ed), *39th ACM SIGPLAN-SIGACT Symposium on Principles of Programming Languages, POPL 2012*. ACM Press.

Borceux, F. 2008. *Handbook of Categorical Algebra (3 Volumes)*. Encyclopedia of Mathematics and its Applications, vols 50–52. Cambridge University Press.

Burstall, R. M. 1969. Proving properties of programs by structural induction. *The Computer Journal*, **12**, 41–48.

Byrd, W. E. and Friedman, D. P. 2007. alphaKanren: a fresh name in nominal logic programming. Pages 79–90 of: *Proceedings of the 2007 Workshop on Scheme and Functional Programming*. Université Laval Technical Report DIUL-RT-0701.

Calvès, C. 2010. *Complexity and Implementation of Nominal Algorithms*. Ph.D. thesis, King's College London.

Calvès, C. and Fernández, M. 2008. A polynomial nominal unification algorithm. *Theoretical Computer Science*, **403**, 285–306.

Calvès, C. and Fernández, M. 2010. Matching and alpha-equivalence check for nominal terms. *Journal of Computer and System Sciences*, **76**, 283–301.

Cheney, J. 2004. *Nominal Logic Programming*. Ph.D. thesis, Cornell University.

Cheney, J. 2005a. Relating higher-order pattern unification and nominal unification. Pages 104–119 of: Vigneron, L. (ed), *Proceedings of the 19th International Workshop on Unification, Nara, Japan, UNIF'05*. LORIA.

Cheney, J. 2005b. A simpler proof theory for nominal logic. Pages 379–394 of: *Foundations of Software Science and Computational Structures 8th International Conference, FOSSACS 2005, Proceedings*. Lecture Notes in Computer Science, vol. 3441. Springer.

Cheney, J. 2005c. Toward a general theory of names: binding and scope. Pages 33–40 of: *Proceedings of the 3rd ACM SIGPLAN Workshop on Mechanized Reasoning about Languages with Variable Binding, MERLIN '05.* ACM Press.

Cheney, J. 2006. Completeness and Herbrand theorems for nominal logic. *Journal of Symbolic Logic,* **71**(1), 299–320.

Cheney, J. 2009. A simple nominal type theory. Pages 37–52 of: *Proceedings of the International Workshop on Logical Frameworks and Metalanguages: Theory and Practice, LFMTP 2008.* Electronic Notes in Theoretical Computer Science, vol. 228. Elsevier.

Cheney, J. 2010. Equivariant unification. *Journal of Automated Reasoning,* **45**, 267–300.

Cheney, J. 2012. A dependent nominal type theory. *Logical Methods in Computer Science,* **8**(1:08).

Cheney, J. and Urban, C. 2008. Nominal logic programming. *Transactions on Programming Languages and Systems,* **30**(5), 1–47.

Church, A. 1940. A formulation of the simple theory of types. *Journal of Symbolic Logic,* **5**, 56–68.

Ciancia, V. and Montanari, U. 2010. Symmetries, local names and dynamic (de)-allocation of names. *Information and Computation,* **208**(12), 1349–1367.

Clarke, E. M., Grumberg, O. and Peled, D. A. 2000. *Model Checking.* The MIT Press.

Clouston, R. A. 2009. *Equational Logic for Names and Binders.* Ph.D. thesis, University of Cambridge.

Clouston, R. A. 2013. Generalised name abstraction for nominal sets. In: *16th International Conference on Foundations of Software Science and Computation Structures, FoSSaCS 2013, Proceedings.* Lecture Notes in Computer Science. Springer.

Clouston, R. A. and Pitts, A. M. 2007. Nominal equational logic. Pages 223–257 of: Cardelli, L., Fiore, M. and Winskel, G. (eds), *Computation, Meaning and Logic, Articles dedicated to Gordon Plotkin.* Electronic Notes in Theoretical Computer Science, vol. 172. Elsevier.

Crole, R. L. 1993. *Categories for Types.* Cambridge University Press.

de Bruijn, N. G. 1972. Lambda calculus notation with nameless dummies, a tool for automatic formula manipulation, with application to the Church-Rosser theorem. *Indagationes Mathematicae,* **34**, 381–392.

Dowek, G. and Gabbay, M. J. 2012. Permissive nominal logic. *Transactions on Computational Logic,* **13**(3).

Dowek, G., Gabbay, M. J. and Mulligan, D. P. 2010. Permissive nominal terms and their unification: an infinite, co-infinite approach to nominal techniques. *Logic Journal of the IGPL,* **18**(6), 769–822.

Dreyer, D., Neis, G. and Birkedal, L. 2010. The impact of higher-order state and control effects on local relational reasoning. Pages 143–156 of: *Proceedings of the 15th ACM SIGPLAN International Conference on Functional Programming, ICFP 2010.* ACM Press.

Felleisen, M. and Hieb, R. 1992. The revised report on the syntactic theories of sequential control and state. *Theoretical Computer Science,* **103**, 235–271.

Fernández, M. and Gabbay, M. J. 2007. Nominal rewriting. *Information and Computation,* **205**(6), 917–965.

Fernández, M. and Rubio, A. 2012. Nominal completion for rewrite systems with binders. Pages 201–213 of: Czumaj, A., Mehlhorn, K., Pitts, A. M. and Wattenhofer, R. (eds), *39th International Colloquium on Automata, Languages and Programming, ICALP 2012, Proceedings, Part II*. Lecture Notes in Computer Science, vol. 7392. Springer.

Fernández, M., Gabbay, M.J. and Mackie, I. 2004. Nominal rewriting systems. Pages 108–119 of: *Proc. 6th ACM-SIGPLAN Symposium on Principles and Practice of Declarative Programming, PPDP'04*. ACM Press.

Ferrari, G., Montanari, U. and Pistore, M. 2002. Minimizing transition systems for name passing calculi: a coalgebraic formulation. Pages 129–158 of: Nielsen, M. and Engberg, U. (eds), *5th International Conference on Foundations of Software Science and Computation Structures, FoSSaCS 2002, Proceedings*. Lecture Notes in Computer Science, vol. 2303. Springer.

Filinski, A. and Korsholm Rohde, H. 2004. A denotational account of untyped normalization by evaluation. Pages 167–181 of: Walukiewicz, I. (ed), *Foundations of Software Science and Computation Structures, FoSSaCS 2004*. Lecture Notes in Computer Science, vol. 2987. Springer.

Fiore, M. P. and Hur, C.-K. 2008a. On the construction of free algebras for equational systems. *Theoretical Computer Science*, **410**, 1704–1729.

Fiore, M. P. and Hur, C.-K. 2008b. Term equational systems and logics. *Electronic Notes in Theoretical Computer Science*, **218**, 171–192. Proceedings of the 24th Conference on the Mathematical Foundations of Programming Semantics, MFPS XXIV.

Fiore, M. P., Plotkin, G. D. and Turi, D. 1999. Abstract syntax and variable binding. Pages 193–202 of: *14th Annual Symposium on Logic in Computer Science, LICS 1999*. IEEE Computer Society Press.

Freyd, P. J. 1992. Remarks on algebraically compact categories. Pages 95–106 of: Fourman, M. P., Johnstone, P. T. and Pitts, A. M. (eds), *Applications of Categories in Computer Science, Proceedings LMS Symposium, Durham, UK, 1991*. LMS Lecture Note Series, vol. 177. Cambridge University Press.

Gabbay, M. J. 2000. *A Theory of Inductive Definitions with α-Equivalence: Semantics, Implementation, Programming Language*. Ph.D. thesis, University of Cambridge.

Gabbay, M. J. 2002. FM-HOL, a higher-order theory of names. In: Kamareddine, F. (ed), *Workshop on Thirty Five years of Automath, Informal Proceedings*. Heriot-Watt University, Edinburgh, Scotland.

Gabbay, M. J. 2007. General mathematics of names. *Information and Computation*, **205**(7), 982–1011.

Gabbay, M. J. 2009. A study of substitution, using nominal techniques and Fraenkel–Mostowski sets. *Theoretical Computer Science*, **410**(12-13), 1159–1189.

Gabbay, M. J. 2011. Foundations of nominal techniques: logic and semantics of variables in abstract syntax. *Bulletin of Symbolic Logic*, **17**(2), 161–229.

Gabbay, M. J. 2012. Finite and infinite support in nominal algebra and logic: nominal completeness theorems for free. *Journal of Symbolic Logic*, **77**(3).

Gabbay, M. J. and Cheney, J. 2004. A sequent calculus for nominal logic. Pages 139–148 of: *19th IEEE Symposium on Logic in Computer Science, LICS 2004*. IEEE Computer Society Press.

Gabbay, M. J. and Ciancia, V. 2011. Freshness and name-restriction in sets of traces with names. Pages 365–380 of: *Foundations of Software Science and Computation Structures, 14th International Conference, FoSSaCS 2011*. Lecture Notes in Computer Science, vol. 6604. Springer.

Gabbay, M. J. and Mathijssen, A. 2008. One-and-a-halfth-order logic. *Journal of Logic and Computation*, **18**(4), 521–562.

Gabbay, M. J. and Mathijssen, A. 2009. Nominal (universal) algebra: equational logic with names and binding. *Journal of Logic and Computation*, **19**(6), 1455–1508.

Gabbay, M. J. and Pitts, A. M. 1999. A new approach to abstract syntax involving binders. Pages 214–224 of: *14th Annual Symposium on Logic in Computer Science, LICS 1999*. IEEE Computer Society Press.

Gabbay, M. J. and Pitts, A. M. 2002. A new approach to abstract syntax with variable binding. *Formal Aspects of Computing*, **13**, 341–363.

Gabriel, P. and Ulmer, F. 1971. *Lokal Präsentierbare Kategorien*. Lecture Notes in Mathematics, vol. 221. Springer-Verlag.

Gadducci, F., Miculan, M. and Montanari, U. 2006. About permutation algebras, (pre)sheaves and named sets. *Higher-Order and Symbolic Computation*, **19**, 283–304.

Goguen, J. A., Thatcher, J. W., Wagner, E. G. and Wright, J. B. 1977. Initial algebra semantics and continuous algebras. *Journal of the ACM*, **24**, 68–95.

Gordon, A. D. and Melham, T. 1996. Five axioms of alpha-conversion. Pages 173–191 of: *Theorem Proving in Higher Order Logics, 9th International Conference*. Lecture Notes in Computer Science, vol. 1125. Springer.

Gordon, M. J. C. and Melham, T. F. 1993. *Introduction to HOL. A Theorem Proving Environment for Higher Order Logic*. Cambridge University Press.

Harper, R. 2013. *Practical Foundation for Programming Languages*. Cambridge University Press.

Harper, R., Honsell, F. and Plotkin, G. D. 1993. A framework for defining logics. *Journal of the ACM*, **40**, 143–184.

Hodges, W. 1993. *Model Theory*. Encyclopedia of Mathematics and its Applications, vol. 42. Cambridge University Press.

Hofmann, M. 1999. Semantical analysis of higher-order abstract syntax. Pages 204–213 of: *14th Annual Symposium on Logic in Computer Science, LICS 1999*. IEEE Computer Society Press.

Johnson, D. L. 1997. *Presentations of Groups*. 2nd edn. London Mathematical Society Student Texts, vol. 15. Cambridge University Press.

Johnstone, P. T. 2002. *Sketches of an Elephant, A Topos Theory Compendium, Volumes 1 and 2*. Oxford Logic Guides, nos. 43–44. Oxford University Press.

Joyal, A. and Moerdijk, I. 1995. *Algebraic Set Theory*. London Mathematical Society Lecture Notes in Mathematics, no. 220. Cambridge University Press.

Klop, J.-W., van Oostrom, V. and van Raamsdonk, F. 1993. Combinatory reduction systems, introduction and survey. *Theoretical Computer Science*, **121**, 279–308.

Kripke, S. A. 1965. Semantical analysis of intuitionistic logic I. Pages 92–130 of: Crossley, J. N. and Dummett, M. A. E. (eds), *Formal Systems and Recursive Functions*. North-Holland, Amsterdam.

Kurz, A., Petrişan, D. and Velebil, J. 2010. Algebraic theories over nominal sets. *CoRR*, *abs/1006.3027*.

Lakin, M. R. and Pitts, A. M. 2009. Resolving inductive definitions with binders in higher-order typed functional programming. Pages 47–61 of: Castagna, G. (ed), *18th European Symposium on Programming, ESOP 2009, Proceedings*. Lecture Notes in Computer Science, vol. 5502. Springer.

Lambek, J. 1968. A fixpoint theorem for complete categories. *Mathematische Zeitschrift*, **103**, 151–161.

Lambek, J. and Scott, P. J. 1986. *Introduction to Higher Order Categorical Logic*. Cambridge University Press.

Lassen, S. B. 1998. *Relational Reasoning about Functions and Nondeterminism*. Ph.D. thesis, Department of Computer Science, University of Aarhus.

Levy, J. and Villaret, M. 2010. An efficient nominal unification algorithm. Pages 209–226 of: Lynch, C. (ed), *Proceedings of the 21st International Conference on Rewriting Techniques and Applications, RTA 2010*. Leibniz International Proceedings in Informatics (LIPIcs), vol. 6. Schloss Dagstuhl–Leibniz-Zentrum für Informatik.

Levy, J. and Villaret, M. 2012. Nominal unification from a higher-order perspective. *ACM Transactions on Computational Logic*, **13**(2), 10:1–10:31.

Lösch, S. and Pitts, A. M. 2013. Full abstraction for nominal Scott domains. Pages 3–14 of: Cousot, R. (ed), *Proceedings of the 40th ACM SIGACT-SIGPLAN Symposium on Principles of Programming Languages, POPL 2013*. ACM Press.

MacLane, S. 1971. *Categories for the Working Mathematician*. Graduate Texts in Mathematics 5. Springer-Verlag.

MacLane, S. and Moerdijk, I. 1992. *Sheaves in Geometry and Logic. A First Introduction to Topos Theory*. Springer-Verlag.

Markowsky, G. 1976. Chain-complete p.o. sets and directed sets with applications. *Algebra Universalis*, **6**, 53–68.

Martin-Löf, P. 1971. Hauptsatz for the intuitionistic theory of iterated inductive definitions. *Foundations of Mathematics*, **63**, 179–216.

Mason, I. A. and Talcott, C. L. 1991. Equivalence in functional languages with effects. *Journal of Functional Programming*, **1**, 287–327.

Mathijssen, A. 2007. *Logical Calculi for Reasoning with Binding*. Ph.D. thesis, Eindhoven University of Technology.

McKinna, J. and Pollack, R. 1999. Some type theory and lambda calculus formalised. *Journal of Automated Reasoning*, **23**.

Menni, M. 2003. About N-quantifiers. *Applied Categorical Structures*, **11**, 421–445.

Miller, D. A. 1991. A logic programming language with lambda-abstraction, function variables, and simple unification. *Journal of Logic and Computation*, **1**, 497–536.

Miller, D. A. 2000. Abstract syntax for variable binders: an overview. Pages 239–253 of: Lloyd, J. *et al.* (eds), *Computational Logic, CL 2000, First International Conference, Proceedings*. Lecture Notes in Artificial Intelligence, vol. 1861. Springer.

Milner, R. 1977. Fully abstract models of typed lambda-calculi. *Theoretical Computer Science*, **4**, 1–22.

Milner, R. 1989. *Communication and Concurrency*. Prentice Hall.

Milner, R., Parrow, J. and Walker, D. 1992. A Calculus of Mobile Processes (Parts I and II). *Information and Computation*, **100**, 1–77.

Milner, R., Tofte, M., Harper, R. and MacQueen, D. 1997. *The Definition of Standard ML (Revised)*. The MIT Press.

Moggi, E. 1989. *An Abstract View of Programming Languages*. Tech. rept. ECS-LFCS-90-113. Department of Computer Science, University of Edinburgh.

Moggi, E. 1991. Notions of computation and monads. *Information and Computation*, **93**(1), 55–92.

Montanari, U. and Pistore, M. 2000. π-Calculus, structured coalgebras and minimal HD-automata. In: *25th International Symposium on Mathematical Foundations of Computer Science, Bratislava, Slovak Republic, Proceedings, MFCS 2000*. Lecture Notes in Computer Science, vol. 1893. Springer.

Mosses, P. D. 1990. Denotational Semantics. Pages 577–632 of: Leeuwen, J. van (ed), *Handbook of Theoretical Computer Science*, vol. B. North-Holland.

Murawski, A. S. and Tzevelekos, N. 2012. Algorithmic games for full ground references. Pages 312–324 of: *39th International Colloquium on Automata, Languages and Programming, ICALP 2012, Proceedings*. Lecture Notes in Computer Science, vol. 7392. Springer.

Needham, R. M. 1989. Names. Pages 89–101 of: Mullender, S. (ed), *Distributed Systems*. ACM Press.

Nipkow, T. 1993. Functional unification of higher-order patterns. Pages 64–74 of: *Proceedings of Eighth Annual IEEE Symposium on Logic in Computer Science, LICS 1993*. IEEE Computer Society Press.

Nipkow, T., Paulson, L. C. and Wenzel, M. 2002. *Isabelle/HOL, A Proof Assistant for Higher-Order Logic*. Lecture Notes in Computer Science, vol. 2283. Springer-Verlag.

Norrish, M. 2004. Recursive function definition for types with binders. Pages 241–256 of: *Theorem Proving in Higher Order Logics, 17th International Conference*. Lecture Notes in Computer Science, vol. 3223. Springer.

Odersky, M. 1994. A functional theory of local names. Pages 48–59 of: *Conference Record of the 21st Annual ACM Symposium on Principles of Programming Languages, POPL 1994*. ACM Press.

Petrişan, D. L. 2011. *Investigations into Algebra and Topology over Nominal Sets*. Ph.D. thesis, Department of Computer Science, University of Leicester.

Peyton Jones, S. L. 2001. Tackling the awkward squad: monadic input/output, concurrency, exceptions, and foreign-language calls in Haskell. Pages 47–96 of: Hoare, A., Broy, M. and Steinbruggen, R. (eds), *Engineering Theories of Software Construction*. IOS Press.

Pfenning, F. and Elliott, C. 1988. Higher-order abstract syntax. Pages 199–208 of: *Proceedings of the ACM SIGPLAN Conference on Programming Language Design and Implementation, PLDI 1988*. ACM Press.

Pientka, B. and Dunfield, J. 2010. Beluga: A framework for programming and reasoning with deductive systems (system description). Pages 15–21 of: *Automated Reasoning, 5th International Joint Conference, IJCAR 2010, Proceedings*. Lecture Notes in Computer Science, vol. 6173. Springer.

Pierce, B. C. 1991. *Basic Category Theory for Computer Scientists*. The MIT Press.

Pierce, B. C. 2002. *Types and Programming Languages*. The MIT Press.

Pitts, A. M. 1996. Relational properties of domains. *Information and Computation*, **127**, 66–90.

Pitts, A. M. 2000. Parametric polymorphism and operational equivalence. *Mathematical Structures in Computer Science*, **10**, 321–359.

Pitts, A. M. 2002. Operational semantics and program equivalence. Pages 378–412 of: Barthe, G., Dybjer, P. and Saraiva, J. (eds), *Applied Semantics, Advanced Lectures, International Summer School, APPSEM 2000, Caminha, Portugal.* Lecture Notes in Computer Science, Tutorial, vol. 2395. Springer.

Pitts, A. M. 2003. Nominal logic, a first order theory of names and binding. *Information and Computation*, **186**, 165–193.

Pitts, A. M. 2005. Typed operational reasoning. Chap. 7, pages 245–289 of: Pierce, B. C. (ed), *Advanced Topics in Types and Programming Languages.* The MIT Press.

Pitts, A. M. 2006. Alpha-structural recursion and induction. *Journal of the ACM*, **53**, 459–506.

Pitts, A. M. 2011. Structural recursion with locally scoped names. *Journal of Functional Programming*, **21**(3), 235–286.

Pitts, A. M. and Gabbay, M. J. 2000. A metalanguage for programming with bound names modulo renaming. Pages 230–255 of: Backhouse, R. and Oliveira, J. N. (eds), *Mathematics of Program Construction. 5th International Conference, MPC2000, Ponte de Lima, Portugal, July 2000. Proceedings.* Lecture Notes in Computer Science, vol. 1837. Springer.

Pitts, A. M. and Shinwell, M. R. 2008. Generative unbinding of names. *Logical Methods in Computer Science*, **4**(1:4), 1–33.

Pitts, A. M. and Stark, I. D. B. 1993. Observable properties of higher order functions that dynamically create local names, or: what's new? Pages 122–141 of: *Mathematical Foundations of Computer Science, Proc. 18th International Symposium, MFCS 1993.* Lecture Notes in Computer Science, vol. 711. Springer.

Pitts, A. M. and Stark, I. D. B. 1998. Operational reasoning for functions with local state. Pages 227–273 of: Gordon, A. D. and Pitts, A. M. (eds), *Higher Order Operational Techniques in Semantics.* Publications of the Newton Institute. Cambridge University Press.

Plotkin, G. D. 1973. *Lambda-Definability and Logical Relations.* Memorandum SAI-RM-4. School of Artificial Intelligence, University of Edinburgh.

Plotkin, G. D. 1975. Call-by-name, call-by-value and the lambda calculus. *Theoretical Computer Science*, **1**, 125–159.

Plotkin, G. D. 1977. LCF considered as a programming language. *Theoretical Computer Science*, **5**, 223–255.

Plotkin, G. D. 1981. *A Structural Approach to Operational Semantics.* Tech. rept. DAIMI FN-19. Aarhus University. Reprinted in Journal of Logic and Algebraic Programming 60–61 (2004), 17-139.

Plotkin, G. D. 1985. *Lectures on Predomains and Partial Functions.* Notes for a course given at the Center for the Study of Language and Information, Stanford.

Poswolsky, A. and Schürmann, C. 2009. System description: Delphin—a functional programming language for deductive systems. Pages 113–120 of: *Proceedings of the International Workshop on Logical Frameworks and Metalanguages: Theory and Practice, LFMTP 2008.* Electronic Notes in Theoretical Computer Science, vol. 228. Elsevier.

Pottier, F. 2005. An overview of Cαml. Pages 27–52 of: *ACM SIGPLAN Workshop on ML (ML 2005).* Electronic Notes in Theoretical Computer Science. Elsevier.

Pottier, F. 2007. Static name control for FreshML. Pages 356–365 of: *Twenty-Second Annual IEEE Symposium on Logic In Computer Science, LICS 2007*. IEEE Computer Society Press.

Pouillard, N. 2012. *Namely, Painless: A Unifying Approach to Safely Program with First-Order Syntax with Binders*. Ph.D. thesis, Université Paris Diderot (Paris 7).

Pym, D. J. 2002. *The Semantics and Proof Theory of the Logic of Bunched Implications*. Applied Logic Series, vol. 26. Springer.

Rado, R. 1964. Universal graphs and universal functions. *Acta Arithmetica*, **9**, 331–340.

Robinson, J. A. 1965. A machine oriented logic based on the resolution principle. *Journal of the ACM*, **12**, 23–41.

Sangiorgi, D. 2011. *An Introduction to Bisimulation and Coinduction*. Cambridge University Press.

Sangiorgi, D. and Walker, D. 2001. *The π-calculus: a Theory of Mobile Processes*. Cambridge University Press.

Ščedrov, A. 1984. *Forcing and Classifying Topoi*. Memoirs, no. 295. American Mathematical Society.

Schöpp, U. 2006. *Names and Binding in Type Theory*. Ph.D. thesis, University of Edinburgh.

Schöpp, U. and Stark, I. D. B. 2004. A dependent type theory with names and binding. Pages 235–249 of: *Computer Science Logic, CSL 2004*. Lecture Notes in Computer Science, vol. 3210. Springer.

Schürmann, C., Despeyroux, J. and Pfenning, F. 2001. Primitive recursion for higher-order abstract syntax. *Theoretical Computer Science*, **266**, 1–57.

Schwinghammer, J. and Birkedal, L. 2011. Step-indexed relational reasoning for countable nondeterminism. Pages 512–524 of: Bezem, M. (ed), *20th Conference on Computer Science Logic, CSL 2011*. Leibniz International Proceedings in Informatics. Schloss Dagstuhl-Leibniz-Zentrum für Informatik.

Scott, D. S. 1982. Domains for denotational semantics. In: Nielson, M. and Schmidt, E. M. (eds), *Automata, Languages and Programming, Proceedings 1982*. Lecture Notes in Computer Science, vol. 140. Springer.

Sewell, P., Zappa Nardelli, F., Owens, S., Peskine, G., Ridge, T., Sarkar, S. and Strniša, R. 2010. Ott: effective tool support for the working semanticist. *Journal of Functional Programming*, **20**(1), 71–122.

Shinwell, M. R. 2005a. *The Fresh Approach: Functional Programming with Names and Binders*. Ph.D. thesis, University of Cambridge. Available as University of Cambridge Computer Laboratory Technical Report UCAM-CL-TR-618.

Shinwell, M. R. 2005b. Fresh O'Caml: nominal abstract syntax for the masses. Pages 53–76 of: Benton, P. N. and Leroy, X. (eds), *2005 ACM SIGPLAN Workshop on ML (ML 2005)*. Electronic Notes in Theoretical Computer Science. Elsevier.

Shinwell, M. R. and Pitts, A. M. 2005a. *Fresh Objective Caml User Manual*. Tech. rept. UCAM-CL-TR-621. University of Cambridge Computer Laboratory.

Shinwell, M. R. and Pitts, A. M. 2005b. On a monadic semantics for freshness. *Theoretical Computer Science*, **342**, 28–55.

Shinwell, M. R., Pitts, A. M. and Gabbay, M. J. 2003. FreshML: programming with binders made simple. Pages 263–274 of: *Eighth ACM SIGPLAN International Conference on Functional Programming, ICFP 2003*. ACM Press.

Shoenfield, J. R. 1977. Axioms of set theory. Pages 321–344 of: Barwise, J. (ed), *Handbook of Mathematical Logic*. North-Holland.

Stark, I. D. B. 1994 (Dec.). *Names and Higher-Order Functions*. Ph.D. thesis, University of Cambridge. Also published as Technical Report 363, University of Cambridge Computer Laboratory, April 1995.

Statman, R. 1985. Logical relations and the typed lambda calculus. *Information and Control*, **65**, 85–97.

Staton, S. 2007. *Name-Passing Process Calculi: Operational Models and Structural Operational Semantics*. Ph.D. thesis, University of Cambridge. Available as University of Cambridge Computer Laboratory Technical Report Number UCAM-CL-TR-688.

Terese. 2003. *Term Rewriting Systems*. Cambridge Tracts in Theoretical Computer Science, vol. 55. Cambridge University Press.

Turner, D. C. 2009. *Nominal Domain Theory for Concurrency*. Ph.D. thesis, University of Cambridge. Available as University of Cambridge Computer Laboratory Technical Report UCAM-CL-TR-751.

Turner, D. C. and Winskel, G. 2009. Nominal domain theory for concurrency. Pages 546–560 of: Grädel, E. and Kahle, R. (eds), *Computer Science Logic*. Lecture Notes in Computer Science, vol. 5771. Springer.

Tzevelekos, N. 2008. *Nominal Game Semantics*. Ph.D. thesis, University of Oxford. Available as Oxford University Computing Laboratory Technical Report RR-09-18.

Tzevelekos, N. 2011. Fresh-register automata. Pages 295–306 of: *38th Annual ACM SIGPLAN-SIGACT Symposium on Principles of Programming Languages, POPL 2011*. ACM Press.

Urban, C. 2008. Nominal reasoning techniques in Isabelle/HOL. *Journal of Automatic Reasoning*, **40**(4), 327–356.

Urban, C. and Berghofer, S. 2006. A recursion combinator for nominal datatypes implemented in Isabelle/HOL. Pages 498–512 of: *3rd International Joint Conference on Automated Reasoning, IJCAR 2006*. Lecture Notes in Computer Science, vol. 4130. Springer.

Urban, C. and Kaliszyk, C. 2011. General bindings and alpha-equivalence in Nominal Isabelle. Pages 480–500 of: Barthe, G. (ed), *Programming Languages and Systems, 20th European Symposium on Programming, ESOP 2011, Proceedings*. Lecture Notes in Computer Science, vol. 6602. Springer.

Urban, C., Pitts, A. M. and Gabbay, M. J. 2004. Nominal unification. *Theoretical Computer Science*, **323**, 473–497.

Urban, C., Berghofer, S. and Norrish, M. 2007. Barendregt's variable convention in rule inductions. Pages 35–50 of: *Proceedings of the 21st Conference on Automated Deduction, CADE 2007*. Lecture Notes in Artificial Intelligence, vol. 4603. Springer.

Wadler, P. 1992. Comprehending monads. *Mathematical Structures in Computer Science*, **2**, 461–493.

Westbrook, E. 2008. *Higher-Order Encodings with Constructors*. Ph.D. thesis, Washington University in St Louis.

Westbrook, E., Stump, A. and Austin, E. 2009. The calculus of nominal inductive constructions: an intensional approach to encoding name-bindings. Pages 74–83 of: *Proceedings of the Fourth International Workshop on Logical Frameworks and Meta-languages: Theory and Practice, LFMTP 2009*. ACM Press.

Winskel, G. 1993. *The Formal Semantics of Programming Languages*. Foundations of Computing. The MIT Press.

Index of notation

Index

Printed in the United States
by Baker & Taylor Publisher Services

Printed in the United States
by Baker & Taylor Publisher Services